THE CAMBRIDGE COMPANION T(
FEMINIST THEOLOGY

D1504348

Feminist theology is a significant movement within contemporary theology. The aim of this *Cambridge Companion* is to give an outline of feminist theology through an analysis of its overall shape and its major themes, so that both its place in and its contributions to the present changing theological landscape may be discerned. The two sections of the volume are designed to provide a comprehensive and critical introduction to feminist theology which is authoritative and up to date. Written by some of the main figures in feminist theology, as well as by younger scholars who are considering their inheritance, it offers fresh insights into the nature of feminist theological work. The book as a whole is intended to present a challenge for future scholarship, since it engages critically with the assumptions of feminist theology, and seeks to open ways for women after feminism to enter into the vocation of theology.

CAMBRIDGE COMPANIONS TO RELIGION
A series of companions to major topics and key figures in theology and
religious studies. Each volume contains specially commissioned chapters
by international scholars which provide an accessible and stimulating
introduction to the subject for new readers and non-specialists.

Other titles in the series
THE CAMBRIDGE COMPANION TO CHRISTIAN DOCTRINE
edited by Colin Gunton
ISBN 0 521 47118 4 hardback   ISBN 0 521 47695 8 paperback
THE CAMBRIDGE COMPANION TO BIBLICAL INTERPRETATION
edited by John Barton
ISBN 0 521 48144 9 hardback   ISBN 0 521 48593 2 paperback
THE CAMBRIDGE COMPANION TO DIETRICH BONHOEFFER
edited by John de Gruchy
ISBN 0 521 58258 x hardback   ISBN 0 521 58751 6 paperback
THE CAMBRIDGE COMPANION TO LIBERATION THEOLOGY
edited by Christopher Rowland
ISBN 0 521 46144 8 hardback   ISBN 0 521 46707 1 paperback
THE CAMBRIDGE COMPANION TO KARL BARTH edited by John Webster
ISBN 0 521 58476 0 hardback   ISBN 0 521 58560 0 paperback
THE CAMBRIDGE COMPANION TO CHRISTIAN ETHICS
edited by Robin Gill
ISBN 0 521 77070 x hardback   ISBN 0 521 77918 9 paperback
THE CAMBRIDGE COMPANION TO JESUS edited by Markus Bockmuehl
ISBN 0 521 79261 4 hardback   ISBN 0 521 79678 4 paperback
THE CAMBRIDGE COMPANION TO FEMINIST THEOLOGY
edited by Susan Frank Parsons
ISBN 0 521 66327 x hardback   ISBN 0 521 66380 6 paperback

Forthcoming
THE CAMBRIDGE COMPANION TO THE GOSPELS edited by Stephen C. Barton
THE CAMBRIDGE COMPANION TO ST PAUL edited by James D. G. Dunn
THE CAMBRIDGE COMPANION TO MEDIEVAL JEWISH THOUGHT
edited by Daniel H. Frank and Oliver Leaman
THE CAMBRIDGE COMPANION TO ISLAMIC THEOLOGY
edited by Timothy J. Winter
THE CAMBRIDGE COMPANION TO REFORMATION THEOLOGY
edited by David Bagchi and David Steinmetz
THE CAMBRIDGE COMPANION TO JOHN CALVIN
edited by Donald C. McKim
THE CAMBRIDGE COMPANION TO MARTIN LUTHER
edited by Donald C. McKim
THE CAMBRIDGE COMPANION TO POSTMODERN THEOLOGY
edited by Kevin Vanhoozer

THE CAMBRIDGE COMPANION TO

FEMINIST THEOLOGY

Edited by Susan Frank Parsons

Margaret Beaufort Institute of Theology Cambridge

CAMBRIDGE
UNIVERSITY PRESS

PUBLISHED BY THE PRESS SYNDICATE OF THE UNIVERSITY OF CAMBRIDGE
The Pitt Building, Trumpington Street, Cambridge, United Kingdom

CAMBRIDGE UNIVERSITY PRESS
The Edinburgh Building, Cambridge CB2 2RU, UK
40 West 20th Street, New York, NY 10011-4211, USA
477 Williamstown Road, Port Melbourne, VIC 3207, Australia
Ruiz de Alacón 13, 28014 Madrid, Spain
Dock House, The Waterfront, Cape Town 8001, South Africa

http://www.cambridge.org

First published 2002

Printed in the United Kingdom at the University Press, Cambridge

Typeface Severin 10/13 pt   *System* LaTeX 2_ε [TB]

A catalogue record for this book is available from the British Library

ISBN 0 521 66327 x hardback
ISBN 0 521 66380 6 paperback

Contents

Notes on contributors   *page* ix
Preface   xiii
Acknowledgements   xviii

Part one   *The shape of feminist theology*

  1 The emergence of Christian feminist theology   3
     ROSEMARY RADFORD RUETHER

  2 Feminist theology as intercultural discourse   23
     KWOK PUI-LAN

  3 Feminist theology as philosophy of religion   40
     PAMELA SUE ANDERSON

  4 Feminist theology as theology of religions   60
     RITA M. GROSS

  5 Feminist theology as post-traditional thealogy   79
     CAROL P. CHRIST

  6 Feminist theology as biblical hermeneutics   97
     BRIDGET GILFILLAN UPTON

  7 Feminist theology as dogmatic theology   114
     SUSAN FRANK PARSONS

Part two   *The themes of feminist theology*

  8 Trinity and feminism   135
     JANET MARTIN SOSKICE

  9 Jesus Christ   151
     MERCY AMBA ODUYOYE

  10 The Holy Spirit and spirituality   171
      NICOLA SLEE

  11 Creation   190
      CELIA DEANE-DRUMMOND

Contents

12 Redeeming ethics   206
SUSAN FRANK PARSONS

13 Church and sacrament – community and worship   224
SUSAN A. ROSS

14 Eschatology   243
VALERIE A. KARRAS

Index of biblical citations   261
Index of names   262
Index of subjects   266

Notes on contributors

Pamela Sue Anderson is Fellow in Philosophy and Christian Ethics at Regent's Park College, University of Oxford, GB. She is the author of *Ricœur and Kant: Philosophy of the Will* (Atlanta, GA: Scholars Press, 1993) and *A Feminist Philosophy of Religion: The Rationality and Myths of Religious Belief* (Oxford: Blackwell, 1998).

Carol Christ is Director of the Ariadne Institute for the Study of Myth and Ritual in Molivos, Lesvos, Greece. She is the author of *Diving Deep and Surfacing* (Boston, MA: Beacon Press, 1991), *Laughter of Aphrodite: Reflections on a Journey* (New York: Harper and Row, 1987), and *Rebirth of the Goddess* (London: Routledge, 1998), and co-editor of *Womanspirit Rising: A Feminist Reader in Religion* (New York: Harper and Row, 1979) and *Weaving the Visions: New Patterns in Feminist Spirituality* (San Francisco, CA: HarperCollins, 1989).

Celia Deane-Drummond is Professor of Theology and the Biological Sciences at Chester College of Higher Education, University of Liverpool, GB. She is the author of *A Handbook in Theology and Ecology* (London: SCM Press, 1996), *Theology and Biotechnology: Implications for a New Science* (London: Geoffrey Chapman, 1997), *Ecology in Jürgen Moltmann's Theology* (Edwin Mellen Press, 1997), and *Creation Through Wisdom* (T. & T. Clark, 2000).

Bridget Gilfillan Upton is Lecturer in New Testament at Heythrop College, University of London, GB. This is her first published paper in addition to numerous book reviews.

Rita M. Gross was Professor of Religion at the University of Wisconsin – EauClaire, USA. She is the author of *Unspoken Worlds* (Belmont, CA: Wadsworth, 1989), *Buddhism after Patriarchy: A Feminist History, Analysis and Reconstruction of Buddhism* (New York: State University of New York Press, 1992), *Feminism and Religion* (Boston, MA: Beacon Press, 1996), and *Soaring and Settling: Buddhist Perspectives on Contemporary Social and Religious Issues* (New York: Continuum, 1998).

Valerie Karras is Assistant Professor of Greek Patristics in the Department of Theological Studies, Saint Louis University, USA. She is the author of a number of articles, including 'Patristic Views on the Ontology of Gender', in *Personhood:*

Orthodox Christianity and the Connection between Body, Mind and Soul, edited by J. Chirban (Westport, CT: Bergin and Garvey, 1996), 'The Incarnational and Hypostatic Significance of the Maleness of Jesus Christ According to Theodore of Stoudios', *Studia Patristica*, 82 (1996), 'The Orthodox Perspective on Feminist Theology', in *The Encyclopedia of Women and Religion in North America*, edited by R. S. Keller and R. R. Ruether (Bloomington, IN: Indiana University Press, 2000), and 'Beyond Justification', in *The Joint Declaration on Justification: Its Ecumenical Implications*, edited by M. Root and Wm. G. Rusch (Collegeville, MN: Liturgical Press, 2001).

Kwok Pui-lan is William F. Cole Professor of Christian Theology and Spirituality at Episcopal Divinity School in Cambridge, Massachusetts, USA. She is the author of *Chinese Women and Christianity 1860–1927* (Atlanta, GA: Scholars Press, 1992), *Discovering the Bible in the Non-Biblical World* (New York: Orbis Press, 1995), and *Introducing Asian Feminist Theology* (Sheffield Academic Press, 2000).

Mercy Amba Oduyoye is Director of the Institute of Women in Religion and Culture at Trinity Theological College in Ghana. She is the author of *Hearing and Knowing: Theological Reflections on Christianity in Africa* (New York: Orbis Press, 1986) and *Daughters of Anowa: African Women and Patriarchy* (New York: Orbis Press, 1996), and co-editor of *The Will to Arise: Women, Tradition and the Church in Africa* (New York: Orbis Press, 1992) and *With Passion and Compassion: Third World Women Doing Theology* (New York: Orbis Press, 1993).

Susan Frank Parsons is Director of Pastoral Studies at the Margaret Beaufort Institute of Theology, Cambridge, GB. She is the author of *Feminism and Christian Ethics* (Cambridge University Press, 1996) and *The Ethics of Gender* (Oxford: Blackwell, 2001), the editor of *Challenging Women's Orthodoxies in the Context of Faith* (Aldershot: Ashgate Press, 2000), and co-editor of *Restoring Faith in Reason* (London: SCM Press, 2002).

Susan A. Ross is Associate Professor of Theology at Loyola University, Chicago, Illinois, USA. She is the author of *Extravagant Affections: A Feminist Sacramental Theology* (New York: Continuum, 1998), and co-editor of *Broken and Whole: Essays on Religion and the Body* (Lanham, MD: University Press of America, 1995).

Rosemary Radford Ruether is Georgia Harkness Professor of Applied Theology at the Garrett-Evangelical Theological Seminary in Evanston, Illinois, USA. She is the author of numerous articles and books, including *Sexism and God-Talk: Towards a Feminist Theology* (London: SCM Press, 1983), *Gaia and God: An Ecofeminist Theology of Earth Healing* (San Francisco, CA: HarperCollins, 1994), *Womanguides: Readings Towards a Feminist Theology* (Boston, MA: Beacon Press, 1996), *Women and Redemption: A Theological History* (London: SCM Press, 1998), and *Introducing Redemption in Christian Feminism* (Sheffield Academic Press, 1998).

Nicola Slee is a freelance theologian and writer based at the Queen's Ecumenical Foundation, Birmingham, GB. She is the author of *Easter Garden* (London: Collins,

1990), of *Remembering Mary* (National Christian Education Council, 2000), and of the Hockerill lecture, 'A Subject in Her Own Right: The Religious Education of Women and Girls' (Hockerill Education Trust, 2001).

Janet Martin Soskice is Reader in the Faculty of Divinity of the University of Cambridge, GB. She is the author of numerous articles and of *Metaphor and Religious Language* (Oxford: Clarendon Press, 1987), and the editor of *After Eve: Women, Theology and the Christian Tradition* (London: Marshall Pickering-Collins, 1990).

Preface

Amongst the more energetic and enthusiastic forms of theology that emerged during the latter half of the twentieth century, feminist theology took up its place to become one of the prominent ways in which women have found theological voice and have allowed the wisdom of faith to be rooted in their lives. While its provenance is located in the Western Christian tradition, its bearing formed by the philosophical assumptions and political ideals of the Enlightenment, feminist theology has become something of a common discourse entered into by women of other faith and intellectual inheritance. Its now universal vocabulary of the rights of women, of the dignity and value of women's lives, of the urgency for their economic and social liberation, and of the prospect for human fulfilment within creation, has become one of the primary means both of communication between women, and of assertion of their status in global politics and in the church. Feminist theology has thus grown up with modernity, and so likewise extends itself as a network of interconnected relationships that are to be ever more inclusive of diversities and adaptable to changing circumstances. Its special attentiveness to women's experiences, its reaching out to touch and to raise up women amid the daily business of life, its concern for the paths that women must walk, are characteristic features in which are expressed the desire of women to be faithful witnesses to the truth of the Gospel that sets us free, and signs of hope in the blessedness that is yet to come.

Feminist theology has developed, particularly since the 1970s, as a special field of inquiry within departments of theology and religious studies. With greater numbers of women entering higher education and preparing for a variety of ministries within the Christian churches at that time, it is not surprising that traditional disciplines of all kinds were being reshaped according to the new questions and concerns that then appeared. These were critical of the sources and methods employed among the various specialisms of theology, as they were also constructive in bringing insights from the experience and wisdom of women to bear on some of the major issues that had arisen within the discipline. In early days, women found perhaps the most congenial of doctrinal frameworks to be those of political theology or of liberation theology, for these were configured in the dialectical pattern that women also used to challenge the status quo, and to find alternative resources from women themselves for revisioning the theological task in the context of the wider society. Theology that is called 'feminist' may be understood in this light as theology that nurtures hopes for the liberation of humanity into a just and equitable political order in which our life together, as women and men, might be more happily realised. This twofold approach of critique and reconstruction will be evident in the chapters that follow, and examples of the particular issues women have addressed will be found.

In addition to this, the study of the phenomenon of religion itself, as well as of the texts and traditions of people of other faith, has been a growing area of academic inquiry. As knowledge of and interaction with peoples of diverse cultural and religious backgrounds was expanding in the late twentieth century, so opportunities for the development of intercultural and interfaith relationships became available. Ordinary women from all parts of the world began to know one another, to discover common problems, to be challenged by unfamiliar ways of life, of speaking, and of understanding, and to be returned to their own traditions with new questions. This has led to a scholarly interest in the place of women in religious practices, institutions, and beliefs, and in the impact of these things upon women's lives and welfare. Here the methods of the human and social sciences have been especially useful in exploring the patterns of social organisation and language, the cultural symbols and values, and the systems of belief that structure women's lives and self-understanding. Feminist theology in this light may be understood as theology that uses the analytical tool of gender to investigate the contexts and practices of religion and of religious bodies, and to suggest ways in which these might become more conducive to women's full participation as believers, and so more adequate as historical signs of divine goodness.

The contributors to this *Companion* have, in one way or another, been influenced by feminist theology in these forms. They have written some of its major texts; they have taught it in a variety of places; they have learned and been influenced by its ways of reasoning. The incisiveness of the gender critique and the proposed reconstruction of theology in a number of different areas are thus evident in these pages, as the contributors seek to describe what feminist theology has been about, and to assess the part it has played, and should continue to play, in shaping contemporary theological efforts as well as the life of the church.

For some time, however, it has been recognised that feminist theology is a complex manifestation of both the promise and the problematic of modern thinking, and thus that its reception is marked by the intellectual turmoil that comes in modernity's wake. While many of its main ideas have swept through Western culture with great moral fervour, contributing not insignificantly to a theological kind of political correctness, it has also brought along with it the very provocations that are so troublesome to us as we bear this inheritance. The sign of this difficulty is not pluralism, for the diverse strands of feminist discourse, the often contradictory types of feminism that indicate it is no unified phenomenon, and the multiple voices with which it now speaks – these are all things that feminist theologians claim to value and to be able to accommodate within an ever-expandable relational web. What is thought-provoking for the theologian is the way in which feminist theology has represented, on behalf of women, the expectation of modern secular reforms that divine providence could legitimately be taken into human hands, and this, in the context of a universe believed to be without God. It has required, for this undertaking, a cluster of assumptions, regarding identity, agency, history, and nature to name but a few, that are themselves both unstable and philosophically questionable, and that have become more obviously and bewilderingly known to be so in the time called postmodernity. That feminist theologians have sought to provide a divine matrix to replace the absent God, and to hold back the tides that threaten this accomplishment by their presence in ecclesial and academic institutions, are poignant indications of tenacity, now rendered so very fragile.

This disturbance is also noticeable in the chapters that follow, for, insofar as the contributors are engaged in their own primary task of theological reflection, they are thereby responding anew to the questions of faith that appear in our present context. For each step that seems to be sure-footed and secure, firmly established on the solid ground of feminist theological orthodoxy, there is another that falters, tripped up by what is now being encountered and thrown back to begin again the patient work of seeking understanding. The intellectual and spiritual effort to be undertaken in observance of what is happening here, so that what lies in this problematic place may be prepared for the coming of faith, is the work to which those who associate with feminist theology are now called.

The chapters in this *Cambridge Companion* have been grouped into two sections. Following a chapter on its emergence, the first section considers the overall shape of feminist theology. The basic presuppositions, the frameworks of understanding, the methods, and some of the contentious issues of feminist theology are set out and analysed in order to disclose what kind of theology it is. Each contributor has written from within a specialism, and has investigated the ways in which feminist theologians address some of the important questions that arise there. They have been forthcoming also in making their own contributions to these debates and to drawing the reader's attention to the relevant resources. In the second section, the themes that have been of particular importance in Christian feminist theology are investigated. Organised according to a doctrinal scheme, these chapters bring the reader into the midst of a number of the substantive issues that engage the attention of theologians today, and show how it is that feminist theologians may approach these matters with the mind and heart of faith. Here, too, there is original thinking and an attempt to open windows onto the future direction of feminist theological work.

There are inevitably both subjects and perspectives that are missing from such a collection. The availability of people to write this kind of piece is normally unpredictable, but is surely intensified in this case by the enormous pressures under which women in academia are now working, and by the demands of daily survival upon women in places of risk in which such things as writing seem a luxury. This disparity so ill-fits the hopes in which feminist theology was born. Nevertheless, the feminist commitment to diversity, however that is to be construed, and to speaking for and so representing oneself in the public forum, are things that this *Companion* has sought in some modest way to respect. If it gives the reader an outline of feminist theology and a fair indication of its place in the present theological landscape, and if it offers companionship to those who would follow through what is beginning to be learned here, then it will have done its work well enough.

For there is an important sense in which, whatever personal responses one may make to feminist theology, and whether or not it is the popular theology of choice in the highly stylised culture of the postmodern university, women and men of faith will at some points encounter the questions it has worked through regarding our humanity, our place in the scheme of things, and the way of the divine presence in our midst. These matters remain, and the service of faithful women has been to keep them nurtured, to be angry at their disappearance under the accoutrements of cultural production, to prophesy concerning the loss of the church's own *raison d'être*, and to proclaim the coming of God wherever they find themselves with their very lives. The finest ministry of feminist theologians within modernity is to be understood in these terms, as a reminder of God's goodness in our creation and faithfulness in bringing us to our end.

That we find ourselves in another situation, and that these matters require of us a new vocabulary, a critical reading of the texts from which we have learned, and again a costly discernment in which we also will be changed by what comes to be known – these things are cause for rejoicing that the well of wisdom ever deepens as we drink of it, and for hope that, after all, it is in us the divine is to be born. Such are the affirmations of Christian feminist theologians made in the light of the resurrection, in the early dawn as one approaches the point where a new thing is about to happen. In giving themselves over to the coming of the Lord, in letting their lives be taken up into the astonishment of what arrives from without, in this moment, there is that speechless joy which is to become the birthplace of the Gospel (Matthew 28^{1-10}, Mark 16^{1-8}, Luke 24^{1-12}, John 20^{11-18}). Here at the place of a meeting, women find themselves disclosed in the morning sun, their bodies poised expectantly over the line that divides darkness and light, their eyes receptive to the most tender turnings of one moment into another. It is a disclosure that beckons them into the journey of truth undertaken by all theologians, each in their own time, as God takes hold of their souls. For women today to be carried into such vocation anew is the desire in which this volume has been prepared and so is presented to you.

Acknowledgements

The Editor wishes gratefully to acknowledge the generosity of the contributors in writing their chapters for this volume, and the enthusiasm and goodwill they have shown for the project. Their fine efforts of scholarship and patience through the editorial task are very much appreciated.

Thanks also are due to Kevin Taylor and those who work with him at Cambridge University Press for their help in the production of the text.

Each *Companion* is so called because it is to accompany readers in their intellectual journey and thus to befriend them in the advent of truth. This is an appropriate occasion then to thank all of our companions who walk along with us, providing what is needful without our asking, sharing food and conversation that so nourishes the soul, and directing our notice to whatever awaits us. For their forbearance and charity, we have reason also to be grateful, for these are things that hold us in proper humility. So it is that faith knows companions to be signs of the tenderness of a good and loving God. To my own, and especially to Mark, a huge thank you.

The publisher has used its best endeavours to ensure that the URLs for external websites referred to in this book are correct and active at the time of going to press. However, the publisher has no responsibility for the websites and can make no guarantee that a site will remain live, or that the content is, or will remain, appropriate.

Part one

The shape of feminist theology

1 The emergence of Christian feminist theology

ROSEMARY RADFORD RUETHER

In this chapter, I will trace the emergence and development of feminist theology in Christianity. I start by asking what counts as feminism, what counts as feminist theology, and what social and cultural conditions allow it to emerge. Feminist theology is not just women doing theology, for women have done theology that does not question the masculinist paradigms of theology. Nor is feminist theology simply the affirmation of 'feminine' themes in theology. What has been called 'feminine' in Western thought has been constructed to complement the construction of masculinity. Thus, the adding of feminine to masculine themes in theology mostly enforces the dominant gender paradigm.

Feminism is a critical stance that challenges the patriarchal gender paradigm that associates males with human characteristics defined as superior and dominant (rationality, power) and females with those defined as inferior and auxiliary (intuition, passivity). Most feminists reconstruct the gender paradigm in order to include women in full and equal humanity. A few feminists reverse it, making females morally superior and males prone to evil, revalorising traditional male and female traits.[1] Very few feminists have been consistently female-dominant in their views; more often there has been a mix of egalitarian and feminine superiority themes. I take the egalitarian impulse of feminism to be the normative stance, but recognise the reversal patterns as part of the difficulty of imagining a new paradigm of gender relations which is not based on hierarchy of values.

Feminist theology takes feminist critique and reconstruction of gender paradigms into the theological realm. They question patterns of theology that justify male dominance and female subordination, such as exclusive male language for God, the view that males are more like God than females, that only males can represent God as leaders in church and society, or that women are created by God to be subordinate to males and thus sin by rejecting this subordination.

Feminist theologians also seek to reconstruct the basic theological symbols of God, humanity, male and female, creation, sin and redemption, and the church, in order to define these symbols in a gender-inclusive and egalitarian way. In so doing they become theologians, not simply critics of the dominant theology. Feminist theologians engage in this critique by reclaiming nascent egalitarian and positive female themes in the Christian tradition and developing them in new ways to apply to gender relations such as: female symbols for God (the Wisdom tradition); humanity, male and female, both created in God's image (Genesis 1²⁷); the distinction of male and female overcome in Christ in a new inclusive humanity of redemption (Galatians 3²⁸); and both males and females called to prophecy (Acts 2¹⁷). But the mere presence of such themes in the tradition does not constitute a feminist reading of them. For the latter to come about, certain cultural and social conditions are necessary. There needs to be a new stance towards knowledge that recognises that symbols, including theological symbols, are socially constructed, rather than eternally and unchangeably disclosed from beyond. Those in power construct cultural symbols to validate their own power and the subjugation of women; social relations, such as class, race, and gender, are not eternally given by God as the 'order of creation', but are social constructs, and, as such, can be changed.

These cultural shifts of consciousness about the nature of truth and knowledge depend on certain social conditions. Women must gain education and agency in some social institutions that enable them to gain a voice. Women's claims of cultural agency must be organised as a movement or community of discourse that supports women's (and men's) critique of the dominant gender paradigm. Women must gain education and agency in the church as those allowed to learn, speak, and be heard as theologians.

These cultural and social conditions did not exist adequately (they still do not exist fully) until the late 1960s. Liberal and Marxist critiques of ideology and society had been somewhat assimilated into modern culture, and women gained some access to theological education, teaching, and ministry in some theological schools and churches. Hence the major emergence of feminist theology dates from the late 1960s. However, feminist theology was not born *ex nihilo*. Some of the conditions for feminist theology also existed in earlier eras. Women in these earlier eras made some beginnings of a critique and reconstruction of sexist paradigms in religion.

Among many female spiritual writers of the Middle Ages, such as Hildegard of Bingen and Julian of Norwich, one finds women able to gain some theological education, to claim and be accepted by some other women and men as producers of theological writing, teachers, and preachers. One finds in their writing affirmations of positive female symbols, particularly drawing on the Wisdom imagery for God, and women's spiritual equality of soul in redemption.[2] What is lacking is a culture that can critique the dominant paradigm and imagine changes of social relations between the genders.

In the Renaissance and Reformation eras from the fourteenth to the seventeenth centuries, one finds a few writers that apply the Protestant critique of the medieval church, and the humanistic claims to a critical rereading of theological texts, to gender relations. Most of Reformation and humanist critique was used to re-enforce traditional gender roles. Among those who spoke from the new humanistic education to claim a fuller humanity for women is Christine de Pizan, an Italian writing in France between 1390 and 1429. In the context of current debates about women's 'nature' as good or evil, Christine de Pizan's *The Book of the City of Ladies* defended women's capacity for virtue against misogynist diatribes by churchmen and poets.[3]

Another proto-feminist humanist is the German Agrippa von Nettesheim. His 1529 essay 'On the Nobility and Preeminence of the Female Sex' mixed defences of women's equality with claims to their moral superiority. Most notably, Agrippa declared that the subjugated state of women is not based on either their natural inferiority or the will of God, but simply is due to male 'tyranny' and will to power over women.[4] But these proto-feminist voices remain isolated and do not become a movement or influential community of discourse.

Seventeenth-century England saw something closer to a movement of feminist discourse arising from two sources in different social contexts: radical, apocalyptic Christianity among the popular classes, and humanism among the leisure class elite. The first type of feminist theology is exemplified by Margaret Fell and the Quaker movement. Fell's 1666 essay, 'Women's Preaching Justified according to the Scriptures', reconstructed New Testament Christianity to claim women's agency as preachers. For Fell, women's public preaching is not simply allowed by Christ, but is the foundational condition for the birth of the church as a movement of redemption.[5]

The second type of feminism is found in a figure such as the Anglican humanist, Mary Astell. Her 1694 book, *A Serious Proposal to the Ladies*, argues for equality of education for women as a precondition of their equality in soul development in this life and the life to come.[6] Both these expressions of seventeenth-century English feminism reflect the emergence of small communities of discourse that counter the dominant culture. They can be seen as the first *movement* of feminist theology. But they remained marginalised because women were still so totally excluded from the dominant church, educational, and cultural institutions. That gender relations could be recon-structed legally, politically, and economically was still mostly inconceivable.

Revolutionary liberalism and socialism in the late eighteenth and nine-teenth centuries mostly used their arguments against the hegemony of the aristocracy and the capitalist class to re-enforce male domination. But they gave new tools to some women to apply to gender relations. A few social critics in France, England, and the United States, Olympe de Gouge, Mary Wollstonecraft, Abigail Adams, and Frances Wright,[7] sought to apply lib-eral and socialist principles to changed social organisation to allow women's equality in a new society.

In the mid-nineteenth century, these calls for gender equality become an organised movement seeking women's property rights, higher education, civil and political rights. In the United States, feminism arose in conjunc-tion with the abolitionist movement against slavery. In this context, one finds some of the first systematic efforts to challenge the sexist paradigms of Christian theology that upheld the ideology of male domination. Key figures in this American development of nineteenth-century feminist theol-ogy are Sarah Grimke ('Letters on the Equality of the Sexes and the Condition of Women', 1837), Lucretia Mott (Sermons, 1840–79), and Elizabeth Cady Stanton (especially *The Women's Bible*, 1895).[8]

Both Grimke and Mott built on the Quaker tradition that had allowed women's preaching and ministry since the seventeenth century. They based their theological critique on their interpretation of the equality of the sexes in the image of God, arguing that this represents God's original intent for social equality. This, they claim, has been wrongly betrayed by male domi-nance. Sexism is a sin against women and God, distorting God's intention for creation. Equality between the sexes must go beyond personal relations to social reconstruction, redeeming society and restoring creation. Stanton takes a more radical view of the Scriptures, seeing them not simply as mis-read by later sexist theology, but as themselves a product of sexism. In her *Women's Bible*, Stanton attacks the Bible itself as sexist, and envisions a feminist theology and ethic emancipated from it.

The 'first wave' of feminism of the 1840s–1920s resulted in a partial emancipation of women. Women were allowed access to higher education, property rights, and the vote in the United States. Similar developments took place in liberalised societies elsewhere, such as in England. But these changes were absorbed into ongoing ways of enforcing gender hierarchy, based particularly on sexual division of labour. The nineteenth century be-ginnings of feminist theology as part of an organised feminist movement was largely forgotten, overwhelmed by a social gospel that re-enforced the male family wage and women's domestication and then the neo-orthodox renewal of classical patriarchal Christianity. It remained until the late 1960s, with a renewed feminist movement in the United States, for feminist theology to be reborn and to discover its earlier predecessors.

The late 1960s in the USA represented a conjunction of two developments that supported the emergence of a more fully developed feminist theology. First, the civil rights and anti-war movements brought a wide-ranging critique of racial, class and militarist patterns that defined American society. Initially these movements ignored gender and re-enforced male dominance on the Left. Feminism emerged from two sources: liberal white women in education, government, and the professions seeking fuller inclusion of women in these institutions; and women of the Left stung by the sexist chauvinism of leftist men. This second group of women shaped a radical feminism that envisioned transformed social and sexual relations, including heterosexual dominance.[9]

Secondly, women in the Christian churches, particularly in liberal Protestantism, had been gradually acquiring access to theological education and ministry from the late nineteenth century: Congregationalists (1853), Unitarians, Universalists, Methodist Protestants (1870–80s). This development flowered from 1955 to 1975 with a number of mainline Protestant denominations approving women's ordination: mainline Methodists and Northern Presbyterians (1956), Lutherans (1965), Episcopalians (1975).

By the 1970s, the opening of ordination to women brought increasing numbers of women students into theological schools. More and more women earned doctoral degrees in theological fields and entered teaching faculties. Feminist theology for the first time gained an institutional basis in Christian theological education. The growing presence of women as students, ministers, and teachers in churches meant that feminism had to be translated into feminist theology. Women in these teaching and ministerial roles had to engage in critique and reconstruction of a tradition that had historically excluded them and justified their exclusion theologically, in order to mandate their own new inclusion and leadership.

Yet these developments among liberal Protestants do not explain the prominence of Catholic women among the American feminist theologians: Mary Daly, Rosemary Ruether, Elizabeth Schüssler Fiorenza[10] who begin their feminist theological work in the late 1960s to mid-1970s, to be followed by a number of others, such as Margaret Farley, Mary Jo Weaver, Elizabeth Johnson, and Susan Ross.[11] The emergence of Catholic women as equal participants in feminist theology reflects another conjunction of movements in the mid-1960s, namely the Second Vatican Council and the eager reception of Vatican II reform among a wing of American Catholics. Progressive Catholic nuns adopted a feminist critique of the church and applied it to the renewal of their religious communities.

A new ecumenism between Catholics and Protestants allowed many Catholic women to gain a critical theological education at liberal Protestant strongholds, such as Princeton, Yale, Harvard, Union, and Chicago theological schools, and to shape careers in theological education at Protestant schools or at university departments of religion. A few found a base in liberalised Catholic universities, such as Fordham and Notre Dame, and the Jesuit seminaries (although at the end of the twentieth century their careers there are under threat due to the new effort of the Vatican and American Catholic bishops to reassert control over Catholic theological education).[12]

Ironically the very intransigence of the Roman Catholic Church toward women's aspirations for equality in the church may have spurred theological energy, while liberal Protestantism's openness to women in ordained ministry lessened the challenge. While Protestant women poured into theological education between 1970 and 2000, becoming 40–60 per cent of the students in the theological schools of these denominations, much of their energy was drawn off into the pastoral ministry, often in low-paid positions with long hours of work, leaving little time for theological reflection and writing.

Catholic women, lacking this outlet and rebuffed by official church seminaries, attended instead interdenominational theological schools, such as those mentioned above. The Vatican's defence of women's exclusion from ordination on grounds of theological anthropology (i.e. women cannot image Christ, and are not, by their very nature as female, ordainable) spurred the need for Catholic women to examine and critique the theological rationales for these arguments. The Catholic Women's Ordination Conference that arose in 1975 took conscious aim at the theology and scriptural exegesis of the Vatican position.[13]

By 1982, some American Catholics were becoming disenchanted with the prospects of being ordained in such a clerical system. They began to shape the 'women–church movement' as free liturgical communities for the nurture of feminist spirituality, worship, and social service. For Catholic feminist theologians, such as Rosemary Ruether and Mary Hunt, these autonomous feminist liturgical communities also became venues for the imagining of more radical feminist theology and liturgy.[14]

Ordained Protestant women needed to conform their ministries within largely unchanged communities of patriarchal religious discourse. These limitations meant that the women–church idea soon spread to Protestant women as well. Some Protestant feminist theologians and pastors began to shape feminist liturgical communities, to supplement the limitations of their work in official churches. In the 1990s, Protestant feminist theologians, such as Letty Russell and Rebecca Chopp, were situating their ecclesiology in the context of the idea of women–church.[15]

American women theologians emerged as feminist theologians through various life histories and contexts. Several pioneer feminist theologians were educated in a pre-feminist context and then transformed their own thought by the inclusion of feminist critique. For example, Mary Daly began her educational journey in the late 1950s through a desire to be fully accepted in doctoral work in Catholic scholastic philosophy. Rebuffed in this quest, she moved to Europe where she attained a doctorate in Catholic theology and then a second one in Catholic philosophy at the University of Fribourg.[16]

In Europe, Daly was influenced by reading the feminist philosophy of Simone de Beauvoir. Returning to teach at Jesuit Boston College in 1968 (where she has remained throughout her career until her ouster in 1999),[17] she became increasingly radicalised by her application of feminist critique to an intransigent church. This drew Daly from feminist reform to a radical rejection of Christianity and all patriarchal cultures, and an effort to think of feminist spirituality outside of and against 'phallocratic' discourse, a development somewhat parallel to French feminists, such as Irigaray.[18]

Rosemary Ruether, as a Catholic growing up in an ecumenical context, and Letty Russell as a Presbyterian followed somewhat parallel paths. Both were deeply shaped by participation in the Civil Rights and Anti-War movements of the 1960s: Ruether through work in the Delta Ministry in Mississippi in 1965 and teaching at Howard University School of Religion, á black Protestant Divinity School (1965–76), and Russell through working as a minister in the innovative East Harlem Protestant parish in the same period. Both developed their first theological reflections in the context of a liberation theology critical of class and race oppression, and then expanded and transformed this paradigm through feminism in the early 1970s.

Other important American feminist theologians of this first generation are Sallie McFague and Beverly Harrison. Trained in neo-orthodoxy, McFague pioneered work in epistemological questions of theological language. Beginning in 1982, she developed a series of books that translated this inquiry into feminist and ecological terms.[19] Ethicist Beverly Harrison situated her work in class, race, and gender terms in the early 1970s. Harrison's teaching has been crucial to the training of a second generation of feminist theologians and ethicists at Union Theological Seminary in New York City.[20]

Carter Heyward was one such feminist theologian to emerge under Harrison's tutelage. An Episcopalian, Heyward shaped her theological identity in the 1970s in the struggle for women's ordination in that church, justifying her own participation in the first wave of 'illegal' ordinations in her 1975 book, *A Priest Forever*. Her 1980 doctoral dissertation, published under the title, *The Redemption of God*, pioneered a feminist view of God as the matrix of 'right relation', decisively challenging the traditional male, transcendental view of deity. Heyward was also the first feminist theologian to begin to write explicitly as a lesbian. Through her work and that of other lesbian feminists, such as Mary Hunt, the critique of 'heterosexism' has become an additional optic for viewing the patterns of sexism in Christian theology.[21]

By the late 1970s and early 80s, enough feminist theologians were established on teaching faculties of theological schools that the new generation of students could study and write their dissertations out of a feminist paradigm, rather than having to invent that paradigm over against a theology that ignored gender issues, as had been the case with the pioneer writers of the early 1970s. Feminist theology was becoming an established part of the discourse of American theological schools. By the 1990s, liberal theological schools had five to ten women scholars across theological fields and even more conservative schools employed some women faculty.

Feminists from evangelical churches have also sought to develop their distinctive theological voice. Letha Scanzoni and Nancy Hardesty pioneered an evangelical approach to women's liberation in their 1986 volume, *All We're Meant to Be*. Evangelical feminists eschew a radical critique of the Bible and affirm its adequacy for women's emancipation from sexism in church and society. The magazine, *Daughters of Sarah*, and the Evangelical Women's Caucus (both discontinued) for a while nurtured feminist readings of Christianity that held on to more traditional views of biblical authority.

American feminist theology was also diversifying as African American, Hispanic, and Asian women entered theological schools. Many found their feminist theological teachers oblivious to racial differences in women's experiences, just as the earlier generation had found their male teachers oblivious to gender differences. Yet the roots of many feminist theologians in the Civil Rights struggle made them ready to hear such questions. African American, Hispanic, and Asian women began to gain their distinctive theological voices.

African American women claimed the name of 'Womanism' for their theological perspective, rooted in the conjunction of sexism and racism in American society. Delores Williams, Jacquelyn Grant, Katie Cannon, Emilie

Townes, Linda Thomas, Marcia Riggs, Cheryl Gilkes, Shawn Copeland, Karen Baker-Fletcher, and Jamie Phelps are among this emerging generation of womanist theologians.[22] Hispanic women, such as Ada María Isasi-Díaz, also began to claim their theological voice out of their cultural context, coining the name 'Mujerista' theologians.[23]

Many Hispanic and Asian women are immigrants or visitors who remain 'cross-border' theologians. Some Hispanic feminists, such as Mexican Maria Pilar Aquino teaching in San Diego, identify more with the networks of feminist theologians in Latin America. Aquino calls herself a Latina Feminist, rather than a Mujerista theologian.[24] Asian women, such as Kwok Pui-lan and Chung Hyun Khung, received their theological training and are presently teaching in the USA, but speak more from their Asian contexts in Hong Kong and Korea.[25]

American women from other religious traditions have also begun to find their feminist voice. Judith Plaskow pioneered Jewish feminist theology with her 1990 book *Standing Again at Sinai*. Buddhist women, particularly American converts, began to examine both the religious practice and the teachings of Buddhism from a feminist perspective. Rita Gross' 1993 *Buddhism after Patriarchy* is the pioneering text for a feminist reading of Buddhism. Some feminists who began in Christian theological studies concluded that patriarchy is too deeply entrenched in this tradition to be capable of feminist transformation. Carol Christ has been a major voice for American religious feminists who have turned to Wiccan or neo-pagan spirituality for sustenance.[26]

In the 1900s, American feminist theology increasingly reflects both American cultural diversity and many new dimensions of social concerns. The ecological crisis has reshaped the way feminists look at human–nature relations, causing many feminist theologians to write from an 'ecofeminist' perspective. Ruether and Daly had such concerns already in the early 1970s,[27] and McFague has reshaped her theological work to situate it in the human–nature relation. Epistemological questions, often sparked by postmodern challenges, have also become an important area of feminist theological discourse.[28]

Feminist theological writing has proliferated, with more and more specialised work in all fields, such as Hebrew Scripture, New Testament, church history, ethics, pastoral psychology, preaching and worship, as well as systematic theology. These are no longer confined to a feminist 'ghetto' in professional theology, but are found in most areas of inquiry. Yet the hostility of many churches to feminist questions has widened the gap between church and academy. More and more women are coming to theological schools to train for ministry, yet many still come with little knowledge of feminist theological thought and are even warned against it by their pastors.

This chapter has dwelt at some length on American contributions to the emergence of feminist theology, but by the 1980s European, Latin American, Asian, and African women were also finding their distinctive feminist theological voices. American feminist theology emerged slightly earlier and helped spark developments in other continents for several reasons. As a nation of immigrants with no established church since the American Revolution, religion in America is extremely plural and lacks the anticlericalism more typical of Europe. This means that new social movements, including feminism, find bases in some parts of the churches, rather than being expressed as secular liberal or Marxist movements hostile to the churches (although this also exists).

The plurality of churches also means a plurality of church colleges and theological schools that offer a base for education and employment for feminist theologians. The greater rigidity of theological faculties in European universities has provided much less opportunity for feminist scholars. France, with its strong anti-clerical tradition against Roman Catholicism, still has no significant movement of feminist theology, even though it has strong expressions of feminism and feminist theory. In Germany, women were first ordained in the 1960s, and feminist theology began to be explored among women theological students. But German feminist scholars have seldom been offered theological chairs.

Yet some pioneer feminist theology began in Europe in the mid-1960s. Elizabeth Grossmann[29] taught for years in Japan because she was unable to obtain a professorship in Germany. Kari Børresen's feminist reading of Augustine and Aquinas was written in French in 1968, to be rediscovered and translated into English in 1981.[30] Dorothee Sölle started her theological writing with a Marxist liberation perspective. She became explicitly feminist in her writings in the 1980s, partly spurred by conversations with feminists at Union Theological Seminary where she taught for many years.[31] Sölle's has been a theology distinctively rooted in the German experience of Nazism, the Holocaust, and the Anti-War movement. In Holland, Catharina Halkes held the first chair of feminist theology at the University of Nijmegen in 1983, providing a base for the training of Dutch women. Halkes has focussed on feminist theological anthropology and, more recently, ecofeminism.[32]

In England, a number of university theological faculties have become bases for feminist study and teaching since the mid-1980s. Mary Grey (who was Halkes' successor at Nijmegen), Ursula King at Lancaster and then Bristol

University, Elaine Graham at Manchester, Grace Jantzen at King's College London and now Manchester, Christine Trevett at Wales, Lisa Isherwood at St Marks and St Johns in Plymouth, and Janet Martin Soskice in Cambridge are among a rising generation of women theologians offering feminist theological studies in Britain. Daphne Hampson at St Andrew's University in Scotland has become the spokesperson for a post-Christian theology that rejects the adequacy of Christianity for a feminist revisionist reading.[33]

Irish women are also shaping a distinctive theological voice, represented by theologians such as Mary Condren, Katherine Zappone, and Ann Marie Gilligan.[34] The School of Feminist Theology of Britain and Ireland and its journal, *Feminist Theology*, have nurtured a larger community of feminist discourse. The feminist theological network, Women in Theology (WIT), gave a forum for British women theologians to exchange views. Significantly it was discontinued in 1999 because the growing presence of feminist theologians in British universities was seen to have made it no longer necessary. The European Society of Women for Theological Research, founded in 1985, networks European feminist theologians and holds a conference in various European venues every two years.

Roman Catholic women are well represented in European feminist theology. Børresen, Halkes, Grey, King, Isherwood, Condren, Zappone, and Gilligan are Catholics. Yet their feminist work has emerged primarily in an ecumenical context. The theological schools of Holland, Protestant and Catholic, have been receptive to feminist theology, even mandating it as a required theological subject for all students at the foundational level. This has given a base for a number of women to teach feminist studies there. Yet the increasingly reactionary stance of the Vatican has affected the re-forming élan of Dutch Catholicism. Many Dutch Catholic feminists have turned away from any hope of church reform to pursue feminist theory on a more academic level or to focus on social issues, such as violence against women.

Catholic women in predominantly Catholic countries in Europe find it hard to establish a base in university or church controlled settings. Mary Condren received her doctoral degree from Harvard Divinity School in Cambridge, Massachusetts. The Mount Oliver Institute of pastoral theology where she taught briefly was closed by the local bishop. Irish feminists have developed their own networks. They publish the journal of feminist spirituality, *Womanspirit*. Feminist theologians also find great barriers in Italy and Spain. Italian feminists often teach through other fields such as art history. Church historian Carla Ricci teaches in this field under the faculty of Political Science at the University of Bologna.[35]

Rosemary Radford Ruether

The 1980s also saw a lively development of feminist theology in Latin America, Asia, and Africa. Latin America had feminist movements in the 1920s that sought civil rights for women. A new wave of feminism in the 1970s focussed on issues of sexuality, reproductive rights, and violence to women. More like France than the United States, Latin American feminism has been secular and anti-clerical against Roman Catholic dominance. In the late 1960s, Latin American male theologians, such as Gustavo Gutiérrez, developed a liberation theology that centred on poverty and the dependency of Latin American economies on neo-colonial domination. These liberation theologians ignored gender issues and mostly were oblivious to racial sub-cultures, indigenous peoples, and Africans.

In the mid-1970s, Latin Americans joined with African and Asian theologians to create the Ecumenical Association of Third World Theologians (EATWOT). This association became a base for mutual support for theologies of the 'South' that challenge North American and European hegemony. African and Asian theologians questioned the Latin American emphasis on class analysis and economic exploitation, arguing for the need in their contexts to discuss religious and cultural plurality. A few women theologians began to be present at these meetings: Mercy Amba Oduyoye from Ghana, Virginia Fabella and Mary John Manazan from the Philippines, Marianne Katoppo from Indonesia, Sun Ai Park from Korea, Ivone Gebara and Elsa Tamez from Latin America. When they challenged the lack of attention to gender issues, initially they received a cold shoulder from their male colleagues, who were disposed to regard feminism as a 'First World' and 'bourgeois' issue.

In 1983 at a joint meeting of EATWOT and First World (North American and European) liberation theologians in Geneva, the women theologians from all continents joined together to support the Third World women in their demand for attention to gender issues. The result was the foundation of the Women's Commission of EATWOT that supported a process by which Third World women could contextualise their own theological reflections in their national and regional situations. This resulted in a series of consultations of women theologians; first national meetings and then continental (Asian, African, and Latin American) conferences. In 1986, an intercontinental meeting took place that brought women theologians together from the three regions.[36]

The Women's Commission has continued as an intercontinental network whose leaders meet regularly. They have helped nurture networks of communication, journals, and conferences in each region. In 1994, a fourth conference brought Third and First World feminist theologians together, with some inclusion of Eastern European and Middle Eastern representatives.[37] In Latin America, a few theological schools provide feminist theological training. Most notable is the Latin American biblical University in Costa Rica, with Elsa Tamez as president, that draws students from all over Central America, the Caribbean, and Latin America. The Methodist Theological Institute in Sao Paulo Brazil, with Nancy Cardoso Pereira and Ivone Richter Reimer, the Pontifical Catholic University in Rio de Janeiro with Margarida Brandao, Maria Clara Bingemer, and Ana María Tepedino, Wanda Deifelt at the Lutheran Seminary in Sao Leopoldo, Brazil are among these schools.[38]

Several grassroots feminist networks organise women's ministries, conferences, and publications, such as Talitha Cumi in Lima, Peru and the Conspirando Collective in Santiago, Chile. Catholic women's religious orders, particularly the Maryknoll Sisters and lay missioners, provide important support for these initiatives. Theologians, such as Ivone Gebara[39] (teaching in Sao Paulo after the progressive seminary created by Helder Camera in Recife, Brazil, was closed by a new conservative bishop) has focussed particularly on an ecofeminist theological method. Ecofeminism is also central to the work of *Con-spirando*, which subtitles itself as *Revista Latinoamericana de Ecofeminismo, Espiritualidad y Teologia*. Indigenous and African Brazilian feminist perspectives are also beginning to emerge in Latin America.

African women theologians have been organising through the Circle of Concerned African Women Theologians, developing a journal and other publications. In the 1960s, African and black theological movements emerged in African nations struggling against Western neo-colonialism. African theologies focussed on values of traditional African cultures and their integration into biblical hermeneutics and Christian theology. Black Theology was shaped in South Africa in the struggle against apartheid,[40] with input from James Cone and the Black Theology movement of the United States. As in Latin America, women and gender issues were largely ignored.

African women theologians have claimed their distinctive voice by bringing together the themes of inculturation and liberation. They question the romanticisation of traditional African cultures, pointing out their oppression of women. They also critique the sexism of the Christian tradition and its alliance with colonialism, but find positive resources in it for women's emancipation. African women evaluate traditional practices such as polygamy and menstrual taboos, the women's work roles, sexuality, reproduction, and family life. The treatment of widows and inheritance, the pervasive belief in evil spirits, and the scapegoating of women as witches in times of misfortune are areas of particular concern.

African women also find areas of empowerment for women in traditional culture, as cult leaders and healers, as farmers and craftswomen, as liberators in myth and folk story. They also claim the Christian traditions of the equality of all persons in God's image. They see Jesus as ancestor and liberator who sides with the poor and the oppressed. They claim the church as spirit-filled healing community and redemptive hope for a new era of justice and peace, rereading these themes from an African women's perspective.[41]

African women theologians work ecumenically from both mainline Protestant and Catholic traditions. They belong to the small educated professional classes of their societies. Many got their doctorates in Belgium, Britain, or the United States. They teach at university departments of religion and pastoral institutes. Mercy Amba Oduyoye, formerly Deputy General Secretary of the World Council of Churches in Geneva, has been a major organiser for the promotion of the African women's theology.[42] Recently she returned to Ghana to develop the work of the Trinity Theological College in Legon. Another leading writer and organiser is Musimbi Kanyoro, a Kenyan Lutheran, presently General Secretary of the World YWCA in Geneva, and Co-ordinator of the Circle of Concerned African Women Theologians.

Other leading African women theologians are Rosemary Edet (deceased), a Nigerian Roman Catholic Sister who taught Religious Studies; Bette Ekeya, a lay Catholic teaching in African traditional religions at the Nairobi University; Teresa Okure, a Catholic sister with a doctorate in Scripture who teaches at the Catholic Institute of West Africa in Port Harcourt, Nigeria; Elizabeth Amoah, a Methodist teaching in African Religions at the University of Ghana in Legon, and Teresa Hinga, a Kenyan lay Catholic presently teaching at DePaul University in Chicago, USA.

Asian women theologians have a history of inter-Asian organising that goes back to the early 1980s. In 1982, Sun Ai Park, an ordained Korean women whose husband was a leader in the World Council of Churches, created the Asian women's theological journal, *In God's Image*. The journal has grown into a major publication with contributors across Asia. In 1988, Sun Ai Park founded the Asian Women's Resource Center for Culture and Theology for publication and the organisation of conferences. The journal and Center has continued after Sun Ai Park's death in 1999 and presently is based in Kuala Lumpur, Malaysia.

Asian women have strong national networks in several countries, most notably the Philippines, Korea, and India. In the Philippines, Mary John Manazan, President of St Scholastica College, has founded a Women's

Institute that sponsors conferences and publications of Filipina women's literary, sociological, and theological writings, in English and Tagalog. Filipina feminist theologians see themselves as developing a feminist reading of the 'theology of struggle' that emerged in the Philippines in the struggle against dictatorship and economic oppression. They are interested in reclaiming pre-colonial Filipino myth and stories that empower women.[43]

Filipina Protestant women, such as feminist theologian Elizabeth Tapia, professor at the United Theological Seminary in Cavite, are an integral part of this circle. Although the Catholic women cannot be ordained, they have a strong independent base for their social activism and theological reflections through their women's religious orders. They are also closely related to the Filipina feminist movement. Mary John Manazan, for example, has also been the president of Gabriela, the main umbrella organisation for Filipina feminism.

While Christians are the majority population in the Philippines, in South Korea they are about a third of the population, mostly Protestants. Much of Korean Protestantism is conservative and has been slow to ordain women. But there is a progressive wing of Christians who have been involved in the struggle against dictatorship. This struggle sparked the Korean liberation theology movement, 'Minjung' (People's) theology in the 1960s. Male Minjung theologians initially ignored gender issues. Korean women involved in the popular struggle, however, began to develop their own networks for action and theological reflection.

The Korean YWCA, Church Women United, and the Korean Association of Women Theologians are among such networks. Sun Ai Park and the Asian Women's Resource Center, located in Seoul for many years, was also a major catalyst. Korean Christian women have taken up several issues specific to their history: the reunification of North and South Korea, the abuse of women in the sex-tourist trade (an issue for women in many Asian countries), and advocacy for Korean slave workers in Japan who were survivors of Hiroshima and Nagasaki. The demand for reparations to Korean women enslaved as sex workers by the Japanese military during the Second World War had become a particular focus.

Korean feminist theologian, Chung Hyun Khung has made this issue central to her reflections on the sufferings of Korean women. Chung writes particularly on the theme of *han* (unrequited suffering) and the healing of women from their particular *han* (*han-puri*), bringing together a powerful mix of biblical liberation themes, Korean religious images drawn from Buddhism and shamanism, pictorial images and dance in her presentations.[44] Korean women theologians have also supported the struggles of exploited women workers, and a small women–church movement that gathers women across classes developed through this struggle.

In India, Christians are a tiny percentage of the population. Christians include educated elites and those drawn from tribal and 'untouchable' groups. Networks of feminist theology have developed among Catholics and Protestants. The All India Christian Women's Council and WINA (Women's Institute for New Awakening) have held conferences on feminist theology and sponsored research and publication. Local groups, such as Satyashodak (Searchers for Truth) in Bombay work on issues of women in church and society. The Lutheran Seminary in Gurukul has made both women and 'Dalit' (Untouchable) theology areas of particular attention.[45]

Indian feminism has done significant work on issues of oppression of women in society. Female feticide and dowry deaths (the killing of brides to obtain another dowry from another bride), both expressions of the low status of women in Indian society, have been particular foci of concern. Feminist theology in India is supported by both a lively movement at the grassroots level and women's studies in sociological and historical issues at universities.

This very brief survey of the emergence of feminist theology, particularly in the last thirty years of the twentieth century, has made it evident that feminist theology is global. Christian women theologians across the globe are concerned with common themes of critique of sexist symbols in Christianity and the reconstruction of the symbolism for God, Christ, humanity and nature, sin, and salvation, to affirm women's full and equivalent humanity. But women theologians in each context take up issues particular to their societies and histories and draw on cultural resources before and beyond Christianity to envision a more just and loving world.

Notes

1. Mary Daly is the best-known feminist separatist. Her view has been developed in works such as *Pure Lust: Elemental Feminist Philosophy* (Boston, MA: Beacon Press, 1984).
2. For Hildegard and Julian see Rosemary R. Ruether, *Women and Redemption: A Theological History* (Minneapolis, MN: Fortress Press, 1998), pp. 81–92, 104–11.
3. Trans. Earl Jeffrey Richards (New York: Persea Books, 1982); also Pizan's *The Treasure of the City of Ladies*, trans. Sarah Lawson (New York: Penguin Books, 1985).
4. See Ruether, *Women and Redemption*, p. 130.
5. See edition edited by Christine Trevett (London: Quaker Home Service, 1989). Also Ruether, *Women and Redemption*, pp. 138–40.

6. Unabridged republication of London 1701 edition (New York: Source Book Press, 1970). For Astell's life and thought, see Ruth Perry, *The Celebrated Mary Astell: An Early English Feminist* (University of Chicago Press, 1986).

7. French revolutionary republican Olympe de Gouge (1745–93) who died by the guillotine under Robespierre, is best known for her *Declaration of the Rights of Women and Citizen* (1793). See excerpt in Frederick C. Griffin (ed.), *Woman as Revolutionary* (New York: New American Library, 1973), pp. 46–9. English feminist Mary Wollstonecraft (1759–97) is best known for her 1792 tract, *A Vindication of the Rights of Women*, Modern paperback edition (New York: W. W. Norton, 1967). Abigail Adams' challenge to her husband, John Adams, to 'remember the ladies' and include them in the rights of the American constitution, is found in Miriam Schneir (ed.), *Feminism: Essential Historical Writings* (New York: Vintage Books, 1972), pp. 3–4. British Feminist Frances Wright (1795–1852) lectured widely on feminism in the United States in 1828–9 and founded an Owenite socialist community in Tennessee. Her views are found in her *Course of Popular Lectures*. See excerpts in Schneir, *Feminism*, pp. 20–4. For a biography of Frances Wright, see Celia M. Eckhardt, *Fanny Wright: Rebel in America* (Cambridge, MA: Harvard University Press, 1984).

8. For Sarah Grimke's letters, see Larry Ceplair, *The Public Years of Sarah and Angelina Grimke: Selected Writings, 1835–1839* (New York: Columbia University Press, 1989), pp. 204–72. For Mott's thought, see Dana Green (ed.), *Lucretia Mott: Her Complete Speeches and Sermons* (New York: Edwin Meller Press, 1980). Stanton's *The Women's Bible* published in 1895 was reprinted by Arno Press in 1974. For a study of the theology of these three figures, see Ruether, *Women and Redemption*, pp.160–76.

9. For an account of the emergence of liberal and radical feminisms in the late 1960s, see Rosemary R. Ruether, *Christianity and the Making of the Modern Family* (Boston, MA: Beacon Press, 2000), ch. 6. For a personal account of the sexism of the male Left as a spur to the emergence of radical feminism, see Jo Freeman, *The Politics of Women's Liberation* (New York: McKay Co., 1975).

10. Mary Daly's break with Christian feminist reform was signalled by *Beyond God the Father* (Boston, MA: Beacon Press, 1973). Rosemary Ruether's foundational book on feminist theology is *Sexism and God Talk* (Boston, MA: Beacon Press, 1983); Fiorenza's is *In Memory of Her* (New York: Crossroads, 1983).

11. Margaret Farley is a feminist ethicist teaching at Yale Divinity School. Among her major writings are 'Feminist Consciousness and the Interpretation of Scripture', in Letty Russell (ed.), *Feminist Interpretation of the Bible* (Philadelphia, PA: Westminister Press, 1985), pp. 41–51 and 'New Patterns of Relationship: Beginnings of a Moral Revolution', in Walter J. Burghardt (ed.), *Religious Freedom 1965–1975* (New York: Paulist Press, 1977), pp. 64–7. Mary Jo Weaver is a historian teaching at Indiana University. Among her writing is *New Catholic Women* (Bloomington, IN: Indiana University Press, 1995) and *Springs of Water in a Dry Land* (Boston, MA: Beacon Press, 1993). Elizabeth Johnson teaches at Fordham University. Her first major book was *She Who Is: The Mystery of God in Feminist Theological Discourse* (New York: Crossroad, 1993). Susan Ross teaches at Loyola University in Chicago and has authored *Extravagant Affections: A*

Feminist Sacramental Theology (New York: Crossroad, 1998). A major collection of Catholic feminist theological writings is Catherine M. LaCugna (ed.), *Freeing Theology: The Essentials of Theology in Feminist Perspective* (San Francisco, CA: HarperSanFrancisco, 1993).

12. For the demand by the American Catholic bishops that Catholic theologians teaching at Catholic universities receive an episcopal *mandatum*, see 'Catholic U. Moves to Tighten Control over Religious Studies Faculty', in the *National Catholic Reporter* (17 Dec. 1999), pp. 3–4.

13. For a critique of the 1976 Vatican Declaration against women's ordination, see Leonard and Arlene Swidler (eds.), *Women Priests: A Catholic Commentary on the Vatican Declaration* (New York: Paulist Press, 1977). For the proceedings of the first Catholic Women's Ordination Conference, see Anne Marie Gardiner (ed.), *Women and Catholic Priesthood: An Expanded Vision* (New York: Simon and Schuster, 1979).

14. See Rosemary R. Ruether, *Women–Church: The Theology and Practice of Feminist Liturgical Communities* (San Francisco, CA: Harper and Row, 1986); Mary Hunt and Diane Neu, *Women–Church Source Book* (Silver Spring, MD: WATER, 1993).

15. Letty Russell, *The Church in the Round: Feminist Interpretation of the Church* (Philadelphia, PA: Westminster, 1993); Rebecca Chopp, *The Power to Speak: Feminism, Language and God* (New York: Crossroad, 1992), pp. 72–8.

16. Mary Daly's biography is found in her *Outcourse: The Be-Dazzling Voyage* (San Francisco, CA: HarperSanFrancisco, 1992).

17. Daly has followed the practice of teaching women separately from men. A male student has sued the college for being excluded from her class and Boston College responded by an enforced retirement of Daly from their faculty. Daly is suing the college: see 'Law Firm Forces Mary Daly's Hand', in the *National Catholic Reporter* (5 Mar. 1999), pp. 3–4. Daly's most recent book is *Quintessence: Realizing the Archaic Future: A Radical Essential Feminist Manifesto* (Boston, MA: Beacon Press, 1998).

18. For Daly's definitions of her distinctive wordage, see her *Webster's First Intergalactic Wickedary of the English Language* (Boston, MA: Beacon Press, 1987).

19. Sallie McFague, *Metaphorical Theology: Models of God in Religious Language* (Philadelphia, PA: Fortress, 1982); *Models of God: Theology for an Ecological, Nuclear Age* (Philadelphia, PA: Fortress, 1987); *The Body of God: An Ecological Theology* (Minneapolis, MN: Fortress, 1993).

20. Beverly Harrison's major collection of essays is Carol Robb (ed.), *Making the Connections* (Boston, MA: Beacon Press, 1985); her major book is *Our Right to Choose* (Boston, MA: Beacon Press, 1983).

21. Carter Heyward, *A Priest Forever* (Cleveland, OH: Pilgrim Press, 1999); *The Redemption of God: A Theology of Mutual Relation* (Washington, DC: University Press of America, 1982); *Touching our Strength: The Erotic as the Power and the Love of God* (San Francisco, CA: HarperSanFrancisco, 1989); Mary Hunt, *Fierce Tenderness: A Feminist Theology of Friendship* (New York: Crossroad, 1991).

22. Delores Williams' major book is *Sisters in the Wilderness: The Challenge of Womanist God-Talk* (Maryknoll, NY: Orbis Press, 1993). Almost all the major womanist theologians are represented in Emilie Townes' volume, *A Troubling*

in my Soul: Womanist Perspectives on Evil and Suffering (Maryknoll, NY: Orbis Press, 1993). Letha Scanzoni and Nancy Hardesty, *All We're Meant to Be* (Nashville, TN: Abingdon, 1986), first published in 1975.

23. Ada María Isasi-Díaz, *En la Lucha: Elaborating a Mujerista Theology* (Minneapolis, MN: Fortress Press, 1993) and *Mujerista Theology* (Maryknoll, NY: Orbis Press, 1996).

24. Aquino's major book, *Nuestro Clamor por la Vida* (1992) was published in English, *Our Cry for Life* (Maryknoll, NY: Orbis Press, 1993).

25. Kwok Pui-lan teaches at the Episcopal Seminary in Cambridge, MA and is author of *Discovering the Bible in the Non-biblical World* (Maryknoll, NY: Orbis Press, 1995). Chung Hyun Khung teaches at Union Seminary in New York and is author of *The Struggle to be the Sun Again: Introducing Asian Women's Theology* (Maryknoll, NY: Orbis Press, 1990).

26. Carol P. Christ, *Laughter of Aphrodite: Reflections on a Journey to the Goddess* (San Francisco, CA: Harper and Row, 1987) and *Rebirth of the Goddess: Finding Meaning in Feminist Spirituality* (Reading, MA: Addison Wesley, 1997).

27. Rosemary Ruether, *New Woman, New Earth: Sexist Ideologies and Human Liberation* (San Francisco, CA: Harper, 1975) and *Gaia and God: An Ecofeminist Theology of Earth Healing* (San Francisco, CA: Harper Collins, 1994). Mary Daly, *Gyn/Ecology: The Metaethics of Radical Feminism* (Boston, MA: Beacon Press, 1978).

28. For example, Mary McClintock Fulkerson, *Changing the Subject: Women's Discourses and Feminist Theology* (Minneapolis, MN: Fortress, 1994). Sally McFague, *Models of God: Theology for an Ecological, Nuclear Age* (Philadelphia, PA: Fortress Press, 1987); *The Ecological Theology* (London: SCM Press, 1993).

29. Grossmann had a chapter on 'Mann und Frau' in her habilitation in 1964. She continued to write on Medieval and Renaissance women writers: see Helen Schweigen-Straumann, 'Zum Werdegang von Elisabeth Grossmann', in Theodor and Helen Schweigen-Straumann (eds.), *Theologie zwischen Zeiten und Kontinenten* (Basel: Herder Verlag, 1993), pp. 483–8.

30. Kari Børresen, *Subordination and Equivalence: The Nature and Role of Women in Augustine and Thomas Aquinas* (reprint Kampen: Kok Pharos Press, 1995).

31. Dorothee Sölle, *The Strength of the Weak: Toward a Christian Feminist Identity* (Philadelphia: Westminster, 1984).

32. Catharina Halkes, *Met Miriam is het Begonnen* (Kampen: Kok Pharos Press, 1980). Her book on ecofeminism has been translated into English as *New Creation: Christian Feminism and the Renewal of the Earth* (London: SPCK, 1991).

33. Daphne Hampson, *Theology and Feminism* (Oxford: Basil Blackwell, 1990).

34. Condren's major book on Irish history and spirituality is *The Serpent and the Goddess: Women, Religion and Power in Celtic Ireland* (San Francisco, CA: Harper and Row, 1981); Zappone has published *The Hope for Wholeness: A Spirituality for Feminists* (Mystic, NY: Twenty-Third Publications, 1991).

35. Carla Ricci's major book is *Maria di Magdala e le molte altre: Donne sul cammino di Gesu?* (Naples: Editor Auria, 1991), in English: *Mary Madgalene and Many Others: Women Who Followed Jesus*, trans. Paul Burns (Minneapolis, MN: Fortress, 1994).

36. The papers from the 1986 intercontinental meeting were published as Virginia Fabella and Mercy Amba Oduyoye (eds.), *With Passion and Compassion: Third World Women Doing Theology* (Maryknoll, NY: Orbis Press, 1988).
37. The papers from this conference were published as Mary John Manazan et al. (eds.), *Women Resisting Violence: Spirituality for Life* (Maryknoll, NY: Orbis Press, 1996).
38. For a collection of essays by these and other Latin American feminist theologians, from the Second Encuentro of Latin American women theologians, see Ana María Tepedino and María Pilar Aquino (eds.), *Entre la Indignación y la Esperanza: Teologa Feminista Latinoamericana* (Bogotá, Columbia: Indo-American Press, 1998).
39. Ivone Gebara, *Teología a Ritmo de Mujer* (Madrid: San Pablo, 1995) and *Intuiciones Ecofeministas: Ensayo para repensar el conocimiento y la religión* (Montevideo: Doble Clic, 1998). A volume of her essays in English is *Longing for Running Water: Ecofeminism and Liberation*, trans. David Molineaux (Minneapolis, MN: Fortress, 1999).
40. For an analysis of these two approaches to theology in Africa, see Emmanuel Martey, *African Theology: Inculturation and Liberation* (Maryknoll, NY: Orbis Press, 1993).
41. See *The Will to Arise: Women, Tradition and the Church in Africa*, Mercy Amba Oduyoye and Musimbi Kanyoro (eds.), (Maryknoll, NY: Orbis Press, 1992).
42. Oduyoye's major book is *Daughters of Anowa: African Women and Patriarchy* (Maryknoll, NY: Orbis Press,1995).
43. This approach to feminist theology is expressed in the paper 'Toward an Asian Principle of Interpretation: A Filipino Women's Experience', authored by Rosario Battung, Virginia Fabella, Arche Ligo, Mary John Manazan, and Elizabeth Tapia, and published by the Women's Institute of St. Scholastica College, Manila.
44. See Chung's essay, 'Han-puri: Doing Theology from Asian Women's Perspective', in Virginia Fabella and Sun Ai Park (eds.), *We Dare to Dream: Doing Theology as Asian Women* (Maryknoll, NY: Orbis Press, 1990), pp. 135–46, and 'Your Comfort vs. my Death', in Manazan et al. (eds.), *Women resisting Violence*, pp. 129–40. Chung's multimedia style was represented in her controversial speech at the 1991 World Council of Churches' Assembly in Canberra, Australia, 'Come Holy Spirit: Renew the Whole Creation', available on videotape from Lou Niznik, 15726 Ashland Drive, Laurel, MA, USA.
45. See the essays in V. Devasahayam (ed.), *Dalits and Women: Quest for Humanity* (Madras: Gurukul Summer Institute, 1992).

Selected reading

Rossi, Alice S. (ed.). *The Feminist Papers*, revised and updated edition, Boston, MA: Northeastern University Press, 1993.
Ruether, Rosemary Radford. *Women and Redemption: A Theological History*, Minneapolis, MN: Fortress Press, 1998.
Russell, Letty and Clarkson, Shannon (eds.). *Dictionary of Feminist Theology*, Louisville, KY: Westminster, 1996.
Schneir, Miriam (ed.). *Feminism: Essential Historical Writings*, New York: Vintage Books, 1972.

2 Feminist theology as intercultural discourse
KWOK PUI-LAN

Feminist theology has become a global movement as women with different histories and cultures challenge patriarchal teachings and practices of the church and articulate their faith and understanding of God. Feminist theology is no more defined by the interests of middle-class European and American women and by Eurocentric frameworks and mind-set. Its scope has been much broadened to encompass the theological voices of women from the Third World and from minority communities in the United States. These newer theological partners have created new names for their theological movements, utilised new resources as theological data, challenged established norms of interpretation, and raised significant questions about the production of theological knowledge.

This chapter considers the ways in which feminist theology has been challenged by the emerging awareness of cultural diversity among women, and has creatively forged new insights in the midst of intercultural critique, dialogue, and partnership. Culture is defined by Mercy Amba Oduyoye of Ghana as 'a people's world-view, way of life, values, philosophy of life, the psychology that governs behaviour, their sociology and social arrangements, all that they have carved and cultured out of their environment to differentiate their style of life from other peoples'.[1] As the 'life-world' of a people, culture has become a site of struggle as people who have experienced colonialism, slavery, exploitation, and genocide reclaim their cultural identity and their sense of who they are after a long history of oppression. Women in these marginalised communities have to negotiate their cultural identities in multiple and complex ways, taking into consideration gender, class, race, and other differences. Cultural difference has been a focal point of contention when women debate on identity politics, the politics of 'difference', and solidarity among women across racial, cultural, and religious boundaries. Feminist theology must pay attention to how women from diverse cultural and social contexts articulate their differences as a result of culture, language, and social realities, without assuming that women's experience is everywhere the same. As a theological movement, feminist theology will be strengthened by the multicultural, multivocal, and multireligious character of women's expressions of faith that bear witness to the inclusive and compassionate God.

In celebrating cultural diversity among women and in lifting every voice, women of faith should not lose sight of the new challenges brought about by the age of globalisation and transnationalism. For today, the politics of cultural difference is no more fought only in terms of Third World/First World, black/white, national/global, or racial minority/majority. Women in every part of the world are faced with the impacts of global capitalism and transnationalism that seek to incorporate all sectors of the global economy into their logic of commodification and to assume a homogenisation of global culture, especially through the mass media and the information superhighway.[2] Religious reflection and theological analysis must not be seen as separate domains with their own practices, immune from the global processes of economic restructuring and social and cultural formation. Embedded in the cultural politics of global capitalism, feminist theologians must articulate an alternative vision of cultural resistance, contestation, and difference, as well as solidarity among women.

This chapter will be divided into three parts. The first part discusses the intercultural origins of feminist theology from different parts of the world. The second part focusses on the critique of universalising in Euro-American women's theology and the different attempts to articulate differences among women. The last section discusses the future of feminist theology in the age of globalisation and transnationalism.

THE INTERCULTURAL ORIGINS
OF FEMINIST THEOLOGY

Feminist theology is pluralistic and diverse, rooted in women's religious experiences, struggles, action and reflection, dreams and hopes. When describing this diverse and multifaceted theological movement, scholars tend to give primacy to the contributions of women of European descent. They are considered 'fore-mothers' who have laid the foundation of the discipline, upon which others can build.[3] The assumption is that white feminist theology appeared first on the scene, and its emergence made possible the development of black women's theology, Hispanic women's theology and various Third World feminist theologies. Such a reading is not only Eurocentric, it also mystifies and obscures the profoundly intercultural character of feminist theology. I want to argue that feminist theology is not only multicultural, rooted in multiple communities and cultural contexts, but is also intercultural because these different cultures are not isolated but intertwined with one another as a result of colonialism, slavery, and cultural hegemony of the West. By intercultural, I mean the interaction and juxtaposition, as well as tension and resistance when two or more cultures are brought together sometimes organically and sometimes through violent means in the modern period.

A powerful myth that sustains colonial authority is the construction of 'the West and the rest', which assumes that Western culture and history is qualitatively different and separated from those of the rest of the world. Within this framework, Western women's development of self-consciousness and their theological pursuit are seen as different, having little to do with women in other parts of the world. Such an interpretation is biased and unfounded, as a brief review of both the first- and second-wave feminist movements will demonstrate. Historians have increasingly paid attention to how the leaders of the first wave of women's movement in nineteenth-century America used racial discourses to justify their causes of abolitionism, benevolence, suffragism, missionary ideology, and feminism.[4] Comparing their second-class status to the slaves, they argued that it was not fair for black men to have the vote, while white women with nobler nature and much better education were deprived of the privilege to do so. White women at that time were seen as the angels in the home. The cult of womanhood, defined by gentility and domesticity, was actually based on the image of a 'white lady', whose existence often relied on the exploitation of the labour of black women. At the same time, the expansion of colonies provided new opportunities for women on both sides of the Atlantic to organise mission societies, to raise funds, and to carve out a sphere of influence in the church. In the name of saving their 'heathen' sisters, European and white American women set out to explore new roles as missionaries, explorers, educators, and ethnographers, roles that were previously denied them by the constraints of Victorian gender norms. Women's changing status and their increasing organisational power, both in the church and in the political arena, prompted their critique of church teachings on women and patriarchal elements in the Bible. Elizabeth Cady Stanton published *The Woman's Bible* in such a climate at the end of the nineteenth century.

The second wave of feminism emerged in the wake of the Civil Rights movement and the Black Power movement of the 1960s with the advent of the black consciousness era. The 1960s also saw intense nationalistic struggles in many parts of the Third World, and student protests around the globe. The demand for desegregation and civil liberties within the USA and decolonised struggles abroad heightened white women's awareness of their oppression within the church and society. In *The Church and Second Sex*, Mary Daly argues that the image of the self-sacrificing Eternal Woman in the Catholic church exacts a heavy toll on women's psyche similar to the effects racist myths have on black people.[5] Having worked in East Harlem, Letty Russell introduced the feminist perspective in what she has learned from the Civil Rights movement and liberation theology from Latin America in *Human Liberation in a Feminist Perspective: A Theology*.[6] The emergence of white feminist theology in the contemporary period was not an isolated phenomenon, but was embedded in the larger political, cultural, and social configurations of its time. The construction of white women's selfhood and emancipation was influenced by the intercultural encounter with people of other races and cultures.

The origins of feminist theology from minority communities in the USA and in the Third World are complex, as these women have to challenge sexism within their culture simultaneously with racism, colonialism, and economic exploitation. Tracing the emergence of black feminist consciousness, Katie Geneva Cannon describes how the struggle against white supremacy and male superiority led black women to reread the Bible for sustenance, hope, and empowerment.[7] Patricia Hill Collins has characterised the unique standpoint of black women as 'outsiders-within' because they have a distinct view of the contradictions between white people's actions and ideologies.[8] Black women are not only marginalised by the white society but also by male chauvinism in the black church and black religion. The Black Power movement was dominated by men, and black theology in general has left out black women's stories and experiences.

Underscoring the multiple oppressions of black women, African American theologian Delores Williams uses the biblical figure of Hagar to illuminate black women's struggles for survival, quality of life, and economic empowerment.[9] To counteract stereotypical negative images of black women, black women theologians have discovered the beauty of black women's culture and the strength and moral wisdom of black women. Many have adopted the term 'womanist' as coined by Alice Walker in 1983 to name their theological project. A womanist is a black feminist who is responsible, in charge, outrageous, audacious, and courageous, who loves other women and appreciates black women's culture and history.[10] Delving deeper into their cultural heritage, Karen Baker-Fletcher notes: 'Womanist theologians and ethicists have dusted off forgotten and neglected texts, recovered the memories of living Black women in the aural–oral tradition, and lifted theological and ethical themes from such cultural resources.'[11]

Hispanic/Latina women in the USA name their theological reflection and praxis '*mujerista* theology'. According to Ada María Isasi-Díaz: 'A *mujerista* is someone who makes a preferential option for Latina women and for their struggle for liberation. *Mujerista* understand their struggle for liberation as a communal praxis. They understand that their task is to gather their people's hopes and expectations about justice and peace.'[12] Hispanic/Latino people are racially and culturally diverse, formed by the mixing of different races, languages, and cultures. *Mestizaje* is the mixture of white people and native people in Latin America and Caribbean; *mulatez* is the mixture of white people and black people. *Mujerista* theology comes from *mestizaje* and *mulatez* cultures, formed by the intermingling of Amerindian, African, and Spanish cultural elements to create something new. To unpack the multilayered stories of Hispanic/Latina women and to understand their lived experience, Isasi-Díaz has used ethnographical methods in cultural anthropology.[13] Listening to many stories and multiple voices, *mujerista* theological inquiry becomes more interdisciplinary as new data and methods are used.

Christianity was brought to the Third World with gunboats and cannons in the colonial period. Third World women have ambivalent relationships with Christian culture: on the one hand, Christianity has been an integral part of the colonial discourse, and, on the other hand, Christian women have found liberating vision in the Bible and in their faith. Missionaries brought with them not only the Bible and the Christian religion, but also their cultural assumptions of womanhood, gender roles, and sexuality. Colonial feminism elevated the social status of white women in Western culture and contrasted it with the subordination of women in non-Western cultures. These cultures were seen as 'primitive' and 'uncivilised' because they practised zenanas and harems, female infanticide and suttee, concubinage and polygamy, foot-binding and child marriage. The social progress of other races was measured in terms of how much they conformed to Western middle-class gender relations, which were vigorously promoted by the church and the mission schools.

In the struggle for national independence and in reclaiming cultural identity, Third World men look at colonial feminism with scorn and rein-scribe what they believe to be 'traditional' gender roles. Third World feminist theologians, therefore, have to fight against feminism imposed from outside as well as the misogyny of Third World men who put women down in the name of protecting their national culture. Mercy Amba Oduyoye, for example, has criticised Western feminists' obsession with the issue of female circumcision, without paying attention to survival and economic exploitation of African women. She also challenges African men who create myths of homogenous national and cultural identity: 'Why do I cringe every time I read African self-identity or African authenticity? Then I realized that it is male writers who make me cringe . . . When they acknowledge that the past is not all golden, are they saying that these "ungolden" aspects include the dehumanization of women, and that these should be eliminated?'[14] Similar to Oduyoye, other Third World feminist theologians have to engage in intercultural critique when they articulate their theology. Latin American theologian Elsa Tamez writes:

> A struggle against violence toward women has to place its analysis within its own culture and in relation to the foreign patriarchal imposition of other cultures. If this is not done, we deceive ourselves, because all cultures, in one form or another, to a greater or lesser degree, have legitimized the power of men over women, and this has generated the violence of the superior against the subordinate, who is considered inferior. This violence is, in turn, doubled when one culture dominates another.[15]

Third World feminist theologians have the double tasks of challenging androcentric myths and practices in their culture and in Christianity. They have also creatively used women's cultural resources such as songs, writings, poetry, and performances.[16] Some have begun to use newer tools from post-colonial theory and cultural studies to assist their work.

The emphasis on the intercultural character of feminist theology under-scores that women's contexts, though diverse, are closely connected with one another because of the legacy of slavery, colonialism, and genocide. Though rooted in the experiences of a particular racial or cultural group, feminist theology has always been developed as a result of the interaction or confrontation of different cultures. This insight challenges us to think of culture as fluid and open-ended, constantly reworked by women, and calls for a multifaceted and nuanced discussion of cultural difference, looking for both the points of departure and the areas of intersection and overlapping. At the same time, it safeguards against a monolithic understanding of femi-nist theology through universalising the experiences of one social group or a parochial conception that privileges the epistemological viewpoint of the group to which one belongs.

CRITIQUE OF UNIVERSALISING AND DISCOURSE ON DIFFERENCE

Since the 1980s, the tendency of Euro-American feminist theologians to generalise their experiences as if they speak for all women has been criticised by both white scholars and women of colour. When these feminist theologians charge that traditional male theology has left out women's experiences, they generally have in mind the experiences of middle-class white women. Sheila Greeve Davaney has challenged white feminist theologians' use of women's experience as a foundation or a normative claim for feminist theology. She says the appeal to women's experience is to 'assert a universal and common essence that somehow defined women as women, and that laid the basis for feminist solidarity as well as providing the content for feminist reflection'.[17] She suggests a historicist understanding of women's existence and warns against universalising white women's experience to cover up racial and class privileges.

Euro-American feminist theology is influenced by the intellectual climate and feminist theory developed at the time. The early wave of feminist theory, produced by Sherry Ortner, Gayle Rubin, and Nancy Chodorow in the 1970s, did not pay sufficient attention to cultural and historical specificity. These theorists were trying to search for grand theoretical explanations for the social reproduction of gender and women's universal subordinate status. White feminist theologians, too, assumed that patriarchy was the common enemy of women and set out to exorcise Christianity from its androcentric symbols and practices. But, as Delores Williams points out, black women are not oppressed only by men, but by white women as well. White women's critique of patriarchy is less valid as a tool to analyse black women's oppression because, although white women are oppressed by patriarchy, they at the same time enjoy the protection and privileges accorded to them by the white patriarchal American institutions.[18] Responding to the challenges of women of colour, biblical scholar Elisabeth Schüssler Fiorenza proposes to shift from patriarchy, based on gender dualism, to kyriarchy (the rule of emperor/master/lord/father/husband over his subordinates), to signal more comprehensive, interlocking and multiplicative forms of oppression.[19]

Euro-American feminist theologians find that the understanding of human nature by traditional male theologians is fundamentally flawed because they have failed to take notice that human beings are gendered. Following Valerie Saiving, some feminist theologians believe that women's sin is not pride, disobedience, or egotism because these characteristics reflect the experiences of men who enjoy more power in society than women. Instead, women's problem or sin is the failure to assume responsibility, sloth, the lack of ego, and triviality.[20] Such anthropological understanding locates sin primarily in the individual without placing it in the larger contexts of the social and political. The gendered self that emerges from these theological constructions reflects the experiences of white middle-class women and not the majority of women of colour, who have to assume crucial responsibility for the survival of their family and community.

Rebecca Chopp, in a crucial essay, provides a plausible explanation of why some of the first generation of feminist theologians would universalise their experiences and subscribe to an essentialist viewpoint. She observes that most of these 'liberal', white Protestant and Catholic theologians share the theoretical assumptions of modern theory. She summarises the three-point structure of modern theory as: (1) the belief in a coherent self with an essential structure, (2) the belief that there exists a true form of reason to understand the essential structures of the self and the world, and (3) the belief that history and culture can be communicated and understood through language without ambiguities. Modern theory, Chopp suggests, 'understands itself as uncovering the foundations of existence, objectively stating them for the beneficial use of humankind, and communicating them through the translucent medium of language'.[21]

But Chopp's postmodern critique of the modernist understanding of self, reason, and language does not interrogate the racial prejudice of many of the influential thinkers who shaped modern consciousness, including Locke, Hume, and Kant.[22] The greatest irony of the Enlightenment was that the beliefs of equality, liberty, and dignity of human beings were used to justify slavery and colonialism. Enlightenment thinkers created categories of people based on racial and cultural groupings: the 'exotic', 'oriental', and 'East' and the more specific ones like 'Negro', 'Indian', and 'Jews'. These people were seen either as less than human or as exotic or primitive souls needing the guidance of the Man of Reason. They saw the civilising mission of the West as to bring the benefits of capitalist development and Western civilisation to the colonised to broaden the latter's freedom. The failure to see that other cultures have their logic and reason and the universalising of Western experience are expressions of colonial motive.

Aware of the danger of universalising, womanist, *mujerista*, and feminist theologians around the world have stressed the differences among women, and intense debates around the politics of identity have taken place. As scholars use different theoretical frameworks to discuss identity and subjectivity of women, several discourses on difference have emerged in the past several decades.[23] Although these discourses have their own history and institutional sites, they are not isolated but often overlap with one another. The first discourse emerged in the late 1970s and early 1980s when Jacquelyn Grant, Delores Williams, and other womanist theologians spoke about the 'multiple oppression' or 'triple jeopardy' of black women. In her 1979 article, 'Black Theology and the Black Woman', Grant charges that black women are marginalised as black and as women, as well as discriminated against by the black churches and by black theology.[24] Williams' provocative essay 'The Colour of Feminism' challenges that when white feminist theology ignores the concerns of black and poor women, its claims are exclusive and imperialistic as the Christian patriarchy it opposes.[25] Black feminist scholars have insisted that the universal human, stripped of all particularities, does not exist. The liberal ideal of the equality of human beings based on a shared human nature, upheld by much feminist theology, does not consider the fact that social reality is simultaneously constructed by class, race, and gender. Sheila Briggs argues:

> Within feminism there has been much discussion in recent years of the 'politics of identity', the need to claim one's particular identity as an act of resistance to cultural hegemony of white, male, middle-class society. Yet a woman's identity is not only female. She also has the particularities of race and class, as well as those of sexual orientation, age, type of physical ability – the list could be lengthened to the extent to which actual women experience their lives in a multiplicity of identities.[26]

She further argues that these particularities cannot be subsumed under one paradigm of human difference, for the oppressions of gender, class, and race are not symmetrical and the burden of difference is not evenly distributed in the larger society.

The second discourse emerged out of the recognition of multiple identities of women and the contention that the subject of feminist theology – woman – is discursively constituted. Mary McClintock Fulkerson challenges that the liberal universal subject still looms large in feminist theology, making it impossible to deal adequately with the differences among women. Using poststructuralist theory, Fulkerson argues that there is no 'natural sexed subject', because the subject is constituted through the signifying processes of language. She proposes to move from the liberal subject, whose transcendental and ahistorical character forms the basis of the false universals as 'women's experience', to investigate the multiple subject positions of women, formed by the intersection of different and sometimes competing discourses. The destabilising of the category of 'woman' allows the differences of women to be displayed and investigated. She says: 'The point is not to lose the subject "woman," but to *change the subject* in the sense that the complex production of multiple identities becomes basic to our thinking.'[27] By doing so, she hopes to take seriously that subjects are constructed out of particular social relations and that women's oppression takes multiple forms. Furthermore, the multiple-subject positions of women are formed in relation to and not separated from others' identities. One significant insight from poststructuralism is that our identity is formed by the others it creates, and thus our narration of our own identity must be open to the criticism of the other.[28]

The third discourse of identity also assumes multiple-subject positions, but accents the fluid and hybridised self, situated in-between two cultures or races. Japanese American theologian, Rita Nakashima Brock, argues that the non-dualistic metaphysics and religions of East Asia enable one to develop a more fluid sense of reality. Situating in a variety of worlds, Asian Americans develop a sense of identity that is multiple, transversal, and hybridised. Trying to live with the tension of the competing claims of these different worlds and to hold together all the complex parts of the self, Nakashima Brock proposes the concept of interstitial integrity as a category of theological anthropology. Interstitial refers to the places in-between, and interstitial integrity is the refusal to rest in one place, to make constricting either/or decisions, and to be placed always on the periphery.[29] Living in the interstices, Asian American women can find diverse cultural resources for their spiritual empowerment and sustenance. The notion of the self as multiple and hybridised is also found in *mestizaje* and *mulatez* cultures in *mujerista* theology. *Mujerista* theologians resist assimilation into the white mainstream and insist on embracing and celebrating cultural diversity. Crucial to the self-understanding of Hispanic/Latina women is *la lucha*, their daily struggle to survive and to live fully as human beings. Because Hispanic/Latina women are multiply and contradictorily positioned in more than one culture, they need to resist constantly cultural marginalisation, language alienation, and economic injustice.[30]

The newest discourse of identity is based on the subversive discourse of queer theory, especially in the writings of Judith Butler. In *Gender Trouble*, Butler challenges all forms of gender essentialism, because gender is not 'natural' but constituted by repeated performance: 'The univocity of sex, the internal coherence of gender, and the binary framework for both sex and gender are . . . regulatory fictions that consolidate and naturalise the convergent power regimes of masculine and heterosexist oppression.'[31] Following Butler, Kathy Rudy in *Sex and the Church* debunks the homo/hetero binary that shapes much of the church's current controversy on sexual morality and ordination of gay men and lesbians. Similar to 'men' and 'women', Rudy insists 'heterosexual' and 'gay' are not natural and transhistorical categories, but socially constructed in particular circumstances.[32] The radical questioning of gender and sexual orientation destabilises our thinking of 'woman' and 'lesbian' and challenges the complacency of identity politics based on 'woman's essential nature' or commonalities of lesbian experience. Rudy calls for a sexual ethics that is not based on the old and traditional distinctions of male/female or gay/straight, but on Christian values that clearly mark the differences between moral and immoral sex.[33]

FEMINIST THEOLOGY IN THE AGE OF GLOBAL CAPITALISM

The varied discourses on differences of women and the destabilising of foundational concepts of feminist theology such as self, sex, and gender raise the questions of the future of feminist theology and the possibility of international solidarity and co-operation. As the world is becoming much more linked together because of the global market, women cannot afford to be divided because of their identity politics. Elisabeth Schüssler Fiorenza articulates such a concern:

> In the face of increasing global violence against women as well as the growing neocapitalist exploitation of the so-called two-thirds world and the explosion of an 'informatics of domination', feminist theory cannot stop with the postmodern 'subject-in-language' and its permanent destabilisation, global dispersal, and atomizing regionalisation. It must develop a theoretical discourse and analytic framework that can account for the interaction between cultural–religious, economic, and political spheres of production.[34]

As we face the challenges of the new millennium, feminists of all colours must be conscious of the new forms of violence and injustice brought by global capitalism and information technology. Ethicist Larry Rasmussen argues that there have been three waves of globalisation which fundamentally changed nature and the world.[35] The first wave was colonisation, with conquest, commerce, Christianity, and the spread of European-based civilisation. 'Wild' nature was 'tamed', and so were native peoples. Diversity of peoples, cultures, and nature was disregarded and European men set themselves as the norm of being human. The second wave was post-war development when societies were measured against their level of production and gross national product. Societies would be labelled as 'developed' and 'underdeveloped' in this single progressive scheme based on the criteria of production and science and technology. The way of the life in the West – capitalist democracy, economic progress, and advanced technology – becomes the standard for other societies to model.

We are currently in the third wave of globalisation, which is post-cold-war free-trade capitalism. Rasmussen argues: 'the chief characteristic of globalisation's third wave is the extension and intensification of market society in a capitalist mode in such a way that the logic of the economy is taken to be the logic of society itself'.[36] With the disintegration of the Eastern European bloc and the collapse of the former Soviet Union, capitalism has been hailed as the winning ideology with no competition. Prominent economists have argued that all societies will have to adjust sooner or later to liberal capitalist modernity. In this stage of globalisation, the market is not subjected to the control of individual nation-states, but directed by transnational economic powers defined by corporate interests and their governmental allies. The market-driven economy restructures cultural formations in such a way that they will reinforce the values and interests of capitalist economy. We have already felt the impact of globalisation on many areas of our lives, including knowledge production, media, entertainment, arts, and sports. Politically it will be more difficult to organise against big corporate powers with their flexible capital and as a result people's self-governing and self-organising power will be limited.

This new wave of globalisation and transnationalism affects women's lives in fundamental ways and requires new thinking and creative responses from feminist theologians. Feminist theology is contextually based, but the contexts we live in are inseparably linked together today as never before. A feminist theology and ethics that works for women's liberation and economic empowerment must develop strategies to link the local with the global in its social analysis. For example, transnational industry has created a gendered international division of labour, which makes use of cheap and 'flexible' labour of women in Asia, Latin America as well as Asian and Latina immigrant women in the USA. A new social formation linking women of the different continents takes place in the global restructuring process, in which neo-capitalism, anti-immigrant racism, and patriarchal gender stratification intersect.[37] In response to such new challenges, womanist ethicist Toinette Eugene argues that feminist theologians and ethicists need to develop globalisation ethics and articulate a new moral imagination that fleshes out the moral imperative of 'solidarity with the poor' in new ways. Such an imagination includes the delineation of an alternative ethical system that questions the complex power dynamics of the status quo and the formulation of responsible action and praxis.[38]

Another critical task for feminist theology is to develop an intercultural hermeneutics that heightens our cross-cultural sensitivity and underscores the relation between cultural–religious production and social and economic formation. As I have argued, feminist theology has always been developed in the midst of intercultural encounters of women. More in-depth studies of how women's lives and cultures have been connected globally in the periods of colonialism and development will lay the foundation for critical analysis of our current wave of globalisation. Postcolonial critics who investigate the intersection between gender, race, sexuality, and colonialism have already done some work along these lines. Building on their work, a multicultural and multiracial investigation of the history of the development of feminist theology will elucidate how women's social location shapes their religious ideas. We can learn from the past how religious women have succeeded or failed to work together and form coalitions across economic and racial boundaries. These lessons from the past will be invaluable in strengthening solidarity among women in the future.

This intercultural hermeneutics can learn from and engage in critical dialogue with cultural studies, a field that has stimulated many discussions on popular culture and politics of culture in the fields of humanities and social sciences. Many critics have debunked the myths of the unity and homogeneity of national and cultural identities based on a certain geographical location. Benedict Anderson, for example, argues that stories and narratives play crucial roles in shaping national identity through the construction of an 'imagined community'.[39] James Clifford examines the late twentieth-century phenomenon of de-territorialisation of culture in travel, diaspora, and ethnographical practices and coins the term 'travelling cultures'. Clifford suggests that the conventional emphasis on 'home' and 'dwelling' as shaping individual and cultural identity has largely been replaced by the more fluid travelling-in-dwelling and dwelling-in-travelling.[40] Instead of treating culture as something static and given, feminist critics such as Lisa Lowe, Gloria Anzaldúa, and Trinh T. Minh-Ha have investigated women's hybrid and diasporic identity formed by immigration, exile, and existence in the borderland.[41] These new theoretical approaches push feminist theologians to construct discourse on cultural difference that recognises the formation of new subject positions of women in globalisation and the ambiguous areas of 'in-between'. The strategic use of 'African', 'Asian', 'Latin American', 'womanist', '*mujerista*', and 'white' to name different theological movements must be seen as provisional and contingent, without resorting to a new form of cultural essentialism. The diversity and multiplicity implied in each of these terms must be fully recognised.

Feminist theology in the age of globalisation requires a new understanding of the other, a critical category in feminist theory and theology. In the past, the self/other or the us/them have been constructed largely in a binary way. To assert the self, the difference of the other must be avoided and the boundary of otherness disregarded. Theologian Robert J. Schreiter offers a helpful elucidation of the various strategies to collapse the other into the same:

> The 'us' (1) *homogenises* the other (the other is not really different if you get to know it or them, and so difference is ignored as a peripheral issue; it (2) *colonises* the other (the other is inferior and needs to be raised to a higher level, whereupon the difference will disappear); it (3) *demonises* the other (repressed desire or conflict is projected onto the other and the other is considered a threat to be expunged); it (4) *romanticises* the other (the other is seen to be superior in its otherness, but the otherness is of an exotic nature that does not threaten our way of seeing and doing things); or it (5) *pluralises* the other (we are all different, so difference doesn't make any difference).[42]

Feminist theology in the past has challenged the tendency to universalise the self and highlighted the difference of the other women because of class, race, age, and sexual preference. But the notions of the multiple-subject positions of women and the hybridised self would open new possibilities for the overlapping of identities and for mutual engagement. It is important for women working across differences to challenge the binary and exclusionary construct of the self and the other, and to begin to see the self in the other. Denise Ackermann, a theologian from South Africa who has constantly spoken against apartheid, describes the fluidity between the self and the other in this way:

> the practice of mutual relationship comes when I turn my gaze from myself and '*look*' into the face of the other. It is you and I, they and we, seeing and being seen. In the face of the other I see a true and authentic human being. We both reflect something of the image of God. The practice of relationship means that I acknowledge that I am not complete unto my self. I see myself in the face of the other. I am not fully my self until I can see 'me' in your face. You are the mirror of myself. I am the mirror of yourself. Only when we can see ourselves and each other are we fully human.[43]

This understanding of the mutual interaction between the self and the other applies not only to human relationship but also to human being's relationship to the natural world. Globalisation has threatened the lives of indigenous communities and sustenance economies that poor women depend on for their survival. An emerging concern for feminist theology is *ecological solidarity* in the face of the massive destruction of natural habitat, the patent of genes and natural resources, and the erosion of the spiritual bond between humanity and creation. Theologian Sallie McFague proposes the image of the 'world as the body of God' to recapture the sacramental dimension of creation in an ecological theology.[44] Aruna Gnanadason of India says that women call for 'a wholistic eco-spiritual vision based on care and nurture of the earth and of all those people who have been denied the right to personhood and human dignity'.[45] From many contexts, feminist theologians are developing a spirituality that values cultural and biological diversity, works for the sustainability of the planet and livelihoods for all, and regards earth-keeping as an integral part of women's struggles.

Notes

1. Mercy Amba Oduyoye, 'Contextualisation as a Dynamic in Theological Education', *Theological Education* 30 Suppl. 1 (1993), 109.
2. See Lisa Lowe and David Lloyd (eds.), *The Politics of Culture in the Shadow of Capital* (Durham, NC: Duke University Press, 1997).
3. Diane M. Collier and Deborah F. Sawyer, 'From Isolation to Integration? New Directions in Gender and Religion', in their co-edited work, *Is There a Future for Feminist Theology?* (Sheffield Academic Press, 1999), p. 2.
4. Louise Michele Newman, *White Women's Rights: The Racial Origins of Feminism in the United States* (New York: Oxford University Press, 1999).
5. Mary Daly, *The Church and the Second Sex* (Boston, MA: Beacon Press, 1985), pp. 168–9.
6. Letty M. Russell, *Human Liberation in a Feminist Perspective: A Theology* (Philadelphia, PA: Westminster, 1974).
7. Katie Geneva Cannon, 'The Emergence of Black Feminist Consciousness', in Letty M. Russell (ed.), *Feminist Interpretation of the Bible* (Philadelphia, PA: Westminster, 1985), pp. 30–40.
8. Patricia Hill Collins, *Black Feminist Thought: Knowledge, Consciousness, and the Politics of Empowerment* (London: HarperCollins Academic, 1990), pp. 10–13.
9. Delores S. Williams, *Sisters in the Wilderness: The Challenge of Womanist God-Talk* (Maryknoll, NY: Orbis Press, 1993).
10. Alice Walker, *In Search of Our Mothers' Gardens* (New York: Harcourt Brace Jovanovich, 1983), pp. xi–xii.
11. Karen Baker-Fletcher, 'Passing on the Spark: A Womanist Perspective on Theology and Culture', in Dwight N. Hopkins and Sheila Greeve Davaney (eds.), *Changing Conversations: Religious Reflection and Cultural Analysis* (New York: Routledge, 1996), p. 145.
12. Ada María Isasi-Díaz, 'Theology, Mujerista', in Letty M. Russell and J. Shannon Clarkson (eds.), *Dictionary of Feminist Theologies* (Louisville, KY: Westminster, 1996), p. 295.
13. Ada María Isasi-Díaz, *En la Lucha: A Hispanic Women's Liberation Theology* (Minneapolis, MN: Fortress Press, 1993).

14. Mercy Amba Oduyoye, 'Christianity and African Culture', *International Review of Mission* 84 (1995), 86–7.

15. Elsa Tamez, 'Cultural Violence against Women in Latin America', in Mary John Manazan et al. (eds.), *Women Resisting Violence: Spirituality for Life* (Maryknoll, NY: Orbis Press, 1996), p. 13.

16. Mercy Amba Oduyoye, *Daughters of Anowa: African Women and Patriarchy* (Maryknoll, NY: Orbis Press, 1992); Chung Hyun Kyung, *Struggle to Be the Sun Again: Introducing Asian Women's Theology* (Maryknoll, NY: Orbis Press, 1990).

17. Sheila Greeve Davaney, 'Continuing the Story, but Departing the Text: A Historicist Interpretation of Feminist Norms in Theology', in Rebecca S. Chopp and Sheila Greeve Davaney (eds.), *Horizons in Feminist Theology: Identity, Tradition, and Norm* (Minneapolis, MN: Fortress Press, 1997), p. 200.

18. Delores S. Williams, 'The Color of Feminism: Or Speaking the Black Woman's Tongue', *Journal of Religious Thought* 43:1 (1986), 48.

19. Elisabeth Schüssler Fiorenza, *Jesus: Miriam's Child, Sophia's Prophet* (New York: Continuum, 1994), p. 14.

20. Valerie Saiving Goldstein, 'The Human Situation: A Feminine View', *Journal of Religion* 40 (1960), 100–12; Judith Plaskow, *Sex, Sin, and Grace: Women's Experience and the Theologies of Reinhold Niebuhr and Paul Tillich* (Washington, DC: University Press of America, 1980).

21. Rebecca S. Chopp, 'Theorizing Feminist Theology' in *Horizons in Feminist Theology*, pp. 216–17.

22. David Theo Goldberg, *Racist Culture: Philosophy and the Politics of Meaning* (Oxford: Blackwell, 1993), pp. 14–40.

23. I benefit from the discussion of discourses on identity by Susan Stanford Friedman, though she was not analysing religious discourse, see *Mappings: Feminism and the Cultural Geographies of Encounter* (Princeton University Press, 1998), pp. 20–5.

24. Jacquelyn Grant, 'Black Theology and the Black Woman', in Gayraud S. Wilmore and James H. Cone (eds.), *Black Theology: A Documentary History, 1966–1979* (Maryknoll, NY: Orbis Press, 1979), pp. 418–43.

25. Delores S. Williams, 'The Color of Feminism', *Christianity and Crisis* 45:7 (29 April 1985), 165.

26. Sheila Briggs, 'The Politics of Identity and the Politics of Interpretation', *Union Seminary Quarterly Review* 43 (1989), 169–70.

27. Mary McClintock Fulkerson, *Changing the Subject: Women's Discourses and Feminist Theology* (Minneapolis, MN: Fortress Press, 1994), p. 7.

28. Ibid., p. 12.

29. Rita Nakashima Brock, 'Interstitial Integrity: Reflections toward an Asian American Women's Theology', in Roger A. Badham (ed.), *Introduction to Christian Theology: Contemporary North American Perspectives* (Louisville, KY: Westminster John Knox, 1998), p. 190.

30. Ada María Isasi-Díaz, *Mujerista Theology* (Maryknoll, NY: Orbis Press, 1996), pp. 128–32.

31. Judith Butler, *Gender Trouble: Feminism and the Subversion of Identity* (New York: Routledge, 1990), p. 33.

32. Kathy Rudy, *Sex and the Church: Gender, Homosexuality, and the Transformation of Christian Ethics* (Boston, MA: Beacon Press, 1997), p. 99.
33. Ibid., p. 123.
34. Schüssler Fiorenza, *Jesus*, p. 13.
35. Larry Rasmussen, 'Give Us Word of the Humankind We Left to Thee: Globalisation and Its Wake', *EDS Occasional Papers* 4 (1999), 1–16.
36. Ibid., p. 13.
37. Lisa Lowe, 'Work, Immigration, Gender: New Subjects of Cultural Politics', in Lowe and Lloyd (eds.), *The Politics of Culture*, p. 359.
38. Toinette M. Eugene, 'Globalization and Social Ethics: Claiming "The World in My Eye!"' *Theological Education* 31:1 (1993), 3–33.
39. Benedict R. Anderson, *Imagined Communities: Reflections on the Origin and Spread of Nationalism* (New York: Verso Books, 1983).
40. James Clifford, *Routes: Travel and Translation in the Late Twentieth Century* (Cambridge, MA: Harvard University Press, 1997), p. 36.
41. Lisa Lowe, *Immigrant Acts: On Asian American Cultural Politics* (Durham, NC: Duke University Press, 1996); Gloria Anzaldúa, *Borderlands/La Frontera: The New Mestiza* (San Francisco, CA: Aunt Lute Books, 1987); Trinh T. Minh-Ha, *Woman, Native, Other: Writing Postcoloniality and Feminism* (Bloomington, IN: Indiana University Press, 1989).
42. Robert J. Schreiter, 'Teaching Theology from an Intercultural Perspective', *Theological Education* 26:1 (1989), 19.
43. Denise Ackermann, 'Becoming Fully Human: An Ethic of Relationship in Difference and Otherness', *EDS Occasional Papers* 3 (1999), 9.
44. Sallie McFague, *The Body of God: An Ecological Theology* (Minneapolis, MN: Fortress Press, 1993).
45. Aruna Gnanadason, 'A Spirituality that Sustains Us in Our Struggles', *International Review of Mission* 80 (1991), 33.

Selected reading

Chopp, Rebecca S. and Davaney, Sheila Greeve (eds.). *Horizons in Feminist Theology: Identity, Tradition, and Norm*, Minneapolis, MN: Fortress Press, 1997.
Chung Hyun Kyung. *Struggle to Be the Sun Again: Introducing Asian Women's Theology*. Maryknoll, NY: Orbis Press, 1990.
Collier, Diane M. and Sawyer, Deborah F. (eds.). *Is There a Future for Feminist Theology?* Sheffield Academic Press, 1999.
Fulkerson, Mary McClintock. *Changing the Subject: Women's Discourses and Feminist Theology*, Minneapolis, MN: Fortress Press, 1994.
Isasi-Díaz, Ada María. *En la Lucha: A Hispanic Women's Liberation Theology*, Minneapolis, MN: Fortress Press, 1993.
Manazan, Mary John, et al. (eds.). *Women Resisting Violence: Spirituality for Life*, Maryknoll, NY: Orbis Press, 1996.
Oduyoye, Mercy Amba. *Daughters of Anowa: African Women and Patriarchy*, Maryknoll, NY: Orbis Press, 1992.
Williams, Delores S. *Sisters in the Wilderness: The Challenge of Womanist God-Talk*, Maryknoll, NY: Orbis Press, 1993.

3 Feminist theology as philosophy of religion
PAMELA SUE ANDERSON

BACKGROUND AND CONTEXT: PHILOSOPHY OF RELIGION AND WOMEN

Can feminist theology take the shape of philosophy of religion without contradiction? Philosophy of religion as practised by privileged Anglo-Americans has posed epistemological and ethical problems for women which, in turn, have led to proposals for a feminist philosophy of religion.[1] Before consideration of the latter let us gain background on the opening question.

Women have been excluded by Western philosophy since its earliest days in Ancient Greece. Genevieve Lloyd has argued that the history of philosophy begins by imagining female powers as what have to be excluded by thinkers seeking to be rational. For Lloyd, 'femaleness [is] symbolically associated with what Reason supposedly left behind – the dark powers of the earth goddesses, immersion in unknown forces associated with mysterious female powers'.[2] Today it is a great concern for women, and at least some men, who seek recognition as philosophers of religion, that reason has been defined by the symbolic, if not the actual exclusion of femaleness. To address the problem of gender exclusion, this essay will set the scene for an alternative sketch of rationality.

Certain contemporary theologians have claimed that the modern philosophy which gave philosophy of religion its distinctive shape is 'secular' as opposed to the more 'religious' writings of pre-modern philosophical theology.[3] If we accept either Western philosophy's gender exclusivity or modern philosophy's secularity, it may seem doubtful that philosophy of religion can shape feminist theology. At the same time, contemporary philosophers who seek a feminist standpoint on religious belief and practice may reject engagement with theology in so far as theology's portrait has been constrained by a patriarchal form of religious discourse. The problem is not only with God conceived as father, but with questions of truth, goodness, and justice. The larger context provided by the writings of contemporary feminists will expose the ways in which the points of view of both philosophers and theologians have remained partial.

We can see prominent feminist theologians entering the picture of philosophy advocating less partial methods, tools, and aims for philosophy of religion. So it is possible to write about 'Feminist Theology as Philosophy of Religion'. This involves exploring new dimensions of philosophy and theology. Feminist theology and philosophy of religion have begun to shape each other; there is every possibility that they will be mutually informative in the twenty-first century for women and men.

Before this possibility can be realised, it is necessary to assess critically what constitutes a feminist critique of philosophy. Does a feminist critique necessarily imply the rejection of reason as male and the reversal of values from male to female? Or should a feminist critique of philosophy of religion, in particular, seek to reform sex/gender-biased conceptions and practices, seeking a gradual and sustained transformation? Another way of putting this alternative is, should we give up Athens for Jerusalem? One answer is to give up philosophy for feminist theology, or for a feminist reading of religion. Instead of taking such drastic action against philosophy, consider what feminist philosophers do with their critiques.

Feminist critiques in philosophy include questioning the dominant interpretations of the philosophical texts privileged in the Western canon, interrogating the way in which that canon has been defined by the exclusion of women, and exposing the masculinist biases in specific conceptions and arguments. These feminist critiques offer at least implicit suggestions for the reconstruction of philosophy's canon, conceptions, and claims. For example, in 1984 Lloyd published the first edition of her ground-breaking feminist critique of reason.[4] She elucidates the nature of reason in the philosophical canon from Plato to Simone de Beauvoir, revealing the ways in which rationality has come to be associated with maleness. Historically, maleness as represented in Western philosophy does not carry the same symbolic associations with body, nature, and passion as it does with mind and reason; but embodiment has been conceived as closely associated with women. Philosophers might agree that the capacity to reason is sex-neutral, in the sense that the mind has no sex, but because human minds are embodied minds, differences in rationality are explained by bodily differences.

Take two canonical philosophers, Aristotle and Descartes on reason. Lloyd points out that Descartes rejects Aristotle's account of souls containing both rational and irrational elements; he replaces the Aristotelian soul with a dualism of rational mind and irrational body. Although Descartes'

alternative is different from Aristotle's, it does not have much better implications for the philosopher's understanding of women's symbolic gender.
On the one hand, Aristotle thought of rationality on a continuum on which
women, as defective males, were less rational than men; and yet women's
souls would always contain a rational element. On the other hand, despite
Descartes' own concern to create an equalitarian philosophy whereby reason
is a priori possessed equally by all human minds, given that women were
symbolically associated with the body, his dualistic conception of the rational mind and irrational body aligns women symbolically with irrationality
and men with rationality. So the Cartesian legacy, although perhaps not
Descartes' intentions, serves to justify a sexual division of labour in the
realm of knowledge.

In this way, Lloyd demonstrates that reason in philosophy has been symbolically male, but that the symbolic connections of reason and gender are
complex. Her conclusions encourage the rereading and reconstruction of the
philosophical canon with sensitivity to both the contingency of the maleness
of reason and the possibility of reason's reconceptualisations. Nevertheless,
some feminists read Lloyd advocating the rejection of reason as male and
so philosophy. This reflects the dramatic, as well as the unwittingly controversial, consequences of her critique. The intimate connection between
the ideals of reason and the self-definition of philosophy itself renders the
outcomes of ongoing feminist critiques of reason decisive for the future of
philosophy of religion. For their part, feminist theologians could respond
to a feminist critique of reason by seeking to reconstruct the symbolisation
and role of reason for philosophy of religion.

In confronting philosophy of religion, feminists face a gender-biased,
often sexist, picture. 'Sex–gender' bias has influenced the ways in which
the traditional problems, beliefs, and arguments in philosophy of religion
have been constructed.[5] Philosophy of religion not only emerged in a male
tradition and history which have excluded and devalued women, but, like the
rest of philosophy, it formed rational conceptions and beliefs by opposing
masculine to feminine qualities. Both privileged-male history and masculine
symbols determine the dominant form of philosophy of religion. When
asked about philosophy of religion today, philosophers would be correct to
list the standard topics found in anthologies and textbooks as: arguments
for and against the existence of the theist's God who is a person without a
body (i.e. a spirit) who is eternal, is perfectly free, omnipotent, omniscient,
perfectly good, and the creator of all things; the nature and attributes of this
God; the justification of religious belief as knowledge; the nature of religious
or mystical experience; the problem of evil and question of theodicy; the

problem of religious language; the hope for immortality; and the relation of faith to reason. These topics have shaped a male picture.

Nancy Frankenberry argues that none of 'the new sophisticated military hardware' which currently renders philosophy and religion 'comrades-in-arms' engages the questions posed by feminist inquiry or aims at 'disarmament' of the sexist elements of traditional theism.[6] Ironically, the dominant form of philosophy of religion does not encourage querying what Athens has to do with Jerusalem. Instead, philosophy and religion in their contemporary male forms have entered 'a period of *détente*'. By contrast, the intervention of feminist theologians into philosophy of religion has once again raised the question of the relationship of Athens to Jerusalem. What do contemporary feminist theologians have to do with philosophy of religion? If philosophy of religion is equated with rationally justifying belief in the existence of God who is both male and patriarchal, then the answer would be nothing – except as a subject for radical critique and feminist subversion. As Mary Daly argued in 1973, if God is male, male is God.[7] Every philosopher of religion, then, who assumes and debates the existence and traditional attributes of God has at least subliminally envisioned the divine as male. This raises issues about our conception of the divine, but also about how we live and how we fulfil our yearnings.

If feminist theology is to be embraced as philosophy of religion we must form conceptions which are not oppressive to women, or to socially and materially marginalised persons. For progress to be made, it is necessary that, on the one hand, feminist theologians do not merely accuse philosophers of being exclusively male and, on the other hand, feminist philosophers do not reject the work of theologians as inevitably patriarchal. Instead, progress in overcoming sex–gender biases has been, and can continue to be, made when each feminist thinker becomes critically aware of her own complex of prejudices, i.e. critically conscious of her sexual, gender, racial, class, ethnic, and religious assumptions. Theologians and philosophers can be transformed individually and collectively by thinking from the standpoint of others.

RELIGIOUS EXPERIENCE AND THE SEX–GENDER DISTINCTION

In the second half of the twentieth century, the attraction of philosophy of religion for theologians was generally their empiricist methods of justifying religious belief from, broadly construed, experience. Philosophers of religion such as Richard Swinburne and William Alston have developed, respectively, evidentialist and experientialist justifications for religious belief.

These have been found theologically attractive to (at least some) Christians. For Swinburne, justification of belief in God comes from the probability on the evidence of what takes place.[8] For Alston, warrant of religious, like perceptual, belief rests on the practical rationality of engaging in a doxastic practice (without proof of its reliability).[9] Generalisations should not be made too quickly about what exactly is understood by 'experience' (including certain 'practices') as a likely or reliable way to secure religious beliefs. Yet we can acknowledge a fundamental difference between those philosophers of religion who justify, or warrant, their religious beliefs on the grounds of experience, whether in terms of external evidence or reliable practice, and those who propose other grounds such as a priori principles of reason, or grounds of faith in revelation. There are also contemporary philosophers of religion who reject totally the practice of justification, opting for a non-realist account of religions, religious practices and symbols. (The realist versus non-realist debate will not be discussed here because it is assumed, until shown otherwise, that non-realism could never address feminist concerns with questions of knowing what is, actual right or wrong, and real justice.)

If we build critically upon the argument from religious experience, it is possible to see its attraction for feminist theologians. Twentieth-century feminists challenged the sexism and androcentrism of Christian theology on the basis of women's experiences of exclusion and inequality. Similarly, the feminist challenge to philosophy of religion seeks to subvert the manner in which sexed–gendered experiences of the divine have been unacknowledged, missing, or devalued. This strategy of subversion employs experience, including textual and first-hand testimony (often prior to inscription), to warrant feminist claims about religious belief. For example, we find Sarah Coakley pushing at the parameters of theology on the basis of distinctively gendered experience of God.[10] Coakley employs the tools and methods of philosophy of religion to undermine what has been conceived as gender-neutral experience and what has been justified as true belief.

Coakley has initiated an important reshaping of Christian philosophy of religion, transforming the dominant form of philosophy of religion in the Anglo-American world. Yet she continues to work within the framework of analytic philosophy of religion, while aiming at a gender transformation. In particular, her concern is with the ways in which 'religious (or mystical) experience' – terms she employs with critical caution – can be both reliable ground for feminist knowledge and compatible with Christianity. She seeks to re-thread the connections of mystics to God without throwing out the Christian vision of God's love for us and our love for God. She believes that the Christian mystic's vision and desire are worthy of close epistemological scrutiny, and are potentially truth-conducive. In her more explicitly theological writings, Coakley also questions the relationship of sexuality and spirituality and, then, seeks to weave new answers into accounts of the relationship of sexual and spiritual desire.[11] A new alignment of the sexual and the theological could become a central topic of feminist theology and philosophy of religion. This realignment would no longer cast women as that which distracts from the rational or the divine.

So it is possible to retain the tools of philosophy, while supplementing them with feminist theological insight. As Coakley points out, the first wave of twentieth-century feminist theology was largely liberal and constructivist, but lacked philosophical acuity.[12] This created an initial diremption of feminist theology from philosophy of religion. The latter has been characterised by philosophical acuity, but remained biblically and doctrinally conservative. The conservatism has been evident on questions of gender and sexuality. In this light, feminist theology and philosophy of religion each in their own ways have been partial, if not exclusive. Coakley renders each less partial; yet she gives up neither Christian theology nor analytic philosophy. Instead each should strengthen the other.

A feminist interpretation of texts on 'religious experience' is contained in Coakley's close readings of analytic philosophers of religion. These reveal where male philosophers have been forced to push at the limits of their own principles and empiricist framework. This includes discovery of the profound feelings from which men claim knowledge, yet which exceed their own abstractly rational principles. The task is to step inside the framework of empiricist justifications of religious belief in order to expose the façade of the 'masculine' account of experience. Coakley remains convinced that what some feminists identify as a *male* preoccupation with the *evidence* of religious experience still has a function in cumulative arguments for theism. Yet she admits that a narrow conception of evidence should be broadened to encompass gendered facts and conceptions. Her readings uncover places where Anglo-American philosophers unwittingly appeal to 'feminine'–female qualities, conceptions, or practices, thus indicating the unstable partiality of exclusively male-defined positions.

For example, Coakley examines the texts of Alston, Swinburne, Plantinga, and Wolterstorff with an eye to gendered ways of knowing. She seeks to unravel the gendered standpoint concealed in Alston's notion of doxastic practice of Christian devotion; to exploit the places in Swinburne's argument for the existence of God where he exposes a 'soft' epistemic centre (of reliance on others or trust); and to bring out the elements of vulnerability expressed in Wolterstorff's and Plantinga's 'proper basicality'.[13] Despite themselves, philosophers bring in what they elsewhere devalue as 'feminine' forms of subjectivity, including trust, vulnerability, and suffering. Traces of traditionally 'feminine' qualities indicate places at which feelings, including erotic passion, reveal a bodily relationship between human and divine. This revelation is not compatible with the assumption that achieving the disembodied ideal of the (male) philosopher would bring him closer to a God's-eye view of reality. Instead it confirms a connection of our sexuality and desire for God.

Daphne Hampson, for one, has criticised Coakley's focus on women's vulnerability and religious practices for reinforcing patriarchy by placing female experience in a realm outside of the public domain of male power and knowledge.[14] This may be somewhat unfair. On the one hand, vulnerability, for Coakley, arises in political struggles. On the other hand, we should avoid restricting feminist conceptions of liberating experience to post-Christian or secular life. Instead Coakley enables us to re-conceive the political to include the powerful intensity of religious practices such as prayer. These can have a transformative potential for women and men, especially in their relations to the divine.

Compare this view of women's religious practices with the view of Grace Jantzen. Jantzen criticises the philosophical approach to mysticism which, she insists, has relied upon William James' conception of religious experience: '[it] allows mysticism to flourish as a secret inner life, while those who nurture such an inner life can generally be counted on to prop up rather than to challenge the status quo of their workplaces, their gender roles, and the political systems by which they are governed, since their anxieties and angers will be allayed in the privacy of their own hearts search for peace and tranquillity'.[15] In her Riddell Lectures, Coakley also stresses the weakness of this Jamesian conception.[16] Yet she herself maintains a powerful vigil of the inner life: the intense nature of submission to the divine can, she argues, be subversive. The question is whether this vigilance can change the status quo in philosophy of religion.

Coakley's account of feminist power in the submission of prayer is contentious. Feminist knowledge is entangled with the gender and power which, for her, uniquely shape the claims of women to know God in submission to divine authority.[17] She identifies the epistemic role of vulnerability before God and of eroticism in prayer. In the silence of prayer one is forced to confront both one's own desire for God and one's sexuality. This confrontation is a means to gendered knowledge of the divine. Coakley argues cogently for the crucial role of vulnerability for feminist theology and philosophy of religion.[18] The repression of all forms of vulnerability, except that of women as victims, is dangerous both for Christian theology and for feminism. Coakley brings philosophy of religion into feminist theology to examine the potential veridical force of silent prayer.[19]

Janet Martin Soskice, like Coakley, remains within the Christian tradition and employs the analytic tools of philosophy of religion. Soskice has done influential work on religious language. Her earliest writing established the role of metaphor in depicting reality, and in speaking about God and what is beyond our own definitive knowledge.[20] Subsequently, she raised questions and gave possible answers about the male-biased language and symbolic system of Christian (and other) religious texts. How much can the symbolic language of religion be revised or abandoned, without parting company from the religion itself? Soskice is not about to part with Christianity.[21] Yet she admits that the religious language of Christian texts and scriptures have privileged metaphors of fathers and sons, and not of mothers and daughters. Furthermore, this privileging has led other feminist theologians to become post-Christians and to reject philosophy of religion as biblically and doctrinally conservative. Nevertheless, Soskice manages to hold onto both Christianity and philosophical acuity, in order to maintain realism in theology. She offers insight, frequently incorporating the work of French feminist philosophers, for moulding feminist theology as philosophy of religion.

In the end, the reliance of Christian feminist theologians upon women's 'experience' as both the *locus* and the source of theological reflection has shaped their thinking in distinctive ways. However, the danger in this shape is assuming a fundamental compatibility between religious experience or practice and empirical realist forms of Christian theism. A potentially decisive issue for a feminist form of Christian philosophy of religion is treating sexuality and gender empirically, and then reducing them to sexual difference. This difference is not simply empirical. To move beyond the limitations of the status quo in Christian philosophy of religion, feminist philosophers need more than an empirical depiction of reality; we need to articulate the interplay of bodily, material, and social differences using a revisable conception of the sex–gender distinction.

To employ sex–gender as a conceptual, and not an empirical (biological–social), distinction is important on at least two counts. For one thing, it would help to distinguish a phenomenological level of description of the body as lived (i.e. as given prior to it being made empirically intelligible). This would assume that the body is intuitively apprehended before it is understood or interpreted. Phenomenological description would, then, broaden the fields of both feminist theology and philosophy of religion by introducing an account of the lived body which is given as sexed. For another thing, a dual conception of the lived and interpreted body (i.e. both a phenomenology of the sexed body and a socially situated epistemology of the gendered body) would enable greater understanding of the factors of sex–gender, including sexual, gender, racial, class, ethnic, and religious orientations. We could use this distinction to further Coakley's readings of religious passion and affectivity, uncovering their conditions of possibility prior to the necessary and sufficient conditions of bodily knowledge. Without the conceptual distinction of the lived and interpreted body, empirical claims concerning the gendered body are only contingent. Arguably something more fundamental than the 'facts' or norms of gender is possible and necessary.

If feminist theologians are not careful to extricate themselves from the empiricist framework of Anglo-American philosophers of religion, they will fail to take the picture beyond the status quo. For example, a teenager who grows up in a religious community where heterosexuality is assumed to be a fact, yet experiences desires which are not intelligible in terms of this fact, would not be able to explain such phenomena without access to a prior, lived body. If the lived body as sexed is accessible, this allows for a challenge to the empirical 'facts' which render it unintelligible. Without this distinction there would be no possibility for feminists, lesbians, or anyone else who does not fit the norm (e.g. compulsory reproduction or heterosexuality) to advocate change on the basis of their desires or needs.

EMBODIMENT AND THE QUESTION OF REASON

Admittedly the central problem for feminists with philosophy of religion has been the unacknowledged exclusion of sexual difference, by the unfair privileging of dominant figures of male self-sameness and by the exclusive use of reason. Feminists such as Coakley, Soskice, and Jantzen have made apparent the privileging of male identity in philosophical representations of God's ideally male attributes and in Western philosophers' ideal of pure rationality. The erasure of female identities and sexual differences by a male ideal of rationality and divinity will continue as long as the male tradition of Christian theism is privileged. Yet the ever-present danger is a female reversal of the privileged sex rendering a new form of pernicious partiality. New forms of sexism and racism will be the result of failing to take on board issues of sexual, gender, racial, class, religious, and other strongly held biases.[22] This difficulty can be confronted by rethinking the sex–gender symbolisation of philosophical reason in terms of new feminist social epistemologies and their conditions of possibility; this means dealing with the body and sex–gender as a complex of relations shaped by a number of material and social factors.

The question is, how does sex–gender function in an account of the body? The choices include reading: (i) the body empirically as having certain contingent characteristics due to its gender construction by a culture, or by a set of privileged texts; (ii) the body performatively as expressing characteristics which create, repeat or resist social conventions and constraints; (iii) the body as both given and interpreted. To explain briefly, (i) the empirical reading relies upon sense perception and testimony (including inscription) of what takes place. However, this reading does not explore what is prior to our perception, whether pre-conscious or more fundamental than perception, i.e. as intuitively given; (ii) the performative reading of the body sets up a new relation between the psychic-social and the corporeal. These relations are effects of the body's performance, not vice versa. So this reading reverses the first reading. But the first is not easily reconfigured as the second. Instead the additional reading (iii) is called for; here the proposed conceptual distinction allows for two accounts. The phenomenological account of lived experience reveals the accessibility (even if unintelligible in terms of contemporary norms) of the sexed body as a sustained, general experience; the interpretative account of the body elucidates the gendered body as constituted socially and materially.

For example, we could follow Coakley and read the body empirically, but recognise the empiricist's constraints of the dominant philosophical tradition. Vulnerability and longing both push at the limits of empirical realism; and so Coakley seeks to read the religious longing for transformation into the divine in relation to Judith Butler.[23] Coakley compares Butler's gender performativity and 'obscured longing' for possibilities excluded by compulsory heterosexuality to repeated religious practices and Christian perception of an unending desire for God as found in, for instance, Gregory of Nyssa (c. 330–95).[24] Yet Butler clearly fails to hold a conceptual distinction between the lived and interpreted body: she rejects 'sex' as a bodily given.[25] The difficulty here is prohibiting access to the lived experience of sexed bodies.[26] Although Coakley carefully and cleverly works to avoid either an idealisation of the de-sexed body over and against particular male–female bodies, or a reduction of the given–interpreted body to gendered rhetoric, these alternatives are frequently consequences of attempting to appropriate Butler's complex negotiations of gender and body matters.

Thus the third reading (iii. above) is offered to establish a sex–gender conceptual distinction which would help feminists avoid privileging of a particular white, Western, female body, reducing the body to a rhetoric of resistance or idealising the de-sexed, de-naturalised body. It is not clear that these pitfalls can be avoided with the other accounts of the body (i. or ii. above); these, therefore, seem inadequate for feminist theologians and philosophers who endeavour to reconceive the relationship between human embodiment and the divine.

A question remains concerning the embodiment of reason for those feminists doing philosophy of religion. Both Coakley and Soskice acknowledge the male bias in contemporary philosophy of religion. In particular, they recognise that the symbolisation of reason as male has had pernicious consequences for embodiment, especially women's relations to their own bodies. Yet neither propose to give up reason or philosophy for an emphasis on desire or religious faith. It is crucial for a feminist philosopher of religion that reason is not reduced to the male in philosophy, or the rational subject to a privileged man. Feminist theologians who do not reject the role of reason in thinking about religion would be applauded by feminist philosophers of religion.

To confront what has been found in texts, but often treated as empirical, to be the equation of maleness and reason in Western philosophy, the feminist philosopher has at least two alternatives: to reject reason as a masculinist conception, or to reform our conceptions of reason which have excluded women. Jantzen follows the first alternative; my proposal for a feminist philosophy of religion, as seen in the next section, follows the second. Jantzen departs from both Coakley and Soskice in her recent proposal for a feminist philosophy of religion, and so from feminist theology as philosophy of religion. In particular, Jantzen rejects the philosophical preoccupation with questions concerning the rationality of religious belief. She thinks that this preoccupation with justification and formal reasoning is part of a masculinist obsession with death and a denial of the body; and she insists that the concern with belief is exclusive to the West. Her proposal is to look for signs of the repression of the body, recalling the abjection of the mother at birth. Jantzen is indebted to the psychoanalytic accounts of matricide found in the writings of Luce Irigaray and Julia Kristeva. Her feminist critique of philosophy of religion is structured by her application of a 'Continental' critique of modern philosophy to 'British' philosophy of religion.[27] Her generalisations about 'the Continental' (or sometimes, 'the French') and 'the British' should not be taken as definitive. Instead, they are employed as prototypes for the sake of argument, ideally, for the goal of understanding the standpoint of the other.

Jantzen claims a more radical position than either Coakley or Soskice in her rejection of Christian patriarchy and masculinist philosophy of religion.

In fact, her brand of feminist philosophy of religion is neither strictly Continental nor Anglo-American in approach. Jantzen rejects 'the British' preoccupation with the justification of religious belief, but appropriates ideas from those Continental thinkers who focus, especially, on religion and repression. Jantzen intends to demonstrate the decisive significance of the unconscious for philosophy of religion. British philosophers of religion have not considered repression of desire, the body, birth, and everything associated with the feminine and maternal. According to Jantzen, this has been to their own personal detriment, as well as to render the content for philosophical accounts of religions biased against women and against any thinking which is different from analytic philosophy of religion.[28]

Her ongoing argument is that, if we did consider knowing the differences between a sexist and a more inclusive understanding of desire for the divine, then we would read more widely and probe more deeply into the recesses of our personal and collective unconscious. This would create a revolution in our thinking about religion. Not only would barriers be broken down between thinking on the Continent and thought on the British Isles, but philosophy of religion would take on a new vibrance in human flourishing, desiring goodness and love. Jantzen urges giving up the masculinist obsession of philosophers of religion with belief in immortality and love of death, and embracing, instead, 'the feminist symbolic of natality' and love of life.[29]

Yet, as Harriet Harris demonstrates, a philosopher will be bothered that Jantzen is inconsistent about reason.[30] Despite her unequivocal, written statements for the rejection of the rationality of religious belief as a proper topic for feminists, Jantzen must admit to relying upon reason and belief. She would agree that *the primary agenda* for a feminist philosophy of religion *is a new manner of thinking.* Yet disagreement continues on whether any priority should be given to embodied reason and feminist epistemology. Jantzen claims to *give priority to ethics* over either ontology or epistemology; but reason must function in ethical thinking. We cannot separate reason from either epistemology or ethics. For Jantzen the crucial difference is in what we prioritise. She would not prioritise conceptions of rationality and belief, even though these are presupposed by her ethics and feminist arguments. Contrary to her, it is possible for feminist philosophy of religion to be motivated by an ethical concern without giving priority to ethics.

Feminists, whether theologians or philosophers, agree at some level that openness to diversity is essential for women. Feminist philosophers of religion tend to argue that philosophy of religion should no longer be primarily informed by natural theology and speculative metaphysics. Instead, our distinctive proposals are informed by feminist ethics and feminist epistemologies. But these proposals will, then, distinguish feminist philosophy of religion from feminist theology as philosophy of religion. Yet again feminists in general would reject the universal requirement to think as if disembodied, or from a God's-eye view. Embodiment and thinking from socially situated positions are crucial elements for the reshaping of philosophy of religion; these will enable the reconstruction of its central topics, texts, and concepts for feminist philosophy of religion.

A closer look at Jantzen's use of gender theory and psychoanalysis will not only reveal the crucial role given to embodiment and social situatedness, but will expose a (decisive, for some) weakness in her alternative conception of the divine. It is useful to consider the latter now. Basically, Jantzen makes a strong case for becoming divine, building upon a passage from Irigaray's 'Divine Women': 'God forces us to do nothing except *become*. The only task, the only obligation laid upon us is: to become divine men and women, to become perfectly, to refuse to allow parts of ourselves to shrivel and die that have the potential for growth and fulfilment.'[31] The danger here is to read this literally as an empirical claim for women to become divine.

Amy Hollywood presents a serious criticism of any Irigarayan conception of religion as a projection of the self onto the divine.[32] Essentially, this conception should result in the dissolution of belief in God. To make her case, Hollywood returns to Irigaray's miming of Ludwig Feuerbach and explains the latter's account of projection. Feuerbach's theory of religion as based upon man's projection of his ideal attributes onto a divine being is not complete without the premise that the projection is an illusion.[33] The point is, even in miming Feuerbach, Irigaray must assume that to understand how religion is created by way of projection is to know that there is no divine being, or object of projection, beyond the subject. While Feuerbach argues that, in becoming aware of the projection, the divine attributes should be recognised as man's own, Irigaray explores what it would be to create a projection for women. The problem seems to rest with the implications of Irigaray's miming. It seems unlikely that we can immediately know whether, or how, 'to become divine . . .'

Jantzen suggests that women and men should become 'natals', developing the idea that birth and life should be valued over death and afterlife.[34] So perhaps her use of 'becoming divine' says something about religious flourishing with or without a direct relationship with Irigaray's miming of Feuerbach. Whatever the implications of the latter, Jantzen confirms that new philosophical thinking about religion, the divine, and the recovery and potential of female symbols are all topics for a feminist philosophy of religion.

DISLOCATING THE PRIVILEGED POINT OF VIEW: EPISTEMOLOGY AND ETHICS

Feminist theologians are likely to have an increasingly fruitful dialogue with feminist philosophers of religion. However, to establish the ground for such a dialogue, we need to dislocate the privileged point of view held by Anglo-American philosophers of religion. Feminist interventions in epistemology and ethics can inform the dislocation of the supposedly disembodied subject of philosophy of religion, but also of the naïve realist reliance upon empirical distinctions of sex and gender.

I wrote *A Feminist Philosophy of Religion* as a prolegomenon.[35] The implicit case for a feminist philosophy of religion is only as strong as our ability to think differently and listen to voices different from a 'male-neutral' philosophy. Male-neutral is employed to describe philosophical conceptions, experiences or thoughts which are distinctively male, but are presented with the pretence of sex/gender neutrality. To see beyond such pretence, those women who are trained in, but struggling with, philosophy (of religion) seek to 'make strange what had appeared familiar'.[36] In general, there is still too much uncritical familiarity, and so unquestioning acceptance, accompanying the classical model of traditional theism in philosophy of religion. Whether theist or atheist, we too easily accept the theistic frame of reference and fail to notice how strange *is* the conception of God, i.e. a personal being, without a body, who is the omnipotent, omniscient, omni-benevolent, eternal creator and sustainer of all creation. Why should the overall conception itself remain, while endless debates centre on each of the divine attributes, especially in relation to the ever-popular problem of evil? Feminist theologians, amongst others, have argued that it is far more constructive to try to alleviate suffering than to justify the existence of evil *and* a good, all-knowing, all-powerful, eternal . . . God. Why not consider beginning philosophy of religion with something different from the traditional conception, even different from variations on this basic conception, of a divine being? The feminist motivation for this shift in thinking is both epistemological and ethical.

We might ask, do philosophers themselves aspire to be infinite in proposing the God's-eye view? From various perspectives, the monotheistic conception implicit in such a view seems an outmoded ideal to which Western men aspired. But note that *the aspiration to be infinite* is distinct from *the craving for infinitude*.[37] The latter has an affinity with 'yearning', a cognitive sensibility which has been conceived ethically, politically, and spiritually, following bell hooks:[38] it motivates the search for goodness, justice, and truth without the one who craves, or yearns, ever aspiring to be perfectly good, completely just, and fully rational, i.e. without aspiring to be God. In yearning, our cognitive sensibility takes on an ethical, or moral, urgency. The now obvious question is, whose conception is the God of contemporary philosophy of religion? If not our own, or if a male corruption of who we are, then why seek to either defend or challenge it? Instead, let us consider a shift away from philosophy's privileged Western point of view which has been identified as the God's-eye point of view or the view from nowhere.

This shift in our ways of thinking about religion is part of a process of reforming what remains deeply and generally familiar as a most fundamental framework: that is, our evolving conceptual scheme. Our conceptual scheme – including the language we use, the way we think or reason – is more fundamental than our conception of the divine, but it is related. My reformist approach reaches back to rebuild philosophy at the level of fundamental presuppositions. Philosophers cannot – any more than theologians can – detach themselves completely from their conceptual scheme to achieve an absolutely correct representation of reality. But this does not imply that philosophers have to give up our search for true belief, or for knowledge of reality. Yet *the embodied search*, or inquiry which acknowledges its perspectival nature, *is clearly distinct from the God's-eye view*. Embracing this distinction does not, however, imply that we simply reject belief as 'masculinist', in Jantzen's terms. Arguably we cannot give up belief, or jump outside of our conceptual scheme; this would be like being in the sea without a ship (i.e. without a conceptual scheme). 'Belief' is employed here as a very basic term for 'thoughts taken up – whether in being handed down or, in some sense, being discovered – and held as true'.[39] Certain beliefs may be (wrongly) conceived as male-neutral. Yet recognition of the sexed–gendered perspectives of beliefs is part of a process which can only begin in discerning the sexed–gendered shape of our conceptual scheme.

In particular we can, then, create an alternative sketch of philosophical conceptions of reason and belief. Modern philosophical texts have contained images of the sea as outside the territory of rationality, in relation to the secure – since rational – ground of an island. Kant employs the stormy sea to represent the illusions which threaten and surround the land of truth. In the Kantian picture, the definite line separating the philosopher or seafarer from the sea represents the limits of ordered rationality and pure understanding. But if this line is drawn by men alone and represents the limits to their reasoning, can and should it be pushed back? According to certain feminists, human rationality should be reformed in order to grasp the contents of the marine waters whose turbulence evokes images of desire, birth, and love. By emphasising these additional images, feminists intend to move towards a fully embodied standpoint on reality. More specifically, my reform would include the belief-constructions implicit in imagery which takes the land in Kant's use of sea imagery as the limit of rationality; or the turbulent sea as gendered images of desire and the land's relationship to the sea as reason's relationship to the unknowable; or the horizon beyond the sea as the divinisation of a disembodied reason and so on.

Unlike Kant, who does not describe the philosopher's ship, but consistent with another picture of philosophy, the planks of the philosopher's ship include the mistaken beliefs which are necessarily part of our conceptual scheme. The post-Kantian point of this imagery is that philosophers must rely upon both true beliefs and falsehoods when changing the planks of mistaken beliefs in order to stay afloat. To be without the ship is to be in the sea without any beliefs; this would be impossible! But to qualify philosophical references to a mariner and his ship on the open sea, if these are taken to mean that the rebuilding of a philosophical framework is done by a lone man then they will also have to be supplemented with additional images from feminist philosophers – for whom the subject of knowledge is not a discrete, simple self with its very own set of fully transparent beliefs. Instead feminist epistemologists speak about subjects of knowledge.

Feminist proposals for the reform of philosophy of religion may indeed involve more than supplementation; they may culminate in a transformation of our thinking and living in yet unimagined ways. Replacing the ship's weak planks, in relation to the sea and land (whether these represent desire and reason or not), implies a rebuilding. This may imply a total reconstruction when it comes to male-neutral planks of philosophy of religion which have excluded differences of religion, gender, sexuality, class, race, and ethnicity. The aim would not merely be to modify rules or to produce a checklist of beliefs. Standard questions about God need not be addressed if the intention is *not* to *justify* theistic beliefs. Instead, the focus could be placed upon the *process of* uncovering and reconfiguring beliefs as embedded and variously configured in myths. Shaping this process is the cognitive, ethical, and political sensibility of yearning.

On this last point, Kathleen O'Grady asks of my use of mythical figures, why not consider those non-privileged persons who are actually marginalised from birth?[40] The reply is to encourage movement from the centre of philosophy to the margins by the reconfiguration of female figures in philosophical texts (e.g. Antigone). Within philosophical texts, these figures themselves can be reconfigured by imagining how they could relinquish their privileged positions in acts of dissent. The very process making up feminist reconfigurations represents the crucial movement from a privileged position at the centre to a position of marginality as a source of less partial knowledge. Moreover, these figures, whether mythical or historical rendered mythical, are imagined as part of what Michèle Le Doeuff calls the philosophical imaginary.[41]

Le Doeuff develops a distinctive account of the philosophical imaginary as a style of thinking in images with which past philosophers have denied engagement. Unacknowledged elements in the practice of philosophy are located in the imagery and symbolism of a philosophical text. This constitutes the philosophical imaginary that is not incidental to philosophy as a decorative aspect of a text, but functions to mask aspects of philosophy not readily articulated and to organise the values implicit in the text. An exercise of the philosophical imaginary by feminist philosophers is to imagine alternative thought patterns and intellectual spaces in which they can glimpse possibilities excluded through polarisations of reason and desire. Informed by Le Doeuff, we can look for mythical figures in the texts of philosophy, in order to use them to imagine alternative patterns of thought. Here my thinking is also informed by a distinctive understanding of a standpoint – which is not the same as an empirical stance.

One difficulty with the use of mythical figures, in *A Feminist Philosophy of Religion*, is grasping the crucial role intended for *a feminist standpoint*. Another difficulty is that it is not yet possible to state definitively a single method for a feminist philosophy of religion. More ground needs to be broken by feminist philosophers. So the prolegomenon hangs to a large degree on developing a transformative awareness of sex–gender, including the multiple variables of race, class, ethnicity, sexual, and religious orientations. To develop this awareness, we can employ an epistemological strategy for reinventing ourselves as other. The strategy requires philosophers of religion to struggle to achieve a feminist standpoint, in order to tackle the problem of a hierarchy of values in which reason is valued over desire, male over female, upper class over working class, infinite over finite, power over weakness, centre over margin, and other similar (value) combinations, inherent in philosophical texts.

A feminist standpoint is not the same as a woman's experience or her empirical situation, it is not a female perspective. It is not straightforwardly, in Jantzen's terms, the female imaginary or a feminist symbolic; and it is not an outlook given by birth to all women whatever their particular social location. Instead a feminist standpoint is the achievement of an epistemically informed perspective; this results from a struggle by, or on behalf of women and men who have been exploited, oppressed, or dominated, including women who have been exploited or even oppressed by specific, pernicious, monotheistic beliefs. The struggle is on the level of lived experience where the body is accessible, even before it is intelligible. But embodiment (as a woman) is not a sufficient condition for the production of a feminist standpoint. Formal and substantive principles – concepts of reason, as well as myths – necessarily mediate one's embodiment. Myth and the philosophical imaginary come into the struggle to achieve a feminist standpoint. Looking at myths and the male-neutral representations of beliefs supports a strategy of reform which exposes the exclusive point of view of philosophy of religion: it *begins with taking* the privileged readings of female figures or images of women in *patriarchal texts* out to the margins in order to reconfigure them *from the standpoint of others*. In this way, the familiar in philosophy of religion is rendered strange; and it becomes apparent that a self-conscious awareness of our sex–gender perspectives (with all the material and social factors that go with these) moves us to change conceptions of ourselves, i.e. to reinvent ourselves as other than we have been. Thus, we recognise greater truth, or more true representations of our social and spiritual reality, by thinking from the lives of others.

O'Grady describes the space which is necessary for embracing feminist philosophy of religion: 'this rebirth [of philosophy of religion] can only be situated within the dynamic forces of *yearning* – the place where bodies embrace – where reason and desire come together to both challenge the discipline and reform it'.[42]

Notes

1. The conception of 'philosophy of religion' assumed in this entry derives from the work of contemporary Anglo-American philosophers; cf. Philip L. Quinn and Charles Taliaferro (eds.), *A Companion to Philosophy of Religion* (Oxford: Blackwell, 1997).
2. Genevieve Lloyd, *The Man of Reason: 'Male' and 'Female' in Western Philosophy* (London: Routledge, 1993), p. 2.
3. Philip Blond, 'Introduction: Theology Before Philosophy', in Philip Blond (ed.), *Post-Secular Philosophy: Between Philosophy and Theology* (London: Routledge, 1998), pp. 1–66.
4. Lloyd, *Man of Reason*.
5. Pamela Sue Anderson, *A Feminist Philosophy of Religion: The Rationality and Myths of Religious Belief* (Oxford: Blackwell, 1998), pp. 5–13.
6. Nancy Frankenberry, 'Philosophy of Religion in Different Voices', in Janet A. Kourany (ed.), *Philosophy in a Feminist Voice: Critiques and Reconstructions* (Princeton, NJ: Princeton University Press, 1998), p. 175.
7. Mary Daly, 'Feminist Post-Christian Introduction', in her *The Church and the Second Sex*, second edition (New York: Harper & Row, 1975), p. 38.
8. Richard Swinburne, *The Existence of God*, revised edition (Oxford: Clarendon Press, 1991), especially ch. 14: 'The Balance of Probability', pp. 277–91.

Pamela Sue Anderson

9. William Alston, *Perceiving God* (Ithaca, NY: Cornell University Press, 1991).

10. Sarah Coakley, 'Knowing Otherwise: Gender, Philosophy and "Religious Experience"', Riddell Memorial Lectures, University of Newcastle, 16–18 March 1999.

11. Sarah Coakley, *God, Sexuality and the Self: An Essay 'On the Trinity'* (Cambridge University Press, forthcoming).

12. Sarah Coakley, 'Feminism', in Quinn and Taliaferro (eds.), *A Companion*, p. 601.

13. Alvin Plantinga, 'Reason and Belief in God', in Alvin Plantinga and Nicholas Wolterstorff (eds.), *Faith and Rationality: Reason and Belief in God* (Notre Dame University Press, 1983), pp. 16–93; Nicholas Wolterstorff, 'Introduction' and 'Can Belief in God Be Rational If It has No Foundations', in *Faith and Rationality*, pp. 5–7 and 136–40, respectively; Alvin Plantinga, 'Reformed Epistemology', in Quinn and Taliaferro (eds.), *A Companion*, pp. 383–9. Also see Nicholas Wolterstorff, *Lament for A Son* (London: SPCK, 1997).

14. Daphne Hampson, 'Response', in Daphne Hampson (ed.), *Swallowing A Fishbone? Feminist Theologians Debate Christianity* (London: SPCK, 1996), pp. 121–2.

15. Grace M. Jantzen, *Power, Gender and Christian Mysticism* (Cambridge University Press, 1995), p. 346.

16. Coakley, 'Knowing Otherwise'.

17. Sarah Coakley, *Powers and Submissions: Spirituality, Philosophy, and Gender* (Oxford: Blackwell, 2002).

18. Sarah Coakley, '*Kenosis* and Subversion: On the Repression of "Vulnerability" in Christian Feminist Writings', in Hampson (ed.), *Swallowing*, pp. 82–111.

19. Coakley, *Powers and Submissions*.

20. Janet Martin Soskice, *Metaphor and Religious Language* (Oxford: Clarendon Press, 1985); and 'Religious Language', in Quinn and Taliaferro (eds.), *A Companion*, pp. 197–203.

21. Janet Martin Soskice, 'Turning the Symbols', in Hampson (ed.), *Swallowing*, pp. 17–32 and 125–8.

22. Ellen T. Armour, *Deconstruction, Feminist Theology, and the Problem of Difference: Subverting the Race/Gender Divide* (University of Chicago Press, 1999).

23. Sarah Coakley, 'The Eschatological Body: Gender, Transformation and God', *Modern Theology* 16:1 (January 2000), 61–73. Also see, Sarah Coakley, 'Introduction: Religion and the Body', in Sarah Coakley (ed.), *Religion and the Body* (Cambridge University Press, 1997), pp. 1–14. Cf. Judith Butler, *Bodies that Matter: On the Discursive Limits of "Sex"* (London: Routledge, 1993); Judith Butler, 'For a Careful Reading', in Linda Nicholson (ed.), *Feminist Contentions: A Philosophical Exchange* (London: Routledge, 1995), pp. 127–43.

24. Coakley, 'The Eschatological Body', 61, 66.

25. Butler, *Bodies that Matter*, pp. 2–4.

26. For an incisive argument for the crucial role for feminists of accessibility to the unintelligible body, see Veronica Vasterling, 'Butler's Sophisticated Constructivism: A Critical Assessment', *Hypatia* 14:3 (Summer 1999), 18–26; cf. Butler, *Bodies that Matter*, pp. 2–4, 30–1.

27. Grace M. Jantzen, 'What's the Difference? Knowledge and Gender in (Post) Modern Philosophy of Religion', *Religious Studies* 32:4 (1996), 431–48.

28. Ibid., pp. 431–48.

29. Grace M. Jantzen, *Becoming Divine: Towards a Feminist Philosophy of Religion* (Manchester University Press, 1998).

30. Harriet Harris, 'Divergent Beginnings in Feminist Philosophy of Religion', *Feminist Theology* 23 (2000).

31. Jantzen, *Becoming Divine*, p. 6; cf. Luce Irigaray, 'Divine Women', in her *Sexes and Genealogies*, trans. Gillian C. Gill (New York: Columbia University Press, 1993), pp. 68–9.

32. Amy Hollywood, 'Beauvoir, Irigaray and the Mystical', *Hypatia*, 9:4 (Fall 1994), Special Issue on Feminist Philosophy of Religion, Nancy Frankenberry and Marilyn Thie (eds.), pp. 158–85.

33. Ludwig Feuerbach, *The Essence of Christianity*, trans. George Eliot (Buffalo, NY: Prometheus Books, 1989), especially pp. 12–19 and 270–8.

34. Jantzen, *Becoming Divine*, pp. 143–55 and 234–54.

35. Anderson, *Feminist Philosophy*.

36. Ibid., pp. 134, 160n18. Cf. Terri Elliot, 'Making Strange What Had Appeared Familiar', *The Monist: An International Journal of General Philosophical Inquiry*, 77:4 (October 1994), General Topic on Feminist Epistemology: For or Against? pp. 424–33.

37. This distinction derives from A. W. Moore, *Points of View* (Oxford University Press, 1997), pp. 274–9. Cf. Pamela Sue Anderson, 'Gender and the Infinite', *International Journal for Philosophy of Religion*, 50 (December 2001), 191–212.

38. bell hooks, *Yearning: Race, Gender and Cultural Politics* (Boston, MA: South End Press, 1990), especially pp. 12–13; *Wounds of Passion: A Writing Life* (New York, NY: Henry Holt & Company, 1997), p. xxiii; and *Remembered Rapture: The Writer at Work* (London: The Women's Press, 1999).

39. Anderson, *Feminist Philosophy*, p. 3.

40. Kathleen O'Grady, 'Where Bodies Embrace: Pamela Sue Anderson's *A Feminist Philosophy of Religion*', *Feminist Theology* 20 (1999), 104–6.

41. Michèle Le Doeuff, *The Philosophical Imaginary*, trans. Colin Gordon (London: The Athlone Press, 1989).

42. O'Grady, 'Where Bodies Embrace', 109.

Selected reading

Anderson, Pamela Sue. *A Feminist Philosophy of Religion: The Rationality and Myths of Religious Belief*, Oxford: Blackwell, 1998.

Coakley, Sarah. *Powers and Submissions: Spirituality, Philosophy and Gender*, Oxford: Blackwell, 2002.

Frankenberry, Nancy, and Thie, Marilyn (eds.). *Hypatia: A Journal of Feminist Philosophy* 9:4 (Fall 1994), Special Issue on Feminist Philosophy of Religion.

Hollywood, Amy. *Sensible Ecstasy: Mysticism, Sexual Difference and the Demands of History*, Chicago, IL: University of Chicago Press, 2002.

Irigaray, Luce. *Sexes and Genealogies*, Gillian C. Gill (tr.), New York: Columbia University Press, 1993.

Jantzen, Grace M. *Becoming Divine: Towards A Feminist Philosophy of Religion*, Manchester: Manchester University Press, 1998.

4 Feminist theology as theology of religions
RITA M. GROSS

Not too long ago, I sat in a gathering of feminist theologians. The topic was 'diversity'; numerous complaints about lack of diversity were being voiced, but it was clear that lack of diversity *among* the Christians, not absence of *religious* diversity, was being protested. I pointed out that the diversity among *Christians* represented was far greater than the diversity among *religions*, and that the discussion presumed a Christian context which I, a non-Christian, found problematic. The conversation paused momentarily to allow me to make my comment, then returned to its previous direction, as if I had never spoken. I felt as if I had momentarily surfaced from underwater in some giant ocean, only to have the waters submerge me again immediately. I also noted that I had felt this way before. In earlier days, it had not been uncommon for men to treat women's observations about religious studies or theology in the same way. One of the few other non-Christian feminists locked eyes with me and whispered, 'They just don't get it, do they?' How many times had we said this about men when trying to explain to them what feminism is and why it matters? This was a profoundly discouraging moment for me, a non-Christian pioneer in the feminist study of religion who has spent my life and career as a feminist theologian and scholar of religions involved almost equally in feminist issues and in issues surrounding religious diversity.

Others have also noticed this strange development in feminist theology. As the editors of the recently published anthology *Is There a Future for Feminist Theology?* comment:

> Although we have included diversity in terms of theoretical and methodological issues, what this volume lacks . . . is any dialogue with non-Western contexts. This on-going lack of engagement by feminist theology, and gender theory itself, with experience outside Western culture artificially limits the issues of gender and religion. From our perspective, this is the major task for the next millennium. The

traditional dichotomy between East and West, a meta-narrative of a past age, needs to be dissolved to allow the vast plurality of global experiences to take centre stage.[1]

Ursula King has called feminism 'the missing dimension in the dialogue of religions', noting that if more women became prominent and visible in 'dialogue, this in turn might help to transform the oppressive patriarchal structures of religions'. In the same paper, she notes that Christian 'feminist theology, though wide-ranging and internally very diverse itself, is not yet critically wrestling with the challenge of religious pluralism'.[2]

'Theology of religions' is a relatively new term that has to do with noting the diversity among the religions of the world and developing conceptual tools for relating with and understanding that diversity. Critical to an adequate theology of religions is that it be knowledgeable about and conversant with the great Asian Wisdom traditions; merely raising one's gaze to include other monotheisms does not really constitute serious encounter with religious diversity. To date, theology of religions has been largely a Christian activity,[3] but only because religious diversity is more theologically challenging to monotheisms than to non-monotheistic religions. In a religiously diverse world in which people of the various religions are in constant contact with each other, eventually all religions will have to develop ways of helping their believers understand and live peacefully with the religious diversity that is not going to disappear. In this enterprise of developing theologies of religions, many tools can be and have already been used, including comparative studies, interreligious exchange, and dialogue. As demonstrations of how these various tools can be used and to participate in the adventure of coming to terms with religious diversity in Christian perspective, two books, written by women but containing no explicitly feminist dimensions, are highly recommended: Diana Eck's *Encountering God: A Spiritual Journey From Bozeman to Benares* and Judith Berling's *A Pilgrim in Chinese Culture: Negotiating Religious Diversity*.

Completing the assigned task of this chapter, discussing feminist theology as theology of religions, clearly presents problems, as the above experiences and quotations indicate. Three intertwined issues are involved: the current lack of religious diversity in most feminist theological forums, the lack of any theology of *religious* diversity in most feminist theology, and the relative lack of feminist participation in most formats for interreligious exchange. Indeed, the most extensive 'interreligious' discussion in the literature of feminist theology to date is the relatively acrimonious debate on 'Christian feminist anti-Judaism', which hardly constitutes a theology of religions or an interreligious exchange by the above criteria.[4] A few early books are more inclusive, but studying their tables of contents quickly shows that the vast majority of the articles speak from a Christian context, a few from a Jewish context, and even fewer from Muslim, Hindu, Buddhist, or other religious contexts.[5] Thus, the tasks of this chapter must be largely constructive: discussing how or why the current situation regarding feminist theology and issues of religious diversity came to be, developing feminist grounds for serious feminist attention to religious diversity, and, finally, suggesting how a feminist theology of religions might look. In this brief chapter, only an outline of those tasks can be undertaken.

Feminist theology, as I envision it, is a movement that cuts across tradition lines, influences all religious traditions, and is relevant to all of them. Indeed, in the early years of the feminist theological movement, that was the case, as Christian, Jewish, post-Christian, and Buddhist theologians worked closely together and were about equally visible in the feminist theological movement. Nevertheless, struggle over diversity is not new to the feminist theological movement. 'In retrospect, it is clear that diversity – of aims, concerns, and perspectives – was always present even when feminist gatherings felt unified, exuberant, and triumphant in their stand against patriarchal religion and androcentric scholarship.'[6] By the mid-1980s, cries of outrage about the watchword of early feminist theology, 'women's experience', were widespread. The feminist theological movement had universalised 'women's experience' as white, middle-class, heterosexual experience, it was claimed. Therefore, to be genuinely inclusive, diversity of class, race, culture, and sexual orientation must be taken seriously. Genuine and irreconcilable theological differences also emerged. Experiencing this breakdown of a perceived unified front against patriarchy was traumatic and painful. Why was/is it so difficult to deal with this diversity and disagreement? My own suggested answer is that the difficulty is, in large part, due to 'a deeply entrenched tendency in Western thinking to turn difference into hierarchy . . . If we are different, then one of us must be better.'[7]

Because of deliberate efforts to be more genuinely inclusive, and because excluded groups of women demanded that their voices be heard, many feminist theological gatherings now are more diverse regarding race, class, culture, and sexual orientation. But, somehow, in that process, *religious* diversity was lost. For all their faults, the feminist theological gatherings of the early 1970s *were* more religiously diverse than is common today. It is also worth noting that in most contemporary cultural discourse about diversity, religion is rarely mentioned.

I would argue that, in ignoring religious diversity, feminist theology has stopped short of its goal of genuine inclusivity, even lost ground. Though diversity is usually valued by feminist theologians, the kind of diversity promoted is intercultural diversity *within* Christianity.[8] 'Feminist theology' and 'Christian feminist theology' have been conflated in many arenas of discussion. Unwittingly, Christian feminist theologians, who think of themselves as more inclusive than mainstream theologians, have been co-opted by one of the more archaic, out-of-touch aspects of mainstream theology – its tendency to equate 'religion' with 'Christianity'. Furthermore, as one who works extensively in both feminist theology and in the theology of religions, in my experience, Christian feminist theologians are among the worst offenders in this regard. For non-Christian feminists, this exclusionary practice is insulting, maddening, and frustrating. The place I would least expect to encounter it is in the feminist theological movement to which I have given so much of my life and work. Personal feelings and experience aside, this development is also limiting for the development of feminist theology. Intercultural Christian diversity will not yield the stunning variety of religious options that would come with genuine *interreligious* study and dialogue that also took account of the variety *within* each religion.

Are there feminist grounds for developing theologies of religion and for learning about and thinking about religious diversity? The history of the feminist theological movement itself provides the first major *feminist* reason for being concerned with *religious* diversity. Feminist theology was born from the experience of being excluded by patriarchal religions, and the resulting convictions that the voices of the excluded deserve to be heard and that adequate theology cannot be done on the basis of erasing many voices and limiting the theological voice to the chosen few. The landmark anthology of feminist theology, *Womanspirit Rising* proclaimed in 1979 that 'the **diversity** [emphasis added] within feminist theology and spirituality is its strength'.[9] The second major *feminist* reason for such concern was also articulated already in that early anthology. Though the phrase 'widening the canon' does not appear in that anthology, the concept is implicit throughout it, especially in its concerns with rejecting the binding authority of the past and in searching for new traditions. Since then, the issues of how to use the received canon in feminist ways and where to find new sources with which to do feminist theology have been important to most feminist theologians. For feminists, concern with religious diversity is necessitated by the most basic values of feminist theology – the importance of inclusivity and the necessity to widen the canon.

These feminist reasons for interest in religious diversity mesh with, are different ways of expressing, two reasons why a theology of religions is necessary today. One is ethical and the other is epistemological. The ethical reasons have to do with the facts that religious diversity is a reality, not a mistake, and that religious diversity is part of the experience of most contemporary people. Intolerance and exclusive truth claims may be unavoidable when religions are relatively isolated from each other, but they are lethal when religions must mix and mingle in a common environment, as is the case today. The moral reason thus amounts to the same thing as the feminist value of including the formerly excluded. The epistemological reasons have to do with the illuminating power of the 'comparative mirror',[10] with the truth of the slogan that 'to know one religion is to know none'. They also have to do with the fact that religions other than one's own may well contain ideas and symbols from which feminist theologians might learn something useful. The epistemological reasons thus amount to the same thing as the feminist need to widen the canon, whether through rejecting received patriarchal interpretations or through utilising formerly non-canonical sources.

In keeping with my understanding of feminism as a religious movement that crosses religious boundaries and has similar implications for all religions, I will propose a theology of religions that I believe would be an adequate feminist theology of religions. Though, to date, theology of religions has been largely composed by Christian theologians, I do not believe that an adequate theology of religions would differ significantly from one tradition to another. Theologians of all traditions have to deal with the fact of religious diversity in a morally compassionate and theologically compelling manner; they all need to ask what can be learned from diverse perspectives. In so far as possible, I will pose the conceptual alternatives and provide arguments for the positions I advocate. In such a short chapter, of course, it will not be possible to discuss fully all possible alternatives and arguments; thus it is an invitation to discussion, not a foreclosure of it.

MORAL ISSUES AND FEMINIST VALUES

Feminist values in this area are best expressed as evaluating religious diversity positively and including those who have been excluded. So the first layer of a theology of religions is concerned with the problem of how to understand normatively the fact that other religions besides one's own exist. To date, three positions have been proposed: exclusivist, inclusivist, and pluralist. Because these positions are already well known and developed in mainstream theology of religions, they will only be summarised very briefly here.[11]

The exclusivist claims that her position alone among the world's religions has validity and would be the only religion in an ideal world. This position necessitates negative attitudes towards all other religions, and exclusivists often claim nothing of any value can be found in other religions. The inclusivists say that there is some merit in other religions, that they are not wholly inadequate. But an inclusivist would also claim that, in the final analysis, these other religions are not completely adequate because they are waiting to be 'fulfilled' by the teachings found in the inclusivist's religion. The other religions would be 'better' religions if only they would adopt what the inclusivist most values about her own religion. (This use of the term 'inclusivity' is not the same as that discussed as the feminist value of inclusivity. I use the term here because it is usual in mainstream theologies of religion.) The pluralist would say that no religion is either the only valid religion or the most valid among religions. Rather, each religion provides something valuable and interesting in a giant mosaic. We probably have personal affinities for one among the religions, but that does not elevate the worth of that religion for everyone else. A pluralist is also interested in dialogue with members of other religions and in learning from other religions, whether through the study of that religion or through dialogue.

For a feminist theology of religions, the only suitable candidate among these options is the pluralist position. It is inconceivable that a feminist theologian would go through all the heartache of being excluded from her own religion, and doing the theological work required to include herself back in, only to turn around and make exclusive or inclusive truth claims about the religion that excluded her! Furthermore, as already pointed out, a major value of feminist theology is to include the voices that have not been heard, to widen the circle, to learn how to welcome diversity. It makes no sense for those values to stop when they hit the boundary of one's own religion, and for another set of values to take over at that point. I do not think this would be a controversial point among feminist theologians, even though none has, to my knowledge, explicitly addressed the issue. Because this argument, in my view, holds for feminist theology, it follows that it also holds for 'mainstream' theology.[12]

Other ethical reasons for preferring the pluralist position are not specifically feminist. Only the pluralist position provides ways for different religions to live together peacefully, without competition. The exclusivist or inclusivist positions, if held simultaneously by members of different religions, can only lead to mutual hostility. It is unreasonable to take for oneself a position regarding religious diversity that, if taken by others of a different persuasion, leads to suffering and away from peace, wholeness, and healing. If religions don't provide peace, wholeness, and healing, what good are they?

When the pluralist position is advocated, someone always brings up the spectre of absolute relativism. Does anything go then? Are there no standards, theological or moral? Pluralists are not saying that one cannot evaluate religious phenomena; we are saying that no religion has a monopoly on either truth or falsity, relevant or harmful teachings and practices. Furthermore, every religion has some of each. In evaluating religious phenomena, I would claim that ethical behaviour is far more important than theological doctrines. It is easy to demonstrate, if one studies world religions, that there are many cogent theologies; there is no particular need to rank or evaluate them against one another. If they can be evaluated or ranked at all, the only possible basis for such ranking would be the ethical *consequences* of theological ideas. When a theological doctrine, by itself, harms people who try to believe in it, or when a theological doctrine translates directly into oppressive social practices, then it could be negatively evaluated. Many Jewish and Christian feminists have claimed that the exclusively male language and imagery of deity common in the monotheistic religions is one such example.[13] More generally, I would claim that if people who hold to a set of doctrines are transformed in ethically positive ways by their adherence of those doctrines, they can be evaluated positively, though that does not mean those doctrines are therefore of universal value. If, on the other hand, people are rigid, inflexible, hateful towards those who are different, wasteful of natural resources, or cruel to animals, then the religious doctrines they hold are not working, are not doing their proper job of transforming humans into gentler, kinder, more compassionate beings. According to this standard, all religions have both succeeded and failed, another reason to hold the pluralist position.[14]

EPISTEMOLOGICAL ISSUES AND FEMINIST VALUES

Feminist values affirm the importance of thinking about diverse religions, and so express a feminist need to widen the canon. The ethical dimensions of a feminist theology of religions are quite straightforward and uncontroversial, in my view. The more interesting, and potentially more challenging dimension of any theology of religions is the epistemological dimension, which takes us from accepting a plurality of religions as theologically unproblematic to the necessity of actually learning something about, and possibly from, these religions. The epistemological reasons for developing a feminist theology of religions centre on the effect it could have on one's *own* theological development, and thus the development of feminist theology in one's *own* tradition. There are two possible and interdependent ways of going about this task: learning about and from the various religions through academic study of them and engaging in dialogue with members of these traditions.

Can one claim to do adequate constructive theology, feminist or otherwise, if one knows little or nothing about religions other than one's own? At least at a time such as ours, in which religious diversity is everywhere and information about world religions is readily available, I would claim that one cannot. The theological imperative has always included taking account of the contemporary culture, which now includes what the modern disciplines and modern knowledge tell us about the world. Included in that knowledge is detailed information about the phenomenon of religion in general, as well as information about a great variety of religions. In a pluralistic and post-colonial era, it is inappropriate to proceed with one's constructive work as if that revolution regarding our knowledge about world religions had not occurred. If theologians are not at least somewhat familiar with this material, they are not operating with a full deck and are constructing theology in a vacuum. How could a theologian, feminist or otherwise, make any claims about religion when she is operating with a sample of one?

I would also make this claim because of the power of the 'comparative mirror' to illumine self as well as other. It is hard to imagine looking at religion through the lens of only one religion after one has begun to study and think about religion comparatively, not only because of what has been learned about the possibility of other religious perspectives, but also because one has so many more tools with which to see one's own religion. The phrase 'comparative mirror' denotes, not only learning some information, but using that information in a certain way. A mirror is reflexive, whereas information, by itself, is not. In the comparative mirror, we see ourselves in the context and perspective of many other religious phenomena, inviting, even necessitating self-reflection about our own religious and cultural systems. In that process, 'Our own world, instead of being taken for granted, becomes exposed as *a* world, its contents held up to the comparative mirror and we become a phenomenon to ourselves.'[15] For theological reflection, feminist or otherwise, nothing is so useful as becoming a phenomenon to oneself because in that process, we see and understand ourselves much more clearly. Part of that seeing includes seeing the strengths and weaknesses of the perspectives we take for granted. As we begin to experience that there really are religious *alternatives*, our own perspective must also become an *alternative*, not merely the only viable theological position or something with which we are stuck.

Furthermore, by really looking in the comparative mirror, we will undoubtedly find many alternatives that we would be unlikely to imagine on our own. For example, most feminist theology takes it for granted that we will speak of deity in some way, even if we are very dissatisfied with the symbolism of deity named and spoken of as male-only. But what of a non-theistic religious alternative, such as that modelled by Buddhism? It would be useful to feminist theologians used to working in theistic contexts to contemplate such a possibility, to contemplate the pros and cons of theism itself. Theism looks different in the comparative mirror than it does when one takes it for granted and does not regard it as an *alternative*.

Unlike a beginning student of religion, an experienced constructive theologian will probably begin, not only to learn *about*, but to learn *from* the material revealed in the comparative mirror relatively quickly. This process of learning *from* the data in the comparative mirror needs to be discussed carefully because it contains many potential pitfalls. It must also be admitted that a *feminist* theologian will face challenges when looking into the comparative mirror that may not be faced by a conventional theologian.

Feminists sometimes object to looking into the comparative mirror because all the religions they see there are patriarchal to some degree, and people are tired of studying patriarchal religion. In and of itself, this complaint is true; all major world religions are patriarchal to some extent. However, there is little place else to go for alternatives with which to imagine religion anew. It would be enjoyable to find some religion that fulfilled one's feminist dreams, but that is unlikely. Such religious visions have to be pieced together from the available parts, combined with imagination, stubbornness, and courage. Why limit oneself to the familiar patriarchies in that quest? There are very interesting and very useful religious ideas and practices in other traditions. Furthermore, feminist theologians, especially Christian and Jewish feminist theologians, are more than adept at finding inspiration and reason for going on, despite and within familiar patriarchies. Why should it be different with unfamiliar patriarchal religions? The benefits of finding a really useful and interesting symbol, concept, or practice are greater than the discomfort generated by encountering patriarchy in unfamiliar places.

Nevertheless, for a feminist, one of the trickiest tasks of looking into the comparative mirror is dealing with material that is not only patriarchal in familiar ways but also seemingly immoral and unredeemably oppressive.

Western feminists, religious and secular, have sometimes been eager to criticise and condemn practices that strike them as completely cruel and unbearable for women. Unquestionably, when a feminist studies some unfamiliar religious contexts, she is likely to heave a sigh of relief that *she* does not live in that culture. Some practices, such as African genital operations on women, cannot be evaluated as anything but completely horrific by feminist standards. Nevertheless, we must ask if vocal outrage is the most effective way of responding to such practices.

Quick condemnation of unfamiliar religious or cultural beliefs and practices is one of the great pitfalls of cross-cultural studies in general. The purpose and the promise of such study is not to feel smug and superior. Long experience in teaching unfamiliar religions has given me certain insights about how best to proceed. First, the ground rules of looking into and learning from the comparative mirror *require* suspension of judgment at first, until one is thoroughly familiar with the situation being studied. One *must* first try to understand *why* such practices exist and *what* purposes they serve, according to the viewpoint of the religion being studied. Empathy is the most critical tool for looking into the comparative mirror in ways that do not create further mutual entrenchment and scorn. It must be applied in all cases, even the most unsavoury, *before* appropriate judgments can be made.

If one does not jump to conclusions about how certain religious or cultural phenomena are experienced by projecting from one's experience, but takes more time to reflect on the practice, there may be some surprising conclusions. Some practices that seem undesirable turn out not to be as completely disadvantageous to women as they might seem at first. For example, arranged marriages *can* protect women from the need for self-display, the indignities of the singles bar, and the danger of date rape. Polygyny *can* provide female companionship and help with childcare. Furthermore, every woman who wants to marry can be married in a polygynous culture. Dress codes that require modesty *can* free women from needing to display themselves as sex objects competing to attract the male gaze if women are to find partners.

In other cases, seemingly undesirable conditions are not really very different from what Western women experienced until very recently, or even experience today. In particular, statements about the inferiority of women and the requirement that women should be subservient to male authority stemming from other religious contexts should not sound too different from the home-grown variety.

Finally, outsiders' judgments about women's situations are often made on the basis of *public* observation, of what goes on in public spaces. Women do not usually have authority in public spaces, including religious public spaces; indeed they may not even be present. However, if one knows the situation more intimately, one will discover that women often have a great deal of power behind the scenes, and everyone knows that and takes it for granted. As we have become familiar with the cultural and religious systems of India and China, this point has been demonstrated time and again.

However, some religious ideas and practices remain deplorable to a feminist even after much consideration. Then what? Cross-cultural public denunciations from First World countries and former colonists probably only entrench the situation further. Then resisting changes in women's situation becomes part of national pride and resistance to Westernisation. It does little good to talk about African genital *mutilation* rather than African genital operations, or to decry Muslim practices surrounding gender, to name two of the most inflammatory feminist causes. It would probably be far better quietly to work with *women* from those situations and to support them financially and emotionally.

Though it may seem that we have strayed from a feminist theology of religions into the ethics of cross-cultural study, that is not the case. Theologians are perhaps more apt to make judgments about what they study than are social scientists and scholars of religious studies. Therefore, as theologians become more competent in their knowledge about the vast diversity of religious phenomena and in their theological thinking about religious diversity itself, it is crucial for them to be able to make comparisons and judgments in ways that are not offensive or naïve.

Feminists also sometimes object to looking into the comparative mirror because of the difficulty entailed in becoming somewhat competent in understanding accurately what the comparative mirror is showing. In my experience, this has occurred at all levels of scholarly development, from that of professional scholars who do not attend papers on feminist topics if they are about an unfamiliar religion, to that of students in a goddess seminar who tuned out when we came to the book on Hindu goddesses. When I asked my students, who were all women studies minors and eager to study material on goddesses, why they were not so willing to make the effort to learn about the Hindu materials, I got the same answer from them that I receive from more established scholars. 'Too many foreign words', they said. The apprenticeship required for being able to use the comparative mirror effectively and adequately can be daunting. One *is* required to learn a good bit of terminology (perhaps even a foreign language) and one must empathise one's way into rather different world-views.

On the one hand, an extremely sensitive issue regarding cross-cultural knowledge and exchange is inappropriate appropriation without an adequate apprenticeship. Segments of the feminist spirituality movement have been especially criticised by Native Americans for indiscriminate and unautho-rised borrowing from their traditions.[16] Caution is better than plunging ahead on the basis of insufficient knowledge. On the other hand, though the process of learning about other traditions is never-ending in a certain sense, it is essentially no different from the process by which theologians first learn the ancient texts and languages, and all the theological variants required for competence and theological literacy within their indigenous tra-dition. Theologians are not born with that information already imprinted in their brains; they learn it, usually relatively early in their training. But why stop there? My claim is twofold. First, to do adequate theology in a pluralistic world, one needs information about the whole world, not just one's corner in it. Secondly, the additional perspective on one's own tradi-tion that one gains by this process of looking into the comparative mirror is well worth the effort.

I have already offered the example of studying and contemplating a non-theistic religion like Buddhism to refine one's understanding of the utility and limits of theistic symbolism. Hinduism offers the example of well-nuanced ways of alternating personal and impersonal imagery of the Ultimate, which is an issue with which many feminist theologians are con-cerned. At least as provocative are the many goddesses of Asia, with their colourful symbolism and intricate mythologies. They provide an example of goddesses as integral parts of ordinary peoples' religious lives, not merely as the construct of a small number of Western religious thinkers. I can think of no reason to exclude these materials from the widened canon, to stop short at the borders of Western history and culture.

When feminist theologians do let a wider canon speak to them, there are two ways it can influence their theology. One is by osmosis and the other is by deliberately altering one's theology on the basis of what has been learned from the comparative mirror. By 'osmosis', I mean that study and contemplation of various unfamiliar ideas, symbols, and practices grad-ually begin to affect how one thinks and how one views the world, which, of course, spills over into one's theologising. A good example of the process would be the post-Christian thealogy of Carol Christ, who has studied an-cient goddesses, especially those of Greece, very thoroughly, but who does not simply import wholesale the goddesses she has studied into her theol-ogy. Rather, she constructs a systematic thealogy of the goddess, based on this study and a good bit of creative imagination.[17] In certain ways this pro-cess is more authentic and involves less chance of total misunderstanding and misrepresentation of unfamiliar materials.

The process of direct borrowing and deliberately altering one's theology is more difficult, which is probably one reason why most academically trained theologians avoid it. If academically trained theologians do deliberately alter their theology on the basis of what they see in the comparative mirror, they are more likely to look at marginalised materials from their own tradition than to look at symbols or practices from completely different traditions. A good example of a feminist theologian who engages in this kind of use of the comparative mirror is Rosemary Ruether, especially her books *Sexism and God-talk: Toward a Feminist Theology* and *Women and Redemption: A Theological History*. These books demonstrate clearly how material that was omitted from the official canon of Christianity can be used in constructing deliberately alterative theologies.

Making theological use of materials from outside one's own culture or religion is much more difficult and challenging because it is so easy to use them in inappropriate or superficial ways. Sometimes those whose symbols and practices we might like to learn from do not wish to share them. Native American resentment about the ways in which the New Age and feminist spirituality movements 'borrow' their symbols and practices has already been noted. A wise rule of thumb in such cases might be to look elsewhere if we are told that we are not welcome to these symbols and practices, no matter how attractive they might be to us. In other cases, the materials are so wrenched out of context and reinterpreted that the new theology lacks credibility. Or, as people shop here and there for goddesses and religious practices they like, the result is a 'good parts' synthesis that is superficial.

Most problematic, however, is simply not doing justice to the materials one is borrowing. For example, as a long-time practitioner of Vajrayana Buddhism, I am not thrilled by most appropriations of 'Tantric goddesses' because they miss the whole point of the practice and the symbolism. My own theology is, of course, deeply influenced by these materials, but I have studied them closely for twenty-five years. Thus we find ourselves back to the question of what constitutes a proper apprenticeship. Time and again, I have found this question of apprenticeship to be crucial; religious teachers of many backgrounds, including Native American, will willingly teach committed students willing to serve the apprenticeship.

On the other hand, clearly religious symbols can cross cultural frontiers, change, develop, and become deeply incorporated into new religious contexts. We know this because it has happened. The goddesses of the ancient world became the Virgin Mary. Kwan-yin broke loose from her Buddhist moorings and her former male gender as an Indian Bodhisattva to become one of the most popular and beloved goddesses of China and Japan. There is no reason that, over time, this process could not happen to Western religions, both Christian and post-Christian, as Asian goddesses become more familiar and more beloved. At this point in time, the most likely candidate for finding a home in the West is the Hindu Goddess Kali,[18] though Kwan-yin is also receiving more attention from Westerners longing for goddesses.[19] The meanings of Kali and Kwan-yin and their impact on devotees are quite different in Western appreciations and appropriations of Kali or Kwan-Yin from what they are in Asian contexts. However, with enough time and with widespread veneration of these goddesses, that will not matter. They will have transformed into Western goddesses with Asian roots, who will still be worshipped in Asian contexts as well. This process will be especially interesting because Asian devotees of Kali or Kwan-yin and their European and American devotees can interact easily, if they choose to do so.

Even though feminist theologians do not often engage in the *study of* other religions, this possibility has been discussed at some length because of its potential impact on the development of feminist theology. However, at present, most of the few feminist theologians involved in learning about and learning from other religions do so through the practice of interreligious dialogue, of which Buddhist–Christian dialogue is probably the most developed. In some ways, dialogue is probably an easier and quicker method by which to learn about and learn from unfamiliar religions than study. In dialogue, one is interacting with members of another religious tradition who are usually very well educated and very articulate in that tradition. They serve as a living library ready to correct one's misinterpretations and misunderstandings of the other religion. However, dialogue between relative amateurs without thorough academic grounding in their own tradition could well become a detour.

To those unpractised in dialogue, it is important to understand what genuine dialogue is *not*. It is not a covert missionary activity in which each side tries to prove the superiority of their religion. It is not a debate, with all the adversarial connotations of the term 'debate'. Nor is it an attempt to find some commonality between religions, an attempt to discover that, at the bottom line in an esoteric way, all religions really are the same.

Many people have the misconception that, in conversations or dialogue with people of other religious persuasions, one could not help but try to demonstrate the superiority of one's own position to one's partner. After all, they say: 'You are committed to this religious perspective; you have devoted years to studying and practising it. Clearly you must think that it is the best position.' The question in response is: 'Best for whom?' A pluralistic theology of religions easily accommodates love of and enthusiasm for one's own religious position with deep appreciation of other positions. One does not have to very psychologically sophisticated to realise that religion cannot be a 'one size fits all' phenomenon. There is no reason to expect that the religious symbols and practices to which I can deeply relate have the same resonance for everyone. Being defensive about one's own perspective is the least likely stance for successful dialogue. For this reason, participation in dialogue almost requires a pluralistic theology of religions, or at least a broadly inclusivist theology of religions. One of the major problems in interreligious dialogue is that the people who need it most are the least likely to engage in dialogue.

Debate is also less than ideal as a format for dialogue, and, in fact, it is never used as a format for dialogue, to my knowledge, even though some might think dialogue would be debate. Debate is an exercise in which the most skilled debaters 'win', which does not prove the truth of their position, and the agenda of debate is to score points for oneself, not to understand the other. Furthermore, a skilled debater needs to be able to argue either side of the debate, which makes debate better suited for fine-tuning one's understanding of the intricacies of various theological positions within one's own tradition than for understanding a radically different alternative. Unless both debaters were highly skilled in discussing both religions, debate as a format for interreligious dialogue simply would not work. Even then, it would not prove to be as fruitful as conversation on a common topic.

Probably the most widespread misconception about interreligious dialogue is that its purpose is to find common ground, areas of agreement between the religions, so that mutual suspicions and hostilities can end. After all, if all religions really teach the same things in the long run, what is there to fight about? This understanding of dialogue carries a covert theology of religions with it. Genuine religious diversity is still seen as a problem if this is one's concept of the purpose of dialogue. It is felt that there must be some common meeting point for all the religions, if we could only find it, and that finding it would promote better relations between the religions. But why do we need a common meeting point? Can't we just appreciate the diversity of religions? Most people who have specialised to some extent in interreligious dialogue do not hold the view there is a common ground upon which all the religions can agree, nor do they think that it would be preferable for there to be a common ground for all religions.

Why, then should one engage in interreligious dialogue? In the long run, the purpose of dialogue is the same as the purpose of studying other traditions: to enrich one's own theology with input that one would probably never think of by oneself. The foremost theoretician of dialogue, John Cobb, states that the attitude one brings to dialogue is willingness to listen completely and carefully, and to change as a result of dialogue. He, and many others, would claim that any genuine encounter changes one; therefore, entering interreligious dialogue means being open to theological growth. Nor are the changes predictable ahead of time. Programmed change and genuine encounter are mutually incompatible.

It is important to realise that, while theological growth and change is an assumed outcome of dialogue, the change with which one is concerned is internal change in oneself, *not* affecting the theological thinking of the *other*. That is their prerogative and their issue. For example, in discussing Jewish–Christian dialogue, John Cobb suggests that, while Christians might hope that someday Jews could integrate the story of Jesus into their history and would feel that such a change would enrich Judaism considerably, the reason for Christians to engage in Jewish–Christian dialogue is *not* to make *that* case. 'The Christian purpose in dialogue with Jews must be to change Christianity.'[20]

This principle does not mean that dialogists cannot make suggestions to each other, especially when trust has developed. Dialogue can also provide a way to see ourselves as others see us, if we are open to hearing about the impressions our theologies make on other people. Genuine dialogue produces the reaction, 'I never would have thought of that', regarding assumptions and givens of our own position. But that process is reversible. In genuine dialogue, when mutual trust is established and it is clear that there is no covert missionary agenda, one is free to say to one's dialogue partners: 'You know, I just don't get that belief or that practice. It doesn't make any sense to me. What does it offer you?' One can also make suggestions to one's partners: 'Why don't you consider these ideas or practices. It seems to me that they might be helpful to you.' Finally, of course, one of the genuinely enjoyable aspects of interreligious dialogue is discussing comparisons and contrasts between religions with truly knowledgeable people of goodwill.

That feminism is the missing dimension in religious dialogue was one of the jumping-off points of this chapter. But that voice is missing because the feminists aren't there! In the dialogue contexts in which I participate, Christian feminists' seeming lack of interest in dialogue is often noted and regretted. As with studying other religious traditions, probably feminists hesitate to become involved in such dialogues because they involve dialogue among patriarchal religions. But, at least in some dialogue contexts, there is a great deal of sensitivity to feminist issues and the men are as unaccepting of religious sexism as are the women. For example, the Society for Buddhist–Christian Studies wrote into its bylaws the principle that its board and its officers, as well as speakers in its programmes, will always include parity not only between Christians and Buddhists, but also between men and women. That happened in part because feminists participated in the founding of the society. Granted, other dialogue contexts are more sexist and less welcoming of women. But the academic study of religion, and Jewish and Christian theology were not very welcoming of feminism either when we first demanded entry. Because feminism is a major movement in many religions today, its voices need to be heard in the dialogues among these religions. But feminists themselves are the only ones who can add that voice. Until feminists insist upon entering interreligious dialogue, feminism will continue to be the missing voice in interreligious dialogue.

SUMMARY

Feminist theology's lack of serious attention to any dimension of a theology of religions, to *religious* diversity, is its most serious failing, in my view. This lack of attention is truly difficult to understand, given feminism's emphases on including the unheard voices, on not trying to speak for others, and on the need for new sources for theology. Feminist theologians could benefit greatly from exposure to religious systems that are *truly different*, that are not just culturally diverse variants of Christianity or monotheism but are *truly different*. Furthermore, this lack of attention to the theology of religions and to interreligious dialogue isolates and marginalises feminist theology in the academy and in the world. If we want to change the world, we can hardly do it by retreating to our feminist enclaves and never seriously encountering the rest of the religious world. Ignoring even our feminist colleagues whose *feminist* theologies may be *religiously* different is even more peculiar. If *feminists* of the various religions are not talking with each other, one wonders what has gone wrong with religious feminism.

The claims and arguments put forth in this chapter are all challenging and controversial. But I do not believe they are more challenging and controversial than were the feminist study of religions or Jewish, Christian, and post-Christian feminist theologies when they were first proposed. Besides, someone has to go out on limbs when something important has been ignored!

Notes
1. Deborah F. Sawyer and Diane M. Cutler (eds.), *Is There a Future for Feminist Theology?* (Sheffield Academic Press, 1999), p. 24.

2. Ursula King, "Feminism: the Missing Dimension in the Dialogue of Religions," in John May (ed.), *Pluralism and the Religions: The Theological and Political Dimensions* (London: Cassell, 1998), pp. 40–55.
3. For a survey of Christian theologies of religion, see Paul F. Knitter, *No Other Name?: A Critical Survey of Christian Attitudes Toward the World Religions* (Maryknoll, NY: Orbis Press, 1985).
4. Katherina von Kellenback, *Anti-Judaism in Feminist Religious Writings* (Atlanta, GA: Scholars Press, 1994); Leonare Siegle-Wenschewitz, Judith Plaskow, Marie-Theres Wacker, Fokkelien van Dijk-Hemmes, and Asphodel P. Long, "Special Section on Feminist Anti-Judaism," *Journal of Feminist Studies in Religion* 7:2 (Fall, 1991), 95–125.
5. Diana Eck and Devaki Jain (eds.), *Speaking of Faith: Global Perspectives on Women, Religion, and Social Change* (Philadelphia, PA: New Society Press, 1987); Virginia Ramey Mollenkott (ed.), *Women of Faith in Dialogue* (New York: Crossroad, 1988).
6. Rita M. Gross, *Feminism and Religion: An Introduction* (Boston, MA: Beacon Press, 1996), p. 49.
7. Ibid., p. 51.
8. For a more detailed discussion of this process, see ibid., pp. 49–58.
9. Carol P. Christ and Judith Plaskow (eds.), *Womanspirit Rising: A Feminist Reader in Religion* (San Francisco, CA: Harper and Row, 1979), p. 15.
10. William Paden, *Religious Worlds: The Comparative Study of Religion* (Boston, MA: Beacon Press, 1988), p. 164.
11. A clear, accessible discussion is found in Diana Eck, *Encountering God: A Spiritual Journey From Bozeman to Benaves* (Boston, MA: Beacon Press, 1993), pp. 166–99.
12. For a detailed presentation of my discussion of these arguments, see Gross, 'Religious Diversity: Some Implications for Monotheism', *Crosscurrents* 49:3 (Fall 1999), 349–66.
13. For example, see Carol Christ's famous essay 'Why Women Need the Goddess: Phenomonological, Psychological, and Political Reflections', in Christ and Plaskow (eds.), *Womanspirit Rising*, pp. 273–87.
14. For a fuller development of these arguments, see Gross, 'The Virtues and Joys of the Comparative Mirror', *Boston University School of Theology Focus* (Fall 1999), 9–16.
15. Paden, *Religious Worlds*, p. 165.
16. Cynthia Eller, *Living in the Lap of the Goddess: The Feminist Spirituality Movement in America* (New York: Crossroad, 1993), pp. 74–81.
17. Carol Christ, *Rebirth of the Goddess: Finding Meaning in Feminist Spirituality* (Reading, MA: Addison-Wesley Publishing Company, 1997).
18. Rachel Fell McDermott, 'The Western Kali', in John Stratton Hawley and Diana Marie Wulff (eds.), *Devi: Goddesses of India* (Berkeley, CA: University of California Press, 1996), pp. 281–313.
19. Sandy Boucher, *Discovering Kwan Yin, Buddhist Goddess of Compassion* (Boston, MA: Beacon Press, 1999).
20. John Cobb, *Beyond Dialogue: Towards a Mutual Transformation of Christianity and Buddhism* (Philadelphia, PA: Fortress Press, 1982), p. 49.

Rita M. Gross

Selected reading

Berling, Judith. *A Pilgrim in Chinese Culture: Negotiating Religious Diversity*, Maryknoll, NY: Orbis Press, 1997.

Eck, Diana. *Encountering God: A Spiritual Journey From Bozeman to Benares*, Boston, MA: Beacon Press, 1993.

Gross, Rita M. *Feminism and Religion: An Introduction*, Boston, MA: Beacon Press, 1996.

King, Ursula (ed.). *Religion and Gender*, Oxford: Blackwell, 1995.

May, John (ed.). *Pluralism and the Religions: The Theological and Political Dimensions*, London: Cassell, 1998.

Ruether, Rosemary Radford. *Sexism and God-talk: Toward a Feminist Theology*, Boston, MA: Beacon Press, 1983; and *Women and Redemption: A Theological History*, Minneapolis, MN: Fortress Press, 1998.

5 Feminist theology as post-traditional thealogy
CAROL P. CHRIST

THE EMERGENCE OF
POST-TRADITIONAL THEALOGY

The word *thealogy* comes from the Greek words *thea* or Goddess and *logos* or meaning. It describes the activity of reflection on the meaning of Goddess, in contrast to theology, from *theos* and *logos*, which is reflection on the meaning of God. The adjective 'post' in the title of this chapter is somewhat problematic. If taken to imply that feminist thealogies designated as 'post-traditional' have developed in reaction to the limitations of Christian and Jewish theologies, it would be correct. However, if thought to mean that such thealogies do not look to the past, it would be wrong. Indeed, many 'post-traditional' feminist thealogies might be called 'pre-traditional' in that they claim to be rooted in a past far more ancient than the sacred histories of Christianity and Judaism. Whereas the times of Abraham and Moses were less than 4,000 years ago, post-traditional Goddess feminists locate their origins in the mists of time, in the Upper Palaeolithic, about 30,000 years ago. On the other hand, because Christianity outlawed the explicit practice of all pre-Christian religions (with the edicts of Theodosius, called 'the Great', at the end of the fourth century CE), 'post'-traditional thealogies cannot claim a direct inheritance of pre-Jewish or pre-Christian religious symbols, rituals, or ideas. I have used the word 'post-traditional' rather than 'post-Christian' in this chapter, because the practitioners of 'post-traditional' religion include both Christians and Jews. A number of the most influential proponents of feminist 'post-traditional thealogy', including Starhawk (Miriam Simos), Naomi Goldenberg, Margot Alder, Miriam Robbins Dexter, Gloria Orenstein, Asphodel Long, and Melissa Raphael are from Jewish backgrounds.

Post-traditional feminist thealogy can be traced to seeds sown at the end of the nineteenth century by American suffragists Matilda Joslyn Gage in *Woman, Church, and State* and Elizabeth Cady Stanton in *The Woman's*

Carol P. Christ

Bible.[1] These works did not create a feminist theological movement in their own time. Gage was written out of the history of the suffrage movement because she maintained that Christianity could not be salvaged for women. Stanton, though remembered, lost her standing in the women's rights movement due to the controversy provoked by her contention that biblical texts detrimental to women were created by man, not God.

In the twentieth century, Mary Daly revived these radical views in her groundbreaking work *Beyond God the Father.*[2] During the course of writing that book, Daly, who holds several degrees in Roman Catholic theology, came to the conclusion that Christianity and patriarchy were so intimately linked that it was time for women to leave Christianity behind. At about the same time, a Hungarian refugee named Zsuzsanna Budapest was forming the Susan B. Anthony Coven #1 in Los Angeles and penning the lesbian–feminist spiritual manifesto *The Feminist Book of Lights and Shadows*, lesbian country homesteaders Ruth and Jean Mountaingrove were planning the first issue of *WomanSpirit* magazine (Fall, 1974), and University of California archaeologist Marija Gimbutas was completing *The Gods and Goddesses of Old Europe.*[3]

In these works, the basic outlines of a feminist post-traditional thealogy were proposed. Daly provided a radical critique of the core symbols of Christian tradition, summed up in the phrase 'if God is male, male is God'.[4] Budapest provided an alternative symbol system and ritual practice, calling upon women-identified women to reclaim the ancient religion of the Goddess. Ruth and Jean Mountaingrove provided a forum where women could share non-traditional spiritual experiences, visions, and rituals, many of them affirming the cycles of the female body and an affinity between women and nature. Marija Gimbutas unwittingly supplied the fledgling movement with a history, through her analysis of the symbolism of the Goddess in the religion of palaeolithic and neolithic Old Europe.

Over the course of the following twenty-five years, a broadly based grassroots movement known as the 'women's spirituality', 'feminist spirituality', or 'Goddess' movement took root in North America, Northern Europe, Australia, and New Zealand. This movement was created and is led primarily by women, though it includes growing numbers of men. It overlaps to a certain extent with the (non- or not explicitly feminist) neo-pagan, witchcraft, and Wiccan traditions which preceded it and from which it has drawn some of its core symbolism. In the last years of the twentieth century, hundreds of books on the 'the Goddess' were published and found a wide audience.

THE GODDESS

For many women, Ntozake Shange's words, 'i found god in myself / and i loved her / i loved her fiercely', describe an almost miraculous transformation of the way they view their female bodies, the power of their female selves.[5] To name the divine power as 'Goddess' also causes a profound metaphoric shift in how we view the world. In changing the way we perceive women, the symbol of the Goddess changes the way we understand all that the female body has come to symbolise: the flesh, the earth, finitude, interdependence, death. When the earth is imaged as the body of the Goddess, the female body and the earth, which have been devalued together, are resacralised. Our understanding of divine power is transformed as it is clearly recognised as present within the finite and changing world.

Rituals, both individual and communal, have flourished in response to the rebirth of the Goddess. Images and pictures of the Goddess are placed on altars along with candles, personal symbols, and elements from the natural world, including stones, feathers, flowers, water. Goddess images inspire women to take pride in themselves and encourage men to treat women and children with respect and to affirm their own connection to the life force. The rituals of Goddess religion celebrate the human connection to the cycles of the moon and the seasons of the sun, invoking the mysteries of birth, death, and renewal, joy and gratitude for finite life. They encourage an appreciation of diversity and difference, affirming that darkness and light, springtime and winter, all people and all beings are sacred. Goddess symbols celebrate the body of the Goddess, the human body, and the earth body, motivating participants to embrace embodied life and care for the earth body. Goddess rituals celebrate the sacredness of the earth in its concrete particularity, reminding the community that the ground on which it stands is holy. Goddess rituals and symbols broaden and deepen the understanding of human interdependence to include all beings and all people. Goddess rituals shape communities in which concern for the earth and all people can be embodied.

Not all feminist post-traditional religious reflection is centred in the Goddess movement. Though she uses the word 'Goddess' in her writings, Mary Daly has kept her distance from the Goddess movement. She rejected all forms of fixed or repeated rituals, along with all forms of theism and even panentheism, opting instead for an ontology of 'becoming' in which there are no fixed points. The deity for her is an open horizon in which 'spinsters', 'hags', and 'nag-gnostics' (that is, lesbian feminist women) are the agents of creativity in the universe. Daphne Hampson, in *After Christianity*, argued that the feminist critique of Christianity ought to be followed not by another appeal to non-rational faith, but by a rational theism.[6] Rita Gross, in *Buddhism after Patiarchy*, drew on Buddhist tradition as the starting point for theological reflection.[7] Grace M. Jantzen, in *Becoming Divine*, used the work of French feminist philosopher Luce Irigaray, who was influenced by both Freud and Feuerbach, to argue that the purpose of human moral life is to 'become divine'. Rejecting traditional theism and atheism, and panentheism, Jantzen opted for pantheism as the philosophical backdrop for interpreting Irigaray's notion that the female divine is 'the perfection of our subjectivity'.[8] In this chapter, I will focus on the post-traditional thealogy that arises out of the Goddess movement.

Feminist post-traditional thealogians share a critique of traditional theology with radical or revolutionary feminist Jewish and Christian theologians. All view the image of God as male as detrimental to women; criticise the image of God as a 'dominating other' as being a legacy of hierarchical and stereotypically 'male' understandings of power; concur that the dualistic (Platonic) philosophical tradition that separates body and mind, spirit and matter, finite and infinite, rational and irrational, male and female, must be replaced with more holistic conceptions; question traditional authorities; believe that theology influences social arrangements and social structures; and envision a more just world, not only for women, but also for all the oppressed. Some Christian and Jewish theologians even advocate female divine imagery that sounds suspiciously like it has been taken from the Goddess movement.

Then why does one group continue to work for change from within inherited traditions, while the other works to create spiritual alternatives? Clearly such choices are not made simply on the basis of weighing up the negative and positive elements within the traditions. Other factors are at work. Those who remain within inherited traditions feel greater loyalty to historic communities. This is especially true for some Jewish women who state that abandoning Judaism after the holocaust would give a 'posthumous victory' to Hitler. Those who leave inherited traditions are less willing to live with and within symbol systems (e.g. the Bible, or the language of prayer and liturgy) and hierarchical structures that they find harmful to self and others. Members of these two groups also differ in their perceptions of whether institutions are more likely to be changed from within or without.

For the most part shut out of the academy, the Goddess movement is more spiritual than theological. Having felt silenced by traditional theological discourse, its adherents are rightly suspicious of theological truth claims. They are more interested in religious practice, especially individual and communal rituals, than they are in discussing 'right belief'. None the less, as Carol P. Christ and Melissa Raphael have shown, the movement has an incipient thealogical discourse.[9]

Practice gives rise to questions, and questions give rise to thealogy. Is the Goddess one or many? Nature or more than nature? An image of female power and possibility, or the ground of all being? How do we know what images to use and to what they refer? Traditional theology has grouped these and other questions into categories that include authority, history, divinity, humanity, nature, and ethics. I will address each of these subjects from the point of view of Goddess theology.

AUTHORITY

The source and norm for traditional theologies is revealed tradition (such as is found in the history of a community or in documents such as the Bible, the Torah, the Talmud [which collects the legal decisions of the rabbis], papal decrees, canon law, the decisions of ecclesiastical councils, etc.) and rational thought which reflects on revealed tradition. Progressive theologians in the nineteenth and twentieth centuries recognised that social and historical factors affect both the creation and interpretation of tradi-tions. Feminist theologians add gender to this mix, asserting that women have had little impact on the shaping of the traditions of which they are a part. Women's experiences, both historical and contemporary, they argue, must be allowed to shape traditions. Those who create theology within tra-ditions must wrestle with and reinterpret inherited texts and the symbol systems they enshrine. Feminist theologians run a gamut from those who believe that the interpretation of traditions from a feminist perspective will solve the problem of women, to those who assert that their traditions must be radically transformed or even recreated.

Goddess thealogy, like feminist theology more generally, begins in women's experience. Goddess thealogy often begins with an individual woman's dissatisfaction with the male imagery of biblical religion. Her expe-rience of the Goddess, which may have come to her through reading, dreams, ritual, or meditation, becomes authoritative for her. She may then share her experiences and ideas with friends, start or find a ritual group. While few leaders of the movement aspire to the status of gurus whose authority is un-questioned, certain books, including those of Starhawk, Z. Budapest, Naomi Goldenberg, Carol P. Christ, Charlene Spretnak, Merlin Stone, Asphodel Long, and others have been widely read and influential in the movement.

Goddess history, especially ancient images of the Goddesses, provides inspiration and to some extent validation for contemporary experience. But, because contemporary worshippers of the Goddess have no received tradition into which they must fit (or struggle to fit) their experiences, Goddess history never becomes (as the Bible or tradition does in Jewish and Christian theologies) a final authority. Because each woman's experience is valued, Goddess thealogy is likely to be plural and suggestive, allowing a variety of interpretations of its meaning, not proposing one final truth. Many contemporary followers of the Goddess perceive all theologies (and perhaps even what might be called 'intellectual clarity and consistency') as systems of thinking that have the purpose of creating dogma and stifling creativity and individuality. It is fair to say that there are many different opinions about every thealogical subject that can be imagined, in the movement.

In writing a thealogy of the Goddess movement, I was initially stopped by the lack of models for such discourse. How was I to decide which of the many opinions and ideas floating within the movement (and even in my own mind) was 'right'? My solution was to propose and model 'embodied thinking' as an alternative to 'objective thought'. I argued that 'objective thought' is not possible (on any subject) and that the pretence to it hides the passions and positions of the thinker. Embodied thinking is rooted in the body and experiences of a particular individual, but it avoids being narrowly individualistic through empathy with the positions of others and by opening itself to dialogue in community. In writing *Rebirth of the Goddess*, I examined my own experience and entered into dialogue with others. I engaged my ideas with philosophical reflection and historical research. Though my positions were passionately held, I never claimed that they were the only possible ones. I hoped this method would inspire others, provoking them to reflect on their experiences and to write other thealogies.

HISTORY

'In the beginning . . . God was a woman. Do you remember?' So wrote Merlin Stone in her influential book *When God Was a Woman*.[10] The work of Stone, Gimbutas, and others has led to a great proliferation of research challenging the common assumption that 'in the beginning, God created the heavens and the earth'.

A new myth of beginnings has emerged in the Goddess movement. It goes something like this. In the beginning, humankind worshipped the Goddess as the animating force within nature. Human beings understood themselves as part of the web of life and lived in harmony with each other and all beings. As children of the Goddess, both women and men were valued. At some point (here the story has several variations), this initial harmony was disrupted by patriarchy, violence, and war. Modern culture with its emphasis on the domination of women and nature, hierarchy, greed, consumption, warfare, and destruction of the ecosystem, is a result of this disruption. By remembering the Goddess, human beings can learn again to live in greater harmony with each other and all beings in the universe. No single text or tradition is the source of this new myth. It has emerged through a combination of intuition and historical research.

Many of those who write about Goddess history are self-taught. Opportunities to study the history of the Goddess in academic contexts are limited. The academic field of religious studies encodes biblical prejudices and finds a place for Goddess studies (if any) in 'area studies', which focus on non-Western religions. There, too, androcentric biases structure study. In the fields of classics and archaeology, feminists interested in Goddesses meet analogous prejudices. In addition, the materialist methodology dominant in archaeology is hostile to religion. Those with academic training who write about the Goddess from a feminist perspective often find their work dismissed as marginal, trivial, or wrong, and this discourages others from taking up the subject. Proponents of Goddess history share an enthusiasm for their subject and a sense of outrage at the androcentric biases that have paraded as 'fact' in religious and scholarly texts. Unfortunately, all too many of those who write about Goddess history rely uncritically upon secondary sources. The insights and errors of Robert Graves, for example, are repeated but not questioned or evaluated.[11]

In this context, the work of Lithuanian-born archaeologist Marija Gimbutas has become a storm centre of academic and scholarly controversy.[12] In her works, Gimbutas proposed that the civilisation of 'Old Europe' (*c.* 6500–3500 BCE, and as late as 1450 BCE in Minoan Crete) was distinctly different from the 'Indo-European' civilisation introduced by the carriers of the Indo-European languages (which were spread throughout Europe and all the way to India and China). Gimbutas argued that Old European civilisation was peaceful, sedentary, agricultural, artistic, matrifocal, egalitarian, and worshipped the Goddess. In contrast, the Indo-European civilisation was warlike, mobile, domesticated horses, patrilineal and patriarchal, and worshipped the sky God above all. Gimbutas studied Indo-European cultures for some forty years, and her work on that topic is widely respected by Indo-Europeanists. Her work on Old Europe came later in her career and coincided with the birth of the 'Goddess movement'. It involved painstaking cataloguing of symbolic elements found on thousands of artefacts, combined with analysis of meaning derived from clues found in later written sources and in folk practice. Gimbutas' reconstruction of the religion and culture of Old Europe is regularly dismissed by classicists and archaeologists as 'romantic fantasy'. This is not surprising given that classicists generally have little knowledge of pre-history, while current methods in archaeology preclude the discussion of religion. In my opinion, the work of Marija Gimbutas has yet to be fully engaged by the scholarly community.

In *Rebirth*, I discussed the evidence for what I call 'the Goddess hypothesis'. I reviewed the attempts to suppress the history of widespread worship of the Goddess by authors of the Bible and by Greek authors such as Hesiod. I showed how contemporary androcentric scholarship, such as that of historian of religion Mircea Eliade, relies upon androcentric texts and traditions, and thus is internally structured to uphold a patriarchal myth of origins. I argued that scholars are wedded to the idea that the Greeks were the 'first rational men', to the notion that all 'civilisations' are hierarchical, warlike, and male-dominant, and to the myth that the worship of 'gods' or 'God' promotes and reflects rationality, while the worship of 'goddesses' or 'Goddess' reflects or promotes barbarism, irrationality, orgies, and bloody sacrifice. In addition, most scholars believe in the 'myth of progress' and are horrified by the idea that cultures of the past might be in any way 'better' than our own. Until and unless androcentric thinkers become critical of their own unnamed passions and assumptions, it is unlikely that they will accept *any* evidence as proving widespread worship of the Goddess or as proving that early societies were more peaceful and egalitarian than our own.

DIVINITY

In the popular imagination, God is often thought to be an old white man sitting on a throne in the sky. Rejecting anthropomorphism, traditional theologies define God as transcendent. These views concur in imagining God as somewhere 'out there', separate and apart from the world. Theologians often adopt the view of Plato, expressed in *The Symposium*, that divine power exists totally apart from the changing world.[13] Feminist theologians have criticised 'dualistic thinking' which values the unchanging above the changing, spirit above matter and body, heaven above earth, the rational above the non-rational, light above dark, male above female. Dualistic thinking relegates the female and the body to an inferior realm. It encourages racism in its depiction of rationality as 'light' in the 'darkness' of the material world. Feminist theologians of all stripes argue that dualistic thinking must be replaced with more holistic models.

In contrast to the traditional God, the Goddess is seen as a power inherent in the earth, in nature, and in humanity. The earth is the body of the Goddess. The Goddess as Giver, Taker, and Renewer of life is reflected in the cycles of birth, death, and renewal or regeneration. The Goddess is intimately involved with changing life. Unlike the transcendent God, the embodied Goddess is not alleged to be omniscient (all-knowing) nor omnipotent (all-powerful), in any conventional understanding of these terms.

If asked to become more specific about the meaning of the Goddess, some participants in the movement might refuse, saying that it is enough to experience the power of the Goddess in meditation and ritual. Most would probably agree that the Goddess is not 'out there', in heaven or some place outside of this earth. Some would say that 'we are Goddess'; others that 'Goddess is nature'; still others that 'Goddess' is a kind of 'person' who cares about the world and 'listens' to our prayers.

A large number of Jungian-inspired books on the 'feminine divine' tell us that the symbol of the Goddess asks us to value matter and the body, the darkness, the intuitive, unconscious, the chaotic, the unstructured, the unformed.[14] This is an important corrective to traditional Christian theology, and indeed to Western philosophical traditions in general. For this reason, these books have been inspiring to many women. On a theoretical level, however, the Jungian framework leaves the classical dualisms intact, ascribing the qualities of rationality, light, spirit, and consciousness to the masculine and male divinities. Women or men who want to activate these qualities within themselves are referred to masculine symbols. As a woman who values her mind as well as her body and who has *never once* thought of her mind as 'masculine,' I concur with Naomi Goldenberg's critique of the Jungian theoretical system.

Starhawk, author of *The Spiral Dance* (1979, 1989, 1999) and one of the most important leaders of the Goddess movement, defines the three principles of 'earth-based spirituality' as 'immanence', 'interconnectedness', and 'community'.[15] 'Immanence' is intended to distinguish Goddess religion from the 'transcendent' God and the longing to 'transcend' the earth that characterises traditional Christian and some forms of traditional Jewish spirituality. For Starhawk and for many others, the appeal of the symbol of the Goddess is that it tells us that this earth is our true home and that it locates the divine presence within the earth-body and our own bodies.

While I agree with Starhawk that Goddess religion is 'earth-based', in *Rebirth*, I argued that the philosophical meaning of the word 'immanence' does not do full justice to the meaning of the Goddess. The word 'immanent' was devised as the other half of the polarity 'transcendent–immanent'. It is generally understood to mean that the divinity *is* nature, denying that nature is a unified living organism (as is alleged in the 'Gaia hypothesis') or 'person' who also interacts with individuals in the world and can be addressed in prayer and ritual.

Another question often debated within the Goddess movement is whether the Goddess is to be understood through a monotheistic or a poly-theistic model. 'The Goddess' is invoked under a great plurality of names. Is she one or many? Some argue that only a polytheistic model can do justice to the infinite diversity of the world, which calls for an infinite diversity of names for the Goddess. Others would agree with Marcia Falk that an inclusive monotheism is required to account for the intuition that within diversity there is a unity of being.[16]

In *Rebirth*, I concluded that the Goddess cannot be understood from within the framework of the traditional dualisms. The traditional dua-lisms structure the polarities transcendent–immanent and monotheistic–polytheistic. These terms were created to justify a particular vision of a ra-tional transcendent theistic or monotheistic (masculine or male) divinity whose realm is shining and light. We cannot construct an image of the God-dess on this model. Nor is the Goddess simply the opposite of the God of tradition – immanent, non-rational or unconscious, dark, and plural. Rather, the Goddess incorporates aspects of both ends of the polarities: she is ratio-nal and other than rational; transcendent and immanent; light and dark; one and many.

I believe that process philosophy as formulated in the works of Charles Hartshorne provides a way out of the impasse created by traditional dualistic thinking.[17] In this system of thought, theism and pantheism, as well as immanence and transcendence, are transformed in pan-en-theism. On the one hand, in what is called its 'consequent' or 'immanent' aspect, the deity is understood to be fully embodied in the world: the world is the body of the divinity. On the other hand, in what is called its 'absolute' or 'transcendent' aspect, the divine power is 'more' than the sum of its parts: the divine power is a 'person' who creates of its (world) body a unified living organism and who interacts with perfect love and understanding with each and every individual who makes up its body. Indications that Hartshorne supported feminism without making it a central feature of his thought are scattered throughout his works, and, at the age of ninety-nine, he apologised in print for using masculine language in his writing about 'God' and 'man'.[18]

In *Rebirth*, I defined Goddess as the power of intelligent, embodied love that is the ground of all being, human and non-human. The world is her body. All beings are connected in the web of life. The power of Goddess is a limited power: she must work in conjunction with humans and other beings to achieve her purposes. When we love concretely, intelligently, in our bodies, and in concern for the whole web of life, we are listening to the persuasion offered to us by the Goddess.

NATURE

In traditional theologies, God stands at the top of a hierarchical system, ruling over man and nature. Man, in the image of God, rules over nature. Man is created to serve God, and nature is created to serve man. While some medieval theologies imagined all beings as connected in what was called 'the great chain of being', modern theologies have generally followed modern science in assuming that 'nature' is 'inanimate' matter. Towards the end of the twentieth century, scientists began to question their own assumptions and a growing number of them began to argue that some or all animals have forms of 'consciousness'. Contemporary ecological theologians have charged that traditional religious views contribute to the environmental crisis.

In Goddess thealogy, neither humanity nor divinity is radically distinguished from nature. The earth is the body of Goddess and all beings are understood to be interconnected in 'the web of life'. All life forms are animate. All participate in the cycles of birth, death, renewal, and regeneration. All life forms are different from one another as well as related. Diversity and difference are the great principles of nature. Humanity is different from, but not higher or better than, other beings within nature. Thus it is common in the Goddess movement to refer to the Goddess with non-anthropomorphic imagery: as rain, wind, mountain, cave, light, dark, lion, hawk, bee, sea, sun, moon, pine tree, hyacinth, seed, grain, river, sea. Ecology is an important concern in the Goddess movement.

In traditional Christian theologies, a life which ends in death is not accepted as natural, but is considered to be 'the wages of sin'. Salvation promises transcendence of this earth and eternal life. Goddess thealogy, on the other hand, views death as part of the cycle of life, to be accepted, not denied or feared. This earth is our true home. Death is the appropriate ending to our lives. Every individual death is followed by rebirth and regeneration. Some find it comforting to think of their bodies decaying in the earth, becoming food for the renewal of other life forms. Others, influenced by non-Western traditions, imagine some form of reincarnation. In *Rebirth*, I proposed a conditional life after death as long as one is remembered by the living. When we are no longer needed or remembered, our spirits simply fade away. These views are in flux, as most who propose them will admit that humans really do not and cannot know exactly what will come after life.

What is called 'natural evil' in traditional theologies, namely earthquakes, floods, drought, and so on, is accepted and understood as an aspect of the earth's processes of renewal and regeneration by Goddess thealogy. Though the earth's processes of renewal and regeneration can create human suffering, thealogy takes a wider view, arguing that it would be selfish to call something evil simply because it does not suit us. On the other hand, human-created 'natural' disasters, such as famine and starvation resulting from war or environmental degradation, are not accepted.

In *Rebirth*, I argued that life within nature includes what I called 'irretrievable loss'. There is a plurality of wills and purposes within the web of life. It is a fact of life on earth that life feeds on life. We cannot live without killing other beings to eat. Not every creature that is born will flourish before it dies. Traditional theologies and New Age philosophies often assert that every loss is part of a 'higher plan' or leads to some 'greater good'. Against such views, I argued that, under the conditions of finitude, some losses really are irretrievable and we should not pretend otherwise.

HUMANITY

In traditional Christian theologies, humanity is understood as 'fallen', trapped in a web of sin caused by the 'original sin' of Adam and Eve. In some theologies and in many artistic depictions, 'sin' is disproportionately blamed on Eve. Following the conventions of dualistic thinking, many theologians have claimed that sin stems from the inability of the mind to control the body. And, since women represent the 'body' in relation to men, it follows (according to this way of thinking) that 'man' was tempted by 'woman': therefore, 'woman' introduced sin and death into the world. The doctrine of 'original sin' developed in conjunction with the doctrine of (exclusive) 'salvation through Christ'. All have sinned, so all must be saved. The notions of original sin and fallen humanity are not part of Jewish belief. This does not mean that Jewish thinkers have not interpreted the story of Eve to women's disadvantage; only that they have done it differently than Christians. Judaism does not imagine humanity as 'fallen'; however, it does assert that without the 'fence' around human impulses (including the sexual impulse) created by the 'law', humanity would revert to a shameful state. These religious views have influenced secular culture as well, in what has been called the virgin–whore dichotomy in which women's sexuality continues to be viewed as disruptive and threatening.

The greatest appeal of the image of the Goddess is that it counters all of this. The *naked female body* of the Goddess is *sacred*. She is the Source of Life, the power of birth, death, and renewal. In Goddess thealogy, the female body, female sexuality, and the female power to give birth and nurture life are considered as sacred, reflecting the creative powers of the Goddess as giver of life. Women participants in the Goddess movement affirm that the symbol of the Goddess has changed the way they feel about their bodies and themselves. Critics counter that the image of the Goddess once again relegates women to the realm of the body and nature. They argue that connection of women with the body and nature is the source of the problem in the first place. They propose that severing the symbolic and verbal connections between women and nature is a preferable strategy. Sensitive to such criticisms, adherents of the Goddess movement reply that it is impossible to separate women from their bodies – because embodiment is part of finite life. We cannot ignore, and therefore we must reclaim, the female body. But isn't this 'essentialism'? critics respond. And what about men? Does this leave them out of the sacred picture? The answer to these questions is 'no'. The symbol of the Goddess resacralises not only the female body, but all bodies – including the male body and the bodies of all beings within the world body.

Furthermore, the symbol of the Goddess does not limit women to the realm of the body and nature. This misperception is a legacy of dualistic, androcentric thinking. The Goddess is not a symbol of female sexuality or fertility in a limited sense. The powers of the female body are understood as a metaphor for all the creative powers in the universe. The powers of the body and nature are not separate from the powers of the mind and spirit. Rather, the powers of the mind and spirit arise from within the body and nature. Powers of mind and spirit, including the ability to think and feel, are found in other animals as well as in human beings. These powers are neither male nor female and are found in both men and women. Humans may be the only animals with the power to reflect on the meaning of life, but this ability does not enable human beings to transcend finitude or the body. The human task is not to conquer nature nor to transcend it, but to use all of our capacities including intuition and rationality to create a home for ourselves within the web of life.

As part of the web of life, human beings are thoroughly relational. We are created and sustained by our relationships with others and by communities. The self as an independent agent is a fiction. We learn to love because we are loved. We learn cruelty when we are treated cruelly. Conflict is an inherent and expected part of finite life. Avoidable 'evil' is the created through the failure of relationships to nurture life and love. Evil is not a metaphysical principle, but the product of human failure. Such failures are not only individual, but historical, social, and communal. 'Evil' has a human cause and a human solution. We must change ourselves, our cultures, our social relationships.

ETHICS

Some have viewed the Goddess movement as being primarily about women regaining self-esteem, caricaturing it as self-indulgent, narcissistic, apolitical. In my opinion, the ethical component of Goddess spirituality is one of its chief appeals. In Goddess religion ethics is not based in fear, external obligation, or duty. Ethical behaviour arises from a deep feeling of connection to all beings in the web of life. Patterns of hierarchical domination, unrestrained greed, warfare, sexism, racism, heterosexism, and ecological destruction occur when we forget that humans are part of the web of life. Goddess ethics is about repairing the web of life. Goddess religion offers the hope that human beings can learn again to live in greater harmony with each other and all beings in the web of life.

Because it is rooted in the ambiguity of finite life on this earth, Goddess religion cannot provide us with a new Ten Commandments delivered from 'on high' or even with universal ethical principles. In *Rebirth*, I proposed what I called nine 'touchstones' of the ethics of Goddess religion. They are:

nurture life;
walk in love and beauty;
trust the knowledge that comes through the body;
speak the truth about conflict, pain, and suffering;
take only what you need;
think about the consequences of your actions for seven generations;
approach the taking of life with great restraint;
practice great generosity;
repair the web.

To nurture life is to manifest the power of the Goddess as the nurturer of life. It is to honour, respect, and support mothers and children, to recognise all people and all beings as connected in the web of life, and to embody the intelligent love that is the ground of all being. There are many ways to nurture life: caring for children; tending a garden; healing the sick; creating a hospice for the dying; helping women to gain self-esteem; speaking the truth about violence; replanting forests; working to end war. How different the world would be if we made the nurturing of life the criterion of all that we do. An ethic based in the nurturing of life has a great deal in common with the 'ethic of care' described by psychologist Carol Gilligan as a female mode of ethical thinking.[19] I believe that if men were more involved with the nurturing of life in all its aspects we would recognise the ethic of care as a human mode of moral behaviour.

To walk in love and beauty is to appreciate the infinite diversity of all beings in the natural world including ourselves and other human beings and to sense that everything wants to be loved. When we walk in love and beauty, we open our hearts to the world, to all our relations. We are stunned by beauty and our hearts fill up and spill over with love.

To trust the knowledge that comes through the body means to take seriously that our bodies are ourselves and that sensation and feeling are the guardians of life. It is to experience the joy and pain that come to us through the body, to allow what Audre Lorde called 'the power of the erotic' to lead us to question the denial of pleasure and satisfaction that is inherent in the ethos of domination,[20] and to ground ourselves in the earth and to acknowledge our interdependence in the web of life. Trusting body experience also means never to give ourselves over to any authority – no wise man, no guru, no spiritual teacher, no spiritual tradition, no politician, no wise woman, no one. The ethos of domination has encouraged people to trust external authorities. This has led to great suffering and harm. Not trusting authorities does not mean that we cannot learn from others. Learning from those who have gone before us is part of interdependent life. But nothing should be accepted unquestioningly. Everything must be tested in our own experience.

To speak the truth about conflict, pain, and suffering means not to idealise life, not to deny the realities of our personal and social lives. For many, childhood and other traumas were intensified because conflict was denied, and they were not allowed to feel pain. Denial is also a social phenomenon. Americans can continue to assert that they live in the 'greatest society on earth' only if they deny the violence and ecological destruction that is occurring all around them. Many in Hitler's Germany denied the existence of the gas chambers. Denial is only possible when we sever our minds from our bodies. When we trust the knowledge that comes through our bodies, we feel our own joy and suffering and the suffering and joy of others and the earth body.

Taking only what you need and thinking about the consequences of your actions for seven generations are touchstones that come from the Native Americans. The first acknowledges that conflict – taking the lives of other beings – is inherent in human life, and thus encourages restraint. The second affirms interconnection and asks us to consider not only our own needs, but also the needs of all our relations for seven generations as we take and give back to the circle of life. Seven generations is a very long time. It is about as backward and forward as the human imagination can stretch. We are not asked to hold ourselves to impossible models of perfection, but to consider the consequences of our actions on a scale we can comprehend.

Approaching the taking of life with great restraint is implicit in taking only what we need. I have made it a separate touchstone because those who live in industrialised countries take so much more than we really need without thinking of the lives that are lost, and because as individuals, communities, and societies we so readily resort to violence and warfare to resolve personal, ethnic, and national conflicts.

The 'spirit of great generosity' advocated by Dhyani Ywahoo is an important guide as we work to transform our cultures and societies.[21] Generosity begins with ourselves. If we are to gain the power to act, we must acknowledge that no one of us can take on all the burdens of the world. As we recognise our strengths and forgive our limitations, we can begin to approach others with a generous spirit. Though great harm has been done, very few people or groups have nothing to commend them. When we polarise situations, we make it difficult for our 'adversaries' to change, not to mention that we begin to perceive ourselves unrealistically as 'all good'.

The last touchstone, repair the web, reminds us that we are living in a world where the bonds of relationship and community are broken by violence. Stemming from the Jewish commandment to 'repair the world', this touchstone calls us to transform our personal relationships, our social and cultural institutions, and our relation to the natural world. In our time, those who nurture life must work to establish greater harmony, justice, and peace for all beings on earth. These nine touchstones define the ethos of Goddess religion, providing a framework for ethical decision-making but not a blueprint for action. There are still hard decisions to be made by individuals, communities, and societies. The touchstones of Goddess religion can be embodied in different lifestyles and ethical choices. Our choices are therefore not between absolutes of good and evil, but between relative degrees of healing and harming other people and the web of life. Because we are finite and interdependent, ours will always be an ethics of ambiguity.

Goddess thealogy and ethics inspire us to hope that we can create a different world.

Notes

1. Matilda Joslyn Gage, *Woman, Church, and State* (Watertown, MA: Persephone, 1980, first published in 1893); Elizabeth Cady Stanton, *The Woman's Bible* (Boston, MA: Northeastern University Press, 1993; first published in 1895).
2. Mary Daly, *Beyond God the Father: Toward a Philosophy of Women's Liberation* (Boston, MA: Beacon Press, 1974)
3. Zsuzsanna Budapest, *The Holy Book of Women's Mysteries* (Oakland, CA: Wingbow Press, 1989); originally published as Helen Beardwoman (ed.), *The Feminist Book of Lights and Shadows* (Los Angeles, CA: Susan B. Anthony Coven #1, 1975); Marija Gimbutas, *The Gods and Goddesses of Old Europe 6500–3500 BC: Myths and Cult Images* (London: Thames and Hudson, 1982).
4. Daly, *Beyond God the Father*, p. 19.
5. Ntozake Shange, *for colored girls who have considered suicide when the rainbow is enuf* (New York: Macmillian, 1976), p. 63.
6. Daphne Hampson, *After Christianity* (London: SCM Press, 1996).
7. Rita M. Gross, *Buddhism after Patriarchy* (New York: State University of New York Press, 1992).
8. Grace M. Jantzen, *Becoming Divine: Towards a Feminist Philosophy of Religion* (Bloomington, IN: University of Indiana Press, 1999), p. 275.
9. Carol P. Christ in *Rebirth of the Goddess* (London: Routledge, 1998); Melissa Raphael in *Introducing Thealogy* (Sheffield Academic Press, 1999).
10. Merlin Stone, *When God Was a Woman* (London: Harcourt Brace Jovanovich, 1976), p. 1.
11. See Robert Graves, *The White Goddess: A Historical Grammar of Poetic Myth*, revised edition (New York: Farrar, Straus and Giroux, 1996).
12. See especially Marija Gimbutas, *The Language of the Goddess* (London: Thames and Hudson, 1989) and *The Civilization of the Goddess* (San Francisco, CA: HarperSanFrancisco, 1991).
13. See especially the views attributed to Socrates by Diotima in Plato, *The Symposium*, trans. Walter Hamilton (Baltimore, MD: Penguin, 1951), pp. 93–5.
14. See Naomi Goldenberg, *The Changing of the Gods: Feminism and the End of Traditional Religions* (Boston, MA: Beacon Press, 1979).
15. Starhawk, *The Spiral Dance*, twentieth anniversary edition with a new introduction (San Francisco, CA: HarperSanFrancisco, 1999).
16. Marcia Falk, *The Book of Blessings: New Jewish Prayers for Daily Life, the Sabbath, and the New Moon Festival* (San Francisco, CA: HarperSanFrancisco, 1996.
17. See Charles Hartshorne, *Omnipotence and Other Theological Mistakes* (Albany, NY: State University of New York Press, 1984).
18. Charles Hartshorne in Mohammed Valady (ed.), *The Zero Fallacy and other Essays in Neoclassical Philosophy* (Chicago: Open Court Press, 1997), p. x.
19. Carol Gilligan, *In a Different Voice: Psychological Theory and Women's Development* (Cambridge, MA: Harvard University Press, 1982). See also Sara Ruddick, *Maternal Thinking: Towards a Politics of Peace* (London: The Women's Press, 1989).
20. Audre Lorde, *Sister Outsider: Essays and Speeches* (Trumansburg, NY: The Crossing Press, 1984).

21. Dhyani Ywahoo, 'Renewing the Sacred Hoop', in C. Christ and J. Plaskow (eds.), *Weaving the Visions: New Patterns in Feminist Spirituality* (San Francisco, CA: Harper and Row, 1989).

Selected reading

Adler, M. *Drawing Down the Moon: Witches, Druids, Goddess-Worshippers, and Other Pagans in America Today*, Boston, MA: Beacon Press, 1986.

Christ, C. P. *She Who Changes: Re-Imagining the Divine in the World*, New York: Palgrave/St. Martin's Press, forthcoming.

  Rebirth of the Goddess: Finding Meaning in Feminist Spirituality, New York and London: Routledge, 1998.

  Laughter of Aphrodite: Reflections on a Journey to the Goddess, San Francisco, CA: HarperSanFrancisco, 1987.

Christ, C. P. and Plaskow, J. (eds.). *Womanspirit Rising: A Feminist Reader in Religion*, San Francisco, CA: Harper & Row, 1989.

  Weaving the Visions: New Patterns in Feminist Spirituality, San Francisco, CA: Harper & Row, 1989.

Downing, C. *The Goddess: Mythological Images of the Feminine*, New York: Crossroad, 1991.

Gimbutas, M. *The Language of the Goddess*, San Francisco, CA: HarperSanFrancisco, 1989.

  The Civilization of the Goddess, San Francisco, CA: HarperSanFrancisco, 1991.

Goldenberg, N. *The Changing of the Gods: Feminism and the End of Traditional Religions*, Boston, MA: Beacon Press, 1979.

Hampson, D. *After Christianity*, London: SCM Press, 1996.

Jantzen, G. M. *Becoming Divine: Towards a Feminist Philosophy of Religion*, Bloomington, IN: University of Indiana Press, 1999.

Long, A. *In a Chariot Drawn by Lions: the Search for a Female Deity*, London: The Women's Press, 1992.

Raphael, M. *Introducing Thealogy: Discourse on the Goddess*, Sheffield Academic Press, 1999.

Starhawk (Simos, M.) *Dreaming the Dark: Magic, Sex, and Politics*, Boston, MA: Beacon Press, 1982.

  The Spiral Dance: a Rebirth of the Ancient Religion of the Great Goddess, San Francisco, CA: HarperSanFrancisco, 1979, 1989, 1999.

6 Feminist theology as biblical hermeneutics
BRIDGET GILFILLAN UPTON

'In what sense feminist theology is a biblical hermeneutics will be the central focus of the piece.' The Editor's notes for contributors to this volume of essays provided this *coup de grâce* of a final sentence. To get the words 'feminist', 'theology', 'biblical', and 'hermeneutics' into one sentence raises a breath-taking number of problems of definition and appropriation for writer and reader alike. And when even apparently the most straightforward of these terms, that of 'biblical', opens as many questions as it closes, where can we possibly insert the can-opener to liberate what has become, for many women, a particularly poisonous can of worms?[1] Even if we decide that canonical norms will be satisfactory for our purposes, are we dealing with the text(s) familiar to most Protestant readers, those with Old (or Former, or First) Testament texts based on the Hebrew canon taken over by Martin Luther and the other reformers? Or shall we base our analysis on the longer canon favoured by the Roman Catholic tradition, which incorporates the writings called apocryphal, or deutero-canonical by those who would not grant them a place in the authoritative list? And does it matter? Do these technical issues affect the ways that feminists can read, challenge, appropriate, hate, or be nourished by the texts that our institutions have sanctioned in some way? Or alternatively, do we move on, refusing even a minimalist level of authority for these patriarchally countenanced materials, and opt for a deliberate lack of answers, in an approach which affirms Alicia Ostriker's call for a hermeneutics of indeterminacy, insisting on the multilayered, contradictory indeterminacy of meaning in texts, and prefers to offer a range of readings of particular texts rather than the development of some kind of theoretical meta-narrative.[2]

However, before I embark on short readings of one or two famous texts, both from what we call the New Testament, because that is my area of expertise, it will be appropriate for me to offer a brief survey of developments in feminist biblical studies, a tag which is in itself more monolithic than the material can possibly support.

DEVELOPMENTS IN FEMINIST BIBLICAL STUDIES

It is easy to believe that something called 'feminist biblical exegesis' is new, different, a product of the political feminist developments of the 1970s, but, inevitably, it has much earlier roots. We could look back to the publication in 1895–8 of *The Woman's Bible* by Elizabeth Cady Stanton, who, as a nineteenth-century theorist of suffragist thought, believed, and argued, that the chief cause of women's oppression was 'the perversion of her spiritual nature', her enslavement to a misogynist religion, and, there-fore, that the Bible and its interpreters, as representatives and promulgators of a patriarchal religion, needed to be investigated in order to elaborate ac-curately what the Bible says about the subjugation of women. So, Elisabeth Schüssler Fiorenza can write:

> Cady Stanton's project starts with the realization that throughout the centuries the Bible has been invoked both as a weapon against and as a defense for subjugated wo/men in their struggle for access to citizenship, public speaking, theological education, or ordained ministry.[3]

So, as Schüssler Fiorenza points out, *The Woman's Bible* and its interpre-tive traditions remain positioned within the space defined by patriarchal argument and women's apologetic response to it.

This point of departure for feminist exegesis, which has become quite popular in recent years, and especially since the centenary of the publication of *The Woman's Bible* in 1995, has the benefit of convenience, and inclusion within an academic milieu, but it is worth pointing out that much had been achieved earlier. Marla J. Selvidge's work, *Notorious Voices*, serves as a salutary, and fascinating, reminder that no arbitrary, singular date will serve as a springboard for all the work done in biblical interpretation which could be seen as serving interests similar to those of the twentieth-century critical stance known as 'feminism'.[4]

It is also notable that the development of feminist biblical interpre-tation has been neither linear nor exclusively from the various Christian traditions. Indeed, Jewish writers have generated much of the material that has arisen over the last decades.[5] Because both traditions hold some or all of their scriptures in common, it follows that there has been a preponderance of energy devoted to the material conventionally referred to by Christians as 'The Old Testament'. Even this choice of title, though, raises a number of questions: the sense of 'old' being replaced by 'new' has led some writers to refer to this material as the 'First Testament' or the 'Former Testament'.

Such a designation can also be found derogatory to those for whom the same material represents a totality of scripture, so various attempts to find common ground in titles such as the 'Hebrew Bible' have been made. Even these are problematic, however, as for many early Christian authors the scriptural language was Greek rather than Hebrew, and canonicity itself is a debatable issue. Whatever outcome may eventually be found to be satisfactory, this elementary debate highlights one of the ongoing hermeneutical dilemmas of reading texts which 'belong' in some sense to more than one tradition, and time and energy must be spent in careful conversations across religious and cultural boundaries in attempts to work sensitively with such issues. This dominance has not just been a matter of mass of material; many would consider the feminist readings that have emerged from these writings to have been more radical in some senses than those which consider New Testament texts.[6] Such a perception bears some reflection; it may well be the case that some Christian writers find the Old Testament material less threatening to dearly held belief structures than some of the writings peculiar to their own tradition; on the other hand, it might just be the case that there is more narrative material available in the Hebrew Bible, and it is that which has proved attractive to scholars. It is also evident that a great deal of energy has been expended on the narratives of Genesis 1–3, the creation myths in both traditions, and reading and rereading these stories has proved fruitful in many ways.[7]

Is there anything, then, that can legitimately be called 'feminist exegesis'?[8] Before I go any further, I think that it is worth discussing briefly whether there really is a category that could be recognisable as feminist biblical criticism. Nearly, though not quite all, feminist biblical studies take as their point of departure a critique of patriarchy, which has itself been defined as 'a graded hierarchy of subordination', and assume that every stage of biblical interpretation in the West has been characterised by patriarchal power structures and patriarchal texts, from translation to reading to preaching and praxis within conventional structures. From this it follows that women's voices have often been silenced, not just individually, but in areas such as education as well as formal ecclesiastical structures. As interpreters of patriarchal texts, then, we are working with material which has been awarded a high status of canonical authority, material which represents one side of a conversation, taking little notice of the voices of the poor, the illiterate, the disenfranchised. Orthodoxy is, in a sense, about power, and critically to investigate such orthodoxy is to be subversive to these power structures.

Various critics have attempted their own categorisations of approaches to feminist criticisms; Mary Ann Tolbert notes that definitions of feminism are almost as various as feminist writers, and that a normative canon of feminist tradition is neither available nor desirable; further, she argues that creedal formulations leading to orthodox–heterodox dualisms are precisely the kind of oppressive structures that feminism should reject.[9] She does, however, suggest two general approaches to feminism:

i. That which regards the goal of feminism to be the ascendancy of women; this approach is usually associated with a 'more radical evaluation of the pervasiveness of androcentric structures';

ii. That which understands feminism to be primarily a movement towards human equality in which oppressed and oppressor might finally be reconciled in renewed humanity. Concern is expressed for the condition of both women and men, as oppression is seen to destroy both parties. There is a danger that too great a present desire for reconciliation might risk becoming a feminist apologetic that actually supports the status quo, but the danger of the ascendancy position which consists in a reversal of power within the existing structures rather than abolition of the structure itself should not be overlooked. If oppression is systemic, it is argued, only a radical change of structure will suffice. There are thus different emphases on the spectrum from reconciliation to critical struggle.[10]

Tolbert defines feminist hermeneutics as 'a reading of the text in the light of oppressive structures of patriarchal society' and argues that such a reading can be primarily negative or primarily positive.[11] Some aim at exposing androcentric bias or oppressive intention, leading to an understanding of the texts as unalterably patriarchal and therefore without authority or value. Others highlight the social, religious, and political power of women which has been ignored, overlooked, or hidden by patriarchal hermeneutics, though neither the approaches taken nor the conclusions reached are monolithic.[12] Here, feminist biblical hermeneutics self-consciously grounds its analyses in the experience of women's oppression, and moves on to a variety of readings and responses, generally within a reformist position which does not seek to render the texts in question impotent or meaningless to the modern or postmodern reader. Even within such a reformist position, however, Tolbert sees three relatively distinct responses to the Bible:[13]

i. An argument, typified in the work of Rosemary Radford Reuther, for the discovery of a 'prophetic liberating tradition' of biblical faith from Exodus to Jesus, which becomes the norm by which other biblical texts are judged. This results in the definition of 'central tradition of the

Bible'; a canon within a canon, using a fairly large portion of scripture, with a goal of reconciliation among the various groups who regard the texts as authoritative. The spectrum that could be described as Christianity/Judaism is thus seen as a prophetic call for the liberation of the oppressed.

ii. Scholars whose work could be described as conforming to a remnant standpoint, select or retrieve texts which they believe to be overlooked or distorted by patriarchal hermeneutics, and attempt to uncover counter-cultural impulses within the text. Perhaps the classical work in which this model was developed and demonstrated can be found in Phyllis Trible's *Texts of Terror*.[14] The texts selected can, of course have positive as well as negative implications for their feminist readers, and the remnant of the canon isolated in this way can be used as encouragement as well as goad.

iii. A standpoint, which eschews the present canon, and makes canonical decisions on criteria different from those used in the social and political milieu of early Christianity. Such readings lead to reconstructions of biblical history in various attempts to show that the actual situations of Israelite and Christian religions allowed a greater role for women than the codified texts suggest. Practitioners look for hints about women in the canonical texts, and search non-canonical heterodox second- and third-century texts for further, hidden clues to the function of women in early Christian communities. So canonical writings are themselves seen as products of androcentric hermeneutics, and a wider group of writings is used to underpin an endeavour to hear the silenced voices of women in the earliest Christian churches.[15]

Tolbert expresses her concern that, even given the insights of all these approaches, the question still remains: if one is convinced of the patriarchal nature of the Bible, and yet not persuaded that reconstructions of history can replace the canon, is it still possible to stay within the Christian tradition, or I might add, the canon, or the academic discipline?[16] This question, I believe, remains with us today and will be answered differently by different practitioners.

Perhaps one of the interpretive bases held in common by most approaches is that which Elisabeth Schüssler Fiorenza, among others, has called a hermeneutic of suspicion – a suspicion of a patriarchal system of thinking in which women are often excluded from the symbolic, public, and social forms of communication, and by which femaleness has been devalued and frequently reduced to the role of victim.[17] In practice, this view acknowledges that literary historical artifacts are usually or often the provinces of an educated male elite, who both produce the material pertaining to a particular culture, and are responsible for the collection, transmission, and often the ensuing reception of the material. This is obviously of paramount importance in biblical studies, which is essentially a literary discipline. Further, this hermeneutic of suspicion underpins a variety of different interpretive positions and approaches to the text in question. Perhaps it is worth mentioning, in passing, that, on the principle that the oppressed tend to collude with their oppressors, women, no less than men are com/implicit in patriarchal thought worlds.

Even if these brief comments offer some preliminary framework, nothing has yet been said about method. Janice Capel Anderson, for example, points out:

> There is no single model. Our choice of method – historical, literary or social-scientific – influences our work. So do our religious ties. My account will concentrate on Christian feminist criticism, which focuses on the Christian tradition or sees itself as belonging to that tradition.[18]

She thus raises personal, as well as political issues concerned with the nature of interpretation, not all of which would be shared by other commentators. Feminist analyses have been produced using all the methods current in biblical criticism: historical critical method, literary methods, social, sociological, and anthropological methods, and various combinations of the above. Some of these methods are under as much suspicion from some feminist critics as are the texts themselves. For example, Monika Fander, in *Searching the Scriptures*, contributes a chapter on historical critical method in a section entitled 'Transforming the Master's House: Building a "Room of our Own"', which reflects both Virginia Woolf's title and Audre Lorde's assertion, central to the self-definition of the whole work, that 'the master's tools will not destroy the master's house'.[19]

Fander points out that historical critical method, the bread and butter of twentieth-century exegesis, has been criticised as 'unfeeling, cerebral, irreligious, even godless; of being too philological in its interests and less theological'.[20] The results have not always been as objective as they have been claimed to be, and they can sometimes be suspected as serving masculine interests, though it should be noted that even historical criticism is hardly monolithic, and has offered insights of many kinds, some of which are very positive towards women. In the famous, and often conservative area of text criticism, for example, Romans 16[7] presents an obvious example. Bernadette Brooten suggested that the Junias, outstanding among the apostles, could, and should, be read as the feminine form, Junia.[21] This suggestion has become commonplace in more recent years, although some would still argue for an almost unknown form leading to the masculine name. Surely, even the possibility of a woman called apostle in a Pauline community brings to the fore the debate about the role of an apostle so dear to Paul in much of his correspondence.

Historical critical method is not the only approach to literary texts, of course. Feminist criticism has followed the routes of all modern criticism, and critics have made good use of the range of methods available, from text criticism to reader response methodology, from sociological readings to postmodernist strategies. Studies in English literature have shown how often patriarchal cultures have subsumed the female under a male norm – to be human is male: to be female is to be derivative. Many feminist critics are deeply privileged as well; many would count themselves as such, routinely coming from white, middle-class academic backgrounds in Europe or North America. A range of responses to such privilege has led to a variety of womanist readings, concentrating on the experiences of black women and women of colour, often from North America. Others have developed readings informed by different cultural and religious experiences – from Asia, Latin America, or Africa.[22] So the hypothesis of the 'feminist reader' is hardly monolithic, and we would do well to remember the multiple variables of gender, race, culture, class, and sexual orientation, all of which affect the reading of a text.

Perhaps the dominant group of methods used by feminist critics in the late twentieth century clustered round narrative models of various types. Although this choice was partly a reaction to the perceived ascendancy of the historical critical methods which many found counter-productive, it was also a deliberate selection of a set of methods which respected the vast majority of biblical genres. These methods allow the critic to concentrate both on a close reading of the text itself, and reflect an understanding that the text is at the centre of a communication event, from the so-called implied author to the implied reader or audience.[23] Such readings have illuminated a number of texts in fruitful ways, allowing a concentration on narrative elements such as tempo, plot, and characterisation, this last particularly important when trying to draw attention to female characters in the text. Thus, studies have been made of the women in Mark's Gospel, for example, or the hidden women in Judges, focussing, not just on depictions favourable to women, but on those which show the abusive nature of some texts in their

treatment of the women who appear there. So, narrative criticism is not ide-
ologically neutral, but allows the reader to uncover the patriarchal nature
of the texts we have in the Bible, and pose questions of quite extraordinarily uncomfortable sharpness. Not all is so straightforward, though. Adele
Reinhartz recently wrote:[24]

> I approached this task with the intention of providing a reasoned
> analysis, cataloguing achievements and challenges, and outlining a
> vision of the shape of the field in the twenty-first century. These
> intentions came to naught, however, when I discovered, to my horror,
> that my capacity for reasoned analysis had been damaged by my
> lifestyle. I refer specifically to my near immersion in narrative. From
> Judges and Judith and campus intrigue during the day, A. A. Milne,
> E. B. White and complicated schoolyard anecdotes in the evening, to
> Toni Morrison, Tony Hillerman and/or the evening news at night, my
> days and my thoughts are bounded by stories . . . But what story, or
> stories could I read into, or read out of, the relationship between
> feminist criticism and biblical studies?

Reinhartz proceeds, by an intelligent and entertaining rereading of some
key texts, to show that reading from 'an "investment perspective" does
not . . . render us incapable of hearing the voice of the text, of imagining the
way in which that text might have been heard by its earliest audience, or of
considering its impact on a contemporary reader who is unlike oneself'.[25]
Her immersion in narrative is thus, I think, vindicated by her results. Our
future as readers of these famous and difficult texts requires of us just such
acts of imagination and subversion.

BY WAY OF EXAMPLE, A COUPLE OF READINGS...

I now want to move on to consider two well-known New Testament
texts, the first of which has often been held to be of positive value in feminist readings of the Bible, while the second has usually been experienced
as detrimental to the point of despair for women within the Christian traditions. They thus represent something of the spectrum available to the
interpreter of the Bible.

Mark 14$^{1-10}$(NRSV)

14:1 It was two days before the Passover and the festival of
Unleavened Bread. The chief priests and the scribes were looking for a
way to arrest Jesus by stealth and kill him; 2 for they said, 'Not during
the festival, or there may be a riot among the people.' 3 While he was

at Bethany in the house of Simon the leper, as he sat at the table, a woman came with an alabaster jar of very costly ointment of nard, and she broke open the jar and poured the ointment on his head. 4 But some were there who said to one another in anger, 'Why was the ointment wasted in this way? 5 For this ointment could have been sold for more than three hundred denarii, and the money given to the poor.' And they scolded her. 6 But Jesus said, 'Let her alone; why do you trouble her? She has performed a good service for me. 7 For you always have the poor with you, and you can show kindness to them whenever you wish; but you will not always have me. 8 She has done what she could; she has anointed my body beforehand for its burial. 9 Truly I tell you, wherever the good news is proclaimed in the whole world, what she has done will be told in remembrance of her.' 10 Then Judas Iscariot, who was one of the twelve, went to the chief priests in order to betray him to them.

I have chosen to concentrate on the Markan narrative, and to present it without the parallel texts from the other gospels, though something like this story is common to all four. Indeed, there is a minimum storyline in each of the canonical gospels: a woman anoints Jesus, onlookers raise objections of some kind, and Jesus shows his approval of the woman's action. The contexts, though, are different, as are their places in the various narratives. Many who hear this story hear, behind a particular rendition, echoes of all the other available versions. So we need to remind ourselves that 'Mark', the author of the Gospel, was a consummate storyteller, not the best writer in the Greek language, perhaps, but far more than merely a vehicle for the redactional activity of the other evangelists. And it is, at least partly, as a tribute to Mark that I want to draw attention to his narrative.[26] The other obvious tribute I wish to pay is to Elisabeth Schüssler Fiorenza, whose seminal work, *In Memory of Her*, takes its name from this passage and was the instigator for so much in feminist biblical studies.[27]

Mark 14$^{3-9}$, with its contextualising framework of verses 1–2 and 10, can be read in many ways, and feminists have come to a variety of conclusions about the text. Here Mark uses his famous 'intercalation', or sandwiching technique, not once, but twice. In the immediate context, the heart of the story is sandwiched between references to the plot to put Jesus to death, first by drawing the reader's or hearers' attention to the plot by the authorities to find and arrest Jesus, and then, at the end of the piece, by referring to the activities of Judas Iscariot, known to be the villain since the naming of the twelve in 3^{19}. Thus a context of scheming and danger forms brackets around the story of a woman who understands something about Jesus, and will be remembered for it, even if her name is not. Further, this narrative of anointing, in which this woman pours oil over the head of the living Jesus, forms an extended bracket, an inclusion with the thwarted anointing activity by the women who approach the tomb and find it empty in 16$^{1-2}$. The whole intrigue of the passion narrative, then, is contained between the actions of women who would anoint Jesus, and the immediate emphasis is on this woman, the one who anoints Jesus 'beforehand for burial'.

At a superficial level, this passage can perhaps be read as deeply embarrassing; a woman, escaping from the conventions of patriarchal society, gatecrashes a formal, masculine dinner party in a social gaffe of considerable proportions, drawing agonising attention both to herself and to Jesus. Such a reading would reinforce the view that women, including the woman readers of the Gospel, are unreliable in the public arena, best left to the relative security of the home and family. On the other hand, though, Schüssler Fiorenza used this text to argue for her view that the women disciples who have followed Jesus from Galilee emerge in the Passion narrative as true disciples, and that this woman, in particular, features as a faithful, if unnamed disciple, in contrast to Judas and Peter, who, for different reasons were both unfaithful, if named.[28] It is worth asking, though, if Mark does show women as ideal disciples. Certainly the men have not done too well; they have misunderstood the nature of Mark's Jesus during his ministry. Now Judas will betray Jesus, Peter will deny him, they will sleep when told to watch and pray, and all, including the unnamed young man in the garden, will flee, leaving Jesus alone – not exactly a model of discipleship, it could be argued, and certainly this woman, also unnamed as are most of Mark's women, performs better than they do. But even the named women who appear later in the Gospel, three times, do not seem to understand that in this narrative, Jesus has already been recognised and anointed. And when they reach the tomb, and find his body unexpectedly absent, they are confused and bewildered, go completely to pieces and tell 'nothing to anyone, for they were afraid'. They, no more than their male colleagues, carry out their discipleship role, described in Mark usually in terms of following and serving. As Elizabeth Struthers Malbon would claim, they, like the men are 'fallible followers' rather than ideal disciples, and provide a role model for the community to emulate.[29] Perhaps, then, Schüssler Fiorenza is a little utopian in her efforts to find an egalitarian community within the earliest strand of tradition, an inclusive community of equality between the sexes, which the evidence cannot sustain. We must, I think, be very careful when we attempt to reconstruct some sort of social reality from the limited and selective texts we have at our disposal.

Other critics tend to resist this optimistic view of the place of women in a gospel which, as Joanna Dewey argues, is, like other Christian writings, an androcentric text, one which assumes that men are normative human beings and that women are derivative or inferior. Mark, she argues, is a text about men, for men and in all probability by a man, and women are mentioned only when they are exceptional or in some way required by the plot. Yet here, positively, we have an extraordinary story about a woman, undertaking not the socially inferior task of anointing a man's feet, which would normally be the job of a slave, but of pouring ointment on his head, the symbolic action of an old Testament prophet anointing a priest or king. So this can be read as a highly significant story of a woman accepting and fulfilling this role, empowering Jesus for his own role as Messiah, the anointed one.[30] A woman in a male-dominated world, anointing Jesus through her sign action, is surely a politically dangerous act within a context of betrayal and intrigue, a story where even a kiss will be used as a sign of duplicity and evil. This woman, Mark's woman, of whom Jesus says, 'Truly I tell you, wherever the good news is proclaimed in the whole world, what she has done will be told in remembrance of her', offers the reader a glimpse of the possible. Women in an androcentric world, where men still own most of the resources of land, power, politics, and the church, can engage with a Jesus and with a woman like this, and respond by acting positively in their own right, empowered by this nameless exemplar of long ago.

This type of reading has become quite common in recent years, as feminists have learned strategies to read these texts in ways which can be experienced as liberating, even from within an acknowledgedly androcentric world. Not everyone, of course, reads this material so positively. Walter Schmithals, who regards the narrative as a Markan redaction of an earlier tradition, is clearly discomforted by such a shift in focus. 'One may', he writes, 'well expect such tastelessness from the evangelist's historicising habit, namely at the climax of the narrative to draw the attention away from Jesus to the woman who had come only for the purpose of serving him.'[31] It seems strange that the same is not said about stories, also chosen by Mark, in which the male disciples take the limelight. More importantly, it betrays a reading that does not declare its own perspective, one in which the focus can only be on the woman at the expense of Jesus. Here, surely, the spotlight falls on both. As Luise Schottroff writes, 'it is a product of androcentrism, claiming to be Christology, to separate the (last) verse 9 from the narrative in the name of literary criticism'.[32]

Even this brief treatment of an extraordinarily rich narrative has been sufficient to give some flavour of a range of readings, most of them self-consciously feminist. It is relatively easy for women, starved of positive role models, to experience this text as nourishing, a paradigm of prophetic action which has few rivals in a world which more readily remembers the symbolic action of Judas.

A second type of text is more problematic. How do we develop strategies to read texts that are not just unattractive but downright damaging to women readers and hearers? I want to go on briefly to consider a famously and frankly uncongenial text, 1 Timothy 2^{8-15}, with its very difficult injunction that '[a woman] will be saved through child-bearing, provided she continues in faith and love and holiness, with modesty'. There seems little room here for discovering nourishing or liberating sentiments. Perhaps the best option is to learn to resist these texts, reading 'against the grain' of texts written and interpreted by men with the professed aim of oppressing women.[33] The immediate context of this injunction concerns behaviour in public within the worshipping community:

1 Timothy 2^{8-15} (NRSV)

2:8 I desire, then, that in every place the men should pray, lifting up holy hands without anger or argument; 9 also that the women should dress themselves modestly and decently in suitable clothing, not with their hair braided, or with gold, pearls, or expensive clothes, 10 but with good works, as is proper for women who profess reverence for God. 11 Let a woman learn in silence with full submission. 12 I permit no woman to teach or to have authority over a man; she is to keep silent. 13 For Adam was formed first, then Eve; 14 and Adam was not deceived, but the woman was deceived and became a transgressor. 15 Yet she will be saved through childbearing, provided they continue in faith and love and holiness, with modesty.

A positive and self-conscious attempt to read this text is made by Linda Maloney in her contribution to *Searching the Scriptures*:

The Pastoral letters – 1 Timothy, 2 Timothy and Titus – are simultaneously the most revealing part of the Christian testament, from the point of view of feminist criticism, and the most frustrating. They are the most revealing because nowhere else do we find such concentrated attention devoted to women's roles in early Christian communities: here, almost alone among Christian testament writings, women actually take center stage from time to time. At the same time, these letters are both frustrating and depressing to the Christian woman who reads them: their tone (especially as regards women and their roles) is negative to the point of ferocity, and it is this negative and oppressive quality that has dominated interpretation and authoritative application of these texts in the succeeding two millennia.[34]

Maloney believes that there is 'no point in making another attempt to put the best face on [these letters] as if their intent were benevolent and only we as readers were at fault with our perceptions', and so she proceeds to read them by an act of historical imagination, not as if they represent the final word from a patriarchal authority figure, as they have often been received, but as if they come from someone frightened and defensive, threatened by those he perceives to be opponents, whose half of the correspondence is no longer extant. Perhaps this silent half of the correspondence, she conjectures, consists of women who are exercising authority, women who 'preach, teach, prophesy, travel, preside at worship and preserve certain "Pauline" traditions that are anathema to the author'.[35] This act of imagination gains results which are not so different from the utopian reconstructions I argued against earlier, and there is certainly room for caution. Lone Fatum usefully points out the pitfalls of many feminist reconstructions when she draws attention to the problems of acknowledging our texts as unrelievedly patriarchal and then proceeding to reconstruct underneath them a perfect, though sadly lost, universe.[36]

As we have seen, the material in 1 Timothy that poses most difficulty to women is clustered in chapter 2, quoted above. Women are to dress modestly and decently, be silent (an injunction which is repeated) and not be permitted to teach, a positive counsel of perfection in an androcentric world, and one which has been used throughout the history of interpretation to keep women out of positions of power. These comments on ideal conduct, set over against the requirements of the men who may, indeed must, pray, though without anger or argument, are reinforced by a reference to a rare Jewish tradition, one which does not appear in the mainstream work we call the Old Testament. Here, in a text which has been seen as particularly misogynist, it is argued that Eve alone was responsible for the fall of humanity, and it is radically different from Paul's position that Adam brought sin into the world, though Eve was deceived.[37] In this text, though, women can be saved only through childbirth, a statement which becomes no less shocking with rereading, and one which seems to put women outside the redemptive work of Christ.[38] Furthermore, even when they have had children, they can be saved only as a result of impeccably submissive behaviour. How dangerous the author must have thought women were to deserve such treatment. The woman invading the dinner party of Mark 14^{3-9} seems positively toothless by comparison.

In this situation then, there is much to be said for reading against the grain of the biblical text, and learning strategies that neither deny the presence of texts that are violently hostile to women, nor collude with the sentencing of women to generations of destructive behaviour, authenticated by institutional authority.

In both these readings I have attempted to show, in dialogue with some contemporary critics, that there are ways of reading even difficult texts that provide women with a gleam of hope. Deeper, more painful questions remain. Some scholars have suggested that it is quite impossible for a woman even to read a patriarchal text.[39] Such arguments cannot be ignored, and there is clearly still much to do, methodologically and exegetically.

To what extent feminist theology is a biblical hermeneutic remains, as I believe it always will, debatable. To the extent that women continue to be nourished by, struggle with, love and loathe the texts of the canon, feminist theology will not, and should not, cut free from the imperative to read and interpret these texts. Often the struggle will lead readers to what Elaine Wainwright aptly calls the shattering of 'the dominant narrative encoded not only within the text but also within themselves as a result of the malestream traditioning process over centuries'.[40] Others will choose to move on, and it is for them to decide the parameters of their vision of feminist theology.

Notes

1. Elisabeth Schüssler Fiorenza, perhaps the best known of feminist biblical schol-ars, argues that '[B]ecause women's biblical studies have focussed for too long on the canonical authority of the Bible, a feminist political interpretation for trans-formation must become canonically transgressive . . . Just as the canon must be transgressed, so also must the term "Bible/biblical" be problematised.' Elisabeth Schüssler Fiorenza and Shelly Matthews (eds.), *Searching the Scriptures*, vol. I *A Feminist Introduction* (London: SCM, 1994), p. 9. Such an approach led to the inclusion of a wide variety of writings in a so-called Christian Testament, by no means all of which would be found between the covers of the canonical New Testament.
2. Alicia Suskin Ostriker, *Feminist Revision and the Bible* (Oxford: Blackwell, 1993) p. 86, quoted by Schüssler Fiorenza, *Searching the Scriptures*, I, p. 8. The idea of a meta-narrative is undoubtedly seductive, but, as so often, seduction is best resisted in favour of a range of individual readings, with all their angular quirkiness and resistance to systemisation.

3. Schüssler Fiorenza, *Searching the Scriptures*, I, p. 3.

4. Marla Selvidge, *Notorious Voices: Feminist Biblical Interpretation 1500–1920* (New York: Continuum Press, 1996) contains material on and by a range of women and men who read the Bible in terms of an affirmation, and sometimes critique, of the value of women. Included are famous and less well-known names such as George Fox, Lucretia Coffin Mott, Mary Hays, and Charlotte Perkins Gilman, as well as Elizabeth Cady Stanton and Matilda Joslyn Gage.

5. The literature is enormous, and, rightly, autonomous, but developing relationships between Christian and Jewish scholars in reading texts which are common to their traditions, but fulfilling different functions within them, have been fruitful in many ways. See, for example, various articles in the *Journal of Feminist Studies in Religion*, the founding editors of which were Elisabeth Schüssler Fiorenza and Judith Plaskow, author of *Standing again at Sinai: Judaism from a Feminist Perspective* (San Francisco, CA: Harper & Row, 1990).

6. The essays collected under the editorship of Athalya Brenner in the Feminist Companion Series (Sheffield: JSOT Press) bear ample witness to the breadth and depth of scholarship available on the 'Hebrew Bible'.

7. Examples can be found ad lib. For example, various essays in Brenner (ed.), *A Feminist Companion to Genesis* (Sheffield: JSOT Press, 1993). Interestingly, Mieke Bal, writing from a deliberately non-confessional perspective, chose these narratives for inclusion in her *Lethal Love: Feminist Literary Readings of Biblical Love Stories* (Bloomington, IN: Indiana University Press, 1987).

8. A brief history of feminist interpretation can be found in R. J. Coggins and J. L. Houlden (eds.), *Dictionary of Biblical Interpretation* (London: SCM Press, 1990), pp. 231–4. This article, by Deborah Middleton, covers a range of thinking in European and North American settings.

9. Mary Ann Tolbert, 'Defining the Problem: the Bible and Feminist Hermeneutics', *Semeia* 28 (1983), 113–26.

10. Ibid., 116–17.

11. Ibid., 119.

12. Most of the contributions to *Semeia* 28 fall into this category of reading.

13. This taxonomy is one among many, and is included as a fairly typical example.

14. Phyllis Trible, *Texts of Terror: Literary-Feminist readings of Biblical Narratives* (London: SCM Press, 1992.)

15. Tolbert, 'Defining the Problem', 121–4.

16. Ibid., 124. For a negative answer to this question see Daphne Hampson, 'On not Remembering Her', *Feminist Theology* 19 (1998), 63–83.

17. This hermeneutic of suspicion forms part of a hermeneutical model which Elisabeth Schüssler Fiorenza has developed to provide a framework for the interpretation of biblical texts. The other components include hermeneutics of remembrance, proclamation, and creative actualisation. For further discussion see Elisabeth Schüssler Fiorenza, *Bread not Stone: The Challenge of Feminist Biblical Interpretation* (Boston, MA: Beacon Press, 1984).

18. Janice Capel Anderson and Stephen D. Moore (eds.), *Mark and Method: New Approaches in Biblical Studies* (Minneapolis, MN: Fortress Press, 1992), pp. 105–6.

19. Monika Fander, 'Historical Critical Methods', in Schüssler Fiorenza and Matthews (eds.), *Searching the Scriptures*, I, pp. 205–24.

20. Ibid., p. 206.
21. Bernadette Brooten, 'Junia – Outstanding among the Apostles (Romans 16:7)', in Leonard and Arlene Swidler (eds.), *Women Priests: a Catholic Commentary on the Vatican Declaration* (New York: Paulist Press, 1977), pp. 141–4.
22. See, for example, Cain Hope Felder (ed.), *Stony the Road we Trod: African American Biblical Interpretation* (Minneapolis, MN: Fortress Press, 1991); Hisako Kinukawa, *Women and Jesus in Mark: A Japanese Feminist Perspective* (Maryknoll, NY: Orbis Press, 1994); R. S. Sugirtharajah (ed.), *Voices from the Margins: Interpreting the Bible in the Third World* (Maryknoll, NY: Orbis Press, 1991).
23. Many readings have been based on the work of Seymour Chatman, whose *Story and Discourse: Narrative Structure in Fiction and Film* (Ithaca, NY: Cornell University Press, 1978) provided an interpretive model that proved attractive to many biblical scholars.
24. Adele Reinhartz, 'Feminist Criticism and Biblical Studies on the Verge of the Twenty-First Century', in Athalya Brenner and Carole Fontaine (eds.), *A Feminist Companion to Reading the Bible: Approaches, Methods and Strategies* (Sheffield Academic Press, 1997), pp. 30–9.
25. Ibid., p. 34.
26. It has occasionally been suggested that the Gospel of Mark was written by a woman, but, given the patriarchal nature of many of the assumptions behind the work, I feel that it is, at best, an extremely optimistic hypothesis.
27. Elisabeth Schüssler Fiorenza, *In Memory of Her: a Feminist Theological Reconstruction of Christian Origins* (New York: Crossroad, 1983).
28. Ibid., p. xiv.
29. Elizabeth Struthers Malbon, 'Fallible Followers: Women and Men in the Gospel of Mark', *Semeia* 28 (1983), 29–48.
30. Joanna Dewey, 'The Gospel of Mark', in Schüssler Fiorenza (ed.), *Searching the Scriptures*, II, pp. 470, 501–2.
31. Walter Schmithals, *Das Evangelium nach Markus* (Gütersloh 1979, 1985) quoted in Luise Schottroff, *Lydia's Impatient Sisters: A Feminist Social History of early Christianity* (London: SCM Press, 1995), pp. 50–1.
32. Luise Schottroff, *Lydia's Impatient Sisters*, p. 51.
33. See Judith Fetterly, *The Resisting Reader: a Feminist Approach to American Fiction* (Bloomington, IN: Indiana University Press, 1978).
34. Linda Maloney, 'The Pastoral Epistles', in Schüssler Fiorenza (ed.), *Searching the Scriptures*, II, p. 361.
35. Maloney, 'The Pastoral Epistles', p. 362.
36. Lone Fatum, 'Women, Symbolic Universe and Structures of Silence: Challenges and Possibilities in Androcentric Texts', *Studia Theologica* 43 (1989), 61–80.
37. Ben Sira 25:24. For a detailed reading see Warren C. Trenchard, *Ben Sira's View of Women: a Literary Analysis* (Chico, CA: Scholars Press, 1982.).
38. Maloney, 'The Pastoral Epistles', p. 361; ibid., p. 370.
39. See, for example, Susan Durber, 'The Female Reader of the Parables of the Lost', *JSNT* 45 (1992), 59–78.

40. Elaine Wainwright, 'Rachel Weeping for her Children: Intertextuality and the Biblical Testaments – a Feminist Approach', in Brenner and Fontaine (eds.), *A Feminist Companion*, p. 469.

Selected reading

Brenner, Athalya and Fontaine, Carole (eds.). *A Feminist Companion to Reading the Bible: Approaches, Methods and Strategies*, Sheffield Academic Press, 1997.

Exum, Cheryl. *Plotted, Shot and Painted: Cultural Representations of Biblical Women*, Sheffield Academic Press, 1996.

Newsom, Carol A. and Ringe, Sharon H. (eds.). *The Women's Bible Commentary*, London: SPCK, 1992.

Plaskow, Judith. *Standing again at Sinai: Judaism from a Feminist Perspective*, San Francisco, CA: Harper & Row, 1990.

Schneiders, Sandra M. *The Revelatory Text: Interpreting the New Testament as Sacred Scripture*, New York: HarperCollins, 1991.

Schottroff, Luise, Schroer, Silvia, and Wacker, Marie-Theres. *Feminist Interpretation: the Bible in Women's Perspective*, Martin and Barbara Rumscheidt (trans.), Minneapolis, MN: Fortress Press, 1998.

Schüssler Fiorenza, Elisabeth. *In Memory of Her; a Feminist Theological Reconstruction of Christian Origins*, London: SCM Press, 1983 (2nd edn 1997).

Schüssler Fiorenza, Elisabeth (ed.). *Searching the Scriptures*, vol. II, *A Feminist Commentary*, London: SCM Press 1995.

Schüssler Fiorenza, Elisabeth and Matthews, Shelly (eds.). *Searching the Scriptures*, vol. I, *A Feminist Introduction*, London: SCM Press, 1994.

Selvidge, Marla J. *Notorious Voices: Feminist Biblical Interpretation 1500–1920*, New York: Continuum Press, 1995.

Stanton, Elizabeth Cady. *The Woman's Bible*. Boston, MA: Northeastern University Press, 1993. (Originally published in New York: European Publishing Company, 1895–1898.)

Washington, Harold C., Lochrie Graham, Susan, and Thimmes, Pamela. *Escaping Eden: New Feminist Perspectives on the Bible*, Sheffield Academic Press, 1998.

7 Feminist theology as dogmatic theology

SUSAN FRANK PARSONS

The word 'dogmatic' may seem an odd choice for the title of this consideration of feminist theology. It could fairly be argued that feminists have themselves not been particularly favourable towards things dogmatic, sharing with the wider ethos of Western thought a modern suspicion of that which is handed down from some other place than here, and which does not bear thinking about but is only to be taken as read. Not only have feminists participated happily in the shredding of previously reputable dogmas with the use of critical reason, but many of their writings also reveal a hesitancy about being dogmatic in turn, an apology for what might appear to be so, even a self-effacement from making what might be taken as dogmatic claims. Nevertheless there is an important sense in which feminist theology undertaken by Christian women has been and continues to be dogmatic. It is to investigate the senses in which this is so that this chapter is written.

Accordingly, there are two things to be undertaken here. The dogmas of feminist theology manifest the central convictions out of which it springs, and embody the urgency with which its project developed, most recently in the late twentieth century. There is a pattern of belief that emerges here, and, in the consideration of this, we may come to understand something of the hopes and the struggles that informed not only its work, but that of women today who are its progeny. Feminists have written out of a critical faithfulness to the Christian tradition, and their interpretations of its claims both illuminate dimensions of orthodoxy that may be troublesome, and indicate ways of revision that may take feminists out to, and beyond, the edges of its domain. Coming to terms with our inheritance is not always a comfortable thing, for we are apt to discover both how profoundly we are bound to, and yet how considerably we disagree with, those who bequeath an intellectual and spiritual life to us. So we ask here – what are the central dogmatic convictions that inform Christian feminist theology? And we do so in recognition of the way in which feminist theology is integral to the tradition to which we are also variously related, and within which our own faithful inquiries are to be set.

For this is a question through which we may begin to discern the shape and the prominence of the problematic of gender that has come to figure in modern Western theology. We stand today as women and men, often bemused at the confusion that thinking about gender brings our way, often perplexed at how its severest charges might ever be resolved, and often compromised in the search for truth by our concern to be nice to each other. To ask about the impact of gender on matters of faith both is an expression of our modern theological inheritance, and at the same time brings us to a kind of impasse that bears thinking about more deeply. How we may engage in such an inquiry, and whether the tools forged and handed on to us by feminist theologians will be entirely appropriate for it, are things that press upon our sense of judgment about their dogmatic efforts. To ask after feminist theology with generosity, with humility towards those from and with whom we have learned, and with full integrity in the search for truth, is our task.

This examination is, however, to bring us to ourselves in the theological work that we must undertake, perhaps especially as women, in our own lives, and this is the second concern of the chapter. It would be easy to proclaim the age of feminist theology to be past, as a phenomenon that belonged with modernity and thus is no longer at home in postmodernity. If feminist theology is merely one amongst a number of types or styles of modern theology, then its damage can be limited and its insights contained in an appropriately labelled drawer. Yet the erasure of its fundamental challenges to the theological tradition, of its prophetic witness to the presence of God in places of human anguish, and of its readiness to exemplify that of which it speaks, cannot be right. These things are now woven deeply into the fabric of our thinking, so that we would misunderstand the questions that are before us by such a dismissal.

More than this however, we, too, are placed before the reality of women's vocation to be theologians. It happens. And its happening is not always an occasion for rejoicing in the church or the world, and so its happening puts women at risk, with their families and friends, with their academic careers, with their presence in church. Our discernment of this call and our response to its demands upon us draw women anew into the fundamental work of dogmatic theology, now informed by feminism. What I am to make of the faith I am given? How I am to articulate the reformation of my life by hope? In what way is love? These are the questions in which a theologian's life is immersed. And it is there in the midst of such questions, not for its own sake, but in order that God may come to matter. The work of the dogmatic theologian, to speak of that which is believed, has been courageously undertaken by women throughout the ages, in whose vigorous spirit we, too, may begin once more to say how it is that God appears to us who live in the world.

BEGINNING WITH EXPERIENCE

By the time of Rosemary Ruether's systematic theological book, *Sexism and God-Talk*, she was able to take for granted what had already become a recognisable conviction of feminist theology, namely that women's experience is to be 'a basic source of content as well as a criterion of truth'.[1] The claim that theology begins in experience is nothing new or startling, since Ruether understands all theology to be a reflection upon and a return to human experiences of the divine, of oneself, of others, and of the world. It was certainly not uncommon amongst Protestant and Roman Catholic theologians of the twentieth century to assert that to speak of the divine is to speak of the human, and thus that theological anthropology and the doctrine of revelation are entirely interdependent.[2] What is unique and potentially disturbing is the claim of women that it is to be their experiences from which theology springs and to which it must continually return to test its findings. To give attention to women's experience is to ask that women speak up for themselves and enter with full integrity into theological debates, and it is thereby to throw open to question the unchallenged assumption that men's experiences speak for everyone and are thus, by default, normative for all.

For feminist theologians to announce this new beginning is prophetic, since the continued life of the Judæo-Christian tradition is believed to be in peril. It has been, according to Ruether, caught up in a self-delusion that the foundations of theology are transcendent of history, that an 'authority outside contemporary experience' could or should provide the norm for theology, and that the embodied historical experiences of those who shape the tradition are of no significance. To alert theology to the dangers of these assumptions and to provide an alternative starting point is 'the critical principle of feminist theology', which is to say:

> whatever diminishes or denies the full humanity of women must be
> presumed not to reflect the divine or an authentic relation to the
> divine, or to reflect the authentic nature of things, or to be the message
> or work of an authentic redeemer or a community of redemption.[3]

This is a strong proclamation, made on the basis of experiences of suffering, and bearing upon itself the weight of conviction that the image of the fullness of human being has been both revealed and made possible to us. Thus, neither women, nor the church as a whole, are to be released from the obligation to live out this truth in diverse and changing circumstances.

This interpretative principle is used by feminist theologians to demonstrate the many ways that the presence of women in the theological tradition has been hidden from view, that women have been rendered silent, their natures devalued and their experiences underrated. Such phenomena are explained as the result of a deep seam of prejudice that is called sexism, and that is embedded in all kinds of institutions, known as patriarchal for their persistent division of humanity into two parts of unequal status and power. This radical sin of our humanity is lodged in a set of dualisms which it is the work of feminist theologians to expose. Once seen, the structures may be reformed by those who have been despised and rejected, in whose lives the potential for wholeness may be exemplified, and who thereby become a sign of hope for the restoration of justice in the world.

Beginning with experience is not, however, without its philosophical or theological problems, as feminists only too soon discovered. For whom does a woman speak? While there may be some broad agreement amongst women about their experiences of exclusion or misrepresentation, this interpretative principle makes claims about the significance of these in order to shed light upon them. At some point, a feminist theologian must make some general statements about what is true elsewhere than in the narrative of her own life, and thus about what she herself has no way of knowing if all knowing begins with experience.

Generalisations about women have been part of the problem of sexism, and yet they seem also to be necessary in order to uncover the denial and devaluing of women within the tradition, and to point the way to its overcoming. If, on the other hand, a woman speaks only for herself, there follows a fragmentation of humanity into entirely individual centres of experience, each of whom can only tell what it looks like from here. Particularities abound amongst feminist theologians, who may introduce their writings with strings of qualifying adjectives so that one can locate their voices correctly, and not read them as speaking for anyone other than themselves. This tension between the universal and the particular is a feature of the kind of theological anthropology within which feminist dogmatic theology has been formed.

To say more about this briefly is to note two things. First, for feminist theology to begin with experience means to enter into a rigorous process of discernment, in which one's experiences are tested for their authenticity. Experiences are not of equal worth. Because human lives are caught up in deceitfulness and pride, it is essential that one distinguish those experiences that are distorted, from those in which one is able to recognise, and thus become, one's own true self. This distinction between the 'original' and the 'fallen' nature of human being, Ruether takes to be a 'classical distinction' in Christian theology,[4] and feminist theology extends this now to include women on the same terms. There is little of comfort here for our brothers, from whose reflections this pattern of theological discernment has emerged in the tradition, but who have mistakenly and even perversely installed themselves alone into the middle of it.

Which brings us secondly to the question of Christ. Ruether's conviction in this early book is that something is made known about full humanity in the person of Christ, and that something is made possible for the realisation of this full humanity by Christ's work. Already she was aware that this is desperately problematic for feminist theology, as she shows in posing the question: 'Can a male saviour save women?'[5] That the man Jesus in particular can reveal something of what is authentic for all humanity generally only makes sense for Ruether if one assumes that he exceeds himself, that 'as redemptive person', he is 'not to be encapsulated "once-for-all" in the historical Jesus'.[6] Yet this is surely a claim for an 'authority outside contemporary experience'. All the more important, then, for Ruether to focus her investigation of the redemptive work of Christ on his earthly interactions with people, which exemplify a way of breaking the bondage of sin and of recovering the original image of the divine in which each person is made. Christ thereby makes himself known as the form of 'a new humanity, male and female'. It is this form which calls all of us into redeeming encounters with our neighbours, so that the 'yet incompleted dimensions of human liberation' might be accomplished.[7] This concept of the form of humanity, now inclusive of women, appears at a critical juncture in feminist dogmatics, for it is required to become the bearer of redemption, to which our human experiences, for all their diversity and multiplicity, are now to be conformed.

LIBERATING HISTORY

A second central conviction of feminist theology becomes clear at this point. To begin with experience as interpreted through the principle of full authentic humanity, brings us to the discovery of the nature of sin and points us to the kinds of practices that will release humanity from its bondage to sin and set it on a better path of living. We are to turn reflections upon our experiences as women into practical actions that make a difference to other people and to the world. In this liberating work, the Spirit is active in the midst of the world, overthrowing structures of oppression, and empowering the weak to carry on this movement for change. So Dorothee Sölle speaks of that which is believed by feminist theologians in her book, *Thinking About God: An Introduction to Theology.*[8] Feminist theology is to find its place between an orthodox commitment to right belief, or dogma, from which timeless and universal principles are derived, and a liberal emphasis on the conversion of the individual soul taken at one remove from its social embeddedness. For feminists, the test of theological truth is firmly placed within history, and its accompanying moral concern is to effect positive changes in the world.

Sölle, along with many other political and liberation theologians, is disturbed by the ubiquity of a destructive worldly power that expresses itself in all systems of thought, even in theological thought which ought to be helping us to recognise and overcome it. This power is multifaceted, but nevertheless consistently manifest in the varied strategies of defence exercised by those who have hold of it, and by the disappearance or silencing of those who do not. Something is operative here that is greater than ourselves, and that subsumes even our best and most lofty work into its divisive purposes. Theology as thinking about God has, for Sölle, fallen into its trap. Through its claims about a transcendent deity who rules dispassionately from above the world, it has become another victim to the illusion that this is not a further example of human self-aggrandisement at the expense of one's fellows. Sheer, raw power is assumed to be the force that drives history, making winners and losers in every event, constructing sets of insiders and outsiders with every institution, and legitimating only certain speakers in every discourse. To hear the Gospel is to know that this is not the last word about history, and to be turned into one in whose life the overcoming of this power becomes possible.

For feminist theologians, it has been the exercise of worldly power that has made women into 'non-persons', that is, those who are both actual victims of exclusion and of destruction of the self, and theoretical objects placed into inferior positions to serve the needs of a given discourse. One task of feminist theology is to describe the various forms this social construction of women has taken, and to demonstrate in various situations the impact of powerlessness upon their lives. Their range of activities becomes closely defined and limited, their speech trivial, their presence unremarked, and in all of this is to be found the fear of the powerful that women might act, or speak, or re-present themselves without warning. This task must be completed by a second, however, which is to attend to the subjected memories, the insights of the oppressed, the yearning for freedom amongst the powerless, and to find there a new basis from which to challenge the status quo and unseat its reign. Feminist theology moves forward by tapping into this well of oppression as the pool from which movements of liberation are to develop, and thus also as the paradoxical sign of hope in a world that is still enthralled by the powerful.

Typically, one is expected to find among the oppressed a number of different ways of relating to one another that may offer alternative models of relationship and of community to a world in which social relations are defined by power alone. There is a solidarity in suffering, which means that women in the situation of being non-persons recognise and empathise with one another, but there is also a range of practices – of helpfulness, of affirmation, of tenderness, yes, but furthermore of subversion, of courage, of outspoken witness to justice – which is to be revealed there. These existing practices among the outcast, and others that can be developed with encouragement, are to be recovered, for they are the resource for changes through which the Spirit will move in its overcoming the principalities and powers of this world.

There are two dilemmas here for feminist dogmatic theology. The first is that humanity is expected to save itself from the very thing which is believed to be definitive of its humanity. Few doctrines of sin can be more penetrating than that of structural sin, which may let individuals off the hook in terms of their personal responsibilities, but certainly does little to ameliorate the thoroughly decisive ways in which we are entangled in webs of injustice and deceit that power minutely weaves us into. Everything about us is shaped by forms of power, so that we may be defined as ones constructed by its operations. The significance of the feminist hermeneutic of suspicion lies particularly here, as Sölle asks of each theology – who are its subjects, who are its objects, and what are its methods? And yet we are asked to believe that there is some reserve, some untouched place, some act of care, which is outside these structures and in which power therefore cannot gain a hold. Feminist theologians have announced such a finding, and have called upon women to practise what is known there for the good of the world.

What must be sustained throughout is the conviction that we will not find the same power at work here, as elsewhere in the world, and it is this presumption of innocence which both strains empirical credibility and presents theological difficulties concerning the doctrines of sin and salvation. As Angela West has so keenly observed, 'the excavation of our religious repressions' is a necessary element of the myth of emancipation, but, once it has begun, it has no reason, except by an untypical and unjustified exercise of power alone, to halt its deconstructive efforts.[9] Women can only protect the space of this reserve by discipline amongst themselves, and by warning others to keep their hands off. Not only has this sent women on a continuous search for those amongst them who are the most oppressed, so that this resource may be ever kept pure of the defilements of power, armed with a kind of implicit 'hierarchy of victimhood', which may itself be exploitative,[10] but this demand for practice requires the most huge assertion of ourselves as women, of our wisdom and experience, that the very concepts of structural sin and the ubiquity of power deny us any grounds for claiming in pristine form. Women are left in this conundrum, maintaining their practices of healthy and nurturing relationality in order that even God may be redeemed from power,[11] and offering themselves sacrificially to social and ecclesial institutions so that another way may be opened.

A second difficulty is here, for the sights of these practices are set on historical transformations of existing structures which, for all the talk of liberation, may strike us nevertheless as a confinement of the vision of God's Kingdom and a critical limitation placed upon the human vocation to know, to worship, and to enjoy God forever. That the horizon of feminist concern is firmly set at the possibilities of history, means that its liberating efforts become pragmatic ones of doing the best that one can in the circumstances to improve things.[12] The hope that what we do will be 'good enough' is perhaps rightly modest, but does not express what has been Christian hope throughout much of the tradition. To demand that we only think historically is a strange requirement of modernity, that has torn up thoughts of transcendence as projections of human power, and has left us bereft precisely of the vocabulary in which to speak of that which comes to us from beyond ourselves, which brings *to us* the life on which we rely, and which thereby sets us impatiently on a way of radical conversion of the world to God. The noble efforts of feminist theologians to proclaim an emancipation from what has been the inheritance of history, by means of diverse practices of freedom in our everyday lives and interactions, bear the brunt of this account of history, by agreeing to its terms and by seeking to rescue it simultaneously.

HOME-MAKING

Yet feminist theologians have pursued this understanding of liberating practices by building a theological framework which would underpin and

sustain them. Such has been the undertaking of constructive feminist theologians like Sallie McFague, whose book, *Models of God*, has become itself a
model for this kind of project. Agreeing with feminist convictions concerning the form of authentic humanity, moulded by historical manifestations
of power and yet free to effect changes in history, she sets out to reconstruct
our ways of thinking theologically so that these may be more helpful and
less damaging to the good works grounded in women's experience. At the
beginning of this book, she insists that she is offering 'models', metaphors,
or images, which is to her unremarkable, because she believes all theology to be *'mostly* fiction'.[13] Models of God in the Judæo-Christian tradition
merely project particular situated notions of humanity and of creation onto
the empty screen at the edge of the world, and reinforce those notions by
shaping human behaviour and social life accordingly. In the past, the model
of God as a monarch ruling over a world from which he is ultimately detached, has both projected man's own self-understanding, and imposed an
'assymetrical dualism' throughout the social and the natural spheres.

McFague has no hesitation in claiming that this model is wrong, since it
results in 'the wrong kind of divine activity in relation to the world', not least
in that it 'inhibits human growth and responsibility'.[14] Thus we are urged
to dethrone this false idol, which is at the same time to decentre ourselves
as human beings from our place in the universe as God's subjects, and
to recentre ourselves 'as those responsible for both knowing the common
creation story and helping it to flourish'.[15] Human responsibility, correctly
theologically conceived, is both to give the right interpretation of God and to
undergird this with appropriate revaluations of our activities in the world.
Feminist theologians have shown McFague that the rightness of dogma can
be measured according to its respect for our proper place as human beings
in the total scheme of things, for the holistic scope of its vision, and for the
care it takes for the delicacy of the web of nature in which all created life is
bound together. All of these things are the devalued and subjected insights
of women, that have been waiting to be taken up as the hidden treasures
within the tradition. What has been typically associated with women –
materiality, sexuality, bodiliness, belonging to nature – is to be understood
no longer as the measure of their unworthiness, uncleanness, or defective
nature, but is to be revalued as that which today is most indicative of the
new way of being in the universe that can work 'for the well-being of all
creation'.[16]

Such a deliberate effort of feminist theology to make a home for itself
again exposes dogmatic weaknesses. One of these has to do with consistency in the argument itself. The appeal of McFague's presentation is that

it appears to offer a return to the natural sphere, to the values that are believed to inhere within nature itself, and to a way of living that would be more in tune with nature's own ways. This seems a fine thing to call for in an age of technology which is overtaken by machinery, choked with poisonous pollution of earth, water, and air, and regulated by the demands of productivity. All of these things speak to ecological theologians of the human abuse of God's good creation, of an unchecked impulse to control what is strange or to dissect what is beautiful, and of the centralisation of power to the will of man alone. To recall us to the fact that humanity, too, is created, that we, too, belong in and with nature as ourselves natural beings, has been a significant feature of contemporary feminist efforts.

Yet the more one considers this 'nature' that we are being recalled to, the more strange it appears, for it cannot avoid being itself a construction of culture. At one level, there is a nostalgia at work as images appear before us of lost or forgotten beauties, varieties of living species now endangered, alternative forms of harmonious living with nature, so that we are drawn to consider what we might be missing from the present state of things. At another level, McFague herself concedes that it is our models of nature that give us access to this sphere, and thus that what we are being called to is a better interpretation, a feminised understanding, a correctly revalued nature that will be good for us.[17] Nature is thus no longer a real sphere to which we return, but instead has become a virtual reality that we are exhorted to believe in.

This brings us, secondly, to comment on the imperative character of feminist dogmatic theology which is consolidated so clearly in McFague's writing as she gathers together the cluster of concerns that have appeared in feminisms. Her description of the way we are to be 'at home on the earth' expresses a familiar conviction amongst feminists that there is a matrix of relationality which sustains and nurtures our lives. Feminists have claimed that this matrix, while necessary for life itself, has none the less throughout the Western tradition of thought been resisted, both as a source of value in itself and as the normative pattern for our lives. The binary oppositions that have become lodged in the Western cultural symbolic are the cause of this resistance, and their overcoming requires the rising up of the feminine symbolic, so long denied or devalued. In this enactment is to be performed the reclamation of what feminists take to be ultimate value, and for women to be able to know this, to speak of this, and to bring this alive in their activities in the world gives tremendous moral force to their theological efforts.

Nevertheless, there is a suspicion here – which feminists themselves have taught, namely that every claim to ultimacy should carry a health warning – that here is a human will at work for the purpose of saving the world with its knowledge and restoring those who are lost to the true path by means of its advice. How are feminist theologians to occupy this place with integrity, given their own critical exposure of the human will to power? The dethroning of man and his God is no modest undertaking, but must presume access to another truth. Yet, because it is an interpreted truth, it itself requires an effort of will to concentrate on what would be the right perspective on it and to discipline oneself (and others) to stay within its bounds. That theological truth appears for us after modernity to be nothing more than a performance of the will to power it seeks to overcome, means that its primary call upon us can only be heard as moral injunctions – to value our lives correctly and to transform the world through our actions. In the imperative of home-making, we reach an aporia in feminist dogmatic theology that beckons us to closer consideration.

GENDERING THEOLOGY

Following the course of these central convictions of feminist dogmatics – that there is a form of true humanity available to us, that liberation of the oppressed is to occur in history by our efforts, that the conception of nature held within the feminine imaginary is of ultimate value – discloses to us the kind of theological thinking which has emerged throughout the post-Enlightenment period. Feminism in its diverse forms is a child of this period, being born out of the logic of modern humanistic thought and thus intimately interwoven with its hopes and its dilemmas. To be encumbered with modernity has been an ambiguous blessing for feminists, for implicit in their work has been a dependence upon the available categories of thought that are most in need of overturning. Feminists have themselves been aware of this, and their continued reflections upon these places of difficulty in modernity are indicative of a most serious intellectual attention to our common Western inheritance, an attention that is passionate because women live here. Women's experiences have been shaped in the midst of this problematic in ways that arouse righteous indignation about injustices, stubborn attachment to what humanity must not abandon, and fierce optimism that new ways of life are possible. Yet their efforts have not been for themselves alone.

For the feminist commitment to gendering theology has summoned a wider awareness of the existential and rational implications of the deep configuration of gender that lies within the Western tradition. The construction of women and men within its terms is a phenomenon whose impact upon relationships, society, and academic inquiry has been unavoidable. It is thus through their work that we are able to see what might not have been so obvious to us, and through their witness that we are alerted to the question of what is happening to us. Feminist theologians have been asking about what is going on here, and they have done so with the critical tools bequeathed by the Enlightenment. However, their critique intensifies rather than resolves the dilemmas. It is no disdain of feminist theology that now stays with these questions that have been raised, as ones that continue to trouble us, and that claims no better answers, yet seeks to understand, even here, what it is that faith believes.

THE QUESTION OF HUMANITY

One of the issues that lies at the heart of feminist theological concern is how we are to understand our humanity – as persons made in the image of God, and as women and men who are in some way related but different. As this concern has taken shape, two theological affirmations have come clearly into focus. First, the belief that there is an original form of humanity which has become deeply submerged, and indeed is in danger of being entirely lost to us through ignorance and pride, has set the anthropological context for considerations of gender. Ruether's argument is that this original form as God intended it is multifaceted and richly diverse, with multiple possibilities for its particular historical shape, and that it is the sin of dualistic thinking which puts the lid on this freedom, capturing it in the straitjacket of binarisms that are both false and destructive.[18] To be a woman, as to be a man, is to be trapped in identities put upon us by cultural and linguistic convention, which are reinforced by offering privilege to one and subjecting the other. There is then, secondly, an affirmation that, in Christ, a restoration to this true humanity is made possible, in his own exceeding of the bounds of his maleness, and in his example of what we can do in our own lives as women and men to resist the categorisations imposed by gender. In this way lies the redemption of humanity, the work of which falls in a special way upon women.

Yet it seems, after modernity, that the understanding of our humanness which lies within this theological account is both something that has arisen specifically with Enlightenment assumptions, and thus is not an enduring feature of Western thought, and that it both demands and defeats attempts to resolve the question of gender implicit within it. Humanism in its post-Enlightenment form is constructed around the figure of man, who is assumed to be a rational being, freely self-determining, and who is also bound to the responsibilities of natural life. Characteristic of this humanism is the tension between these two poles of human identity. Each individual is delicately poised in the middle, capable, on the one hand, of exercising a kind of god-like transcendence by means of reason, and, on the other, of enjoying an embodied existence in the world. This conception of the uniquely constituted human being has become such a commonplace of modern thought, in theology and the human sciences alike, that to challenge it shakes the foundations of our most basic intellectual commitments.

Because it is along the line of this polarity that the question of gender has appeared in modern thought, it is perhaps not surprising that some of its most devastating attacks have come from gender theorists, like Judith Butler. While feminists have been busy reclaiming the devalued pole and recentering human life around its potential, Butler has been examining the role that gender categories play in providing us with a human identity, in disciplining our behaviour according to their requirements, and in occupying such a prominent place in our political and intellectual life that we are constantly being returned into their frame. Butler shows, in her book *Gender Trouble*, that gender categories operate by positing an original form, or nature, according to which the specific identity of each individual woman or man can be known, measured, and valued. Feminists have wanted both to acknowledge this construction of identity by gender, and at the same time to reclaim or revalue the identity of women. Yet, if gender is an effect of our thought about what is human, rather than its prior determinant, are we not thrown back rather fundamentally onto the question of whether there is an original form of humanity at all?[19] To claim that there is, is to measure each individual according to conformity with an authorised version, and will always be to miss those who fall outside its terms, however broadly these might be conceived. Yet this remains a modern anxiety for the correct definition of human being and for knowing who counts as human, and within it the problem of gender appears and intensifies.

So, too, the notion of a fallen humanity has played a crucial part in the formation of humanist notions of political and moral responsibility, and has thus necessarily accompanied the new freedoms promoted by Enlightenment thought. Butler again is astute here in noticing how feminist debates have reinforced this belief in a distorted or deformed humanity, and have extended its terms to include gender. Gender dualism is viewed as a further obstacle to this highly prized freedom, which women have been the first to notice, while simultaneously it is the necessary lens through which our vision of this freedom is projected. Butler's reflections on the nature of subjection have pointed to the deep ambiguity of this situation, in which we are always compromised by whatever we fight against.[20] The investment of subjects in the means of their subjection is necessary, she argues, both so that they may identify themselves and know who they are, and so that they can conceive of another way of life without this condition. Such dependency highlights the ambivalence within the word 'subject', that offers freedom to those who are prepared to see and do things its way. So feminists cannot avoid collusion in the gender categories that afford them access to what they consider to be authentic human being, an ambiguity that is evident throughout their analysis of responsibility. This is a dilemma already known to Christian dogmatics since St Paul, who asked how freedom from the law could be possible without repetition of its terms.[21] That feminist dogmatic theology brings us before this same question is poignant evidence of the question of humanity that it harbours.

What emerges from this reading of our situation is this. It could be that the question for dogmatic theology is not that of what a human being is, but, rather, of what it is to be human. To turn into the question of our humanity in this way is to find that we enter the theological task at some risk to ourselves and our inheritance, yet unavoidably thinking with faith at the troubled places of contemporary discourse.

THE QUESTION OF GOD

This is also where we may find the question of God after modernity. Feminist dogmatic theology has agreed with the distinctly modern declaration that the realm of human affairs, historically conceived, is the beginning and end-point of our reflection and action. Accordingly, God is only to be found active and approachable here. Feminist theologians have called it the besetting arrogance of theology to posit the existence of some other realm than this one, and then to give man privileged access to the knowledge of it. The deficiencies of woman in knowing the truth and acting upon it have thus been construed as a distance from this higher place. As we have seen in Sölle's work, the feminist diagnosis of injustice requires the collapse of this distinction, so that the inclusive message of the Gospel can be enacted amongst those deemed non-persons. Women, along with all the outcast, are believed to carry in themselves, in their experiences of rejection and marginality, a different kind of knowledge which, as Mary Grey describes it, is *Sophia* rather than *Logos*.[22] This non-divisive wisdom is evidence of the intimacy of the divine with the world, and it is a hidden treasure that dwells particularly with the oppressed. Its depths are to be plumbed for the motivation it generates to change the existing state of affairs, and for the new practices it teaches us that will heal the rifts of history. The special work of women in redeeming history is thus to dive deep within for this alternative resource, and to come up with the practical means of patiently overcoming evil with good.

This conviction, too, bears the signs of strain in post-Enlightenment thought. On the one hand is what appears to be the most confident expression of human capabilities to change the world through decisive action which, with careful deliberation about means and ends, will make a better dwelling for humanity. Some feminists have been more modest in their claims for effectiveness, and have presumed a woman's willingness to work with rather messy situations that have no very clear-cut or definitive outcomes. Yet there is a presumption that what happens here is up to us, and that the active agency of women, so long suppressed, is now to come to the fore with renewed zeal. On the other hand is the context of history, believed to provide the narrative into which human action is threaded, and the plot of this history makes sobering reading. Feminist analysis suggests that, on the whole, history has not been favourable to the oppressed, and thus that humanity has rather persistently acted against the interests of its own, while feminist theologians seek to encourage belief in the power of the divine acting amongst the subjected to introduce another story of rescue and restoration.

This account of things runs aground in postmodernity for two reasons that can be mentioned here. Firstly, the world of human affairs has become entirely caught up in the dealings of late capitalism, which seems to be an entirely successful and globally operating system of economic management. At work in its relentless operation is the notion that every thing can be put to some use and thus made to serve a human purpose, so that now every thing in the world can become a commodity that is assigned a value. The process of commodification is no longer associated with manufactured things, with the world of production out of which much of the political rhetoric that inspired liberation thought was formed. Rather it is the case that this process no longer requires actual 'things' at all, for whatever we choose can be commodified – our time, the wall of a building, the countryside, religious experience, a conversation, a memory – all of these can be given a value, bought and sold. Indeed this game is so far advanced that values themselves are now marketable, so that enterprising businesses are not only searching for the 'style' that will sell things this year, but have also discovered that there is money to be made out of 'alternative' style – the very source of energy out of which protest and subversion was to come.[23] Now the language of empowerment has become a cliché for everything from shoes to electricity, and the nostalgia for lost opportunities to make a better world is exploited as a style, that has no more credit than a change of clothes. Such is evidence, not of a loss of faith in utopian politics, but of the very out-workings of its logic. Getting our hands on things has come to this.

Furthermore, the distinction upon which the theological turn into the world was constructed has so successfully disintegrated that its convictions can no longer be meaningfully articulated in its terms. The hinge on which the case turned for Sölle was the existence of non-persons who could be identified by their exclusion from, and by an elite that worked securely on, the inside. The conviction that there are insiders and outsiders is continually at work in the arguments for inclusion that feminists have used throughout a range of institutions and discourses, sustained by the confidence that the excluded have a secret sheltered in their own interior. Few feminists have drawn out more thoroughly the full extent of this conviction than Luce Irigaray. Her praise of the bodily interiority of women wherein the 'sensible transcendent' is to be found, her descriptions of women's organs, fluids, breathing, and internal spaces as unique sources of a feminine symbolic, are attempts to speak of a genuine Other in a space dominated by the masculine logic of the Same. This 'within' is the meeting place of the divine for women, perhaps nowhere more alluringly presented than in Irigaray's essay, 'La Mystérique'.[24] Yet one hardly dare articulate the suspicion that this might be a parody of women's spirituality, after all that, a witty rhetorical excess, and the doubt about this already speaks volumes to us of the absence of God just when we most seek reassurance of divine presence. Such doubt is itself reflective of the postmodern situation in which we know that the distinction between inside and outside space has already been dissolved, and that every attempt to reinstate it comes signed with its own logo ready for consumption.

We are so profoundly before the question of God today, yet so utterly shaped by the fact that each attempt to gain access to the divine and hand it on to others is already at a loss for words. So the question for dogmatic theology is perhaps less one of how I come to know God, than it is of how God knows me, and to follow the path of this question is to be led into the divine economy by another way.

THE QUESTION OF REDEMPTION

Running through our consideration of feminist dogmatic theology has been the question of redemption. The search for and proclamation of the means of redemption has characterised the songs and preaching, political action, and intellectual efforts of Christian women, now so meticulously documented in Ruether's recent book *Women and Redemption*.[25] The key dogmatic convictions in terms of which redemption is conceived by feminist theologians have been explored in this chapter, culminating as they do in the work of revisioning that is to be undertaken on behalf of an anguished world. McFague's description of the alternative models in which God, humanity, and the world are to be reconceived draws together many of the threads of feminist orthodoxy, and presses upon us the urgent need of a world waiting for this help. One feature of the postmodern world that renders this understanding of redemption inadequate is that its efforts are already co-opted by the market economy. We can purchase 'the natural' at the corner shop, tested for cruelty to animals and legitimated as a non-exploitative product, so that this fine holistic vision appears now only as a repetition, and not a redemption, of the very Disneyfied world out of which it comes.

Yet it is not the vision alone that is problematic, and to offer another would be a mistake. Rather we must stay with this dilemma until the nub of the issue becomes clear. The emphasis in feminist dogmatic theology has been predominately on method, on the critique of the methods of traditional male theology, and on the development of an alternative method for speaking about God and the work of redemption. It was Mary Daly who warned feminists of the dangers of 'methodolatry', by which she meant the workings of a rigid system of male-stream thought in which the questions of women were not legitimate and their experiences insignificant.[26] For women to claim a method of their own seemed the obvious thing to do, and therefore much feminist attention has been given to determining the methodology that is appropriate for women's experience, the sources upon which it can most helpfully draw, and the norms by which its framework is to be constructed and its work carried out. Yet to approach things in this way is to assume that theology is a project by which something is to be worked out and then accomplished in the world. It is to assume theology to be fundamentally a technique. It is thus not the vision that results from this method which is to be assessed favourably or not. Rather we need to ask a deeper question about whether theology as a method can only ever arrive at some vision or other, some reproduction of what redemption could or should be.

To ask about this is to wonder what has happened in theology to the matter of truth. For Daly's warning might have been prescient in another sense, namely that the concentration upon methods of approaching, knowing, and utilising truth, whether patriarchal or feminist, may miss the point entirely of what is a theologian's responsibility. For is it not the theologian's burden to be the place wherein truth comes to dwell, and thus to be always vulnerable to the havoc caused by its arrival, and yet to be always and astonishingly made ready to bear it? And thus is not the theologian's attention to be given, not so much to discernment of the correct mode of access to this mystery, which will only reveal more of who she is and what her concerns are, as to the reception of what comes to be known in faith? The distance from truth which is presumed to be successfully traversed by method means that already the truth of redemption is one that I must bring to myself, that I may cause to happen in my life by using the correct means. Yet the truth of redemption is one that comes to me. It comes to matter in the fabric of my life, so that I can never avoid the question of how it is that my life is informed by its truth and how it is that my dealings with others are to be redemptive for them. This is to understand that redemption cannot be something fabricated for the sake of the world, but is the possibility for human beings, women and men, to be themselves the birthplace of the divine. To attend to this phenomenon is to recall feminist theology to its most demanding dogmatic task – to articulate the coming of God in the world today.

Notes

1. Rosemary Radford Ruether, *Sexism and God-Talk: Towards a Feminist Theology* (London: SCM Press, 1983), p. 12.
2. See Anne Carr, *Transforming Grace: Christian Tradition and Women's Experience* (San Francisco, CA: Harper & Row, 1988), ch. 6.
3. Ruether, *Sexism*, pp. 18–19.
4. Ibid., p. 19.
5. Ibid., p. 116.
6. Ibid., p. 138.
7. Ibid.
8. Dorothee Sölle, *Thinking About God: An Introduction to Theology* (London: SCM Press, 1990). Originally published as *Gott denken* (Stuttgart: Kreuz, 1990).
9. Angela West, *Deadly Innocence: Feminism and the Mythology of Sin* (London: Cassell, 1995), pp. 162–3.
10. Ibid., p. 169. See also Susan Brooks Thistlethwaite, *Sex, Race and God: Christian Feminism in Black and White* (London: Geoffrey Chapman, 1990).
11. Isabel Carter Heyward, *The Redemption of God: A Theology of Mutual Relation* (Lanham, MD: University Press of America, 1982).
12. See e.g. Elaine Graham, *Transforming Practice: Pastoral Theology in an Age of Uncertainty* (London: Mowbrays, 1996).
13. Sallie McFague, *Models of God: Theology for an Ecological, Nuclear Age* (Philadelphia, PA: Fortress Press, 1987), p. xi (her emphasis).
14. Ibid., p. 68.
15. Sallie McFague, *Body of God: An Ecological Theology* (London, SCM Press, 1993), p. 108.

16. Ibid., p. 212.
17. See especially her *Super, Natural Christians* (London: SCM Press, 1997).
18. See especially her 'Dualism and the Nature of Evil in Feminist Theology', *Studies in Christian Ethics* 5:1 (1992).
19. Judith Butler, *Gender Trouble: Feminism and the Subversion of Identity* (London: Routledge, 1990), ch. 1.
20. Judith Butler, *The Psychic Life of Power: Theories in Subjection* (Stanford University Press, 1997).
21. Romans 7.
22. Mary Grey, *The Wisdom of Fools? Seeking Revelation for Today* (London: SPCK, 1993).
23. See e.g. Naomi Klein, *No Logo* (London: Flamingo, 2001).
24. Luce Irigaray, 'La Mystérique', *Speculum of the Other Woman*, Gillian C. Gill (trans.) (Ithaca, NY: Cornell University Press, 1985). Originally published in French as *Speculum de l'autre femme* (Les Editions de Minuit, 1974).
25. Rosemary Radford Ruether, *Women and Redemption: A Theological History* (London: SCM Press, 1998).
26. Mary Daly, *Beyond God the Father: Toward a Philosophy of Women's Liberation* (Boston, MA: Beacon Press, 1973), pp. 11–12.

Selected reading

Butler, Judith. *Gender Trouble: Feminism and the Subversion of Identity*, London: Routledge, 1990.

Chopp, Rebecca S. and Davaney, Sheila Greeve (eds.). *Horizons in Feminist Theology: Identity, Tradition, and Norms*, Minneapolis, MN: Fortress Press, 1997.

Hogan, Linda. *From Women's Experience to Feminist Theology*, Sheffield Academic Press, 1995.

Irigaray, Luce. *Speculum of the Other Woman*, Gillian C. Gill (trans.), Ithaca, NY: Cornell University Press, 1985.

LaCugna, Catherine Mowry (ed.). *Freeing Theology: The Essentials of Theology in Feminist Perspective*, San Francisco, CA: HarperCollins, 1993.

McFague, Sallie. *Models of God: Theology for an Ecological, Nuclear Age*, Philadelphia, PA: Fortress Press, 1987.

Parsons, Susan Frank (ed.). *Challenging Women's Orthodoxies in the Context of Faith*, Aldershot: Ashgate, 2000.

Ruether, Rosemary Radford. *Sexism and God-Talk: Towards a Feminist Theology*, London: SCM Press, 1983.

Sölle, Dorothee. *Thinking About God: An Introduction to Theology*, London: SCM Press, 1990.

West, Angela. *Deadly Innocence: Feminism and the Mythology of Sin*, London: Cassell, 1995.

Young, Pamela Dickey. *Feminist Theology/Christian Theology: In Search of Method*, Minneapolis MN: Fortress Press, 1990.

Part two

The themes of feminist theology

8 Trinity and feminism

JANET MARTIN SOSKICE

May the deep of uncreated Wisdom call to the deep of the wonderful Omnipotence, to praise and exalt such breath-taking Goodness, which guided the overflowing abundance of your mercy down from on high to the valley of my wretchedness![1]

Gertrude of Helfta opens her book of God's loving-kindness by addressing her God – Wisdom, Omnipotence, Goodness. In addressing the triune God, Gertrude places her book in a well-established Christian tradition. But this is more than a formulaic opening – reflection upon the doctrine of the Trinity has inspired some of the richest writings on love, gift, and grace, a significant part of it written by women, to be found in Christian literature. The doctrine of the Trinity, while by consent a difficult topic on which to preach, informs Christian liturgy and provides the basic frame for the ancient creeds – 'I believe in God, the Father, the Son, and Holy Spirit.' It has a central place in the Christian doctrine of God classically conceived. The Christian doctrine of God holds in tension two convictions seemingly at odds – that God is One, and that there is diversity in the Godhead. A motive for its formulation was the Christian insistence that their faith was monotheistic, even while praying to one God and to Jesus as the Lord.

Although the conviction that Jesus is the Christ marks Christianity out, ideas of diversity within unity were not alien to the Jewish matrix within which Christianity arose. The unity of God was, of course, a fundamental Jewish teaching, but the Rabbis had no difficulty with the idea that God was present to Israel at different times and in different ways. There was a Jewish tradition of different names for the one God which corresponded to these 'presencings'. What was objectionable to the Rabbis was any suggestion (as found in some Jewish gnostic sects and, so it seemed to its critics, in the new movement of Christians) that different names designated different deities. The New Testament language of 'Father' and 'Son' was problematic, not, of course, for reasons of gender inclusivity but because it suggested polytheism.

The doctrine of the Trinity thus arose from the practical and pastoral concerns of the early church. It was reasonable for Christians as well as their critics to ask – 'If there is only one God to whom we can pray, then who is this Jesus and how can we pray to him?' The Christian scriptures already posed the problem. In identifying Jesus with the Lord who 'Let light shine out of darkness' (2 Corinthians 4$^{5-6}$), Paul applied divine titles to Jesus which the devout Jew of his day would have appropriately applied only to the God who created heaven on earth.[2] In virtue of its reliance on Greek philosophical categories and its relatively late formulation (the third and fourth centuries), the doctrine of the Trinity has periodically been accused of being no more than a Hellenistic interloper, an unwarranted philosophical intrusion on the pure form of the Gospels. But we should not confuse the means with the motives for its formulation. The means, the tools at hand, were those of Greek philosophy but the motives were pastoral and apologetic.

The doctrine of the Trinity adds nothing extra to the basic Christian confession. The early creeds are threefold, confessing belief in God, Father, Son, and Holy Spirit. There is no coda to say – 'And, by the way, I also believe in the Trinity.' In confessing belief in 'One God, Father, Son, and Holy Spirit', the believer confesses the Trinity, or better, confesses *a Trinitarian faith*. The doctrine is best seen not as an additional conviction, but rather as providing the frame in which central convictions rest. It is a *grammar* of Christian faith whose function was to safeguard what the early church took to be the central Christian witness.

THE TRINITY IN MODERN FEMINIST LITERATURE

Despite the fact that the early days of feminist theology coincided with a recovery of theological interest in the doctrine of the Trinity, feminist theology in its early days paid little specific attention to the doctrine of the Trinity.[3] It was natural that biblical studies should be the hub of early feminist interest. The pressing questions, for instance those of ordination of women or inclusive language, arose from pastoral theology, ecclesiology, and liturgy. Amongst the customary *loci* of doctrinal theology, Christology was the area of most debate – not least because of its relevance to the practical problems just mentioned – followed by divine Fatherhood. Both topics are related to, but not quite the same as, the doctrine of the Trinity. In pastoral circumstances, Trinitarian formulae, especially the baptismal formula 'In the Name of the Father, the Son and the Holy Spirit', were points of pain but often addressed by means of ad hoc strategies – that is, simply finding different threefold ascriptions and hoping the problem would be put to rest. Substituting ascriptions did little, however, to address the underlying theological issues.

What might these issues be? Feminist theology has reached the stage of maturity to openly admit that a number of different theological positions roost under its rubric. Usually, not always usefully, these are plotted on a line between radical, post-Christian stances and moderate reformist ones. Some of the early exponents of feminist theology, even apart from feminist interests, had their intellectual formation in church traditions where the doctrine of the Trinity had had for some time little prominence. Some nineteenth- and twentieth-century theology, for instance, under the impact of historical criticism and with a post-Kantian distrust of metaphysics, favoured views of Jesus as a pre-eminent teacher, guru, or liberating leader, but not as one divine. Without a reasonably high Christology, the doctrine of the Trinity as classically formulated is redundant – a solution to a problem which no longer exists. If one no longer wishes or can say that God became incarnate in Jesus of Nazareth, and no longer addresses prayers to Jesus as the Christ, then the Trinity becomes superfluous and even appears as androcentrism at its worst, reinscribing in prayer a divinisation of the male sex. The doctrine of the Trinity is, in this sense, not everybody's problem. Mary Daly's *Beyond God the Father* is an example of a feminist classic which feels no need to address the doctrine of the Trinity in its own terms, having cast off its primary components long before. In this book, Daly lampoons the Trinity but does not tackle the doctrine in its own right. And, from her point of view, why should she? Her concerns are, as the book's title indicates, more primordial – dealing with the prior notions of divine Fatherhood and the special status of Jesus. This is not so much an attack on the doctrine of the Trinity as a denial of the foundational elements and problematic for which it is the proposed solution.[4] It seems that for many modern Christians, and not just feminist, the fundamental building blocks of the doctrine of the Trinity are no longer in place. It is easy then, to be entirely rid of the doctrine of the Trinity. There are more interesting problems for those feminist thinkers who wish to retain a high Christology. To summarise – if you do not wish to say 'Jesus is God incarnate', you do not need the Trinity; if you do wish to say this you can scarcely avoid it.

ALWAYS CONTESTED

The doctrine of the Trinity has always been contested. Its formulation was late, its overt biblical basis slight and reliance on metaphysics substantial. In the last three-hundred years of Western Christianity a number of theologians have thought that the doctrine of the Trinity has outworn its usefulness and might now be scrapped. Even Calvin, despairing over the unbiblical philosophical terms in the doctrine's classical formulations, said he wished he could be rid of the lot except that they were so useful in ferreting out heretics.

'Ferreting out the heretics' is stronger language than most now would wish to use, but it cannot be doubted that feminist theology in its reformist branch is often claiming to do precisely that – challenging idolatrous pictures of God. This is an explicit objective for Elizabeth Johnson in *She Who Is*, a book which, by calling our attention to the limitations of all our speaking of God and by developing the *Sophia–Wisdom* symbolism for Christ, seeks to add a new, and less masculinist, perspective to the classical doctrine. Might the doctrine of the Trinity then, in our own time and with our own theological questions, serve the same useful regulative role it has done in the past?

Perhaps the most persistent criticism from feminist theologians is that the doctrine of the Trinity is used to reinforce hierarchy and underwrite the maleness of God. Paradoxically, the original motives for the doctrine were precisely to subvert hierarchical understandings of the Godhead, not reinforce them. A powerful male eminence is not the picture of God favoured by feminist theologians and nor is it consistent with the doctrine of the Trinity. Yet it is not difficult to see why theologians, and not only feminist theologians, have felt that the doctrine underscores hierarchy. Trinitarian formulae developed for one particular purpose so often suggest their opposite. Talk of the One God's 'triunity' readily appears to be tritheism. Walter Kasper writes with great caution and accuracy of the absolute unity of God *despite* the distinction of persons, and the absolute equality of the persons *despite* the dependence of the second person on the first and the third on the first and the second, and so on, but this 'despite' language sounds a little like Orwell's *Animal Farm*: 'All animals are equal but some animals are more equal than others.'[5] Trinitarian language may be introduced, historically, as a corrective to the tendency of idolatry, but how successful has it been? Tritheism may have been despatched early on, but more subtle forms of subordinationism, monarchianism, and deism, all in their way idolatrous, have enjoyed good careers. Feminist criticisms of classical formulations of the doctrine vary from simple rejection of what sounds like a three-men club, to more nuanced critiques of the way in which, despite best efforts, the Father always seems accorded status superior to the other two persons, with the Holy Spirit as a distinct third. The Trinity appears still hierarchical, still male – maleness, indeed, seems enshrined in God's eternity.[6]

THE CASE FOR CONTINUITY

Despite these criticisms it can still be argued that it is the doctrine of the Trinity which saves the Christian doctrine of God from stifling andro-centrism. Custodians of the tradition would be quite wrong to dismiss the feminist criticisms as simply failing to understand the doctrine. It would be more accurate to see these as a clarion call for its renewal.

First and foremost the doctrine preserves the otherness of God – that is, it frees us from the gross anthropocentrism which is ever a threat in religion. The triune God is not male. (I shall return shortly to the language of fatherhood and sonship.) Even though God became incarnate in the man, Jesus Christ. God is not a creature at all, far less a male creature. The baptismal formula contains its own self-subversion – we are baptised 'in the Name' (singular) of the Father, Son, and Holy Spirit, and not 'in the names' (plural) of two men and a mysterious third. 'Father' and 'Son' in the Trinitarian rubrics are not biological offices, and nor are they positions in a hierarchy.

Secondly, the doctrine defeats the covert monarchianism which has been a main target for feminist theology. The 'god' whom feminist theology loves to have is the lonely, spectral father–god, aloof, above, and indifferent. But this is the god of deism and not the God of scripture or the Trinity. The God of scripture is a God who creates freely from abundant love and who is present to this creation. Christian beliefs about Jesus develop this story of love, concern, and intimacy, and the Christian doctrine of the Trinity con-cerns the way that God is 'with us'.[7] As Elizabeth Johnson points out, 'the Trinity is not a blueprint of the inner workings of the godhead, not an offer-ing of esoteric information about God. In no sense is it a literal description of God's "being *in se*"'.[8] Rather it brings out the Christian conviction that God, the eternal creator is fully present to our human history – even to the point of taking human flesh and dying on the cross – and fully present to us now in the Spirit.

Thirdly, the doctrine endorses the fundamental goodness and beauty of the human being, first fruits of the created order, destined to share in the life of God through the Incarnation of the Word. That Jesus was truly and fully human cannot be denied, not just as an empirical claim but as a conviction of Christian orthodoxy. Jesus was not, as some gnostics thought, one who *merely appeared* to be fleshly, *merely appeared* to be born of a woman, *merely appeared* to die. The paradoxical Christian insistence has been on one who is true man and true God. From a current feminist's perspective it may be unfortunate that God should become incarnate as a male, but it is a glory of this teaching that God became fully and truly a sexed human being. Indeed, given Christianity's persistent tendency to debase the body, this endorsement of physicality should be prized. The soteriological stress has always been on the fact that Christ's was a human body rather than some androgynous and spiritualised shell. Human bodies must be either male or female, but Christ is the Saviour not because he is male but because he is human. To this must be added that the second person of the Trinity is also the Word of God, eternally one with the Father, through whom all things were made (John 1).

Fourthly, the doctrine is a challenge, in modern as in ancient times, to philosophies of the One. Those postmodernists who see the history of Western metaphysics as totally subsumed by philosophies of the One must be forgetting the many Christian centuries informed by the doctrine of the Trinity. Indeed, a lot of the delicate philosophical and theological reflection to be found in historical Trinitarian texts bears resemblance in our time to nothing so much as attempts to accommodate the 'Other' without regressing into 'the-other-of-the-same' – that is, an 'other' whose otherness is only functional to the Ego as 'not me'. The doctrine of the Trinity moves us beyond a binarism in which one can only have the one and the other, the higher and the lower, the male and the female. This is the economy of the Other defined by de Beauvoir: 'it is not the Other, who, in defining himself as the Other, establishes the One. The Other is posed as such by the One in defining himself as the One',[9] and developed more recently by Luce Irigaray. The Cappadocians formulated their Trinitarian theology over and against a similar metaphysics of the One in which there can be no genuine otherness, but only the 'Other of the Same'.[10]

In biblical terms, the doctrine of the Trinity defeats a picture of the Godhead as self-enclosed admiration between Father and Son. Three, as philosophers have noted down the ages, is the first in the cardinal series where one gets genuine difference. There is difference in the Trinity, but no hierarchy. Instead the persons only *are* as they are in relation. Catherine LaCugna makes this point, elaborating upon Aquinas: if God's 'To Be' is 'To-Be-Related', then the Son cannot be what the Son is except in relation to the

Father and the Spirit, nor the Father except by relation to the Son and the
Spirit, nor the Spirit what Spirit is except in relation to Father and Son.
The divine life is a perichoretic outpouring of love.[11] Trinitarian theology
presents us with a God who shatters cardinality, a God is three and One,
who cannot be dissected, reified, or circumscribed.

MEETING THE CHALLENGES

If the doctrine of the Trinity has suffered from a distorted male weighting, then the challenge to contemporary theology – and not just to feminist
theology – is to return the balance. There is a precedent in the *locus classicus*
of Western Trinitarian theology, Augustine's *de Trinitate.* In his account of
the *imago dei,* Augustine departs from the then accepted focus of the Son as
true image of God and the human being as created according to this (male)
image. Augustine argues instead that human beings are in the image, not of
the Son, but of the triune God. He had a number of reasons for doing this,
one of which was to avoid subordinationist implications of the idea that the
Son is *only* an image. Another seems to be that too specific a focus on an
'image' which is male might be taken to imply that women were not fully in
the image of God. In his expansion upon 1 Corinthians 11[7] ('A man should
certainly not cover his head, since he is the image of God and reflects God's
glory; but woman is the reflection of man's glory.'), Augustine is specifically
critical of any suggestion that Paul's meaning is that women are somehow
not fully in the image of God.[12] We are renewed in the spirit of our mind,
says Augustine, 'And it is according to this renewal, also, that we are made
sons of God by the baptism of Christ; and putting on the new man, certainly
put on Christ through faith. Who is there, then, who will hold women to be
alien from this fellowship, whereas they are fellow-heirs of grace with us?'[13]
Augustine, conscious of the masculine freighting of the Pauline language,
takes steps against any distortion which might creep in as a result of it.

NAMING THE TRIUNE GOD – FATHER AND SON

How then do we now name this triune God? The Trinitarian confession
seems to take the language of fatherhood and sonship right into the eternal
life of God.

One strategy, arising from the debates concerning inclusive language,
was to desexualise the language of the Trinity altogether and speak, for
instance, of Creator, Sustainer, and Redeemer. There is ample precedent,
especially in the medieval literature, for diverse Trinitarian invocation. It

is important, however, with any formulation to avoid the suggestion that it is only the First Person who creates, only the Second who redeems, and the Third who sustains. This is to buy into neutrality at the risk of collapse into tritheism. Creation is properly the action of all three persons, as are redeeming and sustaining – all acts *ad extra*. All divine activity is, in Christian terms, the activity of the triune God. That being said, there is no reason why such threefold invocations should not have their place in worship where the theological balance is kept.

Although, as Elizabeth Johnson points out, 'it is not necessary to restrict speech about God to the exact names that Scripture uses',[14] the masculine terminology of the New Testament will be with us as long as the New Testament is with us. In sharp contrast to the Old Testament where the ascription of 'father' is altogether rare, 'Father' and 'Son' titles are central to the New Testament writings.[15] Yet to this must be added the fact that Christians have never felt constrained to call the first person only 'Father' or to call Jesus only 'the Son'. Furthermore, the patriarchal ordering implied by the kinship titles was subverted early on by Christian insistence that the Son is one with the Father, equal to the Father, co-eternal with the Father and Spirit. Arians, if we can still use the term, insisted that the Father–Son titles must imply subordination. Their view was rejected.

It is important to see that the 'Father' and 'Son' language is not kept in place by the doctrine of the Trinity, but the other way round. The Trinity is precisely the reflective means by which unacceptable inferences from the primary language of the New Testament have been kept in place – for instance the unacceptable inference from the fact that there are three names – Father, Son, and Spirit – to the idea that there are three Gods, or the unacceptable inference from a Father who is ungenerate and a Son begotten, to the idea that the Father must be superior to the Son. It was of the essence of the earliest defences of the doctrine that the Godhead be understood as life, love, and complete mutuality – the Son is not less than the Father, nor can the Father be Father without Son and Spirit. The Trinity qualifies all our presumptive knowledge of God. For Gregory of Nyssa even the threefold naming, Father, Son, and Holy Spirit, does not describe the divine essence, something we could never do.

FEMINISING THE SPIRIT

Another strategy for balancing the male weighting of the biblical Trinitarian titles has been to emphasise symbolically female characteristics of the Spirit. We can readily uncover a tradition of regarding the Spirit as the maternal aspect of God – brooding, nurturing, bringing new members of the church to life in baptism. There is, too, the early Syriac tradition of styling the Spirit as feminine, following the female gender of the noun in the Semitic languages (ruha' in Syriac, ruah in Hebrew). Again some attempts in this direction have failed to convince feminist and other theologians of their enduring merit for women or, for that matter, for the Trinity. Consider the implications of these remarks of Yves Congar:

> The part played in our upbringing by the Holy Spirit is that of a mother – a mother who enables us to know our Father, God, and our brother, Jesus . . . He (the Spirit) teaches us how to practise the virtues and how to use the gifts of a son of God by grace. All this is part of a mother's function.[16]

Along with deifying one particular and particularly Western version of 'a mother's function' (for why is it not a mother's function to raise crops to feed her family?), the Spirit by implication is here handmaid to the other two (male) persons who are the ones really to be known and loved. Even less satisfactory, as Elizabeth Johnson notes, is the effort by the process theologian, John Cobb, to align the *Logos*, as the masculine aspect of God, with order, novelty, demand, agency, and transformation, while the feminine aspect of God, the Kingdom or Spirit, is linked with receptivity, empathy, suffering, and preservation.[17]

Feminists are surely right to reject what Sarah Coakley has called 'mawkish and sentimentalised versions of the feminine' as both providing warrant for a particular stereotype of the feminine and at the same time feeding the unorthodox suggestion that there is sexual difference in the Trinity. Furthermore, this kind of feminising rhetoric does nothing to counteract the genuine neglect of the Spirit in modern theology, in which the Spirit appears a sort of 'edifying appendage' to the two real persons, those who have faces, the Father and the Son.[18] We must avoid, as Coakley says, subordinating 'the Spirit to a Father who, as "cause", and "source" of the other two persons, remains as a "masculine" stereotype with the theological upper hand'.[19]

None the less, proceeding with proper Trinitarian caution, the prospects are exciting. First, one must avoid tritheism. Susan Ashbrook Harvey points out that Syriac Christians did not posit a female deity alongside or in distinction to a male. Such concrete identities were available in the pagan deities of the Syrian Orient, 'where a triad of mother, father, and son was a common configuration of divinity'.[20] While the Spirit was styled as feminine, and occasionally identified with the Wisdom figure, the feminisation was drawn across to all three persons of the Trinity. The *Odes of Solomon*, probably from the second Christian century have a maternal Spirit but also a maternal Father:

> A cup of milk was offered to me
> And I drank it with the sweetness of the Lord's kindness.
> The Son is the cup,
> And He who was milked is the Father,
> And she who milked Him is the Holy Spirit,

Harvey highlights the wealth of bodily and gendered metaphors but also the way in which they are layered in paradoxical and conflicting sequences:

> Roles are reversed, fused, inverted: no one is simply who they seem to be. More accurately, everyone is *more than* they seem to be – Mary is more than a woman in what she does; the Father and the Spirit are more than one gender can convey in the effort to glimpse their works. Gender is thus shown to be important, even crucial, to identity – but not one specific gender.[21]

In this rhetorical excess, God is not lacking gender, but more than gender – that to which our human experience of gender and physicality feebly but none the less really points.

RHETORICAL EXCESS – JULIAN OF NORWICH

All three persons of the Trinity can be styled in the imagery of the human masculine and the human feminine. But better still is the play of gendered imagery which keeps in place the symbols of desire, fecundity, and parental love while destabilising any over-literalistic reading. This seems to be the strategy of the Old Testament itself, where images of God as bridegroom and father jostle up against one another in a way that would make an overly literalistic reading noxious. A striking medieval instance is Julian of Norwich's *Revelations of Divine Love*. So much has been made of Julian's dramatic styling of Christ as mother that we almost fail to notice the work's splendour as a piece of Trinitarian theology.

Julian makes it clear at the outset that it is the triune God whom she wishes to speak of throughout. Describing her first revelation of Christ crowned with thorns she says:

> At the same moment the Trinity filled me full of heartfelt joy, and I knew that all eternity was like this for those who attain heaven. For

the Trinity is God, and God the Trinity; the Trinity is our Maker and
keeper, our eternal lover, joy and bliss – all through our Lord Jesus
Christ. This was shown me in this first revelation, and, indeed, in
them all; for where Jesus is spoken of, the blessed Trinity is always to
be understood as I see it.[22]

While it has been suggested that she clarifies to avoid accusations of heresy,
her Trinitarianism seems genuine. She confidently sports with threefold
titles throughout the work. In placing great emphasis on Christ as our
Mother, she is at once provocative and altogether orthodox: Jesus was
indubitably male yet, if he is to be the perfection of our humanity he must
also be the perfection of female humanity. She is willing to style all three
persons as Mother. 'God is as really our Mother as he is our Father. He
showed this throughout, and particularly when he said that sweet word, "It
is I".'[23] Jesus is our mother because he made us, but all making, redeeming,
and sustaining is the work of the triune God:

I came to realise that there were three ways to see God's motherhood:
the first is based on the fact that our nature is *made*; the second is
found in the assumption of that nature – there begins the motherhood
of grace; the third is the motherhood of work which flows out over all
by the same grace – the length and breadth and height and depth of it
is everlasting. And so is his love.[24]

Julian follows the route not of displacement but excess, complementing the
gendered scriptural terms of divine Fatherhood and Sonship with maternal
and functional imagery (God is our Maker, Keeper, and Lover). Yet, just as
God can be our Mother as well as Father, Christ is our Maker as well as
Lover, our Keeper as well as Maker, the threefold terms revolve in a text
which, if effusive, is never careless.

In an Augustinian moment she styles the human soul as triune:

Truth sees God: wisdom gazes on God. And these two produce a third,
a holy, wondering delight in God, which is love. Where there is indeed
truth and wisdom, there too is love, springing from them both. And all
of God's making: for he is eternal sovereign truth, eternal sovereign
wisdom, eternal sovereign love, uncreated. Man's soul is God's
creation, and possesses similar properties (only they are created) and
it always does what it was created for: it sees God, it gazes on God, and
it loves God. And God rejoices in his creature; and his creature in God,
eternally marvelling.[25]

This is Julian's vision of deification – the human being caught up in the life of the triune God.

GOD AS LOVE

Despite the abundance of affective and erotic language of lover and beloved in the Old and New Testaments, the primordial model of love in Christianity is not the love between two but the love of the Trinity. To call this the love of the three would be misleading, for the Triunity of God is not a threeness of cardinal numbers, just as the Oneness of God is not a cardinal oneness. This threeness serves not to replace gendered imagery of love, but to exceed it, calling the believer beyond binarism and the fragile limits of our speech. In my opinion, this baffling of gender literalism, as well as having the stamp of antiquity (not just in Julian but in the Cappadocians, Bernard of Clairvaux, and others), is the single most productive strategy for moving beyond overly masculinised conceptions – it allows us to keep the language of scripture and reminds us to attend always to our *grammar in divinis.*

Recent work on the Trinity attends to its place in the Christian language of love. Sarah Coakley suggest that it should puzzle us more that the doctrine of God as three should so frequently find erotic thematisation. The connection between sexuality and spirituality, embarrassing to so many modern theologians, is overt in earlier writers. Coakley points in the writings of Gregory of Nyssa to the same inversion of sexual stereotypes noted by Susan Ashbrook Harvey and to the possibility, following this lead, of an expansion of the self which subverts narrow, modernist rationality. Drawing this together with French feminism, she suggests that this mirroring forth of the Trinitarian image in sexual love would involve at least,

> a fundamental respect each for the other, an equality of exchange, and the mutual *ecstasis*, of attending on the others desire as distinct, *as other.* This is the opposite of abuse, the opposite of distanced sexual control; it is, as the French feminist Luce Irigaray has written, with uncanny insight, itself intrinsically trinitarian; sexual love at its best is not egological, nor even a duality in closeness, but a shared transcendence of two selves toward the other, within a 'shared space, a shared breath: In this relation', she writes, 'we are at least three . . . you, me, and our creation of that ecstasy of ourself in us (*de nous en nous*) prior to any child'.[26]

The love of the Trinity is a template for the fundamentally ethical love which calls us beyond any narcissicism *à deux* to a love creative and open to others.

FUTURE PERFECT?

If achieving a gracious balance is not a night's work, nor should we imagine its goal for the doctrine of the Trinity should be a final, fixed formulation invincible to all criticism. On the contrary, if the doctrine serves as regulative in Christian thought then it will inevitably face new challenges in new circumstances as they come along. In the early church, the challenge was that of polytheism and subordinationism; in the eighteenth century it was that of a deism which left Jesus just a man. In Trinitarian thinking the object is not to find the definitive but to avoid the defective.

Whatever the doctrine's future, Christian teaching in the past has been more androcentric rather than less when the doctrine of the Trinity was abandoned or neglected. If one keeps the New Testament in place and abandons the doctrine of the Trinity for whatever reason (and we have seen that in the past there were many), one is left with the masculine titles unqualified. As recently as the nineteenth century, theologians, avoiding what they felt to be Greek mystification and metaphysics, easily slipped into the cloying piety of 'fathers' and 'sons' with Jesus the ideal 'son' of the ideal 'father'. The Trinitarian theology of the early church is not without difficulty for modern sensibilities, but overly literalistic and proscriptive readings of the masculine titles were kept in place by the recognition that these named the mystery of relations in the triune God.

Without the doctrine of the Trinity in place, one is lead inevitably to such questions as 'how could a father let his son die on the cross?' The Cross is a painful mystery, but the doctrine of the Trinity reminds us that the death is the death of God for us, and not of some subordinate deity or hapless human being drafted into the divine project with cruel intent. As eighteenth-century defenders of the doctrine like Daniel Waterland noted, without the Trinity Christianity quickly descends into cruel barbarism – Why couldn't God accept the sacrifice of a bull or a goat? Why would only a man do? Within a Trinitarian framework it is God Godself who makes sacrifice for us, and not some lesser emissary.[27]

Gertrude, with whom we began, wrote of the depths of 'uncreated Wisdom'. For those for whom the Trinity is important, spiritually and not just as a theological fail-safe, the doctrine has riches yet in store. It unites us to women writers of the Christian past, especially in its language of praise and wonder. It makes us aware how short our speaking must fall of its divine target. It reminds us that theological language is, by virtue of the mysteries with which it deals, complex and on many occasions deliberately self-subverting. Directions in which we can expect growth in Trinitarian reflection are many, including at least: the theology of the body and embodiment; the recovery in the West of Eastern traditions of divinisation; the theology of creation and wholeness, of Wisdom and Word; the ethics of otherness and relationship; and the theology of love.

Notes

1. Gertrude of Helfta, *The Herald of God's Loving-Kindness*, trans. Alexandra Barratt (Kalamazoo, MI: Cistercian Publications, 1991), p. 100.
2. See Alan F. Segal, 'Two Powers in Heaven and Early Christian Trinitarian Thinking', in Stephen Davis, Daniel Kendall, and Gerald O'Collins (eds.), *The Trinity* (Oxford University Press, 1999).
3. Elizabeth Johnson's *She Who Is* (New York: Crossroad, 1992), and Catherine LaCugna's *God for Us* (San Fransrisco, CA: HarperSanfrancisco, 1991), are landmark studies, although the first is an essay in the doctrine of God more generally and the second, while written by a woman with feminist concerns, not a feminist essay as such. See, however, her article on the Trinity, 'God in Communion with Us', in her edited collection, *Freeing Theology: The Essentials of Theology in Feminist Perspective* (New York: HarperCollins, 1993). Marjorie Suchocki has written a study informed by process thought, *God, Christ and Church* (New York: Crossroad, 1986). Sr. Nonna (Verna) Harrison and Sarah Coakley have each written a series of important articles which bear on the topic. Harrison is a patristics scholar in the orthodox tradition; see for instance 'Male And Female in Cappadocian Theology', *Journal of Theological Studies* 41 (October, 1990), 441–71. Virginia Burrus in *Begotten Not Made: Conceiving Manhood in Late Antiquity* (Stanford, CA: Stanford University Press, 2000) discusses the formulation of Nicene doctrine in terms of a crisis of masculinity.
4. Correspondingly, Daly addresses the doctrine almost not at all. Her sections on the most Unholy and the most Whole Trinities use the term rhetorically. *Beyond God the Father* (London: The Womens Press, 1991) pp. 127–31.
5. See Walter Kasper, *The God of Jesus Christ* (London: SCM Press, 1984), p. 280; George Orwell, *Animal Farm* (New York, NY: New American Library, 1946), p. 123.
6. For this kind of criticism see Mary Grey, 'The Core of our Desire: Re-Imaging the Trinity', *Theology* 93 (1990), 363–72.
7. A route to be avoided is one which, in the enthusiasm for being-in-communion, insists that it is only the doctrine of the Trinity which allows Christianity to preach of a God of relationship and love. This has a decidedly anti-Judaic ring to it. For this reason, amongst others, it is well to remember that the doctrine arises as a resolution to New Testament ascriptions of fatherhood and sonship. It is not a Jewish problem or a Jewish answer, although, as already mentioned, the idea of God dwelling with man, an idea intrinsic to the development of Christology, is a Jewish one.
8. Johnson, *She Who Is*, p. 204.

9. Simone de Beauvoir, *The Second Sex*, trans. H. M. Parshley (London: Pan Books, 1988), p. 18.
10. For treatments that develop this theme with reference to Luce Irigaray, see Serene Jones, 'This God Which is No One', in C. W. Maggie Kim, Susan M. St. Ville, and Susan M. Simonaitis (eds.), *Transfigurations: Theology and the French Feminists* (Minneapolis, MN: Fortress Press, 1993), pp. 109–41, and Janet Martin Soskice, 'Trinity and "the feminine Other"', *New Blackfriars*, January, 1994.
11. I have argued that this can be readily styled in the procreative imagery of the human feminine. See Soskice, 'Trinity'.
12. Augustine, *de Trinitate*, volume 3 of the *Library of the Nicene and post-Nicene Fathers of the Christian Church*, ed. Philip Schaff, trans. A. W. Haddan (Grand Rapids, MI: Wm R. Eerdmans, 1956), Book XII:12.
13. Augustine, *de Trinitate*.
14. Johnson, *She Who Is*, p. 7.
15. See Janet Martin Soskice, 'Can a Feminist Call God "Father"?' in Alvin Kimmel (ed.), *The Holy Trinity and the Challenge of Feminism* (New York: Eerdmans, 1992), and also in Teresa Elwes (ed.), *Women's Voices in Religion* (London: Collins, 1992).
16. Yves Congar, *I Believe in the Holy Spirit* (New York: Seabury Press, 1983), vol. III, p. 161.
17. Elizabeth A. Johnson, 'The Incomprehensibility of God and the Image of God Male and Female', *Theological Studies* 45 (1984), 459.
18. Johnson, 'Incomprehensibility', p. 457.
19. Sarah Coakley, '"Feminity" and the Holy Spirit?' in Monica Furlong (ed.), *Mirror to the Church* (London, SPCK, 1988).
20. Susan Ashbrook Harvey, 'Feminine Imagery for the Divine: the Holy Spirit, the Odes of Solomon, and early Syriac Tradition', *St. Vladimir's Theological Quarterly* 37:2&3 (1993), 114.
21. Ibid., 127.
22. Julian of Norwich, *Revelations of Divine Love*, trans. Clifton Wolters (London: Penguin Books, 1966), ch. 4, p. 66.
23. Ibid., ch. 59, p. 157.
24. Ibid., ch. 59, p. 168.
25. Ibid., ch. 44, p. 130.
26. Coakley, 'Living into the Mystery of the Holy Trinity: Trinity, Prayer, and Sexuality', *Anglican Theological Review*, 80:2, 231. See also her '"Batter my heart . . . ": On Sexuality, Spirituality and the Christian Doctrine of the Trinity', *Graven Images* 2 (1995), 74–83.
27. Daniel Waterland, *The Importance of the Doctrine of the Holy Trinity, Asserted in Reply to some Late Pamphlets*, third edition corrected (Cambridge: J. Burges [printer to the University], 1800).

Selected reading

Coakley, Sarah. 'Living into the Mystery of the Holy Trinity: Trinity, Prayer, and Sexuality', *Anglican Theological Review*, 80:2;
  '"Batter my heart . . . ": On Sexuality, Spirituality and the Christian Doctrine of the Trinity', *Graven Images* 2 (1995).

Johnson, Elizabeth. *She Who Is*, New York: Crossroad, 1992.

Julian of Norwich. *Revelations of Divine Love*, Clifton Wolters (trans.), London: Penguin Books, 1996.

LaCugna, Catherine Mowry. *God For Us*, San Francisco, CA: HarperSanfrancisco, 1991.

Soskice, Janet Martin. 'Can a Feminist Call God "Father"?' in Alvin Kimmel (ed.). *The Holy Trinity and the Challenge of Feminism*, New York: Eerdmans, 1992; 'Trinity and "the feminine Other"', *New Blackfriars* (January 1994).

Suchocki, Marjorie. *God, Christ and Church*, New York: Crossroad, 1986.

9 Jesus Christ

MERCY AMBA ODUYOYE

THE CONTEXT

African Christian theology is decidedly contextual, and this contribution on Jesus by an African woman will stay in that mode and reflect the
faith of African Christian women in the African context. Jesus Christ yes-
terday, today, and tomorrow requires that each generation declares its faith
in relation to its today. It is, therefore, natural that the Christologies African
women were fed should reflect the faith of those who brought Christianity to Africa and the African men who did most of the interpretation and
transmission. Having heard all this, African women today can announce in
their own words the one in whom they have believed.

The intention of this chapter is to survey the language of African Christian women about Jesus and, through that, to build up a profile of the
Jesus in their Christianity. We begin with a note on sources, as the expected
'library study' of this subject will yield very little that is of the provenance
of women. We then sample the oral Christology which is our key source, as
most of what is written by African women began as oral contributions to
study groups and conferences. The third section is this writer's assessment
of what is being said about Jesus and why.

In the past thirty years or so, several Christological models have appeared in books written by men theologians of Africa.[1] They share the
emphases of the Western churches but several go beyond these. They are
grounded in the classical Christian approach that identifies 'Saviour myths'
with biblical narratives and attempt the question: 'who is the Saviour?' The
classical divine–human motif is stated as a matter of faith and not debated,
as the early church was wont to do. African theologians transmit as an article of faith the divine–human person whose sacrifice on the cross is salvific.
As a human being, the Saviour is a pastor and an example for human life.
As a human being, his role is like that of the royalty in traditional African

communities, a representative and leader, but it is as divine that the Saviour is victorious over death.

The divinity of the Christ is experienced through the Bible as of the one in control of the universe and history. The Christ controls evil and is a wonder-worker. In times of crises, the Christ is expected to intervene directly on the side of the good, for God is the giver of Good. In the Gospels, the Christ is seen as a healer, an exorcist, and a companion. All these notions feature in African Christologies and influence what women, too, say about Jesus.

In dealing with Christologies in Africa, one finds two major trends, the inculturationist and the liberationist. The first type are those who consciously appropriate Africa's traditional experience of God. We note that the Greek Bible imagery that forms the foundations of traditional Christologies has appropriated beliefs and language from Jewish religion, as well as Græco-Roman paradigms. To talk intelligently about new experience, one cannot but build upon what is known. African religion and culture furnish the language of Christologies that describe Jesus as an ancestor, a king or elder brother. These carry notions of mediatorship and authority. It is as an ancestor that Jesus stands between humanity and God as the spokesperson, as the *Okyeame*; Jesus is interpreter and advocate. We name ourselves Christians after his being the Christ, just as we name our children after our worthy forebears.

We say Christ is king and we see the lives of royal leaders who were compassionate and brave community builders. We see the royal leaders of the Akan, who bear the title *Osagyefo*, the one who saves the battle, the victorious warrior, and we see Jesus as *Nana*, both ancestor and royalty. In several African traditional cultures, the rulers are regarded as hedged by divinity, and so one is able to talk about the Christ being both divine and human without raising the philosophical debates of early Christianity. So praying to and through Jesus follows naturally and is practised as the spirituality of the religion that enables Christians to face the daily realities of life.

Women have employed cultural paradigms to describe their belief in Jesus, but those that are most favoured are the cultural ones that are also liberative. They employ myths of wonder-workers who save their communities from hunger and from the onslaught of their enemies, both physical and spiritual. The women's Christology in large measure therefore falls within the category of the liberationist types. Jesus is the brother or kin who frees women from the domination of inhuman husbands. They relate more easily to the Christ who knew hunger, thirst, and homelessness, and see Jesus as oppressed by the culture of his own people. Jesus the liberator is a paradigm for the critique of culture that most African women theologians do.

The faith in and the language about Jesus that is reviewed here has become written theology within the last two decades or so; none the less they are of African hue and have their roots in African Christianity in particular. The language about Jesus is heard in songs with lyrics created by both women and men, and sung lustily in churches and in TV drama. There are several women's singing groups who have recorded cassettes sold in our streets, and songs are sung by people at work, at play, or while travelling. The name of Jesus is therefore on the lips, in the ears, and before the eyes of all, including those of other faiths.

Ghana, the country of my birth, today wears many placards bearing slogans, which contain the name of Jesus. When you greet anyone in the streets and ask 'How do you do?' they will profess their faith by telling you 'Yesu adom' – by the grace of Jesus. This version replaces the traditional 'by the grace of God', which has become insufficient, as God was in Ghana before Christianity came and our Muslim sisters and brothers punctuate all hopes and plans and inquiries after their state of being with '*Insha Allah*' – by the will of *Allah* (God). Specifying the name of Jesus, therefore, properly claims Christian particularity. Who Jesus is to Ghanaian Christians is written largely in their songs, prayers, and sayings. The first full text of individual spirituality anchored in Jesus and coming from an African woman with no formal schooling is a publication with the English title *Jesus of the Deep Forest*.[2]

THE TEXTS

Jesus of the Deep Forest signifies the place of Jesus in the life of people both rural and urban. It is the prayers they pray to Jesus and the praises they give to him. One could almost say that, of the women 'writing theologians' of Africa, Afua Kuma is the first, and she paved the way by pointing to the central theme of Christology. She became our first source, and will represent the women who weave lyrics about Jesus and pour their hearts out in prayer and praise at all times and in all places, the women whose theology gets 'reduced' into writing by those who can write.

Our second source is the writings of the women who belong to the Ecumenical Association of Third World Theologians (EATWOT) or to the Circle of Concerned African Women Theologians (the Circle). In the 1980s, EATWOT called attention to the Christologies of the Third World and generated a lot of studies on the subject of Jesus. It is in this context that African women members of the association contributed to the publication, *With Passion and Compassion: Third World Women Doing Theology*.[3] The Circle, with its initial focus on religion and culture, had ecclesiology as its main theological schema, but naturally the subject of Jesus looms large in its members' reflection. The first publication of the Circle, *Talitha Qumi!*, features two Bible studies (Luke 8$^{40-6}$, and 1^{42}) and one article on that subject which can aid us in our study. The series of *Circle Books* and reflections published in the Newsletter *Amka* also provide relevant references.[4]

Our third source will be the writings of individual African women in other anthologies. An example of this is Anne Nasimiyu's 'Christology and an African Woman's Experience' in Robert Schreiter's *Faces of Jesus In Africa*.[5] Individually authored books on the subject by women are rare, but there is a chapter on Jesus in this writer's *Hearing and Knowing*. Teresa Okure's opus on mission can, of course, be read from the perspective of Christology and so can Christina Landman's, *The Piety of South African Women*.[6]

ORAL CHRISTOLOGY

In *Jesus of the Deep Forest* by Afua Kuma, our example of oral Christology, one encounters a lot of astonishing reversals of so-called natural laws and unexpected outcomes of simple actions. Jesus is the one who catches birds from the depths of the ocean and fish from the heights of the trees. These reversals are then reflected in a magnificent type of deeds in the lives of people. Jesus, the Great Provider under all circumstances, brings wealth to widows and orphans and is the friend of the aged. Jesus frees children from the fear of *kakae* (the monster) and breaks the will of the murderer. It is Jesus who has accepted the poor and given them glory. Jesus clears the forest of all evil spirits making it safe for hunters. Imagery that is in keeping with the stilling of the storm abounds in oral Christology.

The motif of Saviour and liberator is very strong in this and other reflections on Jesus by women. For Afua Kuma, the Exodus becomes another motif. Jesus is Yahweh of the Exodus, who defeated Pharaoh and his troops and becomes the sun ahead of Israel and lightning behind them. He is given the Akan title '*Osagyefo*, the one who saves the battle' and so we can depend on him to win life's battles. Other biblical images, like good shepherd, healer, and the compassionate one, are seen together with cultural ones such as 'the mighty edifice that accommodates all corners', while provision of hospitality common to both serves the very antidote to death. Whatever the situation, Jesus has the last word. There are no life challenges for which the power of Jesus is found unequal to the task of achieving victory. The following excerpt from *Jesus of the Deep Forest* illustrates the ethos of this publication:

All-powerful Jesus who engages in marvelous deeds, he is the one called Hero *Okatakyi*! Of all earthly dominions he is master; the Python not overcome with mere sticks, the Big Boat which cannot be sunk.

Jesus, Saviour of the poor, who brightens up our faces! *Damfo-Adu*: the clever one. We rely on you as the tongue relies on the mouth.

The great Rock we hide behind: the great forest canopy that gives cool shade: the Big Tree that lifts its vines to peep at the heavens, the magnificent Tree whose dripping leaves encourage the luxuriant growth.[7]

Several images in Afua Kuma come from Gospel-events involving Jesus and women. 'Women recognize his uniqueness and put their cloths on the ground for him. A woman anoints him as Messiah, friend and Saviour.'[8]

Reflecting on Jesus is not simply an intellectual task or one of personal spirituality. Afua Kuma, like many African women theologians, speaks as an evangelist. 'Follow Jesus', says she, and not only will you witness miracles, but for you will come grace, blessings, eternal life, and peace. The cross of Jesus, she says, is like a net with which Jesus gathers in people; it is the bridge from this life to eternal life. The word of Jesus is the highway along which we should walk. She therefore prays to Jesus: 'Use us to do your will for you have cleansed us with your blood.'[9] This saving blood motif is featuring more and more frequently in song and in prayers in this period of deliverance seeking. The royal blood of Jesus, precious and potent, has given us health and happiness for it has overcome and kept at bay the power of demons. This living faith is proclaimed daily in the churches, on store fronts, on vehicles, and even in the designs of clothes people wear.

WRITTEN CHRISTOLOGY

'There is a concrete history that is lived which is prior to the history that is recounted. That lived history in all its concreteness is the ultimate ground of all the history that is written.'[10] Christologies, therefore, are the results of questions asked by succeeding generations of theologians, the interpreters of the history of Jesus. The vocabulary of African women's theology is focussed on Jesus, rarely Christ or Christ Jesus. Few questions are asked beyond that of human response to that history. The oral affirmations ask hardly any questions, but Edet insists that some women do ask questions of this Jesus-Story. As a Nigerian woman she could ask: 'Who is the Christ to the Nigerian Woman? What type of Christ does she know? How does she relate to this Christ?'[11] The spirituality of the majority of African women moves us to conclude that it is the personality of the one about whom the Gospels speak that draws prayer and praise from them. The songs about Jesus proclaim royalty, king of kings. Jesus is the first and the best of all that is counted good in humanity, and best and first of all good professionals who keep human beings and human communities in a state of health and general well-being. Predominant is Jesus the wonder-worker. Essentially, what we get from African women is an affirmation of faith such as is stated by Rosemary Edet: 'Jesus is the Son of God, son of Mary, sent by the Father to our planet to redeem mankind from sin and death and to restore them to grace.'[12]

Snippets from the contributors to this volume follow the same train of reflections as in 'Christ and the Nigerian Woman' in Edet and Umeagudosu.[13] In the same publication, Kwazu writes, 'Jesus was born on earth to reform man who has completely deviated from God's call to being good.'[14] Akon E. Udo affirms, 'God has sent Jesus Christ to the world to break the barriers of culture and sexism, that is why the names of women appear in the genealogy of Jesus Christ.'[15] This inclusiveness of the mission of God is then illustrated by Jesus' example of giving women the mandate to 'Go and Tell' of the resurrection (Mark 16[7]).

In response to this inclusive mission, African women are heard loud and clear singing the redemptive love of Jesus the liberator. Jesus accomplishes God's mission by setting women free from sexism, oppression, and marginalisation through his death and resurrection, and both women and men are made members of God's household and of the same royal priesthood as men.[16] In *Talitha Qumi!*, we read: 'The ultimate mission of Jesus was to bring healing, life and dignity to the suffering. Jesus came to give voice to the voiceless.'[17]

Teresa M. Hinga's contribution in *The Will to Arise: Jesus Christ and the Liberation of Women* offers a section on 'Christology and African Women: The Ambivalence of the Encounter'. Here she discusses two faces of Christ that are prevalent in African Christologies – the Colonial Christ who is a warrior-king, whose followers sang 'Soldiers of Christ arise', battling against other religions and cultures and indeed races, and the Imperial Christ, the conquering Christ of the missionaries who did battle for Africa, on behalf of the missionaries. Africans embraced this version of Christianity as a 'means of social and economic mobility' – hence the reports we have of mass conversions in some parts of Africa. Hinga states that African women were among those who perceived the emancipating impulses of Christianity and turned to it. Women were among those who took refuge at the mission stations. The early missionary period in Africa presented a Christ who had two faces, the conqueror who inspires the subjugation of people and their cultures while promoting the liberation of individuals from the oppression generated by their environment. Jesus of missionary praxis in Africa was an ambiguous Christ. Thus it is that he has acquired many faces on the continent.

The Christ of missionary teaching, mainly biblical, adds complexity to this scenario. Hinga presents three of these dimensions. Personal Saviour and personal friend – accepting people as they are and meeting their needs at a very personal level – Jesus 'friend of the lonely' and 'healer of those who are sick, whether spiritually or physically'.[18] The title 'friend' is 'one of the most popular among women, precisely because they need such a personal friend the most'. Thus the heightened image of Jesus as the Christ who helps them to bear their griefs, loneliness, and suffering is a welcome one indeed.[19] Women's oral Christologies reflect this history and have been translated into the written ones.

Hinga observes that, in the African women's theology, the 'Image of Christ is a blend of Christology with pneumatology. Jesus is seen as the embodiment of the spirit, the power of God, and the dispenser of the same to all who follow him.'[20] This 'pneumatic Christology' is very popular among women. For here Christ is the voice of the voiceless and the power of the powerless on the models sculptured by Afua Kuma. African women do need such a Christ for they are often expected to be mute and to accept oppression. The Spirit empowers them to enjoy a lively spiritual life that cannot be controlled by the official powers of the church. In this way they are able to defy unjust authority and repressive structures and to stand against cultural demands that go against the spirit of Jesus.

The Christ, the iconoclastic prophet – critic of the status quo that 'engenders social injustices and marginalisation of some in society' illustrates 'some of the defining characteristics of the Christ whom women confess':

> For Christ to become meaningful in the context of women's search for
> emancipation, he would need to be a concrete and personal figure
> who engenders hope in the oppressed by taking their [women's] side,
> to give them confidence and courage to persevere.[21]

Jesus has to be the Christ on the side of the powerless to empower them, the one who is concerned with the lot of victims of social injustice and with the dismantling of unjust social structures. However, the concern most heard these days is deliverance from 'Satanic Bondage', and from demons who seem to have become very active in the Africa of the last decades of the twentieth century. The need for deliverance has revived traditional religious methods. Most especially the importance of blood in African religions is reflected in the central place given to the blood of Jesus in women's theological imagery and, indeed, in much of 'deliverance spirituality' of contemporary African Christianity. Just one example should suffice.

Grace Duah, a 'deliverance Minister' in her book, *Deliverance: Fact or Fantasy?*, includes puberty rites for girls in her windows for demon possession, to demonstrate how easily people can come under the influence of demons and so need deliverance. She writes in her introduction:

> Jesus came not only to give us the highest form of deliverance
> i.e. Salvation – Deliverance from a Kingdom of sin and darkness into a
> Kingdom of Righteousness and light – but also to give us deliverance
> from demonic obsession, demonic oppression, and demonic
> possession, as well as all forms of fleshly enslavement.[22]

Rosemary Edet, a foundation member of the Circle, reflects this in her contribution to the Circle's inaugural conference. Looking at the life of Jesus, she points out that 'Christ has triumphed over illness, blood taboos, women's rituals and the conventions of society'.[23] She is, of course, referring to those that are inimical to women's well-being. These are the ones that Grace Duah is referring to as providing opportunity for demons to possess women.

Jesus has become for us a liberator by countering misogynist culture. After all, says Edet, Jesus' humanity is the humanity of a woman; no human father has contributed. The touch of the 'bleeding woman' has become a very important imagery not only for healing, but also for total liberation from all that oppresses women culturally and makes Jesus Saviour *par excellence*, as we saw in the oral Christology. Therefore Obaga, commenting on the salvific role of the Christ, puts her emphasis on the breaking down of walls of hostilities created by religion and culture. She writes: 'The breaking of the wall therefore meant the abolishing of all external customs and taboos of Judaism which created and perpetuated a state of enmity between Jews and Gentiles.'[24] In her discussion of Ephesians 2[15], she calls attention to contemporary gender issues that are a source of subjugation for women in Africa.

In Afua Kuma, as in most of the writings under review, salvation comes to women and men alike. Even so, she does have feminist consciousness. In Edet, this consciousness is overt in the very title that her paper displays, but even here the starting point is the universal appeal. She notes that Jesus is 'sensitive to the oppression of the weak and the helpless, took them on in his incarnation', as a carpenter's son from a nondescript town.[25] This is heightened by his interpretation of Messiahship, which he portrayed 'not as king but as a servant by contradicting in his life and person, the messianic expectation of Israel'. Jessica Nakawombe is even more overt in this regard. She states bluntly that:

> Jesus was born of Mary, a good and godly woman. She was the obedient vessel through which Christ was conceived of the Holy Spirit. She was given a unique part to play in the outworking of God's plan for the salvation of humankind, for the Incarnation and the virgin birth have had a tremendous significance for Christology.[26]

The women cling to the full humanity of the Christ in order to honour their own humanity and to insist on the link between the human and the divine in all persons as it was in Jesus. The church's imagery of Jesus, which marginalises women, is therefore non-biblical, and contemporary women theologians of other continents have traced the history of this state of affairs. For Edet, this process was most evident in the Constantinian era, with its return to the royal ideology of the Davidic Messiah that made the Christ the 'pantokrator', reinforcing the distance between Christ and the feminine.[27] The Jesus of African women's Christology is the Jesus of the Bible and of whatever scholarship aids the identification of this Jesus and the context in which he lived his earthly life.

Another historical development lifted up by Edet is the Aristotelian desecration of womanhood. This desacralisation of the feminine has succeeded in making the totality of the *imago dei* male, says Edet. Consequently women have had to lead the Christian community towards a 'return to the Christ of the gospels, his Person and his words and deeds'.[28] It is in this tradition that African women's Christology stands:

> Africans in general have a holistic view of life which demands a Christ who affects the whole of life for there is nothing that is not the realm of God if it is true that God made everything and keeps them in being. God as father is beneficent but there are good and evil forces operating in the world. These affect humanity. In short, a Nigerian woman is a victim of evil forces like witches, hunger, infant mortality as well as the triple oppression of culture, religion and socio-economy. How does Christ function within this situation? If Jesus did take on himself our weakness and injustice at his incarnation, then he is a suffering Christ, a liberating Christ and a friend.[29]

Continuing the Christological texts of African women, we call attention now to *Passion and Compassion*. In this publication, Térèsa Souga from Cameroun, writing on 'The Christ event', introduces her reflections with what she titles, 'My Act of Faith'. She has as her opening sentence, 'Jesus Christ means everything to me . . . Christ is the true Human, the one who makes it possible for all persons to reach fulfilment and to overcome the historic alienation weighing them down.'[30] Similarly, Afua Kuma would recite the traditional praise of enablers saying: Jesus is the big tree that makes it possible for the climbing plant to reach the sun. Souga's theology is deeply informed by Philippians 2[9−11], an affirmation of faith that enables her to link the suffering and resurrection of Jesus with women.[31] This, she says, is the source and motivation of African women's spirituality. She writes: 'The realism of the cross every day tells me, as a woman of the Third World, that the laws of history can be overcome by means of crucified love.'[32] Jesus bears a message of liberation for every human being and especially for those social categories that are most disadvantaged.

Jesus 'delivers women from every infirmity and suffering'.[33] Souga has in view Africa's threefold captivity – cultural, spiritual, socioeconomic – when she writes, 'there can be no understanding of Jesus Christ outside of the situation in which we seek to understand ourselves'.[34] 'It is by way of these situations that Jesus bears on his person the condition of the weak, and hence that of women' (Luke 2[6−7],[22−4]; John 2[46]).'[35] In the light of Christ, if Jesus is the God who has become weakness in our context, in his identity as God–Man, Jesus takes on the condition of the African woman. Souga surmises that the correlation between women's experience and liberation in Jesus Christ 'leads us to discover that Jesus reveals God in the various kinds of bonds connecting him to women throughout the Gospels'. Paul emphasises the realism of the incarnation with a legacy of faith saying, 'when the times were fulfilled, the son of God was born of a woman'.[36] Afua Kuma would have said Jesus is the royal one who chooses to live as the common poor so that the common poor might appropriate the dignity of being human:

> Looking at Africa, I wondered how I could write on a subject that
> suggests or points towards hope and renewed life in a continent that
> for decades has witnessed unending violence, suffering and death.
> A critical reflection on the resurrected Christ, the one Paul knew and
> wrote about in the epistles, however, reminded me of the crucified
> and suffering Christ who faced violence and death. The awareness
> gave me the courage to write about the labour pains experienced by all
> creation in Africa as a Christian woman.[37]

The image of Jesus as the suffering servant is very prominent in the writings of African women theologians. Most, like Edet and Njoroge, describe Jesus as identifying with the suffering of humanity, especially that of women. In this vein, Edet describes Jesus as 'the revelation of God's self-giving suffering and enduring love to humanity'.[38]

This suffering love moves into healing the hurts of humanity and so Christ the healer is very popular with church women. Ada Nyaga brings out the results of this love among human beings when she writes:

> Similarly, Jesus calls us to revise our ways of thinking and asks us to reconsider what it means to be a woman in our new understanding. Just as Jesus forced the ruler of a synagogue to reconsider what it means to work on the Sabbath, when he showed his compassion for a crippled woman by healing her (Luke 13[10–17]), there is an obvious need today to awaken women and free them from socio-cultural and theological restrictions based on a false understanding of the Bible.[39]

Suffering love operating in the incarnation wipes off the dirt that hides the glory of our true humanity, that which we believe is of the *imago dei*. Healing here includes liberating women from all evil and life-denying forces, enabling the fullness of all we know of perfect womanhood to be revealed. Jesus is the friend who enables women to overcome the difficulties of life and restore to them the dignity of being in the image of God, having annulled the stigma of blood taboos used as a separation of women's humanity. Akon E. Udo affirms that Jesus Christ has broken the barriers of distinction between men and women and used his precious blood to seal the broken relationships and to make men and women one in himself.[40] Amoah and Oduyoye state in *Passion and Compassion* that:

> the Christ for us is the Jesus of Nazareth who agreed to be God's 'Sacrificial Lamb', thus teaching that true and living sacrifice is that which is freely and consciously made; and who pointed to the example of the widow who gave all she had in response to God's love. Christ is the Jesus of Nazareth who approved of the costly sacrifice of the woman with the expensive oil, who anointed him (king, prophet, priest) in preparation for his burial, thereby also approving all that is noble, lovely, loving and motivated by love and gratitude.[41]

Louise Tappa of Cameroon in *Passion and Compassion*, states that '[t]he task of Christology is to work out the full meaning of the reality of the Christ-event for humankind'. The doctrinal Christology, which reduces the Christ to a positive but sublime abstraction, can be and is ignored 'when the time comes to translate it into the life of our communities'. She continues: '[t]hat is why even to the present it has been possible to interpret the doctrines of the incarnation (liberation) and of expiation (reconciliation) in terms that leave intact the social structures and models of our communities, including the church'.[42] Like Afua Kuma, Tappa proposes another procedure, which she says is much simpler, but no less Christological. It is to put more emphasis on the praxis of Jesus himself, even though she occasionally refers also to Jesus' teaching.

SUMMARY AND REFLECTIONS

These works and words of Jesus culled from the reflections of African women on Jesus, constitute the Christologies that they are developing and which embolden them to work and to speak for Jesus towards the liberation of the world in fulfilment of the *missio dei.* 'The Christ of history is the one who defined his mission as a mission of liberation' (Luke 4[18-19]). The Christ of dogma therefore plays only a marginal role in the women's affirmations about Jesus, who defined liberation by his quotation from Isaiah 61, and whose actions revealed that '[t]he truly spiritual is that which embraces all the material and physical life of the human being and our communities' (Mark 5[21-34]).[43]

In the same publication, Amoah and Oduyoye, writing on 'The Christ for African Women', point out that Jesus, the Messiah, is God-sent and the anointed of God. The messianic imagery is very powerful in Ghana and is reflected in Afua Kuma's praises that make references to what priests are teaching when they speak of deliverance. The influence of male theologians is evident in how large the cross looms in the theology of women like Afua Kuma. The cross, she says, 'has become the fishing net of Jesus. It is also the bridge from which Christians can jump into the pool of saving blood that leads to everlasting life.'[44] The emphasis of women, however, is not that we emulate the suffering, but that it becomes the source of our liberation. We do not only admire Jesus, but we are caught in the net of liberation which we believe will bring us into fullness of life:

> The Christ whom African women worship, honour and depend on is the victorious Christ, knowing that evil is a reality. Death and life-denying forces are the experience of women, and so Christ, who countered these forces and who gave back her child to the widow of Nain, is the African woman's Christ.[45]

Ghana must have great hunger in its history, as is evidenced in folk tales and legend. The more recent 1983 drought revives this reality, and so a Saviour is certainly the one who can keep us whole, integrating body and soul and enabling us to enhance the quality of our lives. Jesus of Nazareth was all of this; his earthly life and today his name and spirit keep the liberative ministry alive. With Jesus we do not need guns and bullets to make the enemy disappear, since, as Afua Kuma encourages us, we only need to 'tell Jesus'. 'I'm going to tell Jesus about it, today my husband is a lawyer. How eloquent he is!'[46]

Deliverance from death into life is often discussed by African women in the context of aspects of cultural practice that they experience as negative in their quest for fullness of life:

> This Christ is the liberator from the burden of disease and the
> ostracism of a society riddled with blood-taboos and theories of
> inauspiciousness arising out of women's blood. Christ liberated
> women by being born of Mary, demanding that the woman bent
> double with gynecological disorders should stand up straight. The
> practice of making women become silent 'beasts' of societies' burdens,
> bent double under racism, poverty, and lack of appreciation of what
> fullness of womanhood should be, has been annulled and countered
> by Christ. Christ transcends and transforms culture and has liberated
> us to do the same.[47]

African women's experiences lead them into Christological language that does not come to African men. Hence Tappa can say: 'I am convinced that Jesus died so that the patriarchal God might die and that Jesus rose so that the true God revealed in Jesus might rise in our lives, and in our communities.'[48]

Souga and others have reiterated that it is by self-emptying that we become filled with the spirit of Jesus. What African women reject is the combination of cross and sacrifice laid on them by people who have no intention of walking those paths themselves. They would argue that the calls to take up the cross and that to self-emptying are directed to all who would be called Christians; it is not sensitive to gender, race, or class. Amoah and Oduyoye, commenting on Kuma, highlight the same point.[49]

The vividness of this drama of jumping from bridges into pools of blood, even when blood has been the main source of their marginalisation, signifies the intensity of African women's spirituality of relating their lives to what the life of Jesus means to them. For them, Christology is not words or reasoning about Jesus, but an actuality in their lives. This is a life of faith, not of theological debates. It is a spirituality to overcome evil and oppression and to lift up constant thanks to God.

It is difficult to say whether the language of intimate relationships with Jesus, as used by African women, is to be read as eroticism or mysticism.

What is clear, however, is that their spirituality is the result of this type of Christology. They find an affirmation of their personhood and worth in the person of Jesus, born of a woman without the participation of a man. The significance for them is that 'womanness' contains the fullness of 'humanness'. By this they counter earlier assertions that a woman by herself is not fully human. This eroticism–mysticism enables them to understand suffering as related to crucified love with an anticipation of transformation and shalom.

Hinga has suggested that it is the lack of male companionship that drives women into the near-erotic language of Jesus as husband. Afua Kuma relies on Jesus, her husband, who is a lawyer who liberates her from the hands of oppressive legal procedures with his eloquence. The only time Jesus appeared in the diary of Dutch-Afrikaans woman, Alie Badenhorst (1866–1908), was when even God 'The Strong One, the Powerful Father in heaven' had seemed impotent to deliver her. When she thought her last hour had come, '[s]he left a message for her husband with her son, that she was going to Jesus and that she would wait for him there'.[50] Thus for her – as for many African women, products of the same European missionary theology – Jesus is the last sure haven. While life lasts, however, African women theologians would suggest that Christology should be about reclaiming and reasserting the role of 'Jesus Christ as Liberator and a saviour of women from all the oppressive contexts discussed, and empowerer of women in their contexts of powerlessness, and as their friend and ally in contexts of alienation and pain that women may be confronted with'.[51]

The Christology is reflected in the spirituality. African women produce very intimate, almost erotic language, about Jesus, a genre more akin to mysticism than theology. They sing lustily about 'Darling Jesus'; they sing:

> I am married to Jesus, Satan leave me alone.
> My husband is coming
> To take me away
> Into everlasting love.[52]

Afua Kuma is not afraid of court cases, for her 'husband' Jesus is a most eloquent lawyer. Christina Landman, who has documented *The Piety of South African Women* from diaries, has several examples of this language from both African and Afrikaner women of South Africa under the influence of European Calvinism. In the context of 'racial persecution (black women) and suburban boredom' for white women, pious women escaped 'into the arms of Jesus', who suffered for them and continues to suffer with them. Landman comments: 'where there is suffering, a woman is in control',[53] and oh, how Africa suffers. It is African women's experience that, where there is suffering, the powers that be, usually men, would allow women to take control. Women derive power from caring and being caregivers, a role which puts them on the side of the Christ. The hallowing of suffering however is rejected in the theology of several African women who see this as a source of patriarchal domestication. The cross and suffering of Jesus are not to be perpetuated but rather decried and prevented.

The victorious Christ of Afua Kuma is clearly the Jesus of the writing theologians. Jesus turns death into life and overcomes the life-denying forces that dog our way. He conquers death and restores life to all who believe in him. Having triumphed over death, he has become our liberator by countering women-denying culture. After all – is his own humanity not that of a woman?[54]

My reading of African women's theology is that they have had no problem of particularising the 'Christ of God' in the man of Nazareth. They know of saviours in their own histories; some are men, others are women. Their stance is that the maleness of Jesus is unjustly capitalised on by those who want to exclude women, but that does not detract from the fact that in Jesus' own practice, inclusion is the norm. What Edet says about the humanity of Jesus was that it is the humanity of woman, and African women should and do claim Jesus as their liberator. They claim the soundly constructed so-called feminine traits they find in Jesus – his care and compassion for the weak and excluded. The anti-hunger ministry, healing, and the place of children in his words and works – all go together to create a bonding around women's lives that African women feel with Jesus. He is one of us, knows our world, and can therefore accompany us in our daily joys and struggles.

What alienates some African women is the interpretation of revelation that suggests that before Jesus Africans had not encountered God and that without Jesus all are doomed. The Christian exclusiveness is in large measure not biblical and is therefore not allowed to become an obstacle in the multireligious communities of Africa. African women theologians have often reinterpreted the exclusiveness of John as a directive to walk in the path of Jesus. Elizabeth Amoah would say, 'Jesus is the only way' is a call to the recognition that to make salvation a reality for all, we all should walk in the way of Jesus and live the truth of the implication of a kenotic life.[55]

There has been no need to insist on the Christ as the wisdom of God. The biblical references to *Sophia* as eternally with God, has not played a significant role in this theology. What is clear is that the Wisdom language would be associated with fairness in dealings among humans and fidelity to the will of God that Jesus exemplified. Thus Christology is reflected in the spirituality.

African Christian women attribute the positive outcome of their endeavours to God or Jesus and to the guidance and protection of the Holy Spirit. They learn from biblical narrators and from stories of liberation that others have attributed to their faith in Jesus. They cling to their own faith in the liberating powers of Jesus and expect them to work in their own lives. Living under conditions of such hardship, African women and men have learnt to identify the good, attribute it to God in Christ, and live a life of prayer in the anticipation that the liberative potential of the person of Jesus will become a reality in their lives.

The victory of Jesus is not over other nations and cultures. It is over death and life-denying forces. The Jesus 'who countered these forces and gave back her child to the widow of Nain, is the African woman's Christ'. Jesus of Nazareth, by the counter-cultural relations he established with women, has become for us the Christ, the anointed one who liberates, the companion, friend, teacher, and true 'Child of Woman'. 'Child of Woman' truly, because in Christ the fullness of all that we know of perfect womanhood is revealed. The Christ for us is the Jesus of Nazareth who agreed to be God's sacrificial lamb, thus teaching that true and living sacrifice is that which is freely and consciously made. Jesus of Nazareth, designated 'the Christ', is the one who has broken down the barriers we have erected between God and us as well as among us. The Christ is the Reconciler calling us back to our true selves, to one another and to God, thereby saving us from isolation and alienation which is the lack of community that is the real experience of death.[56]

'The Christ of the women of Africa upholds not only motherhood, but all who like Jesus of Nazareth perform "mothering roles" of bringing out the best in all around them.' The present profit-centred economies of our world deny responsibly to bring life to the dying and to empower those challenged by the multitude of impairments that many have to live with. Justine Kahungu Mbwiti, in a study of Jesus and a Samaritan woman (John 4^{1-42}), draws out several of the images of Jesus that empower African women. As rural women, they see the scandal of the incarnation, the appearance of God in the hinterlands of the Roman Empire as God coming to their rural and slum situations. They relate to Jesus who deliberately shakes what was customary as a sign of renewal that opens for them the space to put critical questions to what was traditional. They referred to the scandalous action in the temple (John 2^{13-16}), and the many violations of the Sabbath (John 5^{1-18}), as affirmation that life is to be lived consciously and conscientiously.

Jesus becomes therefore not just the one by whom God saves; He is Himself the Saviour.[57]

We may conclude with another survey treatment of Christology in African women's theology, in Mabel Morny's contribution to *Talitha Qumi!*, 'Christ Restores to Life'. She states: 'When I think of liberation, a vision comes into my mind. A vision of a fuller and less injured life in a world where people can say "I" with happiness; a vision is a means of restoring life.'[58] Morny tries to develop an understanding of Christ as the liberator of all people; she writes as an African woman within the context of situations in Africa – cultural, social, religious, economic, and political. She writes in a context where women resort to Jesus as the liberator from bondage, all that makes them less than what God intended them to be. Christology becomes a study of the Jesus who responds to African women's experiences of fear, uncertainty, sickness, illiteracy, hunger, aggression by spouse, and distortion of the image of their humanity.

African women theologians think in inclusive terms, hence the emphasis on Jesus for all and particular contexts, peoples, and all situations. At the same time, they wish to maintain the relations the individual could establish with the Christ, as each is unique, and each a child of God. My reading of African women's Christology, as it appears in the writings of the Circle of Concerned African Women Theologians, may therefore be summed up in the words of the workshop on 'Jesus Christ and the liberation of women':

> Jesus Christ is liberator and a saviour of women from all the
> oppressive contexts discussed and empowerer of women in their
> contexts of powerlessness, and their friend and ally in the context of
> alienation and pain that women may be confronted with.[59]

Notes

1. In this series one finds J. N. K. Mugambi and Laurenti Magesi (eds.), *Jesus in African Christianity: Experimentation and Diversity in African Christology* (Nairobi: Initiatives Ltd., 1989); J. S. Pobee (ed.), *Exploring Afro-Christology* (Frankfurt and New York: Peter Lang Verlag, 1992); Enyi Ben Udoh, *Guest Christology: An Interpretative View of the Christological Problem in Africa* (Frankfurt and New York: Peter Lang Verlag, 1988).

2. Afua Kuma, *Jesus of the Deep Forest*, eds. and trans. Peter Kwasi Ameyaw, Fr. Jon Kirby SVD, et al. (Accra: Asempa Press, 1980). The rendering here is by Mercy Amba Oduyoye.

3. V. Fabella and M. A. Oduyoye (eds.), *With Passion and Compassion: Third World Women Doing Theology* (Maryknoll, NY: Orbis Press, 1988)

4. Since the initiation of the Circle of Concerned African Women Theologians in 1989, the following anthologies and four issues of *Amka* have been published: M. A. Oduyoye and M. R. A. Kanyoro (eds.), *Talitha Qumi!: Proceedings of the*

Convocation of African Women Theologians (Ibadan: Daystar Press, 1989 and 1990); M. A. Oduyoye and M. R. A. Kanyoro (eds.), *The Will to Arise: Women, Tradition and the Church in Africa* (Maryknoll: NY: Orbis Press, 1992); Rosemary N. Edet and Meg A. Umeagudosu (eds.), *Life, Women and Culture: Theological Reflections. Proceedings of the National Conference of the Circle of African Women Theologians 1990* (Lagos: African Heritage Research & Publications, 1991); Justine Kahungi Mbwiti and Couthon M. Fassinou, et al., *Le canari d'eau Fraiche ou L'hospitalité Africaine* (Lubumbashi: Éditions de Chemins de Vie, 1996); Musimbi R. A. Kanyoro and Nyambura J. Njoroge (eds.), *Groaning in Faith: African Women in the Household of God* (Nairobi: Acton Publishers, 1996); Elizabeth Amoah (ed.), *Where God Reigns: Reflections on Women in God's World* (Accra: Sam Woode Publishers, 1997); Grace Wamui and Mary Getui, *Violence Against Women: Reflections by Kenyan Women Theologians* (Nairobi: Acton Publishers, 1996); M. A. Oduyoye (ed.), *Transforming Power: Women in the Household of God*. Proceedings of the Pan-African Conference of the Circle of Concerned African Women Theologians (Accra: Sam Woode Publishers, 1997).

5. Robert Schreiter (ed.), *Faces of Jesus in Africa* (Maryknoll, NY: Orbis Press, 1988); Denise Ackermann, et al. (eds.), *Women Hold up Half the Sky: Women in the Church in South Africa* (Pietermaritzburg: Cluster Publications, 1991).

6. Mercy Amba Oduyoye, *Hearing and Knowing: Theological Reflections on Christianity in Africa* (Maryknoll, NY: Orbis Press, 1986); Teresa Okure, *Johannine Approach to Mission: A Contextual Study of John 4$^{1-42}$* (Tübingen: J. C. B. Mohr/ Paul Sieback Verlag, 1988); Christina Landman, *The Piety of South African Women* (Pretoria: C. B. Powell Bible Centre, UNISA, 1999).

7. Kuma, *Jesus*, p. 5.

8. Ibid.

9. Ibid.

10. Rosemary Edet, 'Christ and the Nigerian Womanhood', in Edet and Umeagudosu (eds.), *Life, Women and Culture*, p. 177.

11. Ibid.

12. Ibid. Note that inclusive language, even on the horizontal level, is not common with African women, most of whose mother-tongues have non-gendered pronouns and words for humanity.

13. Ibid., pp. 177–93.

14. A. E. Kwazu, 'Church Leadership and the Nigerian Woman', in Edet and Umeagudosu (eds.), *Life, Women and Culture*, p. 94.

15. Akon E. Udo, 'The Emerging Spiritualities of Women in Nigeria', in Edet and Umeagudosu (eds.), *Life, Women and Culture*, p. 102.

16. Akon E. Udo, 'Women in God's Household: Some Biblical Affirmations', in Amoah (ed.), *Where God Reigns*.

17. Musimbi Kanyoro, 'Daughter, Arise: Luke 8$^{40-56}$', in Oduyoye and Kanyoro (eds.), *Talitha Qumi!*, p. 59.

18. Teresa M. Hinga, 'Jesus Christ and the Liberation of Women in Africa', in Oduyoye and Kanyoro (eds.), *The Will to Arise*, p. 190.

19. Hinga, 'Jesus Christ', p. 191; See also Christine Landman, *The Piety of South African Women*, pp. 19, 51.

20. Hinga, 'Jesus Christ', p. 191.

21. Ibid., pp. 191–2.
22. Grace Duah, *Deliverance: Fact or Fantasy?* no publication details available
23. R. N. Edet, 'Christianity and African Women's Rituals', in Oduyoye and Kanyoro (eds.), *The Will to Arise*, pp. 26–9.
24. M. K. Obaga, 'Women are Members of God's Commonwealth', in Kanyoro and Njoroge (eds.), *Groaning in Faith*, p. 69.
25. Edet, 'Christ', p. 178.
26. J. K. Nakawombe, 'Women in the Kingdom of God', in Kanyoro and Njoroge (eds.), *Groaning in Faith*, p. 47. See also Betty Govinden on the link between Christology and Mariology in Kanyoro and Njoroge, *Groaning in Faith*, pp. 122–3.
27. Edet, 'Christ', p. 183. Note it seems, however, that, for women like Afua Kuma, this 'pantokrator' is not a distant emperor, but the African ruler into whose courts all can run for refuge, for food, for fairness, and fair-play.
28. Ibid., p. 184.
29. Ibid., pp. 184–5.
30. Térèsa Souga, 'The Christ Event from the Viewpoint of African Women: A Catholic Perspective', in Fabella and Oduyoye (eds.), *With Passion and Compassion*, p. 22.
31. Ibid., pp. 28–9.
32. Ibid., p. 22.
33. Ibid., p. 24.
34. Ibid., p. 26.
35. Ibid., p. 28.
36. Ibid.
37. Nyambura Njoroge, 'Groaning and Languishing in Labour Pains', in Kanyoro and Njoroge (eds.), *Groaning in Faith*, p. 4.
38. Edet, 'Christ', p. 185.
39. Ada Nyaga, 'Women's Dignity and Worth in God's Kingdom', in Kanyoro and Njoroge (eds.), *Groaning in Faith*, p. 81.
40. Akon E. Udo, 'Emerging Spiritualities of Women in Nigeria', in Edet and Umeagudosu (eds.), *Life, Women and Culture*, p. 105.
41. Oduyoye and Amoah, 'The Christ for African Women', in Fabella and Oduyoye (eds.), *With Passion and Compassion*, p. 44. The sacrifice involved in the widow's mite, however, does raise a question. Is Jesus only approving her action or also illustrating how religious obligations can rob the poor of even the little they have for sustaining their lives?
42. Louise Tappa, 'The Christ-Event: A Protestant Perspective', in Fabella and Oduyoye (eds.), *With Passion and Compassion*, p. 31.
43. Ibid., pp. 31–2.
44. As quoted by Oduyoye and Amoah in 'The Christ for African Women', p. 43.
45. Oduyoye and Amoah, ibid.
46. Kuma, *Jesus*, p. 42.
47. Oduyoye and Amoah, 'The Christ for African Women', p. 43.
48. Tappa, 'The Christ-Event', p. 34.
49. Oduyoye and Amoah, 'The Christ for African Women', p. 44.
50. Landman, *Piety*, p. 63.

51. Oduyoye and Kanyoro, *Talitha Qumi!*, p. 206.
52. Conversations on Christology with Pastor Pamela Martin, Baptist from Cameroon, November 1999.
53. Landman, *Piety*, p. 29.
54. Edet, 'Christ', p. 187.
55. Conversations on Christology with Dr Elizabeth Amoah, June 1999.
56. Landman, *Piety*, p. 34.
57. J. K. Mbwiti, 'Jesus and the Samaritan Woman', in Oduyoye and Kanyoro (eds.), *Talitha Qumi!*, pp. 63–76. At the time of writing, the name of the country was Zaire and is now the Democratic Republic of the Congo, a nation still crying for *shalom.*
58. Mabel S. Morny, 'Christ Restores to Life', in Oduyoye and Kanyoro (eds.), *Talitha Qumi!*, pp. 145–9.
59. Workshop on 'Jesus Christ and the Liberation of the African Woman', in Oduyoye and Kanyoro (eds.), *Talitha Qumi!*, p. 206.

Selected reading

Brock, Rita Nakashima. *Journeys by Heart: A Christology of Erotic Power*, New York: Crossroad, 1988.
Carr, Anne. *Transforming Grace: Christian Tradition and Women's Experience*, San Francisco, CA: Harper & Row, 1988.
Fabella, Virginia and Oduyoye, Mercy Amba (eds.). *With Passion and Compassion: Third World Women Doing Theology*, Maryknoll, NY: Orbis Press, 1988.
Grant, Jacquelyn. *White Women's Christ and Black Women's Jesus: Feminist Christology and Womanist Response*, Atlanta, GA: Scholars Press, 1989.
Grey, Mary. *Redeeming the Dream: Feminism, Redemption and Christian Tradition*, London: SPCK, 1989.
Johnson, Elizabeth. *Consider Jesus: Waves of Renewal in Christology*, London: Geoffrey Chapman, 1990.
Schüssler Fiorenza, Elisabeth. *Miriam's Child, Sophia's Prophet: Critical Issues in Feminist Christology*, London: SCM Press, 1994.
Stevens, M. (ed.). *Reconstructing the Christ Symbol: Essays in Feminist Christology*, New York: Paulist Press, 1993.
Tamez, Elsa. *Through Her Eyes: Women's Theology from Latin America*, Maryknoll, NY: Orbis Press, 1989.
Wilson-Kastner, Patricia. *Faith, Feminism and the Christ*, Philadelphia, PA: Fortress Press, 1983.

10 The Holy Spirit and spirituality
NICOLA SLEE

INTRODUCTION

The Holy Spirit, it is often noted, has been much neglected in Western theology and, when given serious theological consideration, usually subordinated to the Father and the Son, a kind of Cinderella of the Trinity. Alwyn Marriage comments: 'There is little doubt that our doctrine of the Holy Spirit is one of the least developed areas in mainstream Christianity.'[1] Elizabeth Johnson notes the variety of metaphors employed by contemporary theologians to express this neglect of the Spirit: the Spirit is imaged as 'faceless' (Walter Kasper), 'shadowy' (John Macquarrie), 'ghostly' (Georgia Harkness), or 'anonymous', the 'poor relation' in the Trinity (Norman Pittenger), the 'unknown' or 'half-known' God (Yves Congar); in Johnson's own phrase, the Spirit is the 'forgotten God'.[2]

Multiple reasons may be adduced for this Western neglect of pneumatology: the comparative paucity of scriptural reflection on the Spirit, coupled with the mysterious nature of the scriptural images and narratives which do exist; the pattern of classical theology which proceeded from consideration of the Father to the Son and only 'in third place' to the Spirit so that treatment of the Spirit often received short shrift; the privatisation of the Spirit's activity to the sanctification of the individual in post-Reformation Protestantism, mirrored by the displacement of the Spirit's functions onto the pope, the Blessed Sacrament, or the Virgin Mary in post-Tridentine Catholicism; and, most significant for our reflections, the association of the Spirit in the Bible with female imagery and experience so that the Spirit became marginalised and repressed just as women themselves did.

For, in contrast to the dominant biblical metaphors and models for God and Christ, which are largely masculine, the central biblical metaphors for the Spirit – *ruah*, *shekinah*, and *hokmah* or *sophia* – are either female or gender non-specific, offering support for the notion of a feminine Spirit which, though largely repressed in Christian tradition, has nevertheless persisted,

and re-emerged in our own time in a renewed debate about the appropriateness of naming the Spirit in explicitly female terms. Whatever the merits
or dangers of such female naming of the Spirit, the point here is that the
neglect of the Spirit seems to bear some direct relation to the repression and
marginalisation of women themselves in Christian tradition. The hidden-
ness, anonymity, and invisibility of women is mirrored and reflected in the
facelessness and namelessness of the Spirit in Christian worship, theology,
and life.

At first sight, this neglect of the Spirit appears to be repeated in feminist
theology itself. In comparison with the large body of feminist scholarship
on models of God and on Christology, there is comparatively little sustained
theological reflection on the Spirit. However, the lack of works explicitly
devoted to the Spirit should not be taken as a measure of the liveliness
of feminist pneumatology, but rather as an indication that we must look
elsewhere for the signs of such flourishing. Whilst systematic treatises on
the Spirit are rare, much creative thinking about the person and work of the
Spirit is to be found within the wider feminist reappraisal of God-language,
and within the rapidly expanding field of feminist spirituality. Reflecting
the wider experiential bias within feminist theology, such work is rooted
first and foremost in women's concrete, historical experience, and only gives
rise secondarily to abstract theological reflection.

Mirroring this priority of experience over abstraction, historical spirituality over abstract speculation about the Holy Spirit, I intend in this chapter
first to consider ways in which feminists are engaged in reappropriating
women's spirituality, both from the past and in the present, before going
on to consider how the person and work of the Spirit per se is understood
in the work of some feminist theologians.

RECOVERING WOMEN'S SPIRITUALITY

Women have, of course, always practised faith, prayed, and lived lives of
holiness (often more devoutly than men!); and all the major world religions
honour at least a handful of women saints. In Christianity, women such as
Julian of Norwich, Teresa of Avila, and Catherine of Siena have long been
revered, with their own feast days and traditions of devotion. Nevertheless,
women's experiences of faith have gone largely unrecorded down the ages
and women's spirituality has been a mostly 'hidden tradition'.[3] This is for a
variety of reasons: partly because, until modern times, women's spirituality
was exercised mostly in the home (whether family or religious community)
and thus took expression in the care and nurture of others and in what

Johnson describes as 'the renewal of the fabric of life, the replenishment of physical and spiritual sustenance';[4] partly because, when women did express their faith in more tangible form, it tended to be through small-scale and occasional means such as journals, letters, hymns, poems, or crafts which have not been accorded public recognition; and partly because of more overt male suppression. Women form the largest of the 'groups that did not fit', in Philip Sheldrake's term, into the dominant forms of institutional spirituality which were dictated by a male, clerical and celibate elite, and controlled by the priorities of orthodoxy, conformity to the centre, and the repression of pluralism.[5] As a result, women's spirituality was often forced into marginal, compensatory, or dissenting forms existing in uneasy tension with 'mainstream', clerically sanctioned patterns. Where women such as Teresa of Avila or Julian of Norwich were accorded some recognition, 'their lives were recorded selectively for institutional purposes in such a way as not to disturb time-honoured patterns of attitude and behaviour'.[6]

Though marginalised, sanitised, and repressed, however, the writings and exploits of women of faith have not been entirely lost, and much historical scholarship over the past two or three decades has been dedicated to rediscovering these forgotten female spiritual traditions. Research by Elaine Pagels and others, for example,[7] suggests that, in the early Christian movement, gnostic sects provided a significant *locus* for women's spirituality. Though notoriously difficult to define and delineate, it seems clear that the gnostic communities offered an arena, over and against the increasingly patriarchal structures of the church, where some degree of gender equality was practised. Emphasising an internal *locus* of religious authority in spiritual *gnosis*, rather than in obedience to canon, creed, or bishop, the gnostic communities offered women freedom to exercise leadership and employed feminine images for God in their stories and rites (although, given the extreme dualism and body-denying emphasis of these groups, such imagery is not necessarily entirely positive).

Within the orthodox Christian movement itself, martyrdom, monasticism, and mysticism offered women alternatives to the dominant cultural norms of marriage, motherhood, and domesticity. Early post-canonical records preserve the heroic faith of such martyrs as Perpetua and Blandina, while others, such as Thecla, though thrown to the wild beasts, were miraculously saved.[8] The free commitment of virgins and widows, and the creation of a distinct lifestyle within the Christian community, has roots in the canonical period, and was certainly well established by the late third century.[9] Although religious life, as it developed, came to be much more highly circumscribed for women than for men, as is evident in the far stricter rules of enclosure which applied to women, it nevertheless provided women with a means of education, interior freedom, and spiritual development hardly imaginable within the context of ceaseless childbearing and domestic duty which was the lot of the vast majority.

The late medieval period saw a particularly fecund flowering of women's spirituality within and on the edges of the religious orders, and the development of new forms of religious life for women, each with their own distinctive patterns of prayer and mysticism. Caroline Walker Bynum's work has done much to stimulate awareness of, and deepen interest in, women's spirituality of this era, as well as to demonstrate the inbuilt biases of earlier accounts of medieval mysticism which focussed on male interests and experience, rendering invisible the concerns of women's lives.[10] Bynum describes the range of forms which women's religious life took during this period, from the formation of peripatetic bands which followed wandering preachers to the founding of many new religious orders or the reform of existing orders, and the development of new forms of religious association such as the Beguines and the tertiaries. The Beguine movement – a lay religious movement of women living both singly and in community who took temporary vows of chastity and obedience but maintained their own property and income – has attracted particular interest.[11] Whilst these various forms of religious life were distinctive, Bynum argues that there are discernible differences between male and female religious experience of this period which generally hold true across the varieties of religious life:

> Mysticism was more central in female religiosity and in female claims to sanctity than in men's, and paramystical phenomena . . . were far more common in women's mysticism. Women's reputations for holiness were more often based on supernatural, charismatic authority, especially visions and supernatural signs. Women's devotion was more marked by penitential asceticism, particularly self-inflicted suffering, extreme fasting and illness borne with patience. Women's writing was, in general, more affective . . . erotic, nuptial themes, which were first articulated by men, were most fully elaborated in women's poetry. And certain devotional emphases, particularly devotion to Christ's suffering humanity and to the Eucharist (although not, as is often said, to the Virgin) were characteristic of women's practices and women's words.[12]

It is not difficult to see how these emphases represent a kind of compensatory channelling of women's spirituality into permissible forms. Denied liturgical office, authority had to come from supernatural sources rather than institutional ones; denied the possibility of consecrating the sacraments, women could nevertheless channel their adoration of the Eucharist into intense mystical devotion; denied overt expression, women's sexuality found shape in erotic devotion to Christ; denied official religious power, women could assume control over their bodies and food and thus tacitly transcend patriarchal rule.

Nevertheless, the expression of women's spirituality walked a tightrope between acceptability to the institution and its male leadership, on the one hand, and suspicion, repression, and control on the part of the hierarchy on the other. The history of the Beguine movement provides an illustration of this tension, as do the records of other movements in which women exercised some degree of freedom, such as the Quakers in seventeenth-century England and the Shakers in eighteenth-century America. Despite popular acclaim, the Beguines were viewed with suspicion from the beginning. Their lay composition, loose association, and freedom from direct male control made them an obvious target for clerical repression. Persecution of the Beguines was sporadic during the thirteenth-century and culminated in their condemnation by the Council of Vienna in 1312, which led to widespread persecution, the confiscation of their property, and their absorption into religious orders. Where the institution could not absorb women's spirituality into its own stringently controlled channels, it exorcised it as deviant and heretical, or repressed it in the hope of destroying it altogether.

The recovery of women's lost traditions can lead to mixed reactions from present-day women – and men – of faith. On the one hand, the discovery of the wealth and depth of women's spiritual traditions may evoke joy and a sense of empowerment in contemporary believers. On the other hand, the reality of the suppression and marginalisation of women's traditions can generate anger and pain and increase a contemporary sense of alienation. The more scholarship restores to wider consciousness an awareness of women's hidden spiritual traditions, the more widely recognised it is that these recovered traditions themselves merely represent the tip of an iceberg of submerged histories, most of which, we must assume, are lost for ever, never to be reclaimed from the depths of patriarchal memory. The legacy of this work of recovery is thus a complex one.

CREATING FEMINIST SPIRITUALITY

Alongside the resurgence of interest in women's past spiritual traditions, the last two or three decades have been marked by an extraordinary flourishing of contemporary feminist spirituality movements worldwide. Existing within the mainstream churches, at their edges and, in some cases, in radical opposition to orthodox Christianity, these movements display a confusing yet lively diversity, witnessing in their various ways to the freedom of the Spirit which blows where it will.

Feminist spirituality, in contrast to women's spirituality more generally, arises from the consciousness of women's oppression and is a quest to overcome women's marginalisation in religion as in every other sphere of life. As Anne Carr suggests:

> A feminist spirituality would be distinguished from any other as a spiritual orientation which has integrated into itself the central elements of feminist consciousness. It is the spirituality of those who have experienced feminist consciousness raising . . . A specifically feminist spirituality . . . would be that mode of relating to God, and everyone and everything in relation to God, exhibited by those who are deeply aware of the historical and cultural restriction of women to a narrowly defined 'place' within the wider human (male) 'world'. Such awareness would mean that we are self-consciously critical of the cultural and religious ideologies which deny women full opportunities for self-actualisation and self-transcendence.[13]

Feminist spirituality, in this sense, is a very broad-ranging movement, and takes expression in all of the major world religions, including Christianity, as well as in movements such as paganism and Wicca. There are also many women with no formal allegiance to any religious group who express their spiritual commitments in other ways, perhaps through work for justice, therapy, ecofeminism, or the arts. There is thus no *one* feminist spirituality, but many different traditions, movements, and forms.

Whilst the range and fluidity of these movements defies easy categorisation, it may be helpful to give an indication of some of the different groupings, at the same time as recognising that, in practice, these groupings often overlap or merge with each other at the edges. Perhaps to speak of a spectrum is a more accurate image. At one end of the spectrum, one can identify a broad range of groups and movements within mainstream Christianity which are committed to celebrating past women's spiritual traditions, employing female imagery and symbolism in contemporary worship and prayer, and reshaping the understanding of what it means to follow Christ in the world in the light of women's experiences. Writers such as Elaine Storkey and Margaret Hebblethwaite in England, Kathleen

Fischer and Anne Carr in the United States, Elizabeth Moltmann-Wendel and Catharina Halkes in Germany and the Netherlands, and Mercy Amba Oduyoye and Musimbi Kanyoro in Africa represent such a movement,[14] as does the great outpouring of creative feminist liturgy by groups as well as individuals in many parts of the world.[15]

Moving along the spectrum, there are a whole range of groups which exist rather more on the margins of institutional church life, often in somewhat uneasy tension with the institution and its sanctioned traditions. These groups seek to forge some sort of creative dialogue between orthodox Christian tradition, on the one hand, and other faith traditions or secular movements on the other, in the process developing a distinctive feminist identity which owes much to Christian roots but also draws on other heritages. Here one might include indigenous feminist Christian movements such as those being developed by African, Afro-Caribbean, Indian, Japanese, Chinese, and Latin American women.[16] A vivid example of this movement was witnessed at the World Council of Churches Assembly in Canberra in 1991 when the South Korean theologian Chung Hyun Kyung gave a presentation on the Holy Spirit in which she invoked the Spirit in a multiplicity of images drawn from many traditions.[17] Calling upon 'the presence of all our ancestors' spirits', she named them 'icons of the Holy Spirit' because of whom 'we can feel, touch and taste the concrete bodily historical presence of the Holy Spirit in our midst'.[18] This claim is echoed by thousands of other Christians living in lands where colonial missionary activity ruthlessly suppressed their forebears' spiritual traditions. Now they are reclaiming them and finding ways to integrate indigenous and Christian spiritual sources, in a new naming of the Spirit. Part of this movement of reclamation entails the retrieval of repressed female religious imagery from indigenous traditions. Thus Aruna Gnanadason, an Indian theologian, seeks to reintegrate the worship of Shakti, the Hindu Mother goddess, with the emerging Asian women's spirituality in the church,[19] whilst Hyung Kyung draws on the image of Kwan Yin, the Buddhist goddess of compassion and wisdom, to speak of the Holy Spirit.[20]

Paralleling indigenous Christian feminist movements in Asia and elsewhere, the women–church movement has been particularly significant in North America, Canada, and Europe. Originating in the 1980s in the United States, women–church has now spread to become a 'global movement of women seeking authentic ecclesial communities of justice',[21] although not all such movements would describe themselves by its name. Existing on the margins of institutional church life, 'Womenchurch is neither a new Church nor an exodus from the established churches', according to Mary Grey. Rather, 'it is both an attempt to make it clear, after years of being marginalised from church structures, that *women are church*, and to recover authentic inclusive, justice-based communities, responding to the reality that within the present structures, many women and men receive no nurture in faith'.[22]

As well as women–church and indigenous feminist Christian movements, one might also include in this second broad category of dialogic movements a whole range of groups which, amongst other concerns, are actively engaged in envisioning new forms of relation between men and women and new, more gender-inclusive patterns of spirituality. For example, Matthew Fox's Creation-centred spirituality movement[23] represents one attempt, amongst many, to re-appropriate female spiritual traditions from the past as well as to take seriously women's experiences in the present in the forging of a new spirituality. Again, some of the men's movements which are springing up in the United States and elsewhere are attempting to take seriously the feminist critique of religion and to learn from feminists in the forging of a masculine spirituality which does not simply reinforce patriarchal models of maleness.[24]

Beyond such movements which seek to maintain dialogue between Christian faith and other religious or secular traditions, a third broad category of feminist spiritual movements is dedicated to the celebration of female spiritual power in opposition to, or in protest against, the repression of the female in institutional, patriarchal religion. These would be located at the opposite end of our spectrum. Goddess, Wicca, and witchcraft movements may all be seen as examples of this third grouping which is more antithetical to Christianity, although, even here, there is some overlapping of purpose, for example amongst Christian feminists who draw upon goddess movements in their renaming of the divine. The Wicca or witchcraft movement, which stands in sharp opposition to Satanism and so-called 'black' witchcraft, sees itself as continuing the tradition of historical wise women down the ages who, in all societies, were healers and repositories of natural and spiritual wisdom. The movement is concerned with the performance of sacred rites to help shape or turn energy and events to promote beneficially the affairs of individuals or society.[25] Emphasis is placed upon the Goddess or female spiritual principle, upon the sacredness of matter and upon the development of intuitive wisdom. Whilst Wicca is practised by both men and women, there is a distinctive feminist Wicca movement represented by writers such as Budapest and Starhawk.[26]

The interest in the goddess in contemporary feminist spirituality takes a number of different forms and has different meanings. Carol Christ distinguishes between three such meanings: first, there is the goddess as divine female existing in different cultural manifestations who is invoked in prayer and ritual; second, there is the goddess as symbol of 'life, death and rebirth energy in nature and culture'; third, there is the goddess as affirmation of 'the legitimacy and beauty of female power'.[27] The second and third of these understandings see the goddess as symbol rather than metaphysical reality. Some warn of the dangers of the goddess movement in encouraging a sentimentalised and essentialist notion of female spirituality, and critique some of its adherents' more dubious historical claims.[28] Nevertheless, the representation of divinity in embodied female form which goddess traditions preserve seems to offer many women a means of self-discovery and affirmation, as well as connection to the divine, which other forms of spiritual tradition cannot. As Carol Christ testifies:

> For me and for many others, finding the Goddess has felt like coming home to a vision of life that we had always known deeply within ourselves: that we are part of nature and that our destiny is to participate fully in the cycles of birth, death, and renewal that characterize life on this earth. We find in the Goddess a compelling image of female power, a vision of the deep connection of all beings in the web of life, and a call to create peace on earth.[29]

The imaging of divinity in female form offers both a critique of patriarchal appropriation of divinity and a clear symbol of the goodness, beauty and sacredness of the female.

CHARACTERISTICS OF FEMINIST SPIRITUALITIES

Whilst it may be foolhardy to attempt to generalise about this enormously diverse movement of feminist spiritualities, there do appear to be certain trends or emphases which, if not universal, are nevertheless pervasive enough to invite comment. I shall draw attention here to five such trends which, I suggest, can offer new ways of conceptualising the work of the Holy Spirit in the world.

First, there is a strong emphasis on *desire, eros,* and *passion* in much contemporary feminist spirituality which may be seen as a reconceptualisation of the Spirit's work of inspiring, energising, and enlivening faith in ways which take seriously the human body, emotions, and drives. Matthew Fox suggests that 'a feminist spirituality as distinct from a patriarchal one will value the erotic and teach us disciplines of erotic celebrating, creating and justice-making'.[30] Writers such as Audre Lorde, Carter Heyward, and Mary Hunt have been influential in reclaiming the erotic from the context of sexuality narrowly perceived to a wider social and spiritual setting.[31] Lorde speaks of the erotic as 'an assertion of the life force of women',[32] whilst Heyward conceptualises it as the power of love which drives towards connection and right relation in both interpersonal and transpersonal relations, and which is rooted in the fundamental reality of God who is the power of connection.[33] Such a reclamation of the language of passion and desire leads to a revaluing of the human body and emotions, and a sense of connection between the personal and the political which has always been the hallmark of feminism.

Secondly, there is an emphasis on *relationality, connectedness*, and *community* in feminist spiritualities which invites new ways of grasping the work of the Holy Spirit in forging bonds and creating *koinonia*. This emphasis on relationality is very closely connected to the understanding of eros outlined above, and is particularly evident in the work of Carter Heyward and Mary Grey,[34] but it is also shared by others. For example, Katherine Zappone suggests: 'in its broadest sense, spirituality centres on our awareness and experience of relationality. It *is* the relational component of lived experience.'[35] She goes on to delineate spirituality in terms of right relation to self, to other, to the earth, and to the sacred. Charlene Spretnak speaks of spirituality as a dynamic impulse towards connectedness in human relationships, social structures, and the wider cosmos: 'Spirituality enables us to feel a deep connection between one another. It heals and avoids the fragmented sense that often plagues political movements, in both personal and collective terms. Our bonding is profound.'[36] Carter Heyward and Mary Grey root such an understanding of spirituality in a philosophical and theological analysis of reality which sees connectedness and relationality at the heart of existence, as well as of the essence of divinity. Thus Heyward speaks of God who is intimately related to the world, who is source of all relational power and active justice-seeking, and who calls for the voluntary participation of human beings in making right relation on the earth here and now:

> Without our touching there is no God.
> Without our relation there is no God.
> Without our crying, our raging, our yearning, there is no God.
> For in the beginning is the relation, and in the relation is the power
> that creates the world through us, and with us, and by us, you and I,
> you and we, and none of us alone.[37]

This emphasis on connectedness and relationality in the work of white feminist theologians has been critiqued by some as a denial of difference and the imposition of false connection between those who are divided by injustice and oppression.[38] On the other hand, many so-called 'Third World' feminist theologians echo the emphasis on connection via a stress on the work of the Spirit in building community, not only within the church but within wider society. Elizabeth Dominguez from the Philippines writes of the image of God in terms of 'the community in relationship', marked by interdependence, harmony, and mutual growth,[39] whilst Aruna Gnanadason suggests that this affirmation of community is, in fact, 'the most important characteristic of Asian women's spirituality'.[40] She describes it as 'the search for a community of people where all will find space for creativity and fulfilment, a community that will live in real peace with justice, a community that will be ever alert to its responsibility to give birth to new life by challenging forces of death'.[41]

The search for right relation in communities as well as interpersonal relations is closely connected to the strong note of *judgment* and *justice* in feminist spiritualities, which takes different forms in different cultural contexts and points to the work of the Holy Spirit in convicting of sin and impelling towards righteousness. There is a strong commitment to justice and the redemption of political and structural relationships, so that spirituality is not confined to the interpersonal sphere but extends to the larger web of social structures which undergird and shape personal relationships. This commitment to justice finds expression in an emphasis on liberation and empowerment in the spiritualities of southern hemisphere feminists which, in common with the bias of liberation theologies in general, insists that liberation is not merely an internal affair but requires living out within the conditions of this world. There is an insistence on wholeness and fullness of life as the goal of spirituality, a renewed appreciation of the work of the Spirit in bringing forth and nurturing life.[42]

Alongside the stress on human liberation and empowerment, feminist spiritualities also demonstrate a passionate commitment to the liberation of the earth. The stress on relationality noted above includes a strong sense of connectedness to the earth and to matter, and is thus explicitly incarnational and sacramental. Feminist analysis demonstrates how both the demise of nature and the oppression of women have gone hand in hand, reinforcing and supporting each other within the dualistic framework of patriarchy.[43] Conversely, the liberation of women logically entails the liberation of the earth, and the spiritual praxis of feminists includes a strong commitment to recreating a renewed relation to the earth, reflected in understandings of the universe as the 'body of God', and a stress on the immanence of the divine presence within the world rather than beyond it, as well as in the broad movement of ecofeminist theology and spirituality.[44]

Closely connected to the justice and life orientation of feminist spirituality, there is also a stress on *holism, integration,* and *inclusivity* which highlights the immanent presence of the Spirit at work in the whole created order and in all human efforts towards justice and truth, wherever they are to be found. There is a rejection of dualism which separates super-nature and nature, spirit and matter, humanity and nature, mind and body, spirituality and sexuality; and an affirmation of the essential interdependence of all things. Thus, Carr suggests that 'spirituality is holistic, encompassing our relationships to all of creation – to others, to society and nature, to work and recreation – in a fundamentally religious orientation'.[45] The strong life-orientation of feminist spiritualities leads to a willingness to affirm as good all that makes for life, whatever its source or provenance, and an openness to recognise the work of the Spirit in all justice and peace movements and in all people of goodwill. Thus there tends to be an inclusivity and catholicity in much feminist spirituality, demonstrated in what we described above in terms of a dialogic approach to other traditions and sources of wisdom.

RENEWING THEOLOGY OF THE SPIRIT

Out of this flowering of lived spiritualities, new understandings of the person and work of the Spirit are being forged by feminist theologians, and I have already attempted to indicate what some of these might be in the emphases elaborated above. As well as these emphases characteristic of feminist spiritualities, there is also more explicit and systematic work by feminist theologians to reframe a theology of the Spirit in terms commensurate with women's lived spirituality.

Some feminists have welcomed and embraced an approach shared with a number of contemporary male theologians of speaking of the Spirit as the feminine dimension in God and naming the Spirit in feminine imagery and terms. This approach has ancient roots in early Semitic and Syrian traditions, which took the cue from scriptural female Spirit imagery to speak of the Spirit as the mother who brings to birth Christ in the incarnation, new members of the body of Christ in the waters of baptism, and the body of Christ through the *epiclesis* of the Eucharist. Recent examples of this approach are to be found in Congar's naming of the Spirit as the feminine person in God, Boff's alignment of the Spirit with Mary as the maternal face of God,

Gelpi's reappropriation of the feminine archetype in his theology of 'Holy Breath', and Marriage's notion of the Spirit as 'the mother who lets us go'.[46]

Whilst appreciating the efforts of these theologians to retrieve an ancient tradition, Elizabeth Johnson agrees with Sarah Coakley[47] that the result is unsatisfactory, for a number of reasons. The approach is essentially compensatory rather than radically creative. The overarching framework of such theologies 'remains androcentric, with the male principle still dominant and sovereign', the third female person or principle subordinate to the male.[48] In addition, the female naming of the Spirit relies on essentialising stereotypes of the feminine which is variously identified with mothering, affectivity, darkness, or virginity. The result, as Coakley puts it, 'is often an idealised, mawkish, or sentimentalised version of the "feminine", one that is still covertly negative'.[49] Furthermore, Johnson suggests, the language of 'dimensions' within the Godhead 'ontologises sex in God, making sexuality a dimension of divine being, rather than respecting the symbolic nature of religious language'.[50]

A more radical approach, represented by theologians such as Johnson and McFague, requires a wholesale re-evaluation of all God-language, not simply the feminisation of the Spirit. Thus, these theologians attempt to restate a theology of the Spirit within a wider framework of a reworking of Trinitarian theology per se. Such an approach is to be distinguished from the naming of feminine traits or dimensions in God; rather, it proposes 'speech about God in which the fullness of female humanity as well as of male humanity and cosmic reality may serve as divine symbol, in equivalent ways'.[51] Johnson's impressive study of God-language is a creative example of this approach, in which she attempts a systematic Trinitarian theology rooted in women's experience of the Spirit. In contrast to classical theologies which began either with the unity of divine nature or the 'first person' of the Trinity, Johnson takes her starting point from the Spirit, 'God's livingness subtly and powerfully abroad in the world'.[52] Beginning with interpreted experience of the Spirit, Johnson draws on scriptural traditions of Spirit–Shekinah, Wisdom–*Sophia*, and Mother imagery to develop a Trinitarian theology of Spirit–*Sophia*, 'divinity drawing near and passing by'; Jesus–*Sophia*, 'wisdom made flesh', and Mother–*Sophia*, 'unoriginate origin'. Together, these namings of the *Sophia* God point us towards the triune God, mystery of relation who may be spoken of as 'SHE WHO IS':

> the one whose very nature is sheer aliveness, is the profoundly relational source of the being of the whole universe, still under

historical threat. She is the freely overflowing wellspring of the energy of all creatures who flourish, and of the energy of all those who resist the absence of her flourishing, both made possible by participating in her dynamic act. In the power of her being she causes to be. In the strength of her love she gives her name as the faithful promise always to be there amidst oppression to resist and bring forth.[53]

McFague's development of new *Models of God*[54] shares in common with Johnson a radical critique of patriarchal religious imagery and an attempt to rework the whole Trinitarian schema. The root model McFague offers is the agential–organic one of the world as the body of God, in opposition to the monarchical model of God as transcendent King ruling over his world. 'Spirit' within the terms of this analogy, is to be understood both as breath and life which animates the world (body), and as Holy Spirit which renews and directs life towards ever more inclusive love. 'Spirit' in McFague's theology thus becomes the major metaphor for understanding the agency of God within the world. McFague prefers it to other agential terms such as 'self', 'mind', or 'will' because of its capacity to undercut anthropocentrism and promote cosmocentricism (only a human being has mind or self, whereas spirit has a much broader range); and because it calls attention to relationship at the deepest level as the connection between God and world – 'it underscores the connection between God and the world as not primarily the Mind that orders, controls and directs the universe, but as the Breath that is the source of its life and vitality'.[55] In contrast to Johnson, McFague prefers to maintain gender neutrality in her speech about the Spirit:

> It may be best that, for once in Christian reflection, we let God be 'it'. 'It' (the divine spirit) roams where it will, not focussed on the like-minded (the fathers and the sons – or even the mothers and the daughters), but permeating, suffusing, and energising the innermost being of each and every entity in creation in ways unknown and unknowable in our human, personal categories.[56]

Accordingly, of McFague's three proposed models of God, only one, Mother, is specifically female, whilst the other two – Lover and Friend – may be male or female. McFague develops these models in creative and challenging ways, not as analogues of the personal relationship between God and the individual, but as models of the relation between God and the world. To name God as Mother, for example, suggests new ways of envisaging the relation between the universe and God as intimately interconnected, rather than distinct and separate; it suggests a co-dependency and mutuality between God and the world, for to the Mother, the world is offspring, beloved, and companion; and it points to an ethic of justice rooted in the agapic love of the Mother God who affirms the existence of the world which is her body and desires all to share in the fullness of life.[57]

Such brief summaries of complex and sophisticated theologies cannot do them justice, but may be enough to hint at the creative ways in which Johnson and McFague, and others like them, are reimaging the nature and work of the Spirit in ways which are renewing for all theology and faith.

CONCLUSION

Feminist spiritualities and theologies of the Spirit can both be understood as part of a wider movement within contemporary culture to critique, enliven, and transform institutional forms of faith, and, at the same time, as one of the most significant contributions to that wider movement. Within the maelstrom of this movement, feminist spiritualities partake of both the strengths and weaknesses of other forms of contemporary spirituality: pluriform and dynamic, eclectic and fluid in form, they can be utopian and romantic, strong on experience but weak on doctrine, mirroring rather than critiquing the fragmented society of which they are a part. Not all of these movements are to be applauded; the New Testament injunction to 'test the spirits' is as relevant today as it was then.[58] Yet, at their best, feminist spiritualities are robust and prophetic, charged with energy and commitment, offering both to individuals and to institutions the vision and the means of a transforming and empowering grace. Even as they themselves change, shift, and merge, partaking of the wider movement of spirituality in our time, they may be seen as a sign of the creative, energising, life-giving work of the Spirit: fragile and unstable, capable of corruption and distortion, yet alluring, compelling, and challenging, refusing easy categorisation and inviting participation and response.

Notes
1. Alwyn Marriage, *Life-Giving Spirit: Responding to the Feminine in God* (London: SPCK, 1989), p. 5.
2. Elizabeth A. Johnson, *She Who Is: The Mystery of God in Feminist Theological Discourse* (New York: Crossroad, 1992), p. 130.

3. The phrase is from Lavinia Byrne (ed.), *The Hidden Tradition: Women's Spiritual Writings Rediscovered* (London: SPCK, 1991).

4. Johnson, *She Who Is*, p. 122.

5. Philip Sheldrake, *Spirituality and History*, revised edition (London: SPCK, 1995), p. 75.

6. Sheldrake, *Spirituality and History*, p. 77.

7. See, for example, Elaine Pagels, *The Gnostic Gospels* (London: Weidenfeld & Nicolson, 1980) and K. King (ed.), *Images of the Feminine in Gnosticism* (Philadelphia, PA: Fortress Press, 1988).

8. See source documents in Amy Oden (ed.), *In Her Words: Women's Writings in the History of Christian Thought* (London: SPCK, 1995), pp. 21ff.

9. See Sheldrake, *Spirituality and History*, pp. 116ff.

10. Caroline Walker Bynum, *Jesus as Mother: Studies in the Spirituality of the High Middle Ages* (Berkeley, CA: University of California Press, 1982); *Holy Feast and Holy Fast: The Religious Significance of Food to Medieval Women* (Berkeley, CA: University of California Press, 1987).

11. See Derek Baker, *Medieval Women: Studies in Church History 1* (Oxford: Blackwell, 1978); Bynum, *Jesus as Mother*; Elizabeth Petrov (ed.), *Medieval Women's Visionary Literature* (Oxford University Press, 1986); Fiona Bowie (ed.), *Beguine Spirituality: An Anthology* (London: SPCK, 1989).

12. Caroline Walker Bynum, 'Religious Women in the Later Middle Ages', in J. Raitt (ed.), *Christian Spirituality: High Middle Ages and Reformation* (London: Routledge, 1987), p. 131.

13. Anne Carr, 'On Feminist Spirituality', in Joann Wolski Conn (ed.), *Women's Spirituality: Resources for Christian Development*, second edition (New York: Paulist Press, 1996) p. 53.

14. See, for example, Elaine Storkey and Margaret Hebblethwaite, *Conversations on Christian Feminism: Speaking Heart to Heart* (London: Fount, 1999); Kathleen Fischer, *Women at the Well: Feminist Perspectives on Spiritual Direction* (New York: Paulist Press, 1988); Anne Carr, *Transforming Grace: Christian Tradition and Women's Experience* (San Francisco, CA: Harper & Row, 1988); Elizabeth Moltmann-Wendel, *A Land Flowing with Milk and Honey* (London: SCM Press, 1986); Catharina J. M. Halkes, *New Creation: Christian Feminism and the Renewal of the Earth* (London: SPCK, 1991); Mercy Amba Oduyoye and Musimbi R. A. Kanyoro (eds.), *The Will to Arise: Women, Tradition and the Church in Africa* (Maryknoll, NY: Orbis Press, 1992).

15. For example, Janet Morley, *All Desires Known* (London: SPCK, 1992); Rosemary Catalano Mitchell and Gail Anderson Ricciuti, *Birthings and Blessings: Liberating Worship Services for the Inclusive Church* (New York: Crossroad, 1992); St Hilda Community, *Women Included: A Book of Services and Prayers*, second edition (London: SPCK, 1993).

16. See, for examples, Ursula King (ed.), *Feminist Theology from the Third World: A Reader* (London: SPCK, 1994), part 5.

17. The full text can be found in Michael Kinnamon (ed.), *Signs of the Spirit* (Geneva: World Council of Churches Publications, 1991), pp. 37–47; the opening invocation is in King (ed.), *Feminist Theology*, pp. 392–4.

18. In King (ed.), *Feminist Theology*, p. 391.
19. Aruna Gnanadason, 'Women and Spirituality in Asia', in King (ed.), *Feminist Theology*, pp. 351–60.
20. Chung Hyun Kyung, 'Come, Holy Spirit – Break Down the Walls with Wisdom and Compassion', in King (ed.), *Feminist Theology*, p. 394.
21. Mary Grey, 'Feminist Theology: a Critical Theology of Liberation', in Christopher Rowland (ed.), *The Cambridge Companion to Liberation Theology* (Cambridge University Press, 1999), p. 100.
22. Grey, ibid., p. 101.
23. See Matthew Fox, *A Spirituality Named Compassion* (Scranton, PA: Harper & Row); and *Original Blessing* (Sante Fe, NM: Bear & Co., 1983).
24. See, for example, James B. Nelson, *The Intimate Connection: Male Sexuality, Male Spirituality* (London: SPCK, 1992); and Mark Pryce, *Finding a Voice: Men, Women and the Community of the Church* (London: SCM Press, 1996).
25. See T. C. Lethbridge, *Witches* (Secaucus, NJ: Citadel Press); I. and S. Farrar, *The Witches' Way* (London: Robert Hale, 1984); Sabrina Woodward, 'Wicca', in Lisa Isherwood and Dorothea McEwan (eds.), *An A to Z of Feminist Theology* (Sheffield Academic Press, 1996), pp. 233–6.
26. Z. Budapest, *The Holy Book of Women's Mysteries I & II* (Los Angeles, CA: Susan B. Anthony Coven #1, 1979, 1980); Starhawk, *The Spiral Dance* (San Francisco, CA: Harper & Row, 1979) and *Truth or Dare: Encounters with Power, Authority and Mystery* (San Francisco, CA: Harper & Row, 1980).
27. Carol Christ, 'Why Women need the Goddess: Phenomenological, Pyschological and Political Reflections', in Carol Christ and Judith Plaskow (eds.), *Womanspirit Rising: A Feminist Reader in Religion* (New York: Harper & Row, 1979), pp. 273–87.
28. For example, Pam Lunn, 'Do Women Need the Goddess?', *Feminist Theology* 4 (1993), pp. 17–38.
29. Carol P. Christ, *Rebirth of the Goddess: Finding Meaning in Feminist Spirituality* (New York: Routledge, 1997), p. xiii.
30. Fox, *Original Blessing*, p. 282.
31. Audre Lorde, *Uses of the Erotic: The Erotic as Power* (Freedom, CA: The Crossing Press, 1978); I. Carter Heyward, *The Redemption of God: A Theology of Mutual Relation* (Lanham, MD: University Press of America, 1982), *Our Passion for Justice: Images of Power, Sexuality and Liberation* (New York: Pilgrim Press, 1984), *Touching our Strength: The Erotic as Power and the Love of God* (San Francisco, CA: Harper & Row, 1989); Mary Hunt, *Fierce Tenderness: A Feminist Theology of Friendship* (New York: Crossroad, 1991).
32. Lorde, *Uses of the Erotic*, p. 297.
33. Heyward, *Touching our Strength*.
34. Heyward, *Redemption of God*, *Passion for Justice*, and *Touching our Strength*; Mary Grey, *Redeeming the Dream: Feminism, Redemption and Christian Tradition* (London: SPCK, 1989) and *The Wisdom of Fools? Seeking Revelation for Today* (London: SPCK, 1993).
35. Katherine Zappone, *The Hope for Wholeness: A Spirituality for Feminists* (Dublin: Twenty Third Publications, 1991), p. 12.

36. Charlene Spretnak, 'The Politics of Women's Spirituality' in Spretnak (ed.), *The Politics of Women's Spirituality: Essays on the Rise of Spiritual Power within the Feminist Movement* (New York: Anchor/Doubleday, 1982), p. 397.

37. Heyward, *Redemption of God*, p. 172.

38. See, for example, Susan B. Thislethwaite, *Sex, Race and God: Christian Feminism in Black and White* (London: Chapman, 1990), especially chapter 6.

39. In 'Consultation Report from Theologically Trained Women of the Philippines: A Continuing Challenge for Women's Ministry', *In God's Image* (August 1983), p. 7.

40. Gnanadason, 'Women and Spirituality', p. 357.

41. Ibid.

42. Many of the essays in part 5 of King (ed.), *Feminist Theology*, reflect this life orientation. See, for example, the workshop reflection, 'From Barrenness to Fullness of Life: The Spirit as Enabler', pp. 303–7.

43. The classic statement of this interconnection between women's oppression and the oppression of nature is C. Merchant, *The Death of Nature: Women, Ecology and the Scientific Revolution* (San Francisco, CA: Harper & Row, 1980).

44. On ecofeminist spirituality, see C. Adams (ed.), *Ecofeminism and the Sacred* (New York: Continuum, 1993) and M. MacKinnon and M. McIntyre (eds.), *Readings in Ecology and Feminist Theology* (Kansas City, MO: Sheed & Ward, 1995).

45. Carr, 'On Feminist Spirituality', p. 49.

46. Yves Congar, *I Believe in the Holy Spirit*, vol. 3 (New York: Seabury Press, 1983); Leonardo Boff, *The Maternal Face of God: The Feminine and Its Religious Expressions* (Maryknoll, NY: Orbis Press, 1987); Donald Gelpi, *The Divine Mother: A Trinitarian Theology of the Holy Spirit* (Lanham, MD: University Press of America, 1984); Marriage, *Life-Giving Spirit*.

47. Sarah Coakley, '"Femininity" and the Holy Spirit?' in Monica Furlong (ed.), *Mirror to the Church: Reflections on Sexism* (London: SPCK, 1988), pp. 124–35.

48. Johnson, *She Who Is*, p. 50.

49. Coakley, '"Femininity"', p. 127.

50. Johnson, *She Who Is*, p. 54.

51. Ibid., p. 47.

52. Ibid., p. 122.

53. Ibid., p. 243.

54. Sallie McFague, *Models of God: Theology for an Ecological, Nuclear Age* (London: SCM Press, 1987). See also McFague's *The Body of God: An Ecological Theology* (London: SCM Press, 1993).

55. Ibid., p. 145.

56. Ibid., p. 147.

57. McFague, *Models of God*, pp. 97ff.

58. See 1 John 4[1].

Selected reading

Bynum, Caroline Walker. *Jesus as Mother: Studies in the Spirituality of the High Middle Ages*, Berkeley, CA: University of California Press, 1982.

Byrne, Lavinia. *The Hidden Tradition: Women's Spiritual Writings Rediscovered*, London: SPCK, 1991.

Conn, Joann Wolski (ed.). *Women's Spirituality: Resources for Christian Tradition*, New York: Paulist Press, 1986.

Johnson, Elizabeth A. *She Who Is: The Mystery of God in Feminist Theological Discourse*, New York: Crossroad, 1992.

Marriage, Alwyn. *Life-Giving Spirit: Responding to the Feminine in God*, London: SPCK, 1989.

Oden, Amy (ed.). *In Her Words: Women's Writings in the History of Christian Thought*, London: SPCK, 1995.

Spretnak, Charlene (ed.). *The Politics of Women's Spirituality: Essays on the Rise of Spiritual Power within the Feminist Movement*, New York: Anchor/Doubleday, 1982.

11 Creation
CELIA DEANE-DRUMMOND

Reflection on the relationship between humans and the natural world is an issue of acute concern for most feminists, not just feminist theologians. Interpretations of this relationship range from more conservative conservation approaches to more politically radical ecology frameworks. Emerging from within this debate we can identify forms of spirituality that are centred on the earth, often loosely based round the notion of ecology. While not necessarily articulated as a systematic theology in the traditional sense of the word, those feminist theologians who write about the world as creation do so in the context of this ecofeminist framework. I therefore intend to begin this chapter with a brief review of ecofeminism in general, before moving to a discussion of particular theological interpretations.

THE RISE OF ECOFEMINISM

Ecofeminism is sometimes known as the 'third wave' of feminism, following the liberal-based emancipation movements of the nineteenth century and the more culturally conscious movement of the 1970s. Ecofeminism understood in this way is often associated with the politics of radical ecology. In this case there is a close parallel drawn between the structural oppression of both women and nature through the project of modernity. It was in 1974 that the French writer Françoise d'Eubonne called on women to lead a practical ecological revolution through *ecofeminisme*. Ecofeminism in this sense becomes the means sought for the liberation of both women and nature.

Carolyn Merchant has argued that the definition of ecofeminism needs to be drawn much wider than this, including in its remit a whole range of political perspectives from the first wave of liberal feminism, through to radical political positions.[1] Women's involvement in practical campaigns finds a means of articulation in ecofeminism. Like other forms of feminism, ecofeminism is shaped by praxis, in other words it draws on the practical experience of women while being informed by more theoretical analyses. While liberal ecofeminists sought to challenge governments to change laws so that they were more environmentally friendly, those known as 'cultural' ecofeminists explored the relationship between women and nature within an overall critique of patriarchy. 'Social' ecofeminists examined the social structures underlying oppression through a critique of capitalism, exploring issues of social justice. Clearly, the boundaries between these different groupings are often more blurred than this categorisation implies. However, given this broader definition, ambiguities in ecofeminism start to emerge, especially those associated with the analysis of the cultural links between women and nature.

It is possible to understand all aspects of human experience as bearing the marks of an association between women and nature. For example, emotional ties in relationships are thought to be more characteristic of the psychology of women compared with men, and such ties are deemed to be closer to 'nature', compared with the detached reasoning of the intellect. Secondly, the social roles historically assigned to women are the practical, domestic chores, considered to be more rooted in contact with the 'earth', compared with the roles assigned to men. Finally, the biological basis of women's physiology, including menstruation, childbirth, and so on, roots the experience of women in the natural cycles of the earth. There are various ways to respond to this association of women and nature. One might be to call for direct political action in order to liberate both women and the environment; the cry of the oppressed becomes a joint chorus of women and nature. Another response, which I will return to again below, is to celebrate the association between women and nature as a means of reclaiming women's power. In this case, the power of women may be recast by looking back to the time when the power of women could be expressed in the form of worship of a goddess. However, quite apart from the theological problems of this position, the very attempt to seek out the link between nature and women smacks to many of essentialism. This is the assumption that men and women have an essential human nature that transcends culture and socialisation. Those cultural feminists who seek to express their views in practical ways through an ethic of caring, play on the traditional role of women. Not only is the question of how men might enter the dialogue left unanswered, the structures of oppression seem to be left intact.

Merchant's response to this dilemma is to argue the case for a socialist ecofeminism, one that explores the means of production advocated by capitalist economies and asks what is at stake for women and nature.[2] Furthermore, she suggests that particular forms of production have particular consequences on biological reproduction, for example the effects on the unborn of chemical or nuclear pollutants, or interventionist medical technologies. While her analysis comes from a different starting point compared with traditional cultural feminism, her solution seems to be based more on ideology, rather than politics. She suggests that new forms of socialist ecology could bring human production and reproduction into balance with nature's production and reproduction, leading to a sustainable global environment. This seems to be worked out through an ethic of partnership, with a new consciousness of nature as subject.[3] Yet it is unclear how this idea of partnership would work out in practice. While she appears to admit that state socialism created its own environmental problems, it is not entirely clear what kind of political structure she is seeking to instate.

Consideration of nature as partner brings ecofeminism into dialogue with deep ecology. Many ecofeminists welcome deep ecology, understood as a radical critique of a 'shallow' environmentalism that seeks merely to reform present structures. Both ecofeminism and deep ecology reject a philosophy based on dualism, understood as encompassing not just the human–nature divide, but also the following pairs: mind–body; reason–nature; reason–emotion; masculine–feminine. Those who advocate deep ecology as a philosophy, including writers such as Warwick Fox and Arne Naess, have developed a particular deep ecology platform. It is this form of deep ecology that ecofeminists, such as Ariel Salleh, have had reason to rebut, believing that the deep ecology has failed to consider adequately the particular experiences of oppression of women.[4] Deep ecology is also associated with forms of spirituality known as creation spirituality, which I will return to again below.

THE ALLURE OF THE GODDESS

One of the landmark contributions in the development of an earth-based spirituality is the book by Susan Griffin, *Women and Nature: the Roaring inside Her.*[5] This book is no standard text in theology, but a poetic interpretation of the intense closeness between humanity and nature. Griffin traces the interrelated dualism between soul–flesh; mind–feelings; culture–nature to the terror of patriarchal man faced with mortality. Men choose to oppress women when faced with this terrifying reality. For Griffin, the solution is identification with the earth. Further, the joint voice of women and nature is an impassioned, embodied voice, unashamed in its rejection of the so-called objectivity of patriarchal modes of thought. Even though she does not use the language of spirituality, she seems to hint at this by association.

Carol Christ is more insistent that the crisis that threatens the earth is spiritual as well as economic and social.[6] Both Griffin and Christ believe that reconstruction of an adequate relationship with the natural world must follow deconstruction of existing patterns of thinking. For Christ, ideas, such as the Goddess, Earth, and Life, are all symbolic of the whole of which we are part, so that 'the divinity that shapes our ends is life, death, and change, understood both literally and as metaphor for our daily lives'.[7] Yet there seems to be little notion of any salvific role of the divine, since for her there is no ultimate justice or injustice, the promise of life remains what it is now. Hence, the only essential religious insight is that we are just part of the whole process of life and death.

The practical response is 'to rejoice and to weep, to sing and to dance, to tell stories and to create rituals in praise of an existence far more complicated, more intricate, more enduring than we are'.[8] While such a practice makes us aware of our limitations, it is less certain that such a view will automatically lead to a deeper sense of the inherent value of other beings. Furthermore, her view of the divine that seems to accept all that is seems to offer little hope; when faced with such a divinity, the response could be resignation rather than transformation. Her writing is contradictory in that she envisages the divine as a Spirit who cares, even while denying she has a consciousness. Like much process thought, it is the energy of eros, or the 'passion to connect' that moves the processes of life.[9] We might ask ourselves, what does caring mean without self-awareness? What does caring mean while there is a tolerance of injustice?

Charlene Spretnak is a post-Christian writer who tries to re-claim the idea of the goddess in order to emphasise the notion of divine immanence.[10] She believes that the idea of the goddess is superior to that of a male deity as she can contain the idea of both male and female in the concept of the divine womb. Like Carol Christ, she views the goddess as intricately linked with the processes of life, 'the cosmic dance, the eternally vibrating flux of matter/energy'.[11] Women are pre-disposed to discern 'connectedness' in all things, with a specific spirituality to evoke healing, creative energy. In her book, *States of Grace*, she argues that it is only through an earth-centred spirituality that we can recover a sense of meaning, following the radical deconstruction of postmodernity.[12] All the Wisdom traditions of all religions evoke particular spiritual practice. Drawing on the creation spirituality of Thomas Berry, she welcomes the sense of creativity at the heart of the cosmic processes.[13] She takes up Berry's ideas of *differentiation*, that is the diversity of existence, *subjectivity*, that includes a sense of inner being, and *communion*, that expresses inherent relatedness between all that exists. This new creation story is the answer to the relativist impasse that we find following deconstruction of modernity. She advocates Buddhist meditation as a way of entering into a deeper union with the cosmos. Native American animist spirituality becomes the model for ethical ecological practice.

A way of joining all these strands together comes through the image of Gaia, the goddess of the earth. Goddess spirituality welcomes the body, with its embeddedness in nature. Spretnak rejects the idea that transcendence is the 'sky God' of patriarchy; rather transcendence is the 'sacred whole' or the 'infinite complexity of the universe'.[14] The answer to the loneliness of fragmentation characteristic of modernity, is to discover one's inner connectedness with all that exists, embracing both life and death, celebrating the erotic and sensual. While she seems to recognise that there are some difficulties in close identification between the earth and femaleness as such, she insists that the most important idea to retain is an understanding of the planet as a body, an organism.[15] Yet this admission seems to contradict her call for a reinstatement of goddess spirituality.

We might ask ourselves how far the reinstatement of goddess spirituality might really be advantageous for women. The historical record does not bear the rosy image expected of matriarchal societies. For example, the idea that matriarchal goddesses embraced both male and female principles, as Christ seems to suggest, more likely comes from a desire to see history in this way through an ideologising of the female.[16] Anthropological studies have shown that not all Buddhism embraces a feminine goddess; for example in Burma, where historically women have a high status, there is no goddess at all. Chinese Buddhism, on the other hand, does have a female deity, but China is still a strongly patriarchal society.[17] Janet Biehl is thoroughly unimpressed with any notion that goddess worship will improve the lot of women. Yet Starhawk speaks for this form of ecofeminism when she claims that: 'In ritual we can feel our interconnections with all levels of being, and mobilise our emotional energy and passion towards transformation and empowerment.'[18] But how far can spiritual practice serve as a way of motivating political action? From a theological perspective, there are problems coalescing such variegated forms of spirituality into one morass of cosmic ecodivinity. Such an image of the divine as goddess can seem an alienating, rather than liberating way of perceiving the divine. The close intimacy between women and the earth in the portrayal of the goddess seems to reinforce identification of women and the earth that is the hallmark of the very patriarchy called into question.

THE APPEAL OF ORGANICISM

An approach that perhaps has rather wider appeal is the notion of the organic, as opposed to the mechanistic way of viewing the earth. While romantic beliefs in the idea of the earth as an organism have ancient roots in the philosophy of the Stoics, many contemporary ecofeminist writers are making a concerted effort to draw on this model as a basis for their philosophy. Carolyn Merchant, in particular, in her book *The Death of Nature*, suggests that it was only with the rise of modern experimental science that nature was considered inert.[19] Up until this time, the belief that the earth was alive prevailed, along with a strong sense of the supernatural at work in the created world. She is particularly critical of Francis Bacon, who she believes portrayed nature as a female to be tortured by men of science, his language hinting of the torment of witches. Such language, she suggests, paved the way for the acceptance of the exploitation of nature.[20] However, she does not reject the association of the female with the earth. Rather, she insists that the twin ideas of the earth as mother and as organism served to constrain the activity of humans.[21] This idea seems inconsistent with her notion that the image of the earth as female encouraged exploitation. There are further historical issues worth noting. Merchant draws on the seventeenth-century writer Leibniz for her understanding of cosmic vitalism. However, Merchant incorporates a notion of mutual intersubjectivity that is completely lacking from Liebniz's position.[22] To swing from metaphors of nature as dead or alive seems too crude, and to adopt either wholeheartedly seems naïve.

GAIA AND GOD

Rosemary Radford Ruether has made a substantial contribution to the theological interpretation of ecofeminism, particularly in her book, *Gaia and God*.[23] Building on her earlier pioneering work, *New Woman: New Earth* and *Sexism and God-Talk*, Ruether is anxious to expose what she considers to be the parallels in subjugation of both women and nature.[24] She is also aware that cultural–symbolic ecofeminism is not adequate on its own. Rather, she recognises that there is a need to take account of the economic and social structures that serve to stabilise patterns of oppression.[25] She rejects aspects of the Goddess thealogy which promote religious practices without taking responsibility for actual social contexts of oppression. Nonetheless, like Spretnak, she takes up the new creation story of modern cosmology and weaves it into a new way of thinking about the earth as an interacting organism. Yet, for Ruether, the stark realities of the ecological crisis and the domination of women are never far from her mind, and she interlaces her more theoretical arguments with evocative images and stories.

Her writing is sensitive to the particular theological categories that have become dominant in Western culture, locating a form of dualism in the themes of creation and redemption. In *Gaia and God*, she tries to keep different aspects of the Christian story intact, even while reinterpreting the concepts in a radical way. The idea of God becomes transformed in a revised understanding of covenant, so that the ancient Jubilee laws provided a corrective to exploitative practices, either between humans or against the earth. The special task of humans becomes that of caretakers of the whole community of creation.[26] None the less, humans are ultimately accountable to God for their actions.

The idea of Gaia seems to be related to a recovery of the sacramental tradition, in particular a reworking of the early cosmological images of the presence of the divine. Drawing on Matthew Fox, Teilhard de Chardin, and process theology, Ruether finds resonance with the idea of Gaia, understood as the feminine voice in the heart of matter itself. She admits that a simplistic return to the Goddess is not really adequate; what we need is a 'coincidence of opposites' in the manner that we find in subatomic physics.[27]

However, another strand in Ruether's thinking seems to reinforce the idea of divine immanence, so that any notion of transcendence understood as immortality disappears completely from view. In particular, she insists that mortality itself is not sin, but needs to be embraced as part of life. This strand has continued in her more recent writing, where humanity needs to see itself as part of an organic community, one that accepts that following death it will rise up again in new forms.[28] Similarly, she suggests that our bodily matter 'lives on in plants, animals and soil, even as our own living bodies are composed of substances that once were part of rocks, plants and animals, stretching back to prehistoric ferns and reptiles, before that to ancient biota that floated on the first seas of the earth, and before that to the stardust of exploding galaxies'.[29] Acceptance of our material, earthly nature and its ability to be taken up into the processes of the cosmos is all that we can hope for in the future. While she admits that this 'spirituality of recyling' also 'demands a deep conversion of consciousness', it is less certain how far this can be thought of as a Christian interpretation of future redemption. It is as if the death of Christ on the cross is acceptance of mortality, so we surrender to the 'Great Matrix of Being' that is renewing life through regrowth following death.

Rather than a 'coincidence of opposites', such a view seems to be a restatement of process theology in the form of a new spiritualised naturalism. I am less convinced that such a view will lead to the kind of ecological sensitivity that Ruether is keen to promote. While it is more sophisticated than crude forms of Goddess thealogy, redemption seems to collapse into creation in a way that seems unable to live with the tension between God and Gaia. While the strong dualism that Ruether is keen to rebut is not an option, the collapse of distinctions that her cyclical view seems to imply could lead to resignation, rather than hope.

Anne Primavesi is also drawn to the image of Gaia, though for her it is the reworking of the story of Genesis in both ecological and feminist terms that is a distinctive aspect of her work.[30] Her attempt to recast the story of Genesis according to the story of process theology and Gaia theory seems, at times, to be somewhat forced. It is by no means clear that the science of ecology in itself supports the model she is trying to suggest.

THE EARTH AS GOD'S BODY

An understanding of the organic relationship between the earth and female divinity spills into much ecofeminist theology. However, the idea that the earth is God's body as a way of reimaging the relationship between God and creation is spelt out formally in Grace Jantzen's *God's World: God's Body* and then in Sallie McFague's *The Body of God*.[31] Jantzen suggests that, if human beings are analogous to God, then just as humans can no longer be thought of as split into body and soul, so God must relate to the world as embodiment. At this stage of her thinking she avoided the notion of God as female; rather God is embodied, just as humans are embodied. She suggests that the logic of the idea of transcendence, once understood as difference from the world, leads to a lack of any knowledge about God from the material world. Instead, a reimaging of the idea of the transcendence of persons gives us some clues as to what God's transcendence might be like.

She rejects the idea that God is somehow 'pregnant' with the world, as this implies for her too great a distinction between God and creation. She rejects, in addition, the classic notion of creation out of nothing, posing instead the idea that creation means forming a cosmos out of chaos. Furthermore, rather than thinking of matter as somehow outside God, all of creation becomes the expression of who God is, so that: 'It is God's self-formation, and owes its being what it is directly to God's formative will.'[32] Here the analogy with human persons breaks down, since our bodies are, to a great extent, given. She suggests that God's embodiment is more complete than that of humans as the world is completely expressive of the will of God. She insists that it is the universe, rather than the earth as such, that is the body of God.

Against the charge that this might imply that God is evil, she considers that the theodicy question is just as much a problem for traditional models of creation, where God is responsible for all that is. Once we see the world as the body of God, then God shares in the evil of the world in a spectacular way. Rather than destroying our autonomy, she suggests that the God of love must limit his power over us and thus give humanity the gift of freedom. God as embodiment is costly to God in that God's power is self-limited by the desire to love. Yet, on the other hand, all creatures owe their existence to God, who is the very ground of Being itself, and this is what is meant by the sovereignty of God.

Jantzen's later writing is more explicit about naming the divine as feminine.[33] She has retained her strong rejection of the Platonic dualism that she believes has influenced our understanding of the relationship between God and the world. Furthermore, the consequences of such dualism are a negative attitude towards the body, as epitomised by a rejection of sexuality. Once this became projected into a dualism of male and female, it provided a rationalisation and justification for the misogynism characteristic of Western culture. She suggests that underlying the strong dualism lies a desire not to lose control, so dualism serves to justify controlling attitudes towards the other, be it sexuality, feelings, women, other races, or the earth. The solution is to heal the fear that is at the root of the negative attitudes. Underlying this fear is a rejection of the body. She suggests that the way out of this impasse is to tap into the Spirit of God understood as one who brings liberation and healing.

It seems to me that Jantzen is correct to identify fear as a key factor in motivating oppression, especially in the human community. I have more reservations about whether fear encourages a rapacious attitude to the earth, though the habit of control no doubt spills over into all our attitudes. Yet, if we examine more closely her understanding of Spirit in creation, it seems that this is not Spirit in the traditional sense of Trinity, but rather the Spirit is God, understood as immanent in the world.

In *Becoming Divine*, her most radical book so far, Jantzen suggests that pantheism is the most fruitful way of considering who God is.[34] Moreover, the fear of pantheism is the fear of a loss of identity, defined as the maintenance of boundaries. She believes that once we see God as in the world in a pantheistic way, then, 'Instead of the mastery over the earth which is rapidly bringing about its destruction there would be reverence and sensitivity;

instead of seeing domination as godlike we would recognise it as utterly contradictory to divinity'.[35] However, there is no reason to believe that this change in attitude would follow. She suggests, quite rightly, that it is not enough to simply valorise categories such as women, earth, bodiliness at the expense of men, intellect, and spirit. Yet her pantheistic approach inevitably tries to collapse one into the other, just as dualism forces their separation.

Even, as she claims, the divine cannot be reduced to the earth, it seems that her idea of transcendence is located primarily in the notion of becoming. Following the French feminist philosopher Irigaray, she suggests that transcendence is 'the projected horizon for our embodied becoming'.[36] Rejecting panentheism as too close to dualism leaves her vulnerable to the charge of reinstating the idea of the Goddess. For the transcendental mode of God is the female divine. If anyone rejects this view, this simply comes from the elemental fear of being swallowed up in the maternal womb, a fear of loss of boundaries. Yet it is hard to understand what this transcendence means other than a notion of the person being more than the body.

Again, the 'pantheist symbolic in which that which is divine precisely is this world and its ceaselessly shifting bodies and signifiers, then it is this which must be celebrated as of ultimate value . . . a pantheist symbolic supports a symbolic of natality, a flourishing of the earth and those who dwell upon it'.[37] All worship, it seems, must be directed earthwards in celebration of the interconnectedness of life.

Such notions of flourishing echo the ecological feminism advocated by Chris Cuomo.[38] However, in her case she rejects a focus on the *objects* of oppressive action, in particular women and nature, that she believes is characteristic of many spiritual writers. Instead, she suggests that there needs to be a wider focus on oppressive *systems* in general, so that other forms of oppression such as race, class, and so on come more clearly into view. Jantzen's theology, in proposing a model that is anti-dualistic, seems to go further than just focus on the objects of oppression. However, by identifying the divine as feminine, Jantzen seems to be undermining her own broader approach by reintroducing the idea of the Goddess. Admittedly, for her the divinity is no longer confined simply to this earth, and includes the whole universe in a way that excludes simple correlation of the earth with mother deity in the way implied by the idea of Gaia. While Cuomo attempts to keep her distance from ecofeminists, it seems that positive notions, such as flourishing, are becoming common currency in both the religious and secular forms of ecofeminism.

Sallie McFague's *The Body of God* takes up and develops the ideas put forward in Grace Jantzen's earlier work. Like Jantzen, she argues strongly for an embodied model of God, and, like Merchant, she argues that experimental science has left us the legacy of the machine metaphor for the earth. In particular, she suggests that our way of knowing the earth is faulty. Instead of looking with the arrogant eye that desires to manipulate and control nature, she suggests we need to pay attention to, to become in tune with, the natural world and consider its particular subjects. More recently she has taken this theme further and argued for a particular earth-based spirituality that is fully in touch with the vibrant subjectivity of all creation.[39] She finds common ground with deep ecology and the common creation story of Thomas Berry. Sin becomes a refusal to accept our place in the earth. This echoes to some extent Ruether's suggestion that redemption consists in accepting our own mortality.

McFague is, perhaps, more cautious than Jantzen in suggesting that the entire planet reflects the glory and being of God, but it is *God's back* and not *God's face* that we see in this world. She is also insistent that this is a metaphor or model, so that we are 'invited to see the creator *in* the creation, the source of all existence in and through what is bodied forth from that source'.[40] She spells out another metaphor, namely God as agent in the Spirit of the body, though her overriding concern is to emphasise the idea of the world as the body of God. Like Jantzen, she believes that transcendence emerges from the immanence of God in the body of the world. This model of God is compatible with contemporary science, even while seeming to reject the foundations of that science in subject–object dualism. She argues that the use of the term 'spirit as agent' stresses the relationship of God to the world as one of deep connection, rather than the idea of mind over body.

However, it seems to me that this attempt to control the metaphor of the body in a certain way fails to really take account of the ambiguity of the image itself. If God is to the world as self is to the body, then it is just as possible to view the Spirit and mind acting in concert on the body, as to see the body somehow coerced from within. Indeed the relationship between the body, religious practice, and the self-image of women is one that remains deeply ambiguous. As Mary Douglas suggests, the image that we have of our own bodies is reflected in social structures and thence into our perceptions of the divine. Once we see the body as a *locus* of control, this is mirrored in ritual.[41] Further, particular social conditions are the prototype of our attitudes to the body and this is echoed in our image of the divine.

In both Jantzen's and McFague's model, God's body is imaged as the vehicle of life, vulnerable to external influences, rather than as a communication network, where the head serves to control the function of other parts of the body. Once we reject the Cartesian understanding of the body as having a mind and soul, then it appears that all that is left is the physical body. Sarah Coakley argues that the sweeping supposition that Christianity is inevitably violent and oppressive against all bodiliness needs to be corrected.[42] The very notion of what it means to have a body is fraught with difficulties. The identification of women with a despised and rejected body is only one issue. Others include, for example, the anxiety caused by medical intervention, the sense of identity confusion with exchange of body parts, the pressures of consumerism on women's self-image of the body, the replacement of bodies by the virtual worlds of cyberspace. There are further contradictions in the human experience of the body. On the one hand, the body is affirmed sexually, but on the other punished in exercise and diet; the claim is made that there is nothing but the body, but self-discipline is still encouraged; the body is both 'flaunted', but disappears in 'cyberspace'.[43] All this suggests that behind the image of the body there lurks a powerful dualism that cannot be completely suppressed. I am suggesting that the image of the world as God's body could lead to confusion and ambiguity, rather than to the affirmation of interconnectedness and wholeness.

Quite apart from its effectiveness as a metaphor, there are further theological difficulties with identifying the world with God in the way McFague and Jantzen suggest. For, while this seems to affirm the incarnation, we might ask ourselves what is the distinctive nature of Christ compared with any other human being who shares in the body of God? For McFague, it is simply that: 'The story of Jesus suggests that the shape of God's body includes all, especially the needy and outcast.'[44] Once sin becomes a refusal to accept our place in the world in the way she suggests, it is hard to imagine how Christ's identification with the outcast will really make any practical difference. Her cosmic Christology sits rather uneasily with her idea of the world as God's body, though she attempts to integrate these through a reinterpretation of the Trinity as the invisible face, the visible body, and the mediating spirit.[45] Like other organic models of God, it is hard to appreciate the radical nature of sin and human suffering, in spite of her attempts to do so through a reinterpretation of Christology. Following the process model of theology, she affirms that God suffers with the world, but that through this suffering love comes the possibility of healing and liberation. She seems to suggest that suffering is an inevitable part of the process, even if the love of God is still present to heal. The loss of all sense of God as other makes it hard to appreciate just how we might experience the love of God, apart from that through human persons. Ruth Page's image of God as one who suffers in and with the web of creation is similar in many respects, though she introduces the notion of pan-syn-theism, that is God with us, rather than in us.[46] The advantage of her model is that it helps to preserve the distinction between God and the world, without loss of a sense of intimacy.

SEEKING WISDOM IN ECOTHEOLOGY

Another possible metaphor for an ecotheology that builds on an image of God found in the Jewish tradition is that of Wisdom. Elizabeth Johnson, in her important work, *She Who Is*, attempts to redefine all persons of the Trinity in terms of the divine *Sophia*.[47] Anne Clifford has suggested that the biblical Wisdom literature has much to offer an ecological theology.[48] I have also argued for a recovery of aspects of the Wisdom literature in developing an ecotheology.[49] There has been a recent surge of scholarly interest in Wisdom literature. As the themes of much of this tradition are on the creative activity of God, it seems an appropriate place to start reflection on what it means for God to relate to the world. While the Hebrew writers knew nothing of contemporary science, certain aspects of how God relates to the world through wisdom are worth contemporary development.

The first aspect worth noting is that the activity of wisdom is associated with ethical action and practice. It is in the framework of righteousness before God that wisdom is given as a gift to those who seek her out. This leads to a judgment of wisdom on all acts of unrighteousness, including the oppression of the weak and defenceless. Such oppression would include that against women, but would be wider than this to include racism, classism, and all other systems of domination. While oppression of the earth is not specifically mentioned, the close relationship between God's blessing and the fertility and flourishing of the earth implies human responsibility towards all the creatures of the planet. Furthermore, by situating the divine covenant as the context for divine creative activity, the responsibility of humans towards one another as well as towards the planet is emphasised. It seems to me that this is a more effective way of harbouring the desire of those who seek God, in that it becomes clearer that ethical practice needs to go hand in hand with particular beliefs. As rooted in practice, the Wisdom literature encourages specific human action and transformation in the present, rather than passive resignation that seems to emerge from models of God as a suffering body.

Another aspect of this model is the idea of Wisdom as the feminine divine. Some feminist theologians have used the belief in the goddess of Wisdom, for example the Egyptian Goddess Isis, in order to develop a thealogy. However, the early Hebrew writers were well aware of this understanding of the divine and sought to show how Wisdom could become part of a monotheistic framework. The personification of Wisdom as feminine does not so much imply a goddess, as a feminine face of God. Like Johnson, I suggest that all aspects of the Trinity need to be explored in the light of Wisdom. The gospel of John tries to do just this with his reinterpretation of *Sophia* through his parallel use of the divine *Logos*. This idea is taken up in the cosmological Christic hymns of Colossians and Ephesians. Hence, this offers a way of incorporating a cosmic Christology into the model of how God relates to the world, without losing a sense of Wisdom as partner to God in the initial creative process.

It seems to me that, while Wisdom needs to be reinterpreted in order to be appropriate to our modern understanding of cosmology, it lends itself to a holistic understanding of God, without collapsing all distinctions. God as transcendent Wisdom is no longer to be feared, since Wisdom invites, listens, and implores, rather than dominates. Yet Wisdom is not anti-rational either; both reason and emotion are woven into the image in a way that is neither romantic nor harshly objective. In addition, Wisdom invites us to keep searching. The image of God is never sealed or precluded, but one that unfolds with time while not rejecting our particular history. Even though Wisdom does recognise the distance between God and creation, I suggest that such distance is necessary in order for creation to have genuine hope. Such hope is one that is not content with the cycle of everlasting return, but looks to our future in God, the promise of life not just for humanity, but for the whole cosmos.

Notes

1. C. Merchant, *Radical Ecology: the Search for a Liveable World* (London: Routledge, 1992).
2. Ibid., pp. 196–201.
3. Ibid., pp. 188–9; C. Merchant, *Earthcare: Women and the Environment* (London: Routledge, 1995), pp. 209–24.
4. A. K. Salleh, 'Deeper than Deep Ecology: the Eco-Feminist Connection', *Environmental Ethics*, 6 (1984), 339–45; A. Salleh, 'The Eco-Feminism/Deep Ecology Debate', *Environmental Ethics*, 14 (1992), 195–216.
5. S. Griffin, *Women and Nature: the Roaring inside Her* (London: The Women's Press, 1984).
6. C. Christ, 'Rethinking Theology and Nature', in J. Plaskow and C. Christ (eds.), *Weaving the Visions: New Patterns in Feminist Spirituality* (San Francisco, CA: Harper & Row, 1989), pp. 314–25.
7. Ibid., p. 321.
8. Ibid., p. 324.
9. C. Christ, *The Re-Birth of the Goddess* (London: Routledge, 1999).

10. C. Spretnak, 'Towards an Eco-Feminist Spirituality', in J. Plant (ed.), *Healing the Wounds: the Promise of Ecofeminism* (London: Green Print, 1989), pp. 127–32.
11. Ibid., p. 128.
12. C. Spretnak, *States of Grace: the Recovery of Meaning in a Post-Modern Age* (New York: HarperCollins, 1993); first edition 1991.
13. See e.g. Thomas Berry, *The Dream of the Earth* (San Francisco, CA: Sierra Club Books, 1988); Anne Lonergan and Caroline Richards (eds.), *Thomas Berry and the New Cosmology* (Mystic, CT: Twenty-Third Publications, 1987).
14. Spretnak, *States of Grace*, pp. 135–6.
15. Ibid., p. 145.
16. H. Meyer-Wilmes, *Rebellion on the Borders*, trans. Irene Smith Bouman (Kampen: Kok Pharos Press, 1995), pp. 165–6. Originally published in German in 1980.
17. J. Biehl, *Rethinking Ecofeminist Politics* (Boston, MA: South End Press, 1991), pp. 40–1.
18. Starhawk, 'Feminist Earth-Based Spirituality and Ecofeminism' in J. Plant (ed.), *Healing the Wounds* pp. 174–85, quotation p. 184.
19. C. Merchant, *The Death of Nature: Women, Ecology and the Scientific Revolution* (London: Wildwood House,1982).
20. Merchant, *Earthcare*, pp. 81–7.
21. Merchant, *Radical Ecology*, pp. 43–4.
22. Biehl, *Rethinking Ecofeminist Politics*, pp. 74–7.
23. R. Radford Ruether, *Gaia and God: an Ecofeminist Theology of Earth Healing* (London: SCM Press, 1993).
24. R. Radford Ruether, *New Woman: New Earth: Sexist Ideologies and Human Liberation* (New York: Crossroad/Seabury Press, 1975); *Sexism and God-Talk: Towards a Feminist Theology* (London: SCM Press, 1983).
25. R. Radford Ruether (ed.), *Women Healing Earth: Third World Women on Ecology, Feminism and Religion* (London: SCM Press, 1996).
26. Ruether, *Gaia and God*, pp. 226–7.
27. Ibid., p. 247.
28. R. Radford Ruether, 'Ecofeminism: Symbolic and Social Connections of the Oppression of Women and the Domination of Nature', in R. S. Gottlieb (ed.), *This Sacred Earth: Religion, Nature, Environment* (London: Routledge, 1996), pp. 332–3.
29. R. Radford Ruether, *Introducing Redemption in Christian Feminism* (Sheffield Academic Press, 1998), p. 119.
30. A. Primavesi, *From Apocalypse to Genesis* (Tunbridge Wells: Burns and Oates, 1991); 'Theology and Earth System Science' in Susan F. Parsons (ed.), *Challenging Women's Orthodoxies in the Context of Faith* (Aldershot: Ashgate, 2000); *Sacred Gaia: Holistic Theology and Earth System Science* (London: Routledge, 2000).
31. G. Jantzen, *God's World: God's Body* (London: Darton, Longman and Todd, 1984); S. McFague, *The Body of God: an Ecological Theology* (London: SCM Press, 1993).
32. Jantzen, *God's World*, p. 134.
33. G. Jantzen, 'Healing our Brokenness: the Spirit and Creation', in M. H. MacKinnon and M. McIntyre (eds.), *Readings in Ecology and Feminist Theology* (Kansas City, MO: Sheed and Ward, 1995), pp. 284–98.

34. G. Jantzen, *Becoming Divine: Towards a Feminist Philosophy of Religion* (Manchester University Press, 1998).
35. Ibid., p. 269.
36. Ibid., p. 271.
37. Ibid., p. 274.
38. C. J. Cuomo, *Feminism and Ecological Communities: an Ethic of Flourishing* (London: Routledge, 1998).
39. S. McFague, *Super, Natural Christians* (London: SCM Press, 1997).
40. McFague, *The Body of God*, pp. 133–4.
41. M. Douglas, *Natural Symbols: Explorations in Cosmology* (London: Routledge, 1996), first edition published 1976, pp. xxxiii, 69–74.
42. S. Coakley, 'Introduction: Religion and the Body' in S. Coakley (ed.), *Religion and the Body* (Cambridge University Press, 1996), note 5, p. 5.
43. Ibid., pp. 6–8.
44. McFague, *Body of God*, p. 164.
45. Ibid., pp. 193–4.
46. R. Page, *God and the Web of Creation* (London: SCM Press, 1996).
47. E. A. Johnson, *She Who Is: The Mystery of God in Divine Discourse* (New York: Crossroad, 1994).
48. A. Clifford, 'Feminist Perspectives on Science: Implications for an Ecological Theology of Creation', MacKinnon and McIntyre (eds.), *Readings in Ecology*, pp. 352–4.
49. C. Deane-Drummond, '*Sophia*: the Feminine Face of God as a Metaphor for an Eco-Theology', *Feminist Theology* 16 (1997), 11–31. Further elaboration of these ideas is in C. Deane-Drummond, *Creation through Wisdom: Theology and the New Biology* (Edinburgh: T. & T. Clark, 2000).

Selected reading

Christ, C. *The Re-Birth of the Goddess*, London: Routledge, 1999.
Deane-Drummond, C. *Creation through Wisdom: Theology and the New Biology*, Edinburgh: T. & T. Clark, 2000.
Jantzen, G. *God's World: God's Body*, London: Darton, Longman and Todd, 1984.
   Becoming Divine: Towards a Feminist Philosophy of Religion, Manchester University Press, 1998.
Johnson, E. A. *She Who Is: The Mystery of God in Divine Discourse*, New York: Crossroad, 1994.
MacKinnon M. H. and McIntyre, M. (eds.), *Readings in Ecology and Feminist Theology*, Kansas City, MO: Sheed and Ward, 1995.
McFague, S. *The Body of God: an Ecological Theology*, London: SCM Press, 1993.
   Super, Natural Christians, London: SCM Press, 1997.
Merchant, C. *The Death of Nature: Women, Ecology and the Scientific Revolution.* London: Wildwood House, 1982.
Page, R. *God and the Web of Creation.* London: SCM Press, 1996.
Radford Ruether, R. *Gaia and God: an Ecofeminist Theology of Earth Healing.* London: SCM Press, 1993.
Spretnak, C. *States of Grace: the Recovery of Meaning in a Post-Modern Age.* New York: HarperCollins, 1993.

12 Redeeming ethics

SUSAN FRANK PARSONS

In her *Dialogue* with God, St Catherine of Siena opens a window onto the encounter of a human soul with the divine.[1] By all accounts a woman of considerable independence of mind and forthright courage, involved both in caring for poor and sick people in Siena and in personal interventions in the complex political and ecclesiastical crises that marked fourteenth-century Italy, she was also from an early age deeply informed by prayer. It is not surprising, then, that this sustained prayer handed down to us, among the first texts of Western Europe to be written and printed in the vernacular, should indicate an inseparable relation of action with thought, of work with contemplation. Our interest here, however, is not in the details of her life, for in any case these are often difficult to disentangle from fervent accounts of good works embellished with pious stories. Reading the lives and texts of saints is a hermeneutic exercise of considerable sophistication in itself. Rather our attention is drawn to a pattern of reflection that unfolds in the *Dialogue*, a pattern that is at once so familiar and so strange to contemporary hearing that one might easily miss what it has to say to us. Yet in this pattern something about the distinctiveness of ethics and something about the nature of redemption is disclosed, and together these things may shed light on the desires and the projects of contemporary feminist ethics. So it is my intention here, not to try to figure out the life of St Catherine, but rather to let her figure us out, and so to let her prayer inform what the ethical life of woman might yet become.

The *Dialogue* is shaped around petitions and responses, which in themselves constitute a theological treatise of some considerable stature in the Christian tradition. Her questions are demanding ones in so many senses – because they are anything but trivial, because she seems to be bringing the whole of her life to bear upon them, and because she asks them with expectation, with insistence, that insight be given. So this is a prayer, like St Anselm's in the *Proslogion*, in which faith seeks understanding, and understanding is turned into life.[2] In its opening lines, the pattern of

Catherine's reflection is laid out:

> A soul rises up, restless with tremendous desire for God's honour and
> the salvation of souls. She has for some time exercised herself in
> virtue and has become accustomed to dwelling in the cell of
> self-knowledge in order to know better God's goodness toward her,
> since upon knowledge follows love. And loving, she seeks to pursue
> truth and clothe herself in it.[3]

It is this rising up of a soul to know truth and this willing to be clothed with
its love that suggest the intrinsic connection of ethics with redemption, a
way indeed of redeeming ethics, with which this chapter is concerned.

For this prayer shows us that in ethics there is both a reaching out for,
a stretching oneself towards, that which is most there to be known, which
Catherine believes to be God's goodness, and there is a desire to be turned
into this goodness herself, so that she will herself manifest its love, its 'gentle
truth', *la dolce Verità*, as she calls it. This reaching out for and turning into
goodness is a pattern of ethical thinking that was most carefully described
long before Catherine's day, in the *Nicomachean Ethics* of Aristotle.[4] His
word for this way of knowing, *phronesis*, has unfortunately become so embedded in the more cautious word which is its Latin equivalent, *prudentia*,
that we hardly have a way of saying it, let alone of following its path, in
English. 'Prudence' just doesn't quite get it. But Catherine did, for her prayer
indicates that she well knows the search for the utmost and the conforming
of one's life to it, which is what ethics is fundamentally to be.

Furthermore this is a quest that has to do with salvation. It is assumed in
this prayer that self-understanding and concern for others are inseparable,
that the deepening of insight into one's own existence and experience is also
a growing in the knowledge and love of others. For how could she know the
goodness of God to her own life unless she was also claiming this for others.
So there is no hesitation in Catherine's assumption that her experiences are
common. There is nothing extraordinary about her life or character that
she sets up before God, and certainly no reason for her to insist upon her
own uniqueness. Rather it seems to be that, in her 'cell of self-knowledge',
she has most acutely and tenderly heard the cry for redemption uttered by
a despairing world, at a loss to know what to do about the mess it is in.
That this cry has come to live with her is the burden of her prayer. Yet it
is also clear that she rises up to know what is for her, so that whatever she
receives by way of truth about the redemptive work of God in Christ is to
become true in her own life. What she learns is that she, too, is to become
a redeeming one, in whom redemption is to be performed. And this means

that she will constantly undergo its transformative impact upon her soul, and that everything she does is to become living evidence of the love that is in Christ.

The title of this chapter suggests that this theme of redeeming ethics is what figures in feminist theology, that the prolific writings of women in the field of ethical inquiry and their considerable involvement in the major crises and issues of the day are also informed, as was St Catherine, by a readiness to undertake the search for truth and by a desire to see salvation. Yet the title is also ambiguous, for it hints at the possibility that feminist ethics needs itself to turn again into its own best possibilities as a *redeeming* ethics, to listen anew to what it is that gives it life. And this is a task which requires of us not the repetition of well-worn phrases and slogans, nor more vehement exclamations of what we already think we know. These things cannot bring life in a world, whose dreams are daily being shrivelled by the availability of everything now, and whose deeds are made to appear always under the guise of power. The challenge before feminist ethics is to be redeeming, and this will require of us no less than it required of Catherine – the reaching out to know the utmost that is God's goodness, and the willingness to let love come to matter in us. To see the way that this might be possible for us today is our task here.

PERSONS AND RIGHTS

To speak of persons and of the rights of persons has been a central theme of feminist ethical discourse from its earliest days. Arising amidst enthusiasm for the liberation of man from regimes of inherited rule and established privilege, the rhetoric of early feminist ethical speeches also enjoys the optimism of the age. Women, it was argued, were to be included in this general effort to extend liberty, equality, and fraternity throughout the whole of society, and so the political efforts of feminists were directed to this realisation.[5] This kind of political change began to seem possible with the emergence of a new understanding of the human person, an understanding that feminists ever since have both shared and fought against in almost equal measure. To share in this concept of a person was to provide a most significant vocabulary for the movement of women's liberation, focussed as it was on bringing women out into society as full participants and recognised agents. To struggle with this concept was to give many women a place from which resistance to its damaging implications for their lives and for the wider good has been formulated. Its general outlines may be set out briefly.

It is especially in the thought of Descartes that we find the modern understanding of the human person appearing in a convincing and systematic way. In his *Meditations on First Philosophy*, he sought to establish the grounds of faith in the midst of an upheaval in Western thought that began in mathematics and the natural sciences. In an unsettled philosophical climate that made radical doubt possible, Descartes' intellectual task was to secure the soul in its knowledge of truth. The foundation on which this came to be built was to be seen in 'the natural light of reason', by which he could clearly see the certainty of his own existence as 'a thinking thing', and that of God, as the source and final proof of the natural light itself.[6] The importance of Descartes' argument can hardly be underestimated, for on its basis an understanding of the human person as a centre of reason, comprised of a thinking substance within a corporeal substance, and protected in its individual journey to truth by God, could be developed. Following this concept would come philosophical assertions of human freedom to think, and of the full dignity of the person in this rational activity, as well as political arguments for the basic rights according to which this freedom must be defended, and thus for the social changes required to secure each individual a place of recognition as an independent self. Among these changes would be the claims to ownership of private property and to legitimate participation in the processes of decision-making – ideas that would inspire revolutions in many parts of Europe and North America.

The ethical arguments of feminists first appeared within this complex of ideas, and so a cluster of interrelated projects became important. It mattered first of all to establish that women are thinking things just as men are, and so to claim that in the relevant respects the mind is not sexed, and then to posit an equality of women with men on the grounds of the human dignity they hold in common. To underpin these assertions was the reasonable belief that in God's goodness rested the ultimate and indiscriminate assurance of human worth, in which the natural rights of women were firmly rooted alongside those of their brothers.[7] The politics of liberating women was to follow, so that throughout the nineteenth and twentieth centuries women pressed for the basic rights that had been newly founded by men – to freedom of speech, to ownership of property, to representation in government, to public gatherings, to freedom to vote and – once these began to be secured – to equal participation, to employment and pay, to public education, to equal opportunities throughout all social institutions, to freedom from sexual discrimination and harassment, to decisions about one's own body. All of these things have figured in the feminist ethics inspired by the modern concept of the human person, and, with their realisation, many women have come to be educated, employed, franchised, represented, dignified, property-holding citizens – full persons in their own right.

The persuasiveness of these ideas has been the result of an intellectual struggle to define the distinctiveness of the human person in its most essential elements, according to the light of the new way of reasoning that emerged with modernity. For women to enter into this effort has required of them this same rigour, to discover the central core that ensures one's humanity, and to strip away the peripheral aspects of appearance or inheritance, status or location, that are not crucial to what a person fundamentally is. The involvement of women in anti-slavery movements in the nineteenth century was one of the first feminist applications of this way of thinking, for they were vociferous opponents of any institution that deprived persons of their personhood on the basis of physical characteristics or lower status. The inhumanity of persons to one another was a denial of the very things that were deemed to be utmost evidence of divine goodness. The commitment of women to this basic insight and their tireless work to ensure its realisation in society have been markers of a most serious ethical engagement with matters of justice and the common good. For the vision that sustains them here is of a Kingdom of equal partners to be established here on earth, as the injustices caused by mistaken ideas, misplaced values, and misjudged qualities are swept away, and with this cleansing will be a better world for all. That this vision was to begin to be realised in the church, as the redeemed community, gave urgency to the insistence there too that it 'ought especially to represent this equality of men and women in its institutional life'. So the church would become 'the paradigm of what all social institutions should become', and thus itself 'the bearer of redeemed humanity'.[8]

Yet women have found themselves along the fault-lines of this understanding of human identity, and, just as they have enthusiastically taken hold of the opportunities it opened up for their lives, they have also lived uncomfortably with many of its assumptions and implications. One of the most successful paradigms in the social sciences in recent decades has been that developed from Carol Gilligan's study of women's way of reasoning through moral dilemmas, for this touched a still raw nerve in our consciousness of what it is to be human. *In a Different Voice* suggests that indeed women and men do not think in the same way about things, and that our failure to understand this about one another has led to confusion in the process of mutual decision-making, and to impossible expectations put upon women to conform to an ideal that is not theirs.[9] This finding corroborated what a number of feminist scholars had already begun to suspect, that the foundations of the modern concept of person were dualistic to the core, in precisely the way that feminists had expected to be overcoming. So there was a real question about whether this tool of reason, detached as it was from embodiment and place, could ever bring about justice, for, after all, whose justice and which rationality are we talking about here?[10]

To find a different starting point and to develop an alternative concept of personhood has been the aim of the more recent emphasis on women's experience, by which the embodied and embedded nature of persons could be recognised. Feminists have questioned the 'man of reason' for his suspicion of sensuality and his effort to secure himself outside of the natural and social world, and so for his implicit devaluation of things defined as 'feminine'.[11] Many women consider that the rule of mind over body disallows the body's own knowledge to be received, but there are deep divisions between them over what this might mean. The debate over the right to an abortion, and over the nature of pornography, are two serious ethical issues in which what it means to be an embodied person plays a decisive role. So, too, women have questioned the detachment of persons from social location and structure which results in a widespread ethos of private individualism. To believe that I carry my rights around with me, and that my personhood in its most basic sense is unshaped by relations with others, are ideas that actually serve to reinforce existing structures rather than to change them. So feminists have entered the debate about what sort of society we should live in with renewed vigour.

And these questions are also questions about the relation of human persons to God, for Descartes' was an anxious search for certainty that many women claim does not characterise their own experience of intimacy with the divine. To return women to their own spiritual wisdom about these things has thus been an important task of feminist theological education and writing.[12] Throughout modern discussions of persons and rights, feminists have found themselves both within and without the prevailing model. Their expressed desire has been to find a way for a redeeming ethics that would reveal the image of God shining in the face of each person, and to develop projects that would identify and strengthen the kinds of dealings with one another that affirm this basic human distinction. Whether in our changing climate of postmodernity this way of thinking has become entirely exhausted, such that a redeeming ethics may no longer be formulated or lived in its terms, is the question that lies before feminist ethics today, and in heeding it we are taken anew into our own most original vocation.

CARETAKING RELATIONSHIPS

A second central theme of feminist ethics has been the significance of relationship, for within ties of biological kinship and communal association the human person is born, nurtured, and fulfilled. To attend to relationships is thus to do what is believed most necessary for a person to be at all, and so it is with this attentiveness that feminists have sought to undergird the detached intellect by reminding it of home. The concern for relationships has been called 'care' amongst feminists, in the sense not so much of a worried feeling or a fretting about something, as a positive determination to look after the necessities and to see to it that they are carried out for the benefit of human flourishing. Such has come to be known as an ethics of care, and it has been particularly claimed by feminists to be their own contribution to modern ethical reasoning. As with the discourse concerning persons and rights, so here, too, there is ambivalence in feminist writings concerning this careful ethic. On the one hand, it has been a protest against the illusion that human beings are separate and separable items, called individuals, merely collected together dispassionately in random groups, and an affirmation of the connections between us as life-giving and fulfilling. To take care here means to understand oneself and others to be woven together in a network of relationships, and to keep those relationships sturdy and flexible enough to sustain us. On the other hand, those who object to such an ethic see it as an excuse to return women to what has been deemed their traditional (and devalued) responsibility, and to put upon them the emotional and practical burden of looking after what men have thankfully escaped.

The notion of relationship has also played its part in the formation of ethics in modernity. Particularly in the English-speaking world, an emphasis on sentiment in the moral life was a noticeable feature of ethical writings, and it was here that care for relationships was expressed. In his *Characteristics of Men, Manners, Opinions, Times*, the Earl of Shaftesbury develops this theme in the notion of the *sensus communis*, the sense of the common, by which is meant our fitness for one another.[13] He writes:

> In short, if generation be natural, if natural affection and the care and nurture of the offspring be natural, things standing as they do with man and the creature being of that form and constitution as he now is, it follows that society must be also natural to him and that out of society and community he never did, nor ever can, subsist.[14]

In this work and in those of the Scottish Enlightenment, ethics is understood to be necessarily grounded in fellow feeling, no other argument for mindfulness of our neighbour having any logical force, so that, without this sense, there is nothing ethical and thus nothing human left, but only the sheer brute tyranny of power.[15] Shaftesbury was certainly aware that he was writing in the context of the new world-view of modern mathematics and science, the quantitative and atomistic implications of which he sought to ameliorate in attending to the qualitative and shared sense of common life by which humanity is sustained.

This emphasis as found amongst early feminists shows how keenly women were aware that responsibility for it belonged to them, if not by social obligation, then by nature. To believe that women have a distinctive nature was probably not as controversial a thing to proclaim as it seems to be today, nor was the notion that women's work in home and family was absolutely crucial to the formation of this *sensus communis*. Women as the primary bearers of human virtue, as models and tutors of goodness, as especially fitted for altruism, were not unusual notions in these early forms of feminist ethics. In our day, these notions survive in the ethics of care. Wherever women find themselves, and whatever might be the speculation about whether they are born or made as women, many feminists today choose to pick up the responsibility for relationships, and to urge upon society the importance of care in its various structures, in schools and businesses, courts of law and hospitals. To take this charge seriously is to challenge in a basic way the epistemological assumptions at work when impersonal objectivity, detachment, and rule-oriented thinking take precedence over personal involvement, passionate attachment, and a quite practical everyday respect for the happiness of those with whom one has dealings. It is also to consider the transformation of social structures that will be required, not least in the collapse of boundaries between the public and private realms, in order to follow this way of justice. For not only the heart, but the whole of the body of society is to manifest care.

These things are central to feminist theological reflection, as Mary Grey most carefully and systematically explores in her book, *Redeeming the Dream*.[16] Her description of the various significant ways in which we are related to our own selves, to others, and to the natural world, gives a quite full picture of the complex sets of interactions in which moral decisions are required of us. For Grey, the redemptive nature of these is to be understood as 'right relation', for it is this which the divine presence has created, now sustains, and promises to bring to completion in the future. Believing all things to exist in God's desire for harmonious relationship, draws women of faith to obey this creative purpose by seeking integrity and wholeness in every situation. To build right relation is an intricate undertaking, for one must be able to love one's own self with integrity while being willing to serve the needs of others, one must care for others in a way that does not foster dependency or compromise dignity, and one must attend to the wholeness of nature while relying upon the use of its resources. Difficult dilemmas arise here, and so women wonder about whether their studies should have priority over preparation of family meals, whether their concern for the personal crises of employees is being exploited by a company too busy making a profit to care, whether the same technology that offers them improved diagnosis and treatment of ill-health is destructive to the environment. That God intends us to enter these dilemmas with regard for the healing return of all things into their proper connectedness is the faith that upholds this redeeming ethics.

Here, too, the questions brought to us in a postmodern context are disturbing. The notion of a 'caring society' has been used as a political slogan in Britain to cover obvious signs of failing community services, underfunding of public agencies, and worsening work conditions for carers, to the extent that its rhetoric is treated with some cynicism. This may be only the surface, however, of a much more widespread problem – in the use of care images for advertising, of caring manners taught to telephonists and salespeople, of caring style sold as good management practice, of care as a value added to commodities – 'this futon was made while people were meditating'. Such things speak of a culture in which the media everywhere communicates to us the latest fashion, which is less and less a thing produced, than it is an idea, a good feeling, a 'brand', a virtual item. Public and private realms alike are so invaded, that families, for example, are no longer defined as units bound by kinship, but as a range of cars, a product-line, a caring company, a church, while kinship itself has become utterly dispersed. Once again, the relentless logic of late capitalism to turn everything to its use has rendered an ethic of care both more frantically needed for emergencies, and, at the same time, more utterly drained of redeeming possibilities. The problematic in this crisis raises more than a technical question about how we could promote care more effectively.

What it touches upon is a philosophical question that once again lies at the root of modernity, and this has to do with whether the very concept of an underlying matrix of relationality in which all things are interconnected has not become the necessary accompaniment of a fragmented individualised world, and thus is no longer able to perform the redeeming it announces. The networking of computer-literate consumers can quite happily subscribe to this rhetoric, which is harmless enough, and the matrix of interconnectedness that spans the globe now mimics reports of the relational nature of the divine. If all of these things are already realised in the world we live in, what is there left for us to say? To raise this question of feminist ethics is discomforting, for it reminds us that we bear the inheritance of modernity even into our best efforts to heal its divisions. The extent to which the concept of independent self-motivating rational agents could only be sustained in turn by a concept of some underlying connectedness, intuited through feeling and expressed in care for life-enhancing relationships, is yet another sign of the inscription of gender so deeply scored in post-Enlightenment thinking that women are at a loss to know which way to jump. That we at least have a question about this that lingers in the mind, is perhaps itself indicative of a point at which faithful women are called to search once more for that utmost which is love and that turning of life into its gentle truth.

THE INFORMATION OF THE SOUL

These themes of modern feminist ethics, of persons and rights, and of relationships and care, have opened up paths for political and social changes inspired especially by concern for women's lives. Ethics has been understood as a medium of this change, as the hinge whereupon humanity could be moved from a closed world of hierarchy and prejudice, that constrains development and inhibits fulfilment, out into an open universe of freely chosen noble action and affirmative relationships with self, others, and nature. This understanding of ethics, of its logic and its role, is one that unfolds from within post-Enlightenment humanism as Western culture is shifted into the modern period, and thus one that will serve its interests and promote its whole realisation. The revelation of full human potential became possible through conformity to the truths of reason and service to the ties that bind everything together. This was to be the work of ethics in thinking and in acting. Postmodernity, for all of its craziness, has been in some senses the completion of this wilfulness, carried through to its conclusions and parodied at once. So that it becomes possible in postmodernity to ask what has been unthinkable before – in what sense the agent subject is a real presence, and the network of relationality, the posited and thus already virtual reality that makes its appearance possible.

Feminist scholars have noted already just how closely notions of moral responsibility have been linked to those of gender. It has become more clear, through the work of Michel Foucault and others, that the discipline of the sexed body which gender enforces has been a major factor in the formation of personal identity in modernity.[17] To be a woman is thus no natural phenomenon, but rather the end product of a process of cultural and linguistic formation in which what it is to be a good woman has also been learned. So Simone de Beauvoir argued in the early 1960s: 'One is not born, but rather becomes, a woman.'[18] To follow the trajectory of gender construction through modern ethical thought has been to expose problems in the founding assumptions of feminist ethics. One of these is the assumption that a person is ontologically prior to its appearance in assigned social roles, that a person is an internally coherent subject distinguished by a capacity for reason, or by moral responsibility for a fabric of relationships. Feminists have claimed their inclusion in this notion of subjectivity by insisting upon their equal status as persons, and even upon their greater capacity as women for ensuring the subject's realisation in the most expansive vision of its context of life. Yet if this priority of the subject is questionable, what will happen to the shape and the task of ethics generally, and of feminist ethics in particular?

This question ripples uncomfortably through contemporary ethics which seems to be caught in a most difficult place. The norms for respect of human dignity and basic freedoms which it has established, and the value it has placed on healthy and life-giving relationships, seem to be more desperately required in a violent and exploitative world, while, at the same time, ethics is losing a grip on its own subject. The exposure of this loss has come through the writings of those like Jean Baudrillard, who shows the way in which man is the outcome of an economic system rather than its master. His assumed 'presence' as a producer, and now as a willing consumer, is the subject required for the system of economic value, that '*mirror of production*, in which all Western metaphysics is reflected'.[19] If, as he claims, 'the entire history of consciousness and ethics (all the categories of occidental psycho-metaphysics) is only the history of the political economy of the subject',[20] then ethical thinking has become the tool of the very thing it seeks to control. No one is *responsible* for being co-opted by this system, for we have all already been fashioned in its image.

The implications of this understanding of the human person as 'an ideological structure' have been explored by Judith Butler in relation to gender, for she shows how it is that '"persons" only become intelligible through becoming gendered in conformity with recognisable standards of gender intelligibility,'[21] and thus that concepts of personhood function as regulative ideals for the recognition and appropriate treatment of subjects. It has been Butler's work to demonstrate the operation of a heterosexual matrix embedded in these concepts, and, by its exposure, to question feminist claims both to equality with men, and to the uniqueness of women.[22] Both of these lie within a domain of compulsory gender difference enforced by the law of modern humanism. Her analysis of the interpretative nature of identity, as that which renders us 'intelligible' as persons, is a call for us, too, to think, and this means both to investigate the genealogy of the interpretations within which we have become intelligible, and, further, for us to engage in this interpretative work ourselves. To explore how it is that the metaphysics of substance has come so deeply to inform the soul, and how it still lingers today in ethical discourse is a difficult undertaking. Yet where else are we to think but in the places of most discomfort that trouble the world? Is this not precisely what the example of St Catherine's own ethical thinking recalls us to – that in it, there is a reaching out for the utmost and a turning into its truth which one undergoes in order that there may be love.

To question this fundamental assumption that lies within feminist ethics is to open up new considerations for faithful scholarly reflection. The distinction between action and passion in terms of which the modern notion of agent subjects has been constructed now bears closer investigation. Ethics seems to insist upon our action, so that not to *do* anything about a problem, or not to be able to give counsel about what is to be done, are the most damning indications of complicity in wrong-doing and of moral irresponsibility. If, however, the deliberate subject who supposedly bears this blame is itself the creation of the system of praise and blame, then we are drawn to consider not what we are to do, but what is being done here. To ask about how I am made, and so to ponder the information of the soul by that which lies beyond its grasp is to enter into a most demanding philosophical and theological inquiry. So, too, the agent subject has made itself known through speaking its mind, so that its desires and intentions are revealed, and its perspective on the world properly represented. The notion of making oneself public through language has been considered essential to the feminist ethical project in laying hold of the power to speak.[23] If, however, language is less what I determine to say than that which is spoken through my words, I become a performance of language. Here, too, lies an inquiry that presses upon us, as we ask what is being done in our speaking.[24]

There is, then, the matter of the body. The modern agent subject has taken its place within a natural world, presumed already to be comprised of an enduring substance, matter, that both precedes and forms the body with which the rational intellect comes in some way to be associated. The underlying materialism of such a conception, which is believed naturally to determine the sex–gender of persons, is again open to question in postmodernity. For Butler to consider the Aristotelian suggestion that there are '*modalities* of materialisation' by which the body comes to be materialised, or comes to matter, is to draw our attention to the very distinction between *morphe* and *psyche* in which the modern subject is framed.[25] These are difficult questions for us to consider, yet they have been harboured for some time within the Western philosophical tradition. For women of faith to attend to these matters is to let ourselves be taken to the edges of what is thinkable, and to ask what is to be learned there, in hope that love itself will come to matter.

The question of God is raised here too, for feminist ethics has sought to ground itself now almost entirely in the reality of a profound underlying network of relationships, manifest in women's ways of knowing and doing, but revealing the divine intention for all things. That such relationships might be broken or restored, damaged or healed, is the guiding impulse of ethical behaviour. For Christian women, such a notion is believed to be true to the traditional affirmation of the Trinitarian nature of God, so that the divine, too, is constituted as persons-in-relation. There has still been a lurking suspicion amongst feminists that the Christian creed is incompatible with this relationality, in some fundamental way that those who call themselves post-Christian or post-traditional have been seeking to establish, through a critique of the notion of transcendence. What, however, concerns us here is to inquire about what is going on in this kind of theological–thealogical grounding of ethics. One finds a sincere desire at work here, not to speak of God in a way that gives privilege, or expresses power, or reinforces hierarchies, or establishes exclusions, but rather to speak of God as that in which our commonness as human beings is created and upheld. To be returned always to this commonality in ethical decisions is a reminder of the final insignificance of privilege, power, status, and elitism in God's presence. Yet, for all the goodwill this expresses, the question is whether it is not still an expression of will, and, in that expression, whether there is not at work also the problematic of speaking of God that has been emerging throughout modernity.

We cannot hear these questions without attending to the excruciating investigations of Friedrich Nietzsche into the provenance of our moral ideas, especially of our notions of good and evil. His search takes him, not into an ontological inquiry in which some original form of these things might be shown, but rather into a genealogical one, which asks: 'Under what conditions did man construct the value judgments *good* and *evil*?'[26] To conduct one's thinking in this way is to render questionable the presumption of originality that lies in modern thinking, and to find within it a gilding, glorifying, even transcendentalising of values until their appearance as 'absolute' hides their humble roots in human thought.[27] This question has been used readily enough in feminist ethical writings to challenge the pretension of gender ideals, and to demonstrate the workings of power that elevate these to an untouchable place. Such is the thinking that lies within its hermeneutic of suspicion. What is also carried out in Nietzsche's inquiry, however, is the turning of humanity fully into time, so that its thoughts and moral ideals are understood as formed within history, and thus as unfoldings of the conditions for thinking prevalent at a given time. For Nietzsche, the history of morals reveals a humanity subject to the recurrent cycles of history, which only the strong-willed can overcome through noble effort securing their lives against time's victims. This account of what ethical thinking is doing, when read into modernity's project is more disturbing, as Nietzsche knew.

Since feminist ethics has ostensibly rejected the place beyond history, secured by man's will to power, and has accused the Nietzschean method of attacking the very ideas that are most essential to its own project, we must ask whether feminists have entirely heard what is being said here.[28] In so many respects, the discourse of contemporary feminist ethics displays precisely the recycling of values that Nietzsche foretold, as words like reclaim, recover, revalue, and reconstruct become the methodological keys to feminist thought. This turning into history, willingly, as a reaffirmation of that which Nietzsche thought to overcome, is precisely to succumb to his logic without further question. It is for this reason that I am sceptical of the efforts at a reverse Platonism, which seeks to secure the self in its relationality, believing this to be a protection against death itself. So that when Grace Jantzen, for example, says that, 'It is within the world, not in some realm beyond it . . . that the horizon of our becoming must occur', I wonder whether this is actually to defy Nietzsche's foresight, or to confirm it.[29] For Nietzsche said these things in recognition of the nihilism that has come over humanity since the death of God, the notice of which was the burden of his writing and the overcoming of which he could not foresee.

Yet in what would such overcoming consist? Feminist ethics is not alone here in facing the desperate question this poses for all kinds of ethical thinking in postmodernity. The loss of a significant political language, which does anything other than repackage old values in a new style, or which can effectively resist the logic of cultural reproduction that takes on the guise of every opponent, is evidence of the exhaustion of ethics, as we are turned out into the world with nothing left to say. Here it is no longer appropriate to speak of recovering something that has been hidden by historical events, or of revaluing something that was misunderstood in its first appearance, or of reconstructing something that can provide a new framework for our lives, for this is precisely to re-enter the self-consumption characteristic of the postmodern. What else is there to eat? These very methods, these techniques for an overcoming, exactly re-site us as postmodern, and can appear as nothing other than the very will to power that is most morally condemned. Nor in them can there be a speaking of God, for Nietzsche heard 'the cry for redemption' from the heart of this 'confining circle',[30] and knew that humanity would not save itself from its plight.

Is this the place where Catherine teaches us? Is this where her heart and mind come to meet ours with food for thought that might inform our souls today? Catherine shows us that to reach out for the utmost, to think to the limit of the thinkable in the midst of thought's most perplexing questions, is not to *will* to understand things more clearly, so that in the search for truth I may grasp that which I most want to get hold of. This is not her way of speaking. Her frequent use of the word, *voglio*, is said in the first instance of God, who *wants* her to know his truth, 'for I loved you before you came into being', and so of God who draws her desire for truth out of her own self-knowledge and into its ways of compassion.[31] For this, she must be receptive. For what is happening here is that, in reaching out, one is taken on, one is met, by that which one seeks. So that increasingly as she rises up and runs forward, as her petitions proceed, she is led into truth by its getting hold of her life. She expresses this through the description of her meeting with Christ crucified, for there is the figure who appears at the aporias of thought, and the more open she is to receiving him at these crucial points, the more is opened to her the bridge of divine love. It is thus that her thinking is praying, and thus that she may speak of what comes to her in this thinking, what happens to her, in the sense of what occurs *to her* in her thinking. For she is being changed into that which she seeks, her heart and mind converted into its tenderness, her soul informed by its gentle truth. So it is that 'by love's affection', she is made into another Christ, *un altro Cristo*.[32]

Thereby she shows us the way of *phronesis*, the way of knowing that ethics is to perform, and so her *Dialogue* teaches us how to enter into this way and to let ourselves be changed by that which we most seek. Catherine knew this to be a redeeming way. Her appeals to church leaders and politicians are not always very effective. She does not make fine public speeches, nor engage in original scholarly research and writing. She is not particularly known for miracles that happen in her presence, nor is there record of outstanding acts of charity that would distinguish her. A list of the ostensible signs of this redeeming would be hard to compile. Yet, in a way that Aristotle did not know, Catherine knew the truth which lies at the horizon of our knowing to be love, and she knew love to be that which so grips the soul in its very essence and so firmly plants itself into the body's own life, that she is entirely claimed by its call upon her, by its demand that she be only love. It is love that informs her tears for the world, so that her common sense of the human plight becomes both pity and outrage. It is love that tears her out of a normal healthy well-adjusted life and shows her that there is more to living than this, that it is only in love's truth that her life matters. It is love that teaches her its peace that passes understanding, and so throws her into the world's turmoil, with truth that can hardly be said, for words fail us, and yet is to be done, enacted, carried out in her life. In this is Catherine's wisdom for a redeeming ethics.

Such thoughts are not entirely alien to feminist ethics, for the search for truth and the longing for redemption have also informed its thought and action. This chapter has traced the ways in which these things have been manifest in the major themes of feminist ethics that have emerged with the Enlightenment in Western culture. They are indications of a readiness to enter fully into the life of one's people and to turn it into something good and just and kind. These same things call upon us today, and ask of us that we seek the truth that can bring the world to love in our time. That our situation is now shaped by the postmodern is no cause for dismay and brings no frantic clinging to things past. Rather are we as faithful women to attend to the places that are unbridgeable by the world's wisdom, and to refuse to let these go from us until love has made itself known there. This is the depth of our prayer which is the most challenging way of thinking that there is, and this is the place for the soul's information by love, which must always live on the sacraments of love, and so this is the redeeming ethics into which we are called by love's gentle truth.

Notes

1. St Catherine of Siena, *The Dialogue*, trans. Suzanne Noffke OP, Classics of Western Spirituality series (New York: Paulist Press, 1980). Dictated and written in 1377–8.
2. St Anselm, *Proslogion*, trans. M. J. Charlesworth, bilingual edition (University of Notre Dame Press, 1979). Written in 1077–8 during his time at the Benedictine abbey of Bec in France.
3. St Catherine, *Dialogue*, no. 1, p. 25.
4. Aristotle, *Nicomachean Ethics*, trans. H. Rackham (Cambridge, MA: Harvard University Press, 1999), see especially Book VI. Written between 336 and 322 BCE and edited by his son, Nicomachus, after his death.
5. Some of these early texts are collected in Alice S. Rossi (ed.), *The Feminist Papers*, revised and updated edition (Boston: Northeastern University Press, 1993).
6. René Descartes, *Meditations on First Philosophy*, trans. George Heffernan, bilingual edition (University of Notre Dame Press, 1990). Based on the second edition published as *Meditationes de prima philosophia, in quibus Dei existentia,*

et animae humanae a corpore distinctio, demonstrantur (Amsterdam: Louis Elzevir, 1642).

7. See especially Mary Wollstonecraft, *A Vindication of the Rights of Women*, reprinted in Rossi (ed.), *Papers*. First published in Britain in 1791.

8. R. Radford Ruether, *Sexism and God-Talk: Towards a Feminist Theology* (London: SCM Press, 1983) p. 104.

9. Carol Gilligan, *In a Different Voice: Psychological Theory and Women's Development* (Cambridge, MA: Harvard University Press, 1982).

10. See the different models discussed in Alasdair MacIntyre, *Whose Justice? Which Rationality?* (London: Gerald Duckworth & Co. Ltd., 1988).

11. Genevieve Lloyd, *The Man of Reason: 'Male' and 'Female' in Western Philosophy* (London: Methuen, 1984).

12. See e.g. Rebecca S. Chopp, *Saving Work: Feminist Practices of Theological Education* (Louisville, KY: Westminster John Knox Press, 1995).

13. Anthony Ashley Cooper, Third Earl of Shaftesbury, *Characteristics of Men, Manners, Opinions, Times*, Cambridge Texts in the History of Philosophy (Cambridge University Press, 1999). First published in 1711, Shaftesbury's own copy being held in the British Library.

14. Shaftesbury, 'The Moralists, a Philosophical Rhapsody', in *Characteristics*, p. 287.

15. See the studies of this period by Joan Tronto, *Moral Boundaries: A Political Argument for an Ethic of Care* (London: Routledge, 1993); Susan James, *Passion and Action: The Emotions in Seventeenth-Century Philosophy* (Oxford: Clarendon Press, 1997).

16. Mary Grey, *Redeeming the Dream: Feminism, Redemption and Christian Tradition* (London: SPCK, 1989).

17. See e.g. Michel Foucault, *The History of Sexuality* in 3 volumes (London: Penguin, 1990–2). Published as *Histoire de la sexualité* (Paris: Editions Gallimard, 1978–84).

18. Simone de Beauvoir, *The Second Sex*, trans. H. M Parshley (New York: Bantam Books, 1961) Published as *Le deuxième sexe* (Paris: NRF/Gallimard, 1949).

19. Jean Baudrillard, 'The Mirror of Production', in Mark Poster (ed. and trans.), *Selected Writings* (Oxford: Polity Press, 1988), p. 113 (his emphasis). Published as 'Le miroir de la production: ou, l'illusion critique du matérialisme historique' (Paris: Galilée, 1975).

20. Jean Baudrillard, 'For a Critique of the Political Economy of the Sign', in *Selected*, trans. Charles Levin, p. 67. Published as 'Pour une critique de l'économie politique du signe' (Paris: Gallimard, 1972).

21. Judith Butler, *Gender Trouble: Feminism and the Subversion of Identity* (London: Routledge, 1990), p. 16.

22. Butler writes: 'I use the term *heterosexual matrix* throughout the text to designate that grid of cultural intelligibility through which bodies, genders, and desires are naturalised.' *Gender Trouble*, p. 151, n. 6.

23. See e.g. Rebecca Chopp, *The Power to Speak: Feminism, Language and God* (New York: Crossroad, 1989).

24. See Judith Butler, *Excitable Speech: A Politics of the Performative* (London: Routledge, 1997).

25. Judith Butler, *Bodies that Matter: On the Discursive Limits of 'Sex'* (London: Routledge, 1993), p. 35.
26. Friedrich Nietzsche, *The Genealogy of Morals: An Attack*, trans. Francis Golffing (Garden City, NY: Doubleday & Co., 1956), p. 151. Published as *Zur Genealogie der Moral: Eine Streitschrift* (Leibzig, 1887).
27. Ibid., p. 154.
28. See e.g. Sabina Lovibond, 'Feminism and Postmodernism', *New Left Review* 178 (1989), 5–28.
29. Grace Jantzen, *Becoming Divine: Towards a Feminist Philosophy of Religion* (Manchester University Press, 1998), p. 274.
30. Nietzsche, *Genealogy*, p. 278.
31. St Catherine, *Dialogue*, nos. 3–4, p. 28–9.
32. Ibid., no. 1, p. 25.

Selected reading

Andolsen, Barbara Hilkert, Gudorf, Christine E., and Pellauer, Mary D. (eds.), *Women's Consciousness, Women's Conscience: A Reader in Feminist Ethics*, New York: Seabury Press, 1985.
Cahill, Lisa Sowle. *Sex, Gender and Christian Ethics*, Cambridge University Press, 1996.
Carmody, Denise Lardner. *Virtuous Woman: Reflections on Christian Feminist Ethics*, Maryknoll, NY: Orbis Press, 1992.
Cole, Eve Browning and Coultrap-McQuin, Susan (eds.), *Explorations in Feminist Ethics*, Bloomington, IN: Indiana University Press, 1992.
Frazer, Elizabeth, Hornsby, Jennifer, and Lovibond, Sabina (eds.), *Ethics: A Feminist Reader*, Oxford: Blackwell, 1992.
Grey, Mary. *Redeeming the Dream: Feminism, Redemption and the Christian Tradition*, London: SPCK, 1989.
Parsons, Susan Frank. *Feminism and Christian Ethics*, Cambridge University Press, 1996.
The Ethics of Gender, Oxford: Blackwell, 2001.
Rossi, Alice S. (ed.), *The Feminist Papers,* revised and updated edition, Boston, MA: Northeastern University Press, 1993.

13 Church and sacrament – community and worship

SUSAN A. ROSS

INTRODUCTION

Women's involvement in the church and its worship is neither a new nor an uncontroversial phenomenon. Paul exhorted women to keep their heads covered when praying or prophesying (1 Corinthians 11^{1-16}), and the author of the first letter to Timothy went even further by commanding that women should 'learn in silence and be completely submissive' (1 Timothy 2). But in her groundbreaking book *In Memory of Her*, Elisabeth Schüssler Fiorenza argued that women were active leaders in the early church – indeed, the New Testament evidences their involvement by its very prohibitions. And the work of scholars such as Karen Jo Torjesen and Teresa Berger has added to the evidence for women's place in any consideration of church, worship, ritual, and sacrament.[1] Yet the standard histories of church, liturgy, and sacrament take little if any notice of women's roles and contributions.

Over the last three decades, feminist theologians have engaged in a multipronged approach to the issues surrounding women, church, sacrament, and worship. First, as noted above, feminist theologians have taken a fresh look at the past, showing that, from the beginnings of Christianity, women have been active in ministry and worship, pastoral care and education. This kind of historical work is more than just compensatory, *restoring* women to their *rightful place* in church history. It also has serious theological implications, given the churches' reliance on historical precedent, particularly on early Christianity.

Secondly, the issue of women's ordination, linked of course to historical concerns, has been the focus of much feminist theological attention, particularly by Roman Catholics. But, even for those traditions which do ordain women (and some have only made this decision within the last thirty years), the question arises as to the relationship of ordination to church structure and polity. Should women seek ordination alongside their male colleagues?[2] Or should they push to change church structures so that ministry is less hierarchical?[3]

Within those traditions that continue to ordain only men, the question is how women can continue to worship in liturgical settings that are male-dominated, where lectionary readings fail to reflect women's contributions, where language for God and humanity is overwhelmingly male.[4] And in those traditions that do ordain women, the question is how women ministers can contribute to the transformation of Christianity within church structures which have been, and continue to be, dominated by a male elite.[5] Despite the ordination of women in many mainstream Protestant traditions, and despite the Roman Catholic magisterium's declaration that the issue of women's ordination is *closed*, such questions regarding women's ministries and church structures continue to surface.

Thirdly, the emergence of women's worship traditions and communities has empowered a generation of women who have developed new rituals and practices, many of them revolving around women's distinct experiences. There is an emerging sense of ritual empowerment on the part of women who are able to draw on old traditions as well as new ideas to combine symbols and rituals that remember, celebrate, and lament the lives of those who have been forgotten. These rituals also remember those who have played central roles in the lives of women in the present; they also mark new experiences of women in the present.[6] Ceremonies which honour distinctly female biological experiences, such as menstruation, childbirth, menopause, as well as other experiences which have no ritual precedent, such as sexual assault, divorce, or same-sex commitment have been developed. There is a new body of literature and tradition emerging from this movement which by naming and ritualising these experiences gives them a validity that they otherwise lack.[7]

In some cases, these rituals stand alongside women's involvement in traditional church structures. Indeed, this focus also requires a new look at *traditional* communities of women in the churches, such as sewing groups, prayer groups, altar societies. But, in other cases, women have found that new ritual communities offer a source of inspiration that traditional churches do not provide. The growth of these communities suggests that for many women the role of Christianity in their lives is profoundly changed; moreover, many mainline churches consider the language and symbols of women's ritual practices to be deeply threatening.[8] The question of how to worship is also a painful and divisive one for Roman Catholic women in religious communities who cannot *validly* celebrate a Eucharist without a male priest.[9] Their concerns centre around their autonomy as women's communities, yet their dependence on the male hierarchy for worship.

Fourthly, there is an emerging feminist theology of the sacraments, which includes a variety of *religious practices* that involve the ministry of women. That is to say, women's involvement in pastoral care, religious education (which for children has traditionally been a preserve of women), and sacramental preparation has in recent years come to be seen less in terms of support or as auxiliary to the more significant work of worship leadership and theology, and more as significant church-work in and of itself. Traditional divisions between *official* sacraments and *sacramentals*, as one might find in Roman Catholicism, are being challenged by a generation of feminist theologians who question the criteria for sacramental validity and the *public–private* separation that seems to be at the root of such divisions.[10] Feminist theologians are questioning the very definition of sacrament and the understandings of sacramental power that are so central to traditional practice. They are also delving into psychoanalytic, political, literary, and sociological theories to expand the understanding of sacrament to be more receptive to the concerns of women.[11]

The implications of all these developments are vast. A new theology of church and community, worship and sacrament challenges the power of the established tradition as church communities experience women's leadership and women's ritual and sacramental power.

This chapter will consider issues concerning women's relationship to the Christian churches and their worship. As the editor of an earlier anthology of feminist theology observed, there is much less work done by feminists in sacramental theology – and, I would add, in ecclesiology – than in some other areas of theology, for example, the doctrine of God, Christology, theological anthropology, ethics.[12] The reasons for this are complex, and I will address some of them later in the chapter. But my own work in this area has convinced me that, while there may be a less-developed theology of women, church, and sacraments, there is in churches and among worshippers a great deal of thoughtful involvement by women of every educational and socioeconomic level. A feminist theology of church and sacrament that confines itself only to theory, or even only to all-women's worship, will miss some of the most important dimensions of the phenomena of women, church, and sacrament. Thus my aim in this chapter is to cover both the theory of women's church and worship involvement, as well as some of the grassroots issues that concern women – feminist or not – who consider church and worship participation to be central to their lives.

HISTORICAL CONSIDERATIONS OF WOMEN, CHURCH, AND WORSHIP

The idea that women have always been relegated to the background of church structure and of worship has been recently laid to rest by the work that has been published over the last few decades.[13] Moreover, feminist scholars have challenged the very criteria for historical scholarship in church and liturgy as failing to incorporate gender as an *analytical tool*.[14] In *In Memory of Her*, Elisabeth Schüssler Fiorenza argued that a careful reading of New Testament texts reveals a complex picture of women's active participation in worship and in church leadership, a picture at odds with the standard portrayals of women only minimally involved in Jesus' and Paul's ministries. Women's active participation diminished, however, as Christianity survived its initial years and as the second coming of Christ did not materialise. Conservative forces within the churches began to challenge the radically egalitarian community that had emerged, and women's voices were silenced, at least officially.

Both Teresa Berger and Schüssler Fiorenza alert their readers to the idea that a *generic* or *ungendered* idea of the person in standard texts of biblical scholarship and history conceals much that is significant. Schüssler Fiorenza argues that unless such generic statements explicitly exclude women, they are to be interpreted as including women.[15] Berger observes that it is important to note that, while some statements about worship apply equally to women and men, others are gender-specific, while yet others apply to both genders in different ways.[16] What is important to note for both these writers is that gender serves as a significant historical category.

It is impossible in this brief space to do complete justice to the work of these and other scholars on the situation of women in church and worship in the history of Christianity. Nevertheless, certain themes emerge. First, when Christianity became the 'official' religion of the Roman Empire in the early fourth century, there were serious consequences for women's involvement in the church. As Christianity moved into the public sphere, with public houses of worship and public rituals, women, who had been active in the *house churches*, found themselves excluded from the public sphere of the polis, where Christianity had now found a new home. Berger observes that women were increasingly marginalised from public worship, but at the same time developed forms of worship (prayer, fasting, visiting cemeteries) over which they had some measure of control.[17]

Secondly, the development of religious communities for women had a major impact on their opportunities for church involvement and for worship. Anyone who reads the Fathers of the Church from the first five or six centuries of Christianity cannot but be struck by their frequent references to significant women in their lives, by their concerns about women's deportment, and by their acknowledgment of women's contributions to their scholarship and spirituality.[18] Women's convents and monasteries became a significant force in the church. Recent scholarship has suggested that abbesses often performed sacramental functions, such as hearing confessions in their convents; and the rite of ordination of an abbess bears significant similarities to rites of ordination for clerics.[19]

Women in convents, as well as women living at home with a vowed commitment, also practised forms of piety that had distinct characteristics. Caroline Walker Bynum has studied women whose Eucharistic piety evidenced a particular reverence for Christ's humanity, at a time when women were associated with the flesh and men with the spirit.[20] Such devotion showed a real solidarity with the human Jesus; their practices have been cited by contemporary women theologians, such as Mary Collins, as an example of women taking the Eucharist into their own hands.[21] And the recent resurgence of interest in medieval women, such as Hildegard of Bingen, has shown how actively involved women in the medieval church were in preaching, administration, and the advising of clergy.[22]

Thirdly, the Protestant Reformation had both positive and negative effects on women's religious lives. For the Protestant traditions, marriage was seen by the reformers, particularly Luther, as a real vocation in its own right.[23] And, while the reformers were men of their times and thus took for granted women's inferiority, theologically they opened up opportunities for women that would not be fulfilled for centuries. Luther's conception of the 'priesthood of all believers', with his insistence that all are priests to one another, in effect removed theological barriers to women's ordination, although it would be centuries until this was recognised.[24] While Protestants were highly critical of the vowed religious life, and in large part eliminated this opportunity for Protestant women, the Roman Catholic tradition encouraged the foundation of new religious orders with distinctive missions. There were definite limitations to religious life for women – the cloister was the norm – yet Roman Catholic nuns contributed to religious education, social services for many, particularly the poor, as well as to new forms of piety.[25]

The historical evidence for women's involvement in church and worship is thus rich indeed. Arguments *from tradition* that women have not played a serious role in church leadership or in worship life suffer from a highly limited idea of what involvement constitutes, as well as an ignorance of the extent of women's leadership roles. Women's work in nineteenth-century Protestant missionary movements, the work of women of colour in the anti-slavery and suffrage movements, the work of nuns in colonial Latin America, and women's activism in social justice movements, all counter a picture of church that places women in the background.

THE ORDINATION OF WOMEN

The question of women's ordination is at the centre of any consideration of women in the church and its liturgical life. There is some evidence that women were ordained for certain functions in early and medieval Christianity. In modern Christianity, the issue of women's liturgical leadership has emerged as a consequence of arguments for women's equality. Nevertheless, it is important to note that questions about women's leadership and/or ordination have been raised since the beginning of Christianity and have been treated seriously by thinkers such as Thomas Aquinas.[26]

As I noted above, Luther's theology of ministry in effect opened the door to the ordination of women by rejecting the Roman Catholic conception of ministry as priesthood. In doing so, this theology (re)claimed a more scriptural picture of ministry that included a universal call to ministry, a conception of the pastorate as involving call by the people, and, in general, a more congregational, and less hierarchical, emphasis on ministerial structures.[27] Even before Antoinette Brown Blackwell's ordination in the United States in 1854 by the Congregational Church, women such as Ann Lee, the founder of the Shakers, and Anne Hutchison, a Puritan colonist, were challenging prevailing conceptions of all-male religious leadership.[28] Such efforts were supported by Enlightenment ideas of human equality (as for example those of John Stuart Mill), and it is probably fair to say that the movement for the ordination of women in Protestantism as well as Catholicism has been energised and fuelled by liberal ideas of equality. The more conservative Protestant denominations which continue to ordain only men base their positions on a strict interpretation of biblical texts, some of which were mentioned above.[29] But mainline Protestant denominations began ordaining women in the mid-twentieth century.[30]

The Anglican–Episcopalian debates on women's ordination have been divisive ones. In 1974, eleven American women were *irregularly* ordained to the priesthood by four retired bishops, and it took until 1976 for the General Convention of the Episcopal Church of the United States to recognise these ordinations as valid.[31] Individual dioceses could decide against women's ordination by not sponsoring female candidates for priesthood. In 1992, the Church of England voted to permit the ordination of women to the priesthood. These decisions have had a dampening effect on ecumenical dialogue with the Roman Catholic Church, and some (male) priests have left the Anglican Communion and sought ordination in the Roman Catholic Church because of the decision to ordain women.

Within Roman Catholicism, the issue has revolved around two related conceptions: one of priesthood and one of gender complementarity.[32] In relation to priesthood, official Roman Catholic teaching understands the priest as *another Christ, alter Christus*. Anyone representing Christ must be *recognisable* as a symbol of Christ, 'who was and remains male'.[33] Moreover, according to this argument, Christ called only men to be his apostles. While he could have called women, such as his mother Mary and his companion Mary Magdalen, he did not, and this example is seen to be normative. In relation to gender complementarity, Vatican teaching sees sexuality as an essential dimension of the person, one that goes far deeper than racial or ethnic differences. The *essential* nature of men is to be active, as God is active in creation, and the *essential* nature of women is to be receptive, as humanity is receptive in creation, and as women are receptive in human procreation.[34] Thus Christ is Bridegroom to his Bride the Church, and consequently only men can realistically and adequately represent Christ.

Feminist responses to this argument have wholeheartedly rejected both this conception of priesthood and its *essentialist* understanding of personhood, as well as the biblical and historical warrants for Christ's *example*.[35] First, feminist theologians argue that biblical interpretations that relegate women to the background of apostolic ministry fail to consider the patriarchal situation of church and society at the time the New Testament narratives were written; moreover, they take a more literalist approach to this issue than towards other biblical examples (e.g. holding all goods in common, rejection of violence, the calling of married Jewish men).

Secondly, essentialist ideas of gendered personhood uncritically (and mistakenly) fall into the 'biology as destiny' trap and fail to recognise how ideas of 'woman' and 'man' are also socially constructed. The picture of men as wholly active and women as receptive in procreation has been shown to be false, influenced more by ideologies of female passivity and male aggression than biology.[36] But, even more importantly, the idea that women are *essentially* maternal and nurturing – the picture of womanhood advocated by John Paul II – while men are *essentially* paternal and active is resoundingly rejected, as well as ridiculed, by feminist theologians who charge that the Vatican position is driven by a fear of sexuality and of women's power.[37] Such conceptions of complementarity, feminist theologians argue, violate the theological principle that all human beings are created in the image of God, since men are seen to be *more like God* than are women.[38]

Contemporary discussions of women's ordination in Roman Catholicism have come to revolve more around the nature of the priesthood itself, and whether women would even *want* to be ordained into a celibate, hierarchical – and, some would argue, dysfunctional – clerical system.[39] And, while Protestant women are in seminaries and are ordained in increasing numbers, the problem of the structure of the ordained ministry, and thus of church structure as well, continues to be an issue. Congregational resistance to women pastors, women clergy's difficulty in moving out of associate into senior positions, problems in balancing professional and personal lives, and differences between men's and women's leadership practices all contribute to the sense that women clergy face 'an uphill calling' and a 'stained-glass ceiling'.[40] Yet, as women have entered ministry, either ordained or lay, it is clear that they are changing its practice as well as its face.[41] Even in Roman Catholicism, *priestless parishes* are increasingly headed by women, many of them nuns, who in ways that cannot be measured are transforming people's conceptions of church and ritual leadership.

WOMEN AND WORSHIP

In the early 1970s, I was invited by a friend to participate in an informal gathering of women to celebrate a Eucharist without a priest. We met in her apartment, lit candles, read the Bible and prayed and blessed bread and wine together. It was an exhilarating experience, but also one that made us feel vaguely like criminals. I soon learned that we were not alone, and that women in many other places were doing the same.

At the same time, opportunities for women to participate in official worship were opening up. In Roman Catholicism, women could now do more than bake the communion wafers and wash and iron the altar linens. Women became readers and Eucharistic ministers, and, in 1994, girls were officially allowed to be altar servers.[42] Although, for some, the prospect of a woman in the sanctuary was a shock, women began to take on a much more active role in worship.[43] In Protestant congregations, women took on pastoral leadership and preaching, and moved beyond the traditional role of pastor's wife or children's religious educator.

But both the practice of women's worship communities and women's increasing involvement in the worship traditions of their churches raised important questions: how does women's worship draw on the tradition?

Should traditional practices be changed so as to recognise women's contributions? What (if anything) should be done about the language of traditional liturgies and of the choice of readings?

The issue of language has been one of the most challenging issues for women and worship. By this I mean not only the language used for God, traditional prayers, and lectionary choices, but also the *words of women*. As the title of Rebecca Chopp's book illustrates, *The Power to Speak* is a power that women have begun to claim as their own, challenging understandings of the Word and words.[44] Women's preaching has the power to break open the word of God, *naming grace* in ways that have until now gone unspoken.[45] As the consciousness-raising groups of the 1960s illustrated, naming and speaking one's experiences gives them reality and authority.

Feminist explorations and critiques of worship extend, of course, beyond *inclusion* of women in traditional preaching and presiding roles. The choice of lectionary readings for the church year as well as the kinds of bodily postures worshippers are expected to take raise profound questions about the *formative* role of worship. The ancient formula, *lex orandi lex credendi*, the law of praying is the law of believing – or, we believe what we worship – suggests that liturgy shapes the person, even in ways that we may not be aware of. Thus the exclusion of women from the lectionary suggests that we inherit and transmit a tradition in which women's contributions – such as that of the Egyptian midwives in the Exodus story – are absent.[46] The forms of prayer that we use in asking for forgiveness, in standing (or kneeling) before God, suggest relationships of male dominance and female submission, relationships that are all too often imitated in daily life.[47]

Such examples reveal that *inclusion* of women in the traditional, and male-dominated, worship practices of the churches is not an adequate solution to the question of how women can participate in worship. So, many women have turned to new forms of worship: some take their inspiration from more traditional forms of worship, such as 'WomenEucharist' groups.[48] Others are communities *on the margins* that provide a space for women to celebrate, mark, or lament, as the occasions call for, particular experiences: abortion or miscarriage, sexual assault, a change in one's life situation, a house blessing, 'croning'.[49] Still others, like WATER, are more or less permanent groups which offer a definite alternative to traditional worship.[50] And there are groups that go beyond Christian boundaries to practise a revival of ancient witchcraft and/or worship of the goddess. All of these groups share, in varying ways, a certain set of commitments and practices. Lesley Northup has identified 'emerging patterns in women's ritualizing', and names ritual images (which would include the circle, nature, the body), ritual actions (reflexivity, naming, healing), and ritual characteristics (spontaneity, de-emphasis on formal leadership, non-reliance on texts) as characteristics of women's ritual practices.[51]

These practices challenge the hegemony of the churches' traditional forms of worship and, indeed, challenge the traditional boundaries between official, or valid, worship. Hispanic women, for example, have traditionally maintained altars in their homes; devotions to Mary and processions on feast days are as significant, if not more so, than the Sunday Eucharist that is officially the central worship of the Catholic church.[52] Bible study groups and prayer groups, particularly among Protestant women, help to create a sense of community that for many is more central to their experience of church than Sunday worship.[53] All of these practices suggest that women's worship practices are changing the face of worship.

WOMEN AND THE SACRAMENTS

While there has been considerable discussion in feminist theology about women's *liturgical* participation, both traditional and non-traditional sacramental theology has not received the same amount of attention. My own research into post-Vatican II sacramental theology has revealed that the issue of gender, apart from the question of women's ordination, is addressed rarely, if at all. Important questions regarding gender and sacramentality beg for answers. What assumptions about human nature and embodiment are included in sacramental theology's attention to the incarnation? What understandings of symbol and language serve as a foundation to discussions of presence and meaning? What role do the sacraments play in transforming our moral life?

My own work has been an effort to address these questions.[54] Sacramental theology and feminist theology share some significant concerns: among them, a recognition that God's presence is to be found in and through the material dimensions of life, particularly in the incarnation; a sensitivity to human interdependence and a deep concern for non-human life; and a rootedness in the story of Jesus, whose life was a living sacrament of God's presence in the world. Yet, as the sacraments have become institutionalised rituals of the church, their possibility to break open and reveal God's 'extravagant affections' has been constricted. God's immanent presence in the world and in human embodiment is narrowed to its definitive expression in the bodies of men.[55] Human communal life is regulated by the church and subject to legal strictures on what sorts of sacramental expressions are to be permitted. And the life of Jesus, notwithstanding his emphasis on service to the other and his ambivalent attitude to the demands of the law, is used to legitimate both male domination and ecclesiastical legalism.

A feminist understanding of the sacraments, I argue, needs to allow for a much greater appreciation of the inherent ambiguity of the sacraments as vehicles of God's mysterious and elusive presence in the world. The metaphysical ambiguity surrounding conceptions of the ordering of the world and of God's presence, the expressive ambiguity that is inherent in symbolic and linguistic expression, and the moral ambiguity of a tradition which has both encouraged and demeaned women – all of these speak to the problems of a tradition that has tended to interpret the sacraments through the legal criteria of canon law. While a toleration and appreciation for ambiguity remains a formal criterion for an adequate feminist theology of the sacraments, such a criterion cannot stand alone. Along with it are needed critical understandings of embodiment and sexuality and of language and symbol. And all of these criteria ultimately stand or fall with their ability to advance the full flourishing of women and men – that is to say, there is a final criterion of justice.

The seven sacraments of the Catholic tradition have served as rituals of passage for the Christian life, signs of God's presence in the birthing, nourishing, forgiving, maturing, uniting, healing, and calling of human lives. Yet the theology which has served to explain and understand the sacraments has not, for the most part, taken gender into account – except when it comes to Holy Orders and Marriage. So it is appropriate to ask what kind of theological anthropology is at work in the sacraments. When it comes to embodiment, nearly all of the discussion of body and gender has focussed on the appropriateness of male-only ordination. But a theology of the body has been an important dimension of the current theology of the official Roman Catholic Church, particularly that of Pope John Paul II, and his understanding has had a profound effect on Roman Catholic theological anthropology. This theology, in turn, has important implications for sacramental theology, but it ought to be noted that there are very important implications for sexual ethics as well.

Briefly put, the theological anthropology of John Paul II, as noted above in the discussion of ordination, is *nuptial*, relying on the metaphor of the Bridegroom and Bride to understand human personhood in its sexual differentiation and in relation to God. The Bridegroom (God) is the one who initiates love, and this love is received and responded to by the Bride (humanity). Since the sacraments are the human symbols which the church uses to express its understanding of human and divine relationship, it is appropriate for these symbols to extend this same metaphor. The implications for a theology of holy orders are quite clear, as I have noted above. But the further problem with this anthropology is its dualistic conception of embodiment and relationship.[56]

When it comes to symbol and language, recent psychoanalytic theory has provided some intriguing ways of conceiving human expression. Feminist theorists and theologians have drawn on these theories in both critical and constructive ways to suggest that gender and family socialisation may well play a powerful role in the ways that human beings communicate.[57] My own suggestion here is that psycholinguistic theories that propose language as a way of bridging the gap between the self and the absent (m)other are largely based on the assumption that human selfhood, language, and symbolic communication emerge through a process of separation from the mother. In such a system, women's ritual absence makes sense. But feminist theories propose that women's experiences may not be so much of separation, as are those of men, but more of identification and relation. Thus a feminist sacramental theology is less concerned with absence than with presence, less with separating sacramental life from ordinary life than with finding continuities between the two.

In sum, my conception of a feminist sacramental theology is one where careful distinctions between sacred and secular, male and female, sacrament and 'sacramental' are far less significant than the sacraments' ability to express God's amazing presence in human life, the potential of all life to reveal God's presence, and the importance of relating the hospitality of God's gracious love in every possible dimension of human life. Such a sacramental theology begins not with official definitions but with women's experiences of God, often in the most ordinary of circumstances.

CONCLUSION: CHURCH AND SACRAMENT 'FROM THE GROUND UP'

A feminist theology of church–community and sacrament–worship begins from the ground up. That is to say, women's experiences of community, of celebrating the extraordinary within the ordinary, of ritual and celebration, have provided the basis for a practice of community and worship that does not begin with the traditional theological conceptions of church and sacrament, but rather with a gathered, inclusive, and non-hierarchical community.

But, as feminist theory has reminded us, particularly over the last twenty years, there is no such thing as 'women's experience'.[58] Not all

Susan A. Ross

women experience their relationship to the church in the same way, and women's practices of ritual and worship run the gamut from Wicca to WomenEucharist to women's groups within traditional churches. There are significant differences even among women of the same religious traditions regarding the naming of God, the nature of church leadership, and the value of traditional worship practices. Yet, despite all of these differences, I think that it is still possible to draw some tentative conclusions and propose some issues for future agendas when it comes to issues of church and worship.

First, the history of the church, and therefore its heritage for the present, needs serious revision and renewal. Women's leadership in the ancient, medieval, Reformation, and modern eras has been rendered invisible by the myopia of historians of church and of liturgy. Such historical work, it is crucial to note, is not merely text-writing. Tradition, explicitly for Roman Catholicism and implicitly for Protestantism, serves as a criterion for authenticity. So, as the understanding of the biblical witness has been developed and expanded, new pictures of that tradition that restore women to their place can and do play constructive roles as the churches face the future.

Secondly, church identity and structure have undergone significant challenges by feminist theologians. Elisabeth Schüssler Fiorenza's 'Discipleship of Equals' is one important model for conceiving of the church's self-understanding. It is, I think, fair to say that hierarchy is a *red flag* word for feminist theologians who distrust conceptions of leadership that work on a top-down basis. Like their forebears in all Christian reform movements, feminist theologians turn to the example of Jesus, whose ministry, as described by Sallie McFague, was 'destabilizing, inclusive, and nonhierarchical'.[59] Feminists struggle with issues of leadership among themselves, and issues of inclusivity in leadership.[60] Nevertheless, feminist, womanist, and mujerista theologians have been able to organise in various ways that attempt to model a community that practises as well as preaches justice.[61] For theologies of the church, feminist theologians have often turned to their colleagues in Latin American liberation theology, who see the church as grounded in small communities of reflection and action.[62]

Thirdly, women's rituals have come to empower women as ritual experts in traditions which have long excluded women from direct contact with the sacred. This movement is one of the most revolutionary, as new rituals challenge the primacy of established church traditions. Women's worship groups need to develop ways in which they can be both intentional and yet open to the wider community, and to practise hospitality in ways that they see traditional churches as failing to do.[63] Women's ritual empowerment has become a threat to some in the traditional churches, particularly Roman Catholicism, where strict rules about who *dispenses* sacraments and who does not are being issued so as not to *confuse* the people.[64] But women's leadership in the church, particularly in *priestless parishes*, has resulted in more than one person saying that 'Sister's Mass' is preferable to 'Father's Mass'. Women's rituals have also come to mark events in human life that have heretofore been ritually ignored. Thus the ritual structuring of human life is changed, as experiences such as menarche and menopause, childbirth and croning are seen as significant life markers.

Fourthly, and finally, women's involvement in church and sacrament– community and worship raises urgent questions which will need to be addressed in the future. For example: what kind of doctrine of God is suggested by a radically *immanentist* approach to worship? Given the *horizontality* of women's worship, are ideas and experiences of God's transcendence no longer relevant? Another question: how long will Roman Catholic feminists be able to continue strategies of resistance to hierarchical male leadership? As the numbers of ordained priests decline, how will women continue to participate in church leadership without the structures giving way? What kinds of organisational structures most enhance love and justice? As feminist, womanist, and mujerista theologians have discovered, working together in just and liberating ways is a more difficult task than they have imagined.[65]

If there is anything that can be drawn from this brief study of women's involvement in the church and its ritual life, it is that women have always been involved, and will continue to be involved. But how this involvement will be defined and understood in the future is a question which cannot yet be answered.

Notes

1. Elisabeth Schüssler Fiorenza, *In Memory of Her: A Feminist Theological Reconstruction of Christian Origins* (New York: Crossroad, 1983); Karen Jo Torjesen, *When Women Were Priests: Women's Leadership in the Early Church and the Scandal of their Subordination in the Rise of Christianity* (San Francisco, CA: Harper and Row, 1993); Teresa Berger, *Women's Ways of Worship: Gender Analysis and Liturgical History* (Collegeville, MN: Liturgical Press, 1999).
2. See Elisabeth Schüssler Fiorenza's essay, 'Should Women Aim for Ordination to the Lowest Rung of the Hierarchical Ladder?' in *Discipleship of Equals: A Critical Feminist Ecclesia-logy of Liberation* (New York: Crossroad, 1993), pp. 23–38; the twentieth anniversary meeting of the Women's Ordination Conference in November of 1995 considered the questions of the organisation's goal. There was no consensus as to the best approach. See 'Women Wary about Aiming to be Priests: Catholic Feminists Urge a Wider Goal [20th Anniversary meeting of

the Women's Ordination Congress' (*sic*)], *New York Times* 144 (14 November 1995), p. A12.

3. Letty Russell, *Church in the Round: Feminist Interpretations of the Church* (Louisville, KY: Westminster John Knox Press, 1993).

4. See Marjorie Procter-Smith, *In Her Own Rite: Constructing Feminist Liturgical Tradition* (Nashville, TN: Abingdon Press, 1990); *Praying With our Eyes Open: Engendering Feminist Liturgical Prayer* (Nashville, TN: Abingdon Press, 1995). See also Procter-Smith and Janet Walton (eds.), *Women at Worship: Interpretations of North American Diversity* (Louisville, KY: Westminster John Knox Press, 1993.

5. Barbara Brown Zikmund, Adair T. Lummis, and Patricia M. Y. Chang, *Clergy Women: An Uphill Calling* (Louisville, KY: Westminster John Knox Press, 1998).

6. See Lesley A. Northup, *Ritualizing Women: Patterns of Spirituality* (Cleveland, OH: Pilgrim Press, 1997).

7. See Rosemary Radford Ruether, *Women–Church: Theology and Practice* (San Francisco, CA: Harper and Row, 1985).

8. See, for example, the responses to the 'Re-Imagine' conference in Minnesota in 1993. See *Church and Society* 84:5 (May–June 1994); the entire issue of the journal (published by the Presbyterian church [USA]) is devoted to reflections by Presbyterian women on the conference.

9. See Susan A. Ross, 'Like a Fish Without a Bicycle?' *America*, 181:17 (27 November 1999), 10–13.

10. See Susan A. Ross, *Extravagant Affections: A Feminist Sacramental Theology* (New York: Continuum, 1998).

11. See, e.g. Kelly Rab, 'Nancy Jay and a Feminist Psychology of Sacrifice', in her review of Nancy Jay's *Throughout Your Generations Forever: Sacrifice, Religion, and Paternity* in *Journal of Feminist Studies in Religion* 13 (Spring 1997), 75–89.

12. See Catherine LaCugna's remarks in the Introduction to LaCugna (ed.), *Freeing Theology: The Essentials of Theology in Feminist Perspective* (San Francisco, CA: HarperSanFrancisco, 1993), p. 3.

13. There is a great deal of material available on this subject; see, for example, Carolyn DeArmond Blevins, *Women in Christian History: A Bibliography* (Macon, GA: Mercer University Press, 1995); Agnes Cunningham, *The Role of Women in Ecclesial Ministry: Biblical and Patristic Foundations* (Washington, D.C.: US Catholic Conference, 1976); Ross Shepard Kraemer and Mary Rose D'Angelo (eds.), *Women and Christian Origins* (New York: Oxford University Press, 1999).

14. The phrase is from Berger, *Women's Ways*, p. 6.

15. 'If exegesis, therefore, would take seriously the issue of androcentric language as generic language, we would maintain that any interpretation and translation claiming to be historically adequate to the language character of its sources must understand and translate New Testament androcentric language on the whole as inclusive of women until proven otherwise.' Schüssler Fiorenza, *In Memory*, p. 45.

16. Berger, *Women's Ways*, p. 8.

17. Ibid., pp. 40–61.

18. For an anthology of such contributions, see Elizabeth Clark (ed.), *Women in the Early Church* (Collegeville, MN: Liturgical Press, 1983).

19. See the work done by Gary Macy (College Theology Society paper, June 1999). Thomas Cahill mentions Brigid of Kildare and the significance of women's leadership in Ireland in *How the Irish Saved Civilization* (New York: Doubleday, 1995), pp. 172–6.
20. Caroline Walker Bynum, *Holy Feast and Holy Fast: the Religious Significance of Food for Medieval Women* (Berkeley, CA: University of California Press, 1987).
21. Mary Collins, OSB, 'Women and the Eucharist', Address to the Leadership Conference of Women Religious, 1992 (*Origins*).
22. Barbara Newman, *Sister of Wisdom: St. Hildegard's Theology of the Feminine* (Berkeley, CA: University of California Press, 1987).
23. Martin Luther, 'The Freedom of a Christian', in John Dillenberger (ed.), *Martin Luther: Selections from his Writings* (New York: Doubleday, 1961), pp. 64ff.
24. See ibid.
25. See JoAnn McNamara, *Sisters in Arms: Catholic Nuns Through Two Millennia* (Cambridge, MA: Harvard University Press, 1996). It is worth noting that the ideas of Ignatius Loyola inspired many women who wished to follow his lead in serving Christianity actively. Such efforts, however, were not encouraged by Rome, and the story of Mary Ward serves to illustrate what happened to religious women who wanted to serve outside the cloister. See the biography of Mary Ward by Henriette Peters, *Mary Ward: A World in Contemplation*, trans. Helen Butterworth (Leominster: Gracewing Press, 1994).
26. See 1 Timothy 2^{12} and Thomas Aquinas, *Commentary on the Sentences*, Book IV, Q. 39, art. 1: 'Accordingly, since it is not possible in the female sex to signify eminence of degree, for a woman is in the state of subjection, it follows that she cannot receive the Sacrament of Order.'
27. See Luther, 'The Pagan Servitude of the Church', in Dillenberger (ed.), *Selections*, pp. 345ff; John Calvin, *Institutes of the Christian Religion*, book IV, ch. III, vol. 21 of *The Library of Christian Classics* (Philadelphia, PA: Westminster Press, 1960), pp. 1053–68.
28. See Nardi Reeder Campion, *Mother Ann Lee: Morning Star of the Shakers* (Hanover, NH: University Press of New England, 1990); Elaine C. Huber, *Women and the Authority of Inspiration* (Lanham, MD: University Press of America, 1985).
29. Protestant denominations which do not ordain women include Southern Baptists, Missouri Synod Lutherans, and Mormons. Most of these denominations have opened ordained ministry to men of colour (this only happened in 1978 for the Church of Latter-Day Saints [Mormons]) but have continued to exclude women.
30. See Patricia M. Y. Chang, 'Female Clergy in the Contemporary Protestant Church: A current Assessment', *Journal for the Scientific Study of Religion* 36 (December 1997), 565–73. See also Mark Chaves, *Ordaining Women: Culture and Conflict in Religious Organizations* (Cambridge, MA: Harvard University Press, 1997).
31. On 29 July 1974, four retired Episcopal bishops ordained eleven women in a ceremony in Philadelphia. Two years later, the General Convention of the Episcopal Church voted to approve the ordination of women.
32. See the Vatican Declaration on the Admission of Women to the Ministerial Priesthood (*Inter Insigniores*, 1976). This is available in Leonard Swidler and

Arlene Swidler (eds.), *Women Priests: A Catholic Commentary on the Vatican Declaration* (New York: Paulist Press, 1977); see also John Paul II, *Ordinatio Sacerdotalis* (22 May 1994) and 'Response to a *Dubium* on Ordaining Women to the Ministerial Priesthood' (30 November 1995).

33. 'For Christ himself was and remains a man.' *Inter Insigniores*, para. 27.
34. For papal documents which describe male–female complementarity, see Paul VI, 'On the Regulation of Birth' in *Humanae Vitae* (25 July 1968); John Paul II, *Mulieris Dignitatem* (6 October 1988).
35. See Swidler and Swidler (eds.), *Women Priests*, for Catholic responses to the ordination statement.
36. Margaret A. Farley, 'New Patterns of Relationship: Beginnings of a Moral Revolution', in *Theological Studies* 36 (December 1975), 627–46.
37. Rosemary Radford Ruether, *New Woman, New Earth* (New York: Seabury Press, 1975).
38. See Mary Catherine Hilkert, 'Cry Beloved Image: Rethinking the Image of God', in Ann O'Hara Graff (ed.), *In the Embrace of God: Feminist Approaches to Theological Anthropology* (Maryknoll, NY: Orbis Press, 1995), pp. 190–205; 'Experience and Tradition: Can the Center Hold? Revelation' in LaCugna (ed.), *Freeing Theology*, pp. 59–82; 'Key Religious Symbols: Christ and God' in *Theological Studies* 56 (June 1995), 341–53.
39. For an earlier comment on this issue, see Schüssler Fiorenza, 'Should Women Aim for Ordination?'
40. Zikmund, Lummis, and Chang, *Clergy Women.* In March 2000 in the Evangelical Lutheran Church of America (ELCA), of roughly 11,000 ordained pastors, only 20 women hold the position of senior pastor in a large (over 1,000 members) church. (From a personal communication with the Revd Janice Erickson-Pearson.)
41. See Dorothy Bass (ed.), *Practicing Our Faith: A Way of Life for a Searching People* (San Francisco, CA: Jossey-Bass, 1997).
42. The National Conference of Catholic Bishops of the US eliminated the distinction between male and female altar servers in 1994.
43. 'Vicar "Would Shoot" Women Priests', in *Chicago Tribune*, 10 March 1994.
44. Rebecca Chopp, *The Power to Speak: Feminism, Language, God* (New York: Crossroad, 1989).
45. Mary Catherine Hilkert, *Naming Grace: Preaching and the Sacramental Imagination* (New York: Continuum, 1997).
46. Jean Campbell, 'Lectionary Omissions: Biblical Women and Feminine Imagery', in *Witness* 76 (May 1993); Marjorie Procter-Smith, 'Images of Women in the Lectionary', in Elisabeth Schüssler Fiorenza and Mary Collins (eds.), *Women – Invisible in Theology and Church* (Edinburgh: T. and T. Clark, 1985), pp. 51–62.
47. Marjorie Procter-Smith, '"Reorganizing Victimization": The Intersection between Liturgy and Domestic Violence', in Carol J. Adams and Marie M. Fortune (eds.), *Violence Against Women and Children: A Christian Theological Sourcebook* (New York: Continuum, 1995), pp. 428–43.
48. See Sheila Durkin Dierks, *WomenEucharist* (Boulder, CO: WovenWord Press, 1997).
49. See Ruether, *Women–Church.*

50. Women's Alliance for Theology, Ethics, and Ritual (WATER), co-founded by Mary Hunt and Diane Neu, is based in Silver Spring, Maryland. Information can be found at http://www.his.com/~mhunt/.

51. Northup, *Ritualizing Women*. I draw on ch. 2, 'Emerging Patterns in Women's Ritualizing', pp. 28–49. See also Mary Collins, 'Principles of Feminist Liturgy' in Procter-Smith and Walton, *Women at Worship*; Berger, *Women's Ways*, ch. 4, 'Liturgical History in the Making: The Women's Liturgical Movement'.

52. Ada María Isasi-Díaz, *Mujerista Theology: A Theology for the Twenty-First Century* (Maryknoll, NY: Orbis Press, 1997).

53. Mary McClintock Fulkerson, *Changing the Subject: Women's Discourses and Feminist Theology* (Minneapolis, MN: Fortress Press, 1994).

54. Ross, *Extravagant Affections*.

55. It might be argued that devotion to Mary mitigates this focus on male embodiment as the definitive place for the incarnation. But Marian devotions do not occupy the public and 'official' place in the church's liturgical life that the sacraments do. Nevertheless, these devotions show how women's worship is able to develop outside the church's public devotions. The work of Hispanic theologians such as Orlando Espín and Ada María Isasi-Díaz has been significant in showing the importance of folk religious practices.

56. See *Extravagant Affections*, pp. 127–36, where I suggest that a broader conception of embodiment and relationship might draw more fully on feminist conceptions of the family, as both rooted in the 'natural order' and as socially constructed.

57. For a helpful feminist theological treatment of psychoanalytic theory, particularly that of Jacques Lacan, see Mary Frohlich, 'From Mystification to Mystery: Lonergan and the Theological Significance of Sexuality', in Cynthia S. W. Crysdale (ed.), *Lonergan and Feminism* (University of Toronto Press, 1994).

58. Sheila Greeve Davaney, 'The Limits of the Appeal to Women's Experience', in Clarissa W. Atkinson and Constance H. Buchanan (eds.), *Shaping New Visions: Gender and Values in American Culture* (Ann Arbor, MI: University of Michigan Press, 1987).

59. See Sallie McFague, *Models of God: Theology for an Ecological, Nuclear Age* (Nashville, TN: Fortress Press, 1987), p. 45.

60. See Isasi-Díaz on issues of inclusion and exclusion in *Mujerista Theology*, pp. 18ff.

61. Women–Church Convergence is one example of women gathering together under a common organisation. Further information is available at http://www.luc.edu/orgs/gannon/archives/general/html.

62. See Mary Hines, 'Community for Liberation: Church' in LaCugna (ed.), *Freeing Theology*, pp. 161–84.

63. See Christine D. Pohl, *Making Room: Hospitality as a Christian Tradition* (Grand Rapids, MI: Eerdmans, 1999); Bass (ed.), *Practicing Our Faith*.

64. See 'Some Questions Regarding Collaboration of Non-ordained Faithful in Priests' Sacred Ministry', *Origins* 27:24 (27 November 1997).

65. An example of this difficulty is the Women–Church Convergence meeting in Albuquerque, New Mexico, 16–18 April 1993, where some groups withdrew from the meeting because of concerns over inclusion in the planning process,

Susan A. Ross

and of 'using' Native American traditions. Papers from the conference are available at the Gannon Center, Loyola University, Chicago, IL; further information on the center is available at the website (see note 61 above).

Selected reading

Berger, Teresa. *Women's Ways of Worship: Gender Analysis and Liturgical History*, Collegeville, MN: Liturgical Press, 1999.

Fulkerson, Mary McClintock. *Changing the Subject: Women's Discourses and Feminist Theology*, Minneapolis, MN: Fortress Press, 1994.

Hilkert, Mary Catherine. *Naming Grace: Preaching and the Sacramental Imagination*, New York: Continuum, 1997.

Procter-Smith, Marjorie. *In Her Own Rite: Constructing Feminist Liturgical Tradition*, Nashville, TN: Abingdon Press, 1995.

Ross, Susan A. *Extravagant Affections: A Feminist Sacramental Theology*, New York: Continuum, 1998.

Ruether, Rosemary Radford: *Women–Church: Theology and Practice*, San Francisco, CA: Harper and Row, 1985.

Russell, Letty A. *Church in the Round: Feminist Interpretation of the Church*, Louisville, KY: Westminster John Knox Press, 1993.

Schüssler Fiorenza, Elisabeth. *Discipleship of Equals: A Critical Feminist Ecclesia-logy of Liberation*, New York: Crossroad, 1993.

Torjeson, Karen Jo. *When Women Were Priests: Women's Leadership in the Early Church and the Scandal of their Subordination in the Rise of Christianity*, San Francisco, CA: Harper and Row, 1993.

14 Eschatology

VALERIE A. KARRAS

'Eschatology is . . . Christology and anthropology conjugated in the future tense.'[1]

INTRODUCTION

Eschatology is, to define the word etymologically, 'the study of the *eschaton*', a Greek word meaning 'the furthest end', and usually translated in its theological sense as the 'last days' or, more loosely, the 'end of time'. So, eschatology traditionally has been understood within Christianity as the study of the 'Last Things', particularly in the areas of death, judgment, heaven, and hell, associated in the New Testament with the Second Coming of Jesus Christ. These 'Last Things' have been seen as apocalyptic, retributive, restorative, and, above all, transformative. The one thing that all visions of humanity's and creation's future have had in common is the belief that our future reality will be radically different from our present reality: 'new heavens and a new earth' (Isaiah 65[17]). In sum, for most of Christianity's history, eschatology has been speculation about the ultimate end of humanity and of creation – the advent of the Kingdom of God.

But feminist theologians such as Sallie McFague[2] and Rosemary Radford Ruether[3] are viewing eschatology from a radically new perspective, one which totally rejects or drastically reformulates some traditional Christian beliefs. They have refocussed eschatology from the distant future ('unrealised eschatology') to the here-and-now ('realised eschatology'). Simultaneously, these feminist thinkers have shifted the thematic centre from humanity, as the apex of creation, to creation itself, with humanity removed from centre stage to a supporting position as an interwoven, interdependent component of that creation. In short, realised eschatology has become the ethical culmination of ecofeminism. Ecofeminist eschatology is concerned not with personal immortality but with ecological and cosmic sustainability. The future is envisioned as a return to the pristine past, before human degradation of nature, but with humanity fulfilling its symbiotic potential. Ecofeminism rejects the church as the Body of Christ in favour of the cosmos as the body of God; McFague, for example, relativises the incarnation by transmuting it from the transcendent God's unique and personal union with humanity, to a paradigm for the principle of the universe itself as God's body.

Is 'feminist eschatology', then, an oxymoronic expression? That is, is feminist theology inherently anti-eschatological, at least in so far as the *eschaton* is understood as personal immortality and a distant future spelling the 'end' of the world (or, at least, the radical transformation of creation)? Certainly, most feminist theological literature gives that impression. Creation will not be wholly transformed to what science-fiction enthusiasts might describe as a different dimension of existence. Resurrection and judgment, and so consequently heaven and hell, in a personal sense are non-existent. Even the resurrection of a 'spiritual body' (1 Corinthians 15), understood as radically different from our current biologically based physical existence, is ignored. For Rosemary Ruether, immortality is, at best, simply a possibility which may mean nothing more than the return of our 'energy' to its source. McFague posits the possibility of 'persistent distinctiveness' without tying it to any notion of personal immortality; i.e., different types of inorganic and organic phenomena must be maintained and enjoyed, more or less as they exist now, but none of these individually is immortal *in se* – humanity continues, but perhaps individual persons do not.

Ruether resurrects the argument of an early twentieth-century feminist theologian, Charlotte Perkins Gilman, to articulate her theory that concern with personal immortality is a patriarchal concept arising predominantly from the male psyche. Gilman juxtaposed 'male' and 'female' religion, characterising traditional, patriarchal male religion as death- and future-oriented (hence, the eschatological focus), while describing female religion as life- and present-oriented. But are not man as hunter–warrior and woman as birth-giving/lactating mother equally tied to both life and death? The hunter–warrior kills to sustain and preserve the lives of his kin and tribe; the mother gives nourishment and life, but sometimes at the cost of her own life, a harsh reality for pre-modern women. If men feared death in battle or on the hunt, both of which they engaged in to preserve the lives of those they loved, how must women have feared death in the very act which brought forth new life? Can we legitimately claim that women are unconcerned with the future, that they do not seek personal immortality, that the immanent obliterates the transcendent in the female psyche?

I do not believe so. As a feminist theologian, I have been asked in this chapter to present to the reader an overview of feminist eschatology, and in so doing to ponder the relevance of eschatology to our present human existence as women and men. But, as a believing and practising Eastern Orthodox Christian, I cannot accept wholesale the contours of a realised feminist eschatology which sees the future essentially as a revision of the present based on an idealised past, a future which is predicated more on re-forming humanity and creation than on transforming them. Nevertheless, as a Christian of the East, I also cannot ponder eschatology (the study of 'the end') without reflecting on protology – the study of the beginning – especially, human beginning. This means that I cannot examine human existence and nature ('anthropology' in its theological sense) without ex-amining humanity's relationship not only to the cosmos ('cosmology') but to divinity as well: divinity as relational within itself (the Trinity), and as relational with humanity (the person of Jesus Christ). In other words, it is impossible for me to discuss eschatology without discussing Trinitarian theology and Christology, or *theology*, properly speaking.

METHODOLOGY AND HERMENEUTICS

I will explain shortly why I believe eschatology is inescapably connected to these other areas of theological thought. First, however, I must explain how I understand the theological enterprise differently both from Western feminists and from those of non-Western, historically non-Christian cul-tures, such as Kwok Pui-Lan and Mercy Oduyoye. I am something of a hy-brid, a woman born and raised in a Western Christian society (the United States) but also raised and inculcated with the language, culture, and the-ology of the Christian East (Greek Orthodoxy). The Eastern core of my being forces me to critique certain elements common to both feminist and patriarchal Western methodology, and to offer, in contrast, an historically Orthodox Christian approach to theological inquiry, a methodology which incorporates theology, anthropology, cosmology, and, in our case, feminist eschatology (which, of course, includes the other three).

I undertake this critique by appropriating the hermeneutics of suspi-cion created within feminist thought and reapplying them, from an Eastern Christian perspective, to Western (including classical feminist) theology. This appropriation results in the rejection of certain presuppositions and methodological approaches not only of traditional patriarchal Western Christian theology, but even of modern feminist theological thought. What this means is that, while classical and feminist theology have traditionally been seen as oppositional, they are, from an Eastern Christian perspec-tive, sometimes two sides of the same methodological coin. Perhaps this is because feminist and patriarchal theologians usually share a common (Western) mindset and common (Western) theological building blocks, which lead both groups to think in similar ways while focussing on different concerns. For Orthodox Christians, however, even some of the most basic aspects of the Western way of doing theology are alien to our way of thinking.

I will critique two tendencies in Western theological thought. The first is that of defining the juxtaposition of two different (even opposing) concepts or qualities as mutually exclusive polar opposites (dualism), a tendency evident in philosophy and social history as well as in theology. 'Mutually exclusive' is the key phrase here. The logical extrapolation of this definition of the world is the Hegelian paradigm of thesis, antithesis, and synthesis. The thesis–antithesis model can clearly be seen in feminist theology's rejection of an otherworldly, future-oriented, i.e., unrealised, eschatology in favour of a 'this-worldly', present-oriented, *realised* eschatology. It is similarly seen in feminist theology's emphasis (some might say its exclusive focus) on God's immanence (femaleness) in contrast to what is seen as an overemphasis on God's transcendence (maleness).

The problem with Hegel's theory of the resolution of the tension between thesis and antithesis through synthesis is that, usually, the synthesis can reconcile opposites only by eliminating part of what made them opposites to begin with. As it stands now, patriarchal and feminist eschatologies have not even reached the stage of synthesis. They seem locked in a battle of opposites, which makes their elimination of vital components of the rejected paradigm of the 'other' even more pronounced. Peter Phan has pointed out the deficiencies of such unbalanced eschatologies, whether they be unrealised classical eschatology or realised feminist eschatology. He sees a positive trend in post-Vatican II Catholic theology, particularly in the interrelated areas of anthropology and eschatology, towards a vision of 'pairs of polarities . . . in direct rather than inverse proportion'.[4]

This movement within more traditional theological circles, as well as feminist theology's focus on the relationship between humanity and creation, is generally welcomed in the East. Eastern Christian theology (actually, historical Christian theology in the first few centuries, though not as it developed in the West through scholasticism and the Enlightenment) is not based on the Hegelian model. Instead, as exemplified in the core doctrines of the Trinity and of the person of Jesus Christ, Eastern Christian theology sees complementarity rather than opposition, and – where complementarity is not feasible – holds diametric opposites, in their fullness, together in tension rather than resolving them into a synthetic singularity which waters down or even eliminates one half of the dialectic. This is crucial to understanding eschatology as both realised and unrealised, as simultaneously both 'now' and 'not yet'.

The second critique of Western theological methodology is its tendency to work 'bottom-up', that is, from the created to the Creator. Feminist theologians, including Ruether and McFague, have rightly accused much traditional Christian eschatology of an anthropocentric bias, but they have failed to see the same bias, or a similar one, in much of feminist theology. One example of this is the push to replace the traditional (revealed) names for the persons of the Trinity – Father, Son, and Holy Spirit – with the non-gendered names – Creator, Redeemer, and Sanctifier.

The 'new' names, unfortunately, create more problems than they solve. That is, in addition to the theological problems produced by parcelling out the shared activities of the Trinity to individual Persons within the Trinity (Does God create alone? Does the Son redeem humanity by himself?), these new names show a cosmocentric–anthropocentric focus. True, the advocated names have the important advantage of avoiding a danger far too often realised in practice by patriarchal cultures – thinking of God as male. Certainly, the early Eastern Church recognised that danger; hence, Greek and Syriac Christian writers used feminine imagery for all three Persons of the Trinity and self-consciously disassociated the traditional names from any gender content. For example, the fourth-century theologian and bishop Gregory of Nyssa claimed that one could speak of mother just as well as of father for the First Person of the Trinity since '[b]oth terms mean the same, because the divine is neither male nor female'.[5]

Nevertheless, Gregory and others argued for the irreplaceability of the traditional name 'Father' for the First Person of the Trinity, not only because Jesus Christ had revealed it, but precisely because of the *relationship* it imaged among the Persons of the Trinity. The uniqueness of the Christian message is an understanding of God *not* as an impersonal 'Force' or 'Matrix', but as a being whose very manner of existence is irreducibly personal and interrelational. The beauty of the traditional names for the Trinity is that the names tell us who the Persons of the Trinity are in relationship to each other. In other words, they reveal to us the personal and relational nature of God in God's own Self: three distinct Persons who exist as a community of love and mutual indwelling. So, Eastern Christian writers were well aware of the importance of not understanding the name Father in a human disexual sense. But, they also recognised that, since no single name would be complete, the most important aspect of God's being must be exemplified by God's name – and they valued interpersonal relationality within the Divine over divine function and activity in creation.

By contrast, the feminist names for the Trinity tell us not *who* God is in God's own Self, but *how* God relates to creation in general and to humanity in particular. In other words, instead of God telling us God's 'name' as an expression of who God is, we have decided to name God according to what God does to and for us. The feminist names are therefore simultaneously cosmocentric and anthropocentric. To use a human example, it would be equivalent to telling a woman that, although she thinks of herself most existentially and fundamentally as the mother of her children, we have decided to categorise her and refer to her only by her occupation as a physician. Ironically, then, the traditional names are more feminist, in the sense of interpersonal relationality, than the feminist names.

A THEOCENTRIC APPROACH

As with other areas of theology, so, too, in eschatology I believe that feminist theology is still operating largely within the framework of Western theology. Feminist theologians have rightly critiqued the anthropocentric focus of much traditional Western eschatology. Their solution has been to shift the focus from humanity to creation, replacing the anthropocentric focus of patriarchal Christian theology with the cosmocentric focus of ecofeminism. In reality, however, this is not so much a shift of focus as a broadening of it, a recentring which is not really. Humanity is no longer central in and of itself, but it remains part of the focus as a part of creation. In other words, ecofeminist theology's cosmocentric focus has broadened traditional eschatology's telephoto lens from an extreme magnification focussing on humanity alone to a wider view of the cosmos in which humanity exists, but it has kept the lens focussed in the same direction – creation.

What I propose is that we not merely broaden the vision seen through our lens, but that we reverse the direction in which the lens is pointed: from the created to the Creator, from the cosmos to God. If, as feminist eschatology has rightly noted, our existence as humans can only be seen within the context of our participation in the bionetwork of creation, then both humanity in particular and the cosmos as a whole can only be seen in relation to that which has given them existence and sustains that existence. Ecofeminism's understanding of the cosmos as the body of God is an important attempt to articulate this relationship, but it has inverted the order, thereby making the cosmos – and, derivatively, humanity – normative in and of itself. Thus, the restoration of both the cosmos and humanity is seen primarily as a quantitative process rather than a qualitative one. There is little focus on the future because, if one does not understand the ultimate goal of existence as something transcendent, then that future existence will look similar to the present – it may be 'better', but it won't be substantially *different*.

In reorienting our focus, we necessarily need to distinguish between creation and the Creator. The bottom-up, cosmocentric approach of feminist eschatology is a natural consequence of an ecofeminist theology which, by understanding the cosmos as the body of God, creates a virtual tautology between God and creation (or does the tautology lead to the cosmocentric approach?). Rather than the Uncreated God's relating to and sustaining creation through the Spirit (panentheism), creation becomes a part of God's own being (pantheism). In such a theology, there is relatively little of the transcendent – it does not fit the paradigm – and what little there is almost never is seen as personal. As Phan notes, Ruether's cosmic Matrix of matter–energy or great Matrix of Being[6] is reminiscent of the Buddhist concept of nirvana;[7] certainly it is closer to that than to any Christian understanding of God. McFague recognises more clearly the need for transcendence but, limited by her cosmocentric focus, seems unable to incorporate it intrinsically into her model.

I propose an eschatology, and in fact an entire theological model, which is *truly* top-down, as opposed to the apparent top-down theology of patriarchal Christianity. In other words, I will apply the feminist hermeneutics of recovery, with a twist: like Catherine LaCugna,[8] the forgotten voices which I am recovering are those of the early Christian East, articulating a theology of a tri-personal God who truly is simultaneously immanent and transcendent. This approach starts with God and who God is – it starts, in other words, with *theology* in its classical sense.

Ecofeminism's cosmocentric approach arises from what I believe is the mistake of going beyond a recognition of the value of what is called the 'common story' (the evolutionary theory of creation) in explaining *how* the cosmos came to be and continues to exist, to a model of created existence which employs that common story to explain *why* creation exists as it does. The problem is that, for there to be any room at all for God in this model, God must be understood as being totally revealed within creation.

I cannot accept this tautology. Truly, the cosmos reveals much of God's love, tenderness, power, simplicity, complexity. But can we understand the cosmos as the summation of what God is, and as the norm for our own existence? I think not. Faith includes the belief that the transcendent experiences of men and women through human history are real and are something beyond a communing with nature. A theocentric focus recognises that the cosmos reveals God, but not entirely. The cosmos reveals something of our own purpose and meaning, but a theocentric focus allows us to recognise that this is a derivative revelation which only heightens our thirst for the Source. By relying completely on creation as intercessor and revealer of the Divine, we risk falling into the trap of creating God in the creation's image. In order to understand who we truly are meant to be – and in order truly to become who we are meant to be – we must turn our view and our life towards God.

THEOLOGY – GOD AS TRANSCENDENT – IMMANENT

As I have already mentioned, the extreme immanence of feminist theology is a reaction to the extreme transcendence which characterises patriarchal theology, an example of the thesis–antithesis polarisation of Western theology. And here lies one of the most important differences between Eastern and Western Christian theology, in the understanding of the relationship between God and creation: the question of grace. The extreme transcendence of patriarchal Christianity – God as totally Other – resulted historically in the view that some mediatory element must be created in order for God to communicate with creation and, in particular, with humanity. Thus, in the theology of Thomas Aquinas, grace is created by God because uncreated grace can exist only within the internal life of the Trinity. Feminist theologians, wishing to eliminate the mediatorial gap between God and creation, reacted by identifying God with that creation.

By contrast, the Orthodox East has always holistically understood God's very Being as simultaneously transcendent and immanent, a notion emanating from the Eastern Christian understanding of human salvation as *deification* – true union with God as 'partakers of the divine nature' (2 Peter 1[4]). Salvation is not a juridical notion of justification (being made right with God), but an existential participation in the life of the Trinity, an experience which begins here and now and extends dynamically and eternally into the future. So human persons, while distinct from the transcendent divine nature, are called to be 'gods' by union with the immanent divine nature.

This theology of transcendence–immanence, rooted in the soteriology and the prayer practice of the East, was articulated most fully in the writings of a fourteenth-century monk, archbishop, and theologian, Gregory Palamas.[9] Although acknowledging that God is Other, Palamas rejected a theology based on total transcendence. Yes, Palamas said, God is truly transcendent. But God is not *only* transcendent; God is also immanent. Furthermore, God's participation in the life of creation is not mediated through the mechanism of created grace. No, Palamas averred, God is *truly* immanent. Not only may we stand in God's presence, but we also can and do experience God's own life in a way which unites us to the divine without destroying our human distinctiveness. We can perceive and participate in God's energies – God's own Self as *uncreated* grace – and are thereby transfigured.

Palamas' theology of essence and energies can, I believe, overcome the dichotomy between transcendence and immanence characterised by patriarchal and feminist theology, respectively. It allows us to develop an eschatology which can be future-oriented without ignoring or denigrating the present, because salvation is understood not as an event, but as a continuous activity of humanity's – and, through us, creation's – deifying participation in the life of the Trinity. It permits us to reach for the transcendent God without abandoning the immanent creation (including our own selves); in fact, creation itself is called to be transfigured by God's immanence.

MICROCOSM AND IMAGE OF GOD: THEOLOGICAL ANTHROPOLOGY

This theology of the transfiguration of creation brings us to humanity's distinct role as mediator. But, in order to understand humanity's mediatorial role, we must first understand what it means to be a microcosm, to be human. Many feminist theologians reject the biblical creation story with its emphasis on the special status of humanity vis-à-vis the rest of creation. Instead, they promote a 'common creation story' characterised by humanity's total identity within the evolutionary fabric of creation, usually with no transcendent connection to the divine substantially different from that shared by the rest of the universe. But, we can accept evolutionary theory (the common creation story) as a description of the process of creation and of one aspect of anthropology (the physical and biological aspect) while also retaining the theological truths of the creation accounts in the first chapters of Genesis. In other words, again we must reject an either/or approach, this time with respect to anthropology and biblical interpretation.

In the Yahwist tradition (the second, older creation account), humanity is clearly shown as linked to both creation and divinity, formed of 'dust from the ground' but quickening with God's own 'breath of life' (Genesis 2[7]). The first account (the somewhat younger priestly tradition) describes humanity as the culmination of God's ever-increasingly complex creation: part of creation, but with an important difference. Humanity is understood theologically as unique within the order of creation because it is created according to the image of God (*imago dei*).

What does this mean? Interestingly, as we have seen, for the Christian East sexual differentiation is not understood as being an attribute of God and, therefore, it is not understood as being part of God's image. Certain sex-linked traits may reflect aspects of God's nature (giving life, protecting, nurturing, etc.), but the writers of the East have almost unanimously interpreted Genesis 1[27] ('male and female God made them') in an inclusive sense, not a normative one. In particular, Eastern Christianity does not understand the male human being as the 'normative' human. Both man and woman are created in the image of God, but human differentiation as male and female is not in itself a reflection of who and what God is intrinsically. This will have eschatological significance, as we shall see later in the chapter.

So, what does the 'image' signify? The Eastern Christian distinction between the *image* and the *likeness* of God is important here. According to Genesis 1[26], God decided to create humanity in God's own image and likeness. But Genesis 1[27] states that God created humanity only according to the divine image, with no mention of the likeness. Although this parallel structure went uncommented on in the Jewish tradition, the early writers of the Christian East elaborated from these verses a distinction between image and likeness. The likeness is the realisation of true God-likeness, that is, of virtue and perfection: perfect love. We may grow into the likeness, but we do not possess it automatically; we possess only the potential for it. The image is what gives us this potential. It might be called humanity's 'toolkit', i.e., the qualities or characteristics reflective of the divine nature which make humanity distinct within the order of creation: intellect, reason, creativity, abstract thought, consciousness of right and wrong, and, above all, free will. So, God, rather than creation, becomes normative for humanity. As the Greek theologian Panayiotis Nellas stated, '[t]he category of biological existence does not exhaust man. Man is understood ontologically ... as a theological being. His ontology is iconic.'[10]

In other words, what I am articulating here is a *theological anthropology* (theocentrism) in contrast to both patriarchal anthropological theology (anthropocentrism) and ecofeminist theology (cosmocentrism). Humanity is part of creation, and so includes all aspects of creation, both inorganic and organic: physicality, a vivifying soul, emotions, and feelings. But human beings also possesses the ability to think beyond ourselves and our current condition, to make moral choices based on a rational evaluation of various possibilities and consequences, and consciously to hunger for the Other. It is this 'spirit', the part of human nature which uniquely images and participates in divinity, which makes humanity a true microcosm. Fundamentally, we are created beings who are innately oriented towards our Creator.

HUMANITY AS MEDIATOR

As we said earlier, it is this characteristic of being a microcosm which makes humanity uniquely suited to its role and calling as mediator between creation and Creator. Certainly, humanity is called to be steward, not exploiter, of creation. Ecofeminism has been immensely important here in recalling Christianity to humanity's primordial relationship to nature. The 'dominion' of humanity over creation expressed in the first chapter of Genesis is understood intertextually as stewardship, based on the second chapter's emphasis on humanity's role as gardener or caretaker. This theology of stewardship, which ecofeminism has lifted up as an intrinsic characteristic of human nature, is being embraced by traditional Christian churches and bodies. For instance, the Greek Orthodox Archbishop of Constantinople, Ecumenical Patriarch Bartholomew I, has been one of the first major church leaders to follow the example of ecofeminists in labelling pollution, destruction of the environment, and other forms of ecological insensitivity as 'sin'.[11]

But humanity's calling goes beyond the present-oriented, functional role of steward to the eschatologically oriented, existential role of microcosmic mediator; humanity is called not simply to protect, serve, and preserve creation, but to transform it by uniting it with the Divine. I am recovering here the vision of the seventh-century Greek theologian Maximos the Confessor.[12] As mediator, humanity appears to be the central focus, but Maximos' theology is not anthropocentric because humanity is not the end but the means. Humanity is seen only in relation to other elements of creation and to God, serving as mediator among these elements in its capacity as microcosm, as a 'little world' combining the inorganic and the organic, the physical, the vivifying, and the spiritual.

In Maximos' thought, humanity is called to transcend, through the grace of God, the various divisions which exist within creation. Maximos delineates five divisions, which range from the division between the created and the Uncreated, through that between heaven and earth, to the distinction between male and female within humanity. Maximos' theology of mediation is not dualist; that is, his distinctions or 'divisions' are *not* oppositional in the sense of mutual exclusion. Maximos distinguishes between ('divides') the perceptible and spiritual worlds, for example, but does not see them as antagonistically opposed. Thus, the transcendence of distinctions through human mediation does not mean the obliteration of differences; rather, it is the interrelational unifying of things which are by nature different.

In fact, the only division which Maximos says would be abolished is that between male and female within humanity. Based on theological

anthropology, Maximos sees sexual differentiation as a human characteristic outside the image of God and, unlike the other divisions, irrelevant
to our function as mediator; therefore, it is not a necessary component of
eschatological human nature. Like his predecessors Gregory of Nyssa and
Gregory's sister Macrina,[13] Maximos believes sexual differentiation to be an
aspect of our current biological mode of existence which will be abolished
in the transformation of our entire mode of being. Our current biologically
based body (the 'garments of skin' of Genesis 3^{21}), according to Eastern
Christian thought, is meant to be transformed into another mode of existence which, while still participating in the physical and organic creation,
will be sustained by union with God and therefore have no needs: the spiritual body of the resurrection (1 Corinthians 15^{44}). For Maximos, if there
were any ontological significance to sexual differentiation, then it necessarily would limit how we act and exist, and in so doing would interfere with
our freedom to act ultimately and fundamentally as human beings. In other
words, sexual differentiation with any ontological content (such as instincts
or traits) would be a denial of our complete human freedom.

So, except for the distinction of male and female in humanity, we are
called to transcend the various levels of division not by obliterating one for
the other, nor by abandoning one for the other, but by uniting them all in
ourselves as part of who we are existentially. In this mediatorial task, human persons cannot overcome the final level. Humanity in itself possesses
the attributes of all the previous divisions, but humanity is not itself divine.
So, the final division, that between created and Uncreated, must be overcome by someone who personally incorporates both created and uncreated
natures. That person is, of course, Jesus Christ, who as the *theanthropos*
(the God–human) becomes the ultimate mediator, the only one capable of
transcending and reconciling the final division. Jesus Christ, by personally uniting human nature to the divine, existentially makes possible not
only the transformation and renewal of creation, but also the deification of
humanity. Thus, for Maximos and others in the Christian East, the Incarnation is not contingent on humanity's fall from a state of grace. It is part
of God's eternal plan as the culmination of humanity's mediatorial role in
creation.

ESCHATOLOGY: REALISED AND UNREALISED

This model of humanity as mediator provides us with an eschatological vision which is 'both/and' as opposed to 'either/or'. It is an unrealised
(future-oriented, transcendent) eschatology that simultaneously has realised

(present-oriented, ecofeminist, immanent) implications. It is this vision of humanity already realised as microcosm, together with humanity's not-yet-realised goal of mediator, which provides the rationale for an eschatology which recognises that the Kingdom of God is in our midst (Luke 17²¹) while concurrently seeking it (Matthew 6¹⁰) as something not yet come – now, and not yet.

There is a similarity among patriarchal Western theology, feminist theology, and Eastern Christian theology in the emphasis all place on a future utopian society – the 'Kingdom of God' – as the goal of human existence, a goal which is not yet achieved. Consequently, all three theological threads recognise that the social, political, economic, and cultural inequities of various human societies not only are not normative for humanity, but are an aberration from the condition of paradise and far removed from the Kingdom of heaven. This recognition is not a modern development; it is part and parcel of historical Christianity's understanding of the 'fallen' nature of corporate humanity. For instance, John Chrysostom (a monk–priest from Antioch who became archbishop of Constantinople in 397) in his 22nd Homily on Ephesians identified slavery as 'the fruit of covetousness, of degradation, of savagery'; in homilies on Genesis and 1 Corinthians, he asserted that the subordination of woman was a consequence of humanity's fall from grace. He clearly recognised human inequality as a divergence from the prelapsarian and eschatological norms.[14]

But, while all three of these theological systems agree that the current condition of the human community falls far short of what it is meant to be, they differ as to whether it *can* reach its potential in the foreseeable future. That is, is the Kingdom of God achievable within the bounds of normal history? Can we construct a human society which is radically different from the way human societies are currently structured? This is the essence of the distinction between realised and unrealised eschatology: the former answers 'yes' to this question, the latter answers 'no'.

Historically, Christianity in both its Eastern and Western traditions has had an unrealised eschatology. Despite Chrysostom's recognition of the fallen nature of social inequalities, he did not call for the radical reform of either political or social structures. In fact, like many in both East and West, he considered such inequality normative for our current condition, necessary for the smooth functioning of a society filled with persons driven by ego and passions rather than love and self-emptying. Chrysostom was willing to allow for deviation from this norm where a personal spiritual situation called for it, but such deviation did not, for him, upset the validity of the norm.

Feminist theologians have railed against this apparent resignation to a fallen human condition. They have argued that human society need not inevitably be corrupt, unequal, and abusive; much less can we claim that human inequalities are God-ordained for our own benefit. Rather, we have within ourselves the power (free will) to turn from our egoism and insensitivity and, instead, to create a truly just society. This achievable society would value women, the poor, and the differently abled as equal and contributing members, and would seek not to exploit nature hurtfully for selfishly human ends, but to live in harmony with it in a sustainable way as part of a flourishing and renewable biosphere. This is realised eschatology.

I believe that both realised and unrealised eschatology are partial eschatologies, i.e., they reject, or at least de-emphasise, some part of the biblical witness. The contribution of feminist theology has been to emphasise the (largely missing) realised element of eschatology. I would like to build upon the foundations laid by Letty Russell,[15] Sallie McFague, and Rosemary Ruether, who have sought to make the *eschaton* normative for the present. At the same time, the present and the eschatological future cannot be conflated. A holistic eschatology must incorporate both realised feminist and unrealised patristic methodological approaches without diluting either one, to create an eschatology which is at once both now and not yet, with seemingly contradictory elements coexisting in an unresolved tension.

My Orthodox feminist approach combines radical feminism's rejection of the entire social order with an eschatological focus that recognises that human will and action alone is incapable of transforming the human community into one based on the loving, relational, non-egoistic model of the Trinity. Feminism's emphasis on humanity as community has provided a much-needed corrective to the individualism of much of post-Reformation Western Christianity. But, the most visible feminist theologians have not postulated a future humanity that would exist ontologically in a different manner from the present, and many have been explicitly agnostic on the issue of personal immortality. Thus, feminist eschatology has focussed on the reformation of human social and political structures, what I call an 'outside-in' or surface approach.

Eastern Orthodox Christianity, by contrast, recognises the *eschaton* as a fundamental change in the manner of created existence, including human existence. As we have seen, the main Greek tradition contends that the physical and biological nature of the human person will be radically transformed, to the extent of the abolition of sexual differentiation. Yet, the essence of eschatological humanity already exists; we are microcosms created in the image of God. Thus, the fulfilment of creation's (and humanity's) potential exists not at the level of creation – what humanity does or does not do to nature – but in creation's uniting itself ever more organically to God, through humanity's unique role of mediator.

Political and social reform are incapable of achieving this unifying goal within creation, and between creation and the Creator, because it is achieved not primarily through social action but through personal existence. The unifying action is rooted not in what humanity does, but in humanity's realising fully what it *is*. This is the foundation behind the personal, transformative theology of the Christian East. Fulfilment of human persons, and the eschatological realisation of humanity's potential and purpose, is a transformative process which works from the 'inside out'. When human persons are transformed, then their relational actions towards creation and others are existentially changed as well. Social ethics are thus based on personal transformation, on making the Kingdom of God present 'by redeeming and transfiguring the world', to quote Armenian Orthodox ethicist Vigen Guroian.[16]

However, the mistake often made in the East (and in traditional Christianity in general) is to assume that the dichotomy between present and *eschaton* is so sharp that two different norms must exist, one for this life and another for the resurrection. Nothing could be further from the truth. Only our eschatological existence can be normative for humanity: we are called to seek the Kingdom of God. Historically, Christianity has recognised this in the monastic lifestyle, which is a leap into an eschatological human existence where sexual differentiation is abolished and humanity lives in harmony with creation in a life of communion with God.

But monasticism is not the only way to live eschatologically in the present. All of us are called to mediate the various elements of creation and to mediate between the created and the divine. This is a process, a manner of existence, which must begin in the here-and-now, even if it will not be ultimately fulfilled until the *eschaton*. And this manner of existence has consequences. As Chrysostom and Maximos have noted, distinctions of class, race, and sex will not exist eschatologically because they are not ontologically part of our make-up as human beings. Therefore, if human society does not allow *all* human persons to express uniquely and distinctively the work of the Spirit, of uncreated grace, then it is impeding humanity's fulfilment of God's purpose and plan. The functional equality of all human persons is based not on political rights but on humanity's shared purpose as mediator. Each person fulfils that purpose in a unique and personal way but, as Maximos pointed out, that personal distinctiveness cannot be understood in terms of sexual differences which restrict certain traits or qualities to those of only one sex. Thus, any type of human inequality interferes with humanity's ability to fulfil its ordained purpose as mediator. And, any exploitation of creation is an existential denial of that very purpose. Thus, human inequalities and ecological degradations rightly are called sins. They are a denial of human nature and purpose as God intended it.

CONCLUSION

So, I have proposed a peculiar kind of feminist eschatology which is simultaneously like and unlike both patriarchal and feminist Western eschatologies. It is eschatology based on a circular, Eastern model of doing theology: start with God, move to creation (including humanity), and then bring creation back to God. We start with an understanding of God as existing in a community of distinct persons unified in mutually indwelling love. That love extends beyond God's own Self to the creation of a universe distinct from God and yet connected to God, a universe whose existence and meaning derives from its Creator. Humanity, created in the image of this loving and personally differentiated God, occupies a special place within this creation as a mediator, combining the physical existence of inorganic creation with the vivifying soul of organic creation and the intellectual and spiritual faculties of the spiritual world. Human beings are bodily creatures who participate simultaneously in the life of physical creation and of noetic (intellectual/spiritual) creation. We have a purpose, a calling – to unite the differences and distinctions of the created world within ourselves, not abolishing these distinctions, but bringing them together in an interrelated network which we then, through the person of Jesus Christ, unite with the Divine.

However, the radical nature of the eschatological fulfilment of this mediatorial purpose does not relieve us of current responsibilities. Far from it: the existential character of our personal and corporate human nature as mediator of creation precludes any notion of waiting for some far-off, projected Second Coming. Mediation, like salvation, is not a one-time 'event' but an ongoing process, evolving and developing eternally. Its point of departure, its beginning, is *now* because our human nature, as it exists *now*, is meant to serve as conduit between the Creator and creation. 'The Kingdom of heaven is at hand.' Salvation is transformational, not merely reformative. Personal salvation, the salvation of the human community, and the salvation of creation are inextricably linked through a circular dance of love: God's self-emptying love pours continually out of God's own Self to creation, while humanity acts as the lens focussing the energy and love of God's creation and redirecting it back to God in a never-ending cycle of renewal and transformation.

Notes

1. Peter C. Phan, 'Woman and the Last Things', in Ann O'Hara Graff (ed.), *In the Embrace of God: Feminist Approaches to Theological Anthropology* (Maryknoll, NY: Orbis Press, 1995), p. 222.
2. Sallie McFague, 'Eschatology: a New Shape for Humanity', ch. 7 in *The Body of God: an Ecological Theology* (Minneapolis, MN: Augsburg Press, 1993), pp. 197–212.
3. Rosemary Radford Ruether, 'Eschatology and Feminism', in Susan Brooks Thistlethwaite and Mary Potter Engel (eds.), *Lift every Voice: Constructing Christian Theologies from the Underside* (San Francisco, CA: Harper & Row, 1990), pp. 111–24.
4. Phan, 'Woman and the Last Things', p. 208; see, generally, pp. 207–8 and 221–3.
5. Gregory of Nyssa, On the Song of Songs, 6, 212–13; in Verna Harrison, 'Male and Female in Cappadocian Theology', *Journal of Theological Studies*, new series, 41:2 (October 1990), 441.
6. Ruether, 'Eschatology', pp. 122–3.
7. Phan, 'Woman and the Last Things', p. 221.
8. See especially Catherine Mowry LaCugna, *God For Us: The Trinity and Christian Life* (San Francisco, CA: HarperSanFrancisco, 1993).
9. See Gregory Palamas, *The Triads*, John Meyendorff (ed.), Nicholas Gendle (trans.), Classics of Western Spirituality series (New York: Paulist Press, 1983), sections E, 'The Uncreated Glory', and F, 'Essence and Energies in God', pp. 71–92, 93–111, respectively.
10. Panayiotis Nellas, *Deification in Christ*, trans. Norman Russell (Crestwood, NY: St. Vladimir's Seminary Press, 1987), pp. 33–4.
11. In a statement made during an environmental symposium held in Santa Barbara, CA, 12 February 1998. A further instance of Bartholomew's ecological theology is his speech, dated 1 September 1998, listed as Protocol No. 1048, and available on the Web at the following address: http://www.patriarchate.org/SPEECHES/1998/Sept1.html.
12. See Nellas, *Deification*, for a translation of selected passages from Maximos' *De ambigua*, regarding humanity's role as mediator of extremes or divisions, pp. 211–16. Nellas discusses the cosmological dimension in an ecclesial context in Part III, ch. 1, pp. 163–72. See also Andrew Louth, *Maximus the Confessor* (London: Routledge, 1996), ch. 5, 'Cosmic Theology', pp. 63–77. This book includes Louth's own introduction to and translation of a broader selection of passages from Maximos' *De ambigua*, pp. 155–62.
13. See Gregory of Nyssa, 'The Soul and the Resurrection', Catharine P. Roth (trans.), 'Contemporary Greek Theologians', vol. 5 (Crestwood, New York: St. Vladimir's Seminary Press, 1993), especially ch. 10.
14. Ephesians 6[5–9]. See e.g., John Chrysostom, *Homilies on Ephesians*, vol. 13, *Library of the Nicene and Post-Nicene Fathers*, Philip Schaff (ed.), the Oxford

Translations with additional notes by G. Alexander, J. A. Broadus, and P. Schaff (Grand Rapids, MI: Wm. R. Eerdmans, 1969), Homily 22, p. 159. See also Valerie Karras, 'Male Domination of Woman in the Writings of Saint John Chrysostom' in *The Greek Orthodox Theological Review*, 36:2 (1991), 131–9.

15. E.g. Letty Russell, 'Theology of Anticipation', ch. 4 in *Growth in Partnership* (Louisville, KY: Westminster Press, 1981), pp. 87–109.

16. Vigen Guroian, *Incarnate Love* (University of Notre Dame Press, 1987), p. 24.

Selected reading

Farley, Margaret A. and Jones, Serene (eds.). *Liberating Eschatology: Essays in Honor of Letty M. Russell*, Louisville, KY: Westminster John Knox Press, 1999.

Gilman, Charlotte Perkins. *His Religion and Hers: a Study of the Faith of the Fathers and the Work of our Mothers*, New York: Century, 1923.

Gregory of Nyssa. *The Soul and the Resurrection*, Catharine P. Roth (trans.), Contemporary Greek Theologians, vol. 5, Crestwood, NY: St. Vladimir's Seminary Press, 1993.

Guroian, Vigen. *Incarnate Love*, University of Notre Dame Press, 1987.

Harrison, Verna E. F., 'Male and Female in Cappadocian Theology', *Journal of Theological Studies*, new series, 41:2 (October 1990), 441–71.

Keller, Catherine, 'Pneumatic Nudges: the Theology of Moltmann, Feminism, and the Future', in Miroslav Volf et al. (eds.), *The Future of Theology: Essays in Honor of Jürgen Moltmann*, Grand Rapids, MI: Eerdmans, 1996.

McFague, Sallie. *The Body of God: an Ecological Theology*, Minneapolis, MN: Augsburg Press, 1993.

Nellas, Panayiotis. *Deification in Christ*, Norman Russell (trans.), foreword by Bishop Kallistos of Diokleia. Crestwood, NY: St. Vladimir's Seminary Press, 1987.

Phan, Peter C. 'Woman and the Last Things', in Ann O'Hara Graff (ed.), *In the Embrace of God: Feminist Approaches to Theological Anthropology*, Maryknoll, NY: Orbis Press, 1995, pp. 206–28.

Ruether, Rosemary Radford. 'Eschatology and Feminism', in Susan Brooks Thistlethwaite and Mary Potter Engel (eds.), *Lift every Voice: Constructing Christian Theologies from the Underside*, San Francisco, CA: Harper & Row, 1990, pp. 111–24.

Russell, Letty. 'Theology of Anticipation', in *Growth in Partnership*, Louisville, KY: Westminster Press, 1981, pp. 87–109.

'Authority of the Future in Feminist Theology', in Hermann Deuser, Gerhard Marcel Martin, Konrad Stock, and Michael Welker (eds.), *Gottes Zukunft, Zukunft der Welt: Festschrift für Jürgen Moltmann zum 60. Geburtstag*, Munich: Chr. Kaiser Verlag, 1986, pp. 313–22.

Ware, Kallistos. *The Orthodox Way*, Crestwood, NY: St. Vladimir's Seminary Press, revised edition, 1998.

Index of biblical citations

Genesis 197, 255
Genesis 1 251
Genesis 1 – 3 99
Genesis 1^{26} 252
Genesis 1^{27} 4, 252
Genesis 2^7 251
Genesis 3^{21} 254

Exodus 100, 154

Judges 103–4

Isaiah 61 162
Isaiah 65^{17} 243

Judith 104

Matthew 6^{10} 255
Matthew 28^{1-10} xvii

Mark 103
Mark 3^{19} 105
Mark 5^{21-34} 162
Mark 14^{3-9} 104–7, 110
Mark 16^{1-2} 106
Mark 16^{1-8} xvii
Mark 16^7 156

Luke 1^{42} 154
Luke 2^{6-7} 160
Luke 2^{22-24} 160
Luke 4^{18-19} 162
Luke 8^{40-46} 154
Luke 13^{10-17} 161
Luke 17^{21} 255
Luke 24^{1-12} xvii

John 203
John 1 140
John 2^{13-16} 166
John 2^{46} 160
John 4^{1-42} 166
John 5^{1-18} 166
John 20^{11-18} xvii

Acts 2^{17} 4

Romans 16^7 103

1 Corinthians 255
1 Corinthians 11^{1-16} 224
1 Corinthians 11^7 141
1 Corinthians 15 244
1 Corinthians 15^{44} 254
2 Corinthians 4^{5-6} 136

Galatians 3^{28} 4

Ephesians 203, 255
Ephesians 2^{15} 158
Ephesians 6^{5-9} 259 n. 14

Philippians 2^{9-11} 160

Colossians 203

1 Timothy 108
1 Timothy 2 8–15, 108–10
1 Timothy 2^{11-12} 224, 239 n. 26
2 Timothy 108

Titus 108

2 Peter 1^4 250

Index of names

Abraham 79
Ackermann, Denise 39, 168
Adam 90, 109
Adams, Abigail 6
Alder, Margot 79
Alston, William 43–5
Amoah, Elizabeth 16, 161, 162, 163, 165
Anderson, Benedict 35
Anderson, Janice Capel 102
Anselm 206
Antigone 55
Anzaldúa, Gloria 35
Aquinas, Thomas 12, 140, 229, 250
Aquino, Maria Pilar 11
Aristotle 41–2, 159, 207, 217, 220
Astell, Mary 5
Augustine 12, 141, 145

Bacon, Francis 195
Badenhorst, Alie 164
Baker-Fletcher, Karen 10, 26
Bartholomew I 253
Baudrillard, Jean 216
Beauvoir, Simone de 9, 41, 140, 216
Berger, Teresa 224, 227
Berling, Judith 61
Bernard of Clairraux 146
Berry, Thomas 193, 200
Biehl, Janet 194
Bingemer, Maria Clara 15
Blackwell, Antoinette Brown 229
Blandina 173
Boff, Leonardo 182
Børresen, Kari Elisabeth 12, 13
Brandao, Margarida 15
Briggs, Sheila 31
Brock, Rita Nakashima 32

Brooten, Bernadette 103
Budapest, Zsuzsanna 80, 83, 178
Butler, Judith 32, 49, 126–7, 216–18
Bynum, Caroline Walker 174, 228

Calvin, John 138
Camera, Helder 15
Cannon, Katie Geneva 10, 26
Cappadocian Fathers 140, 146
Carr, Anne 176, 177, 182
Catherine of Siena 172, 206–8, 217, 220
Chardin, Teilhard de 196
Chodorow, Nancy 29
Chopp, Rebecca 9, 30, 232
Christ, Carol P. 11, 71, 83, 179, 193, 194
Chrysostom, John 255, 257
Chung Hyun Khung 11, 17, 177
Clifford, Anne 202
Clifford, James 35
Coakley, Sarah 44–6, 49, 50, 143, 146, 183, 201
Cobb, John 75, 143
Collins, Mary OSB 228
Collins, Patricia Hill 26
Condren, Mary 13
Cone, James S. 15
Congar, Yves 143, 171, 182
Copeland, Shawn 10
Cuomo, Chris 199

Daly, Mary 7, 9, 11, 26, 43, 80, 81, 130, 137
Davaney, Sheila Greeve 29
D'Eubonne, Françoise 190
Deifelt, Wanda 15
Descartes, René 41–2, 209, 211
Dewey, Joanna 107

Dexter, Miriam Robbins 79
Dominguez, Elizabeth 181
Douglas, Mary 200
Duah, Grace 158

Eck, Diana 61
Edet, Rosemary N. 16, 155–6, 158, 159, 160–1, 165
Ekeya, Bette 16
Eliade, Mircea 86
Eugene, Toinette 34
Eve 90, 109

Fabella, Virginia 14
Falk, Marcia 88
Fander, Monika 102
Farley, Margaret 7
Fatum, Lone 109
Fell, Margaret 5
Feuerbach, Ludwig 52, 82
Fischer, Kathleen 177
Foucault, Michel 215
Fox, Matthew 178, 179, 196
Fox, Warwick 192
Frankenberry, Nancy 43
Freud, Sigmund 82
Fulkerson, Mary McClintock 31

Gage, Matilda Joslyn 79–80
Gebara, Ivone 14, 15
Gelpi, Donald 183
Gertrude of Helfta 135, 147–8
Gilkes, Cheryl 10
Gilligan, Ann Marie 13
Gilligan, Carol 93, 210
Gilman, Charlotte Perkins 244
Gimbutas, Marija 80, 84, 85–6
Gnanadason, Anna 37, 177, 181
Goldenberg, Naomi 79, 83, 87
Gouge, Olympe de 6
Graham, Elaine 12
Grant, Jacquelyn 10, 30–1
Graves, Robert 85
Gregory of Nyssa 49, 146, 247, 254
Grey, Mary 12, 13, 127, 178, 180, 213–14
Griffin, Susan 192–3
Grimke, Sarah 6
Gross, Rita M. 11, 82

Grossmann, Elizabeth 12
Guroian, Vigen 257
Gutiérrez, Gustavo 14

Hagar 26
Halkes, Catharina 12, 13, 177
Hampson, Daphne 13, 46, 81
Hardesty, Nancy 10
Harkness, Georgia 171
Harris, Harriet 51
Harrison, Beverly Wildung 9
Hartshorne, Charles 88
Harvey, Susan Ashbrook 143–4, 146
Hebblethwaite, Margaret 176
Hegel, G. W. F. 246
Hesiod 86
Heyward, Isabel Carter 9, 180
Hildegard of Bingen 4, 228
Hillerman, Tony 104
Hinga, Teresa M. 16, 156–7, 164
Hitler, Adolf 82, 93
Hollywood, Amy 52
hooks, bell 53
Hume, David 30
Hunt, Mary 8, 10, 180
Hutchison, Anne 229

Irigaray, Luce 9, 50, 52, 82, 129, 140, 146, 199
Isasi-Díaz, Ada María 11, 27
Isherwood, Lisa 12, 13

James, William 46
Jantzen, Grace 12, 46, 48, 50–2, 54, 56, 82, 197–9, 200–1, 219
John Paul II 230, 234
Johnson, Elizabeth 7, 138, 139, 142, 143, 171, 183–5, 202
Judas (Iscariot) 105, 106
Julian of Norwich 4, 144–6, 172, 173
Jung, Carl 87
Junia(s) 103

Katoppo, Marianne 14
Kant, Immanuel 30, 54–5, 137
Kanyoro, Musimbi R. A. 16, 177
Kasper, Walter 138, 171
King, Ursula 12, 13, 61
Kristeva, Julia 50

Index of names

Kuma, Afua 153–5, 157, 158, 160, 162–3, 164, 165
Kwazu, A. E. 156
Kwok Pui-lan 11, 245

LaCugna, Catherine Mowry 140, 249
Landman, Christina 154, 164–5
Le Doeuff, Michèle 56
Lee, Ann 229
Leibniz, G. W. 195
Lloyd, Genevieve 40–2
Locke, John 30
Long, Asphodel 79, 83
Lorde, Audre 93, 102, 180
Lowe, Lisa 35
Luther, Martin 97, 228, 229

Macquarrie, John 171
Macrina 254
Malbon, Elizabeth Struthers 106
Maloney, Linda 108–9
Manazan, Mary John 14, 16, 17, 22
Marriage, Alwyn 171, 183
Mary 72, 163, 171, 182, 230, 233
Maximos the Confessor 253–4, 257–8
Mbwiti, Justine Kahungi 168
McFague, Sallie 9, 11, 37, 122–3, 130, 183–5, 197, 199–201, 236, 243–4, 247, 249, 256
Merchant, Carolyn 190–2, 195, 200
Mill, John Stuart 229
Milne, A. A. 104
Minh-Ha, Trinh T. 35
Moltmann-Wendel, Elizabeth 177
Morney, Mabel S. 167
Morrison, Toni 104
Moses 79
Mott, Lucretia 6
Mountaingrove, Jean 80
Mountaingrove, Ruth 80

Naess, Arne 192
Nakawombe, J. K. 159
Nasimiyu, Anne 154
Nellas, Panayiotis 252
Nettesheim, Agrippa von 5
Nietzsche, Friedrich 218–19, 220
Njoroge, Nyambura J. 160
Northrup, Lesley A. 232
Nyaga, Ada 161

Obaga, M. K. 158
Oduyoye, Mercy Amba 14, 16, 23, 27–8, 161, 162, 163, 177, 245
O'Grady, Kathleen 55, 57
Okure, Teresa 16, 154
Orenstein, Gloria 79
Ortner, Sherry 29
Orwell, George 138
Ostriker, Alicia 97

Page, Ruth 201
Pagels, Elaine 173
Palamas, Gregory 250–1
Paul 103, 109, 127, 136, 141, 224
Pereira, Nancy Cordoso 15
Perpetua 173
Peter 106
Phan, Peter 249
Phelps, Jamie 10
Pittenger, Norman 171
Pizan, Christine de 5
Plantinga, Alvin 45
Plaskow, Judith 11
Plato 41, 82, 86, 198, 219
Primavesi, Anne 197

Raphael, Melissa 79, 83
Rasmussen, Larry 33–4
Reimer, Ivone Richter 15
Reinhartz, Adele 104
Ricci, Carla 13
Riggs, Marcia 10
Ross, Susan 7
Rubin, Gayle 29
Rudy, Kathy 32–3
Ruether, Rosemary Radford 7, 8, 9, 11, 72, 100, 116–18, 125, 130, 195–7, 200, 243–4, 247, 256
Russell, Letty 9, 26, 256

Saiving, Valerie 9, 29
Salleh, Ariel K. 192
Scanzoni, Letha 10
Schmithals, Walter 107
Schottroff, Luise 107
Schreiter, Robert J. 36, 154
Schüssler Fiorenza, Elizabeth 7, 29, 33, 98, 101, 105, 106, 224, 227, 236
Selvidge, Marla J. 98
Shaftesbury, Earl of 212–13
Shange, Ntozake 81

Sheldrake, Philip 173
Sölle, Dorothee 12, 119–20, 129
Soskice, Janet Martin 13, 47, 48, 50
Souga, Térèsa 159–60
Spretnak, Charlene 83, 180, 193–4
Stanton, Elizabeth Cady 6, 25, 79, 98
Starhawk (Miriam Simos) 79, 83, 87,
    178, 194
Stone, Merlin 83, 84
Storkey, Elaine 176
Sun Ai Park 14, 16, 17
Swinburne, Richard 43–5

Tamez, Elsa 14, 15, 28
Tapia, Elizabeth 17
Tappa, Louise 161–2, 163
Tepedino, Ana Maria 15
Teresa of Avila 172, 173
Thecla 173
Thomas, Linda 10
Tolbert, Mary Ann 99–101
Torjesen, Karen Jo 224

Townes, Emilie 10
Trevett, Christine 12
Trible, Phyllis 101

Udo, Akon E. 156, 161
Umeagudosu, Meg A. 156

Wainwright, Elaine 110
Walker, Alice 26
Waterland, Daniel 147
Weaver, Mary Jo 7
West, Angela 120
White, E. B. 104
Williams, Delores 10, 26, 29, 30–1
Wollstonecraft, Mary 6
Wolterstorff, Nicholas 45
Woolf, Virginia 102
Wright, Frances 6

Ywahoo, Dhyani 94

Zappone, Katherine 13, 180

Index of subjects

anthropology, theological 8, 12, 29–30, 116–17, 251–2
(see also humanity, human being)

Bible (scriptures) 6, 27 97–104, 136, 154, 166, 171, 233
biology 191, 230
body (embodiment) 47–51, 91, 93, 140, 179–80, 197–201, 217–18, 233–5, 256

Christ, Jesus 104–7, 109, 118, 125, 139–40, 144–5, 151–67, 182, 193, 201, 220, 228, 230, 246
Christology 136–7, 151–3, 155–63, 201, 203
colonialism 15, 25–8, 30, 33
'comparative mirror' 36, 67–72
creation 4, 190–203, 243, 248–9, 250–2, 258–9
cross 139, 147, 151, 160, 162–3, 165, 196
culture, cultural xiv, xvi, 4, 15–16, 23–4, 27–8, 103, 152, 158
intercultural 23–37

dialogue 61, 73–6, 177–8
difference(s) 23, 28, 30–1, 76, 253, 258
diversity xvi, 23, 32, 60–4
divinisation 52, 82, 250–1, 253–4
dualism 86, 88, 100, 122, 181–2, 192, 199

earth (world) 81, 87, 89–90, 92, 93–4, 122–3, 181–2, 192–3, 194–5, 197–9, 200, 202
ecclesiology 224–37
ecology 89, 190
ecofeminism 12, 15, 182, 190–2, 194–5, 199, 243–4, 248–9, 253

ecological theology 37, 202–3
education xiii, xvi, 4, 6–18
Enlightenment xiii, 30, 125–6, 212, 215, 221
epistemology 11, 40–57, 64, 66–7, 213
equality 3–4, 6, 30–1, 106–7, 209–10, 255–6, 257–8
eschatology 243–59
realised 243, 246
unrealised 254–8
ethics 34–5, 51, 53–4, 64, 69–72, 92–4, 123–4, 148, 191–2, 202, 206–21
ethic of care 172–3, 191, 212–15
evil 89–90, 91–2, 198
experience, women's 23, 43–8, 62, 83–4, 100, 116–18, 172, 176, 191, 225, 235–7
African women's 152–3, 163, 167

faith xv, 115, 127, 135–6, 151–3, 155, 160, 172, 185, 206, 214, 221
faithfulness xiii, xvi, 106, 114, 221
feminine, femininity 3, 40, 46, 142–4, 182–3, 247

Gaia 195–7
gender 3–4, 29–30, 32–3, 40–1, 42, 44–6, 47, 115, 124–5, 126–7, 144, 146, 215–16, 218–19, 227
global capitalism 23–4, 33–7, 128–9, 214
God 3–4, 42–3, 44, 45–6, 52, 53–5, 80, 82, 86, 89, 122–3, 127–9, 135–48, 180–1, 183, 184–5, 197–202, 207, 209, 211, 218, 220–1, 234, 247, 250–1
Goddess/goddess 71, 79–81, 83–6, 87–90, 91, 92–4, 179, 192–4, 196–7, 199, 202–3, 232
grace 232, 250–1, 257

hermeneutics 35, 97–110, 117, 120, 245–8
Holy Spirit 119, 120, 142–4, 157, 171–85, 193, 198
hope xiii–xiv, xvi–xvii, 94, 110, 121, 197, 203
(*see also* vision)
humanity, human being 90–2, 116–17, 125–7, 139–40, 158–9, 215 (humanism), 234–5, 248, 251, 253–4, 257–9
(*see also* anthropology)

identity, discourse of 30–3, 48, 126, 210
imaginary 55–6
imago dei 141, 159, 231, 251–2, 257
immanence, immanentism 87–9, 184–5, 193–4, 196, 199–200, 233–4, 237
inclusivity 62–3, 129, 167, 232, 235–6
interiority 46, 129

justice 177–8, 181–2, 210–11, 213, 234, 237, 256

Kingdom of God 121, 143, 210, 254–8

liberal, liberalism 4, 31
liberation xiii, 118–121, 154, 156–8 (deliverance), 162–7, 181, 208–9
liberation theology xiv, 119
love 51, 93, 115, 145, 146–7, 148, 156, 161, 180, 184, 207–8, 217, 220–1, 258

modernity xv, 30, 124–6, 194, 215
mujerista theology 11, 27, 30, 35, 236–7
mysticism 46, 163–4, 174–5
myth, mythical 55–7, 84, 86

nature, natural 32–3, 89–90, 122–3, 130, 190, 191–2
nihilism 218–20

ordination, women's 7–8, 10, 224–5, 229–31, 233

person, personhood 119, 142, 208–11, 216–18, 244, 247, 256–7
plurality, pluralism xv, 12, 24, 65–6, 73–4, 173
political economy 216

postmodernity xv, 115, 128–9, 130, 140, 193, 211, 214, 215, 219–20
prayer 46–7, 136, 137, 176, 206–7, 220–1, 232

race, discourse of 10, 25–7, 29–31
reason, rationality 40–2, 50, 54–5, 209–11
redemption, salvation 5, 109, 116, 118, 121, 125, 128, 129–31, 156, 165–6, 196–7, 200, 206–8, 213–14, 220–1, 250, 257–9
Reformation 5, 228
relation, relationality (connectedness) 91–2, 120–1, 180–2, 191, 193, 201, 212–15, 247–8
religion(s) xiv, 60–76
resurrection xvii, 156, 160, 165, 244, 257
rights, human xiii, 208–11
civil 7, 9–10, 14, 25–6
ritual(s) 80–1, 83–4, 87, 158, 178–9, 194, 225, 232–3, 236–7

sacraments 226, 233–5
sexual difference 47–9, 143, 252, 253–4, 256, 258
sin 6, 29, 90, 117, 120, 200–1
soul 145, 207–8, 217, 220–1
spirit, spirituality 71, 82–3, 163, 164, 172–82, 192
standpoint 40, 43, 55–7, 101
subject, subjectivity 31–2, 126–7, 216–18
suffering 17, 117, 120, 160–2, 164–5, 201

thealogy 71, 79–94
theology, feminist xiii–xiv, xv, 3–4, 18, 23, 62, 72, 79, 83, 114–31
transcendence 86–8, 119, 126, 184, 194, 199–200, 218, 248–51, 253
Trinity 135–48
truth xvii, xviii, 4, 40, 54–5, 57, 64, 82–3, 84, 115–16, 119, 123–4, 130–1, 145, 208–9, 215, 220–1

universalising discourse 28–30

values 3, 34, 37, 56, 64–6, 122–4, 180, 214, 218–19
vision 18, 37, 110, 130, 167, 179, 185, 243, 255
(*see also* hope)

Wicca 11, 80, 176, 178, 236
wisdom 4, 127–8, 138, 143, 165, 183,
   193, 202–3
womanist theology 10–11, 26, 30, 35,
   236–7

women–church 8–9, 17, 177–8,
   236–7
worship 86, 176–7, 225, 227–9, 231–3

yearning 43, 53–4, 57, 120, 180